T0210534

Lecture Notes in Computer Science   **9149**

Commenced Publication in 1973
Founding and Former Series Editors:
Gerhard Goos, Juris Hartmanis, and Jan van Leeuwen

More information about this series at http://www.springer.com/series/7409

Pierangela Samarati (Ed.)

Data and Applications Security and Privacy XXIX

29th Annual IFIP WG 11.3 Working Conference, DBSec 2015
Fairfax, VA, USA, July 13–15, 2015
Proceedings

 Springer

Editor
Pierangela Samarati
Università degli Studi di Milano
Crema
Italy

ISSN 0302-9743   ISSN 1611-3349 (electronic)
Lecture Notes in Computer Science
ISBN 978-3-319-20809-1   ISBN 978-3-319-20810-7 (eBook)
DOI 10.1007/978-3-319-20810-7

Library of Congress Control Number: 2015942534

LNCS Sublibrary: SL3 – Information Systems and Applications, incl. Internet/Web, and HCI

Springer Cham Heidelberg New York Dordrecht London

Printed on acid-free paper

Springer International Publishing AG Switzerland is part of Springer Science+Business Media
(www.springer.com)

Preface

This volume contains the papers selected for presentation at the 29th IFIP WG 11.3 Working Conference on Data and Applications Security (DBSec 2015), held in Fairfax, VA, USA, July 13–15, 2015.

In response to the call for papers, 45 papers were submitted to the conference. These papers were evaluated on the basis of their significance, novelty, and technical quality. Each paper was reviewed by at least three members of the Program Committee. The Program Committee meeting was held electronically, holding intensive discussion over a period of two weeks. Of the papers submitted, 18 full papers and six short papers were selected for presentation at the conference.

A conference like this does not just happen; it depends on the volunteer efforts of a host of individuals. There is a long list of people who volunteered their time and energy to put together the conference and who deserve acknowledgment. Thanks to all the members of the Program Committee, and the external reviewers, for all their hard work in the paper evaluation. We are very grateful to all people who gave their assistance and ensured a smooth organization process, in particular Sabrina De Capitani di Vimercati (IFIP WG11.3 Chair) for her guidance and support and Giovanni Livraga (Publicity Chair) for helping with publicity. A special thanks goes to the keynote speakers, who accepted our invitation to deliver keynote talks at the conference.

Last but certainly not least, thanks to all the authors who submitted papers and all the workshop's attendees. We hope you find the proceedings of DBSec 2015 interesting, stimulating, and inspiring for your future research.

July 2015

Sushil Jajodia
Pierangela Samarati

Organization

IFIP WG 11.3 Chair

Sabrina De Capitani di Vimercati   Università degli Studi di Milano, Italy

General Chair

Sushil Jajodia   George Mason University, USA

Program Chair

Pierangela Samarati   Università degli Studi di Milano, Italy

Publicity Chair

Giovanni Livraga   Università degli Studi di Milano, Italy

Program Committee

Vijay Atluri	Rutgers University, USA
Joachim Biskup	Technische Universität Dortmund, Germany
Sabrina De Capitani di Vimercati	Università degli Studi di Milano, Italy
Soon Ae Chun	CUNY, USA
Frédéric Cuppens	Telecom Bretagne, France
Nora Cuppens-Boulahia	Telecom Bretagne, France
Jun Dai	California State University, USA
Carmen Fernandez-Gago	University of Malaga, Spain
William M. Fitzgerald	UTRC, Ireland
Simon Foley	University College Cork, Ireland
Sara Foresti	Università degli Studi di Milano, Italy
Ehud Gudes	Ben-Gurion University, Israel
Yuan Hong	University at Albany, USA
Florian Kerschbaum	SAP, Germany
Sotiris Ioannidis	FORTH, Greece
Adam J. Lee	University of Pittsburgh, USA
Peng Liu	The Pennsylvania State University, USA
Javier Lopez	University of Malaga, Spain
Haibing Lu	Santa Clara University, USA
Catherine Meadows	NRL, USA

Ravi Mukkamala	Old Dominion University, USA
Martin Olivier	University of Pretoria, South Africa
Stefano Paraboschi	Università degli Studi di Bergamo, Italy
Guenther Pernul	Universität Regensburg, Germany
Silvio Ranise	FBK-Irst, Italy
Indrakshi Ray	Colorado State University, USA
Kui Ren	State University of New York at Buffalo, USA
Andreas Schaad	SAP, Germany
Basit Shafiq	LUMS, Pakistan
Scott Stoller	Stony Brook University, USA
Tamir Tassa	The Open University of Israel, Israel
Jaideep Vaidya	Rutgers University, USA
Cong Wang	City University of Hong Kong, Hong Kong SAR
Lingyu Wang	Concordia University, Canada
Meng Yu	Virginia Commonwealth University, Canada
Shengzhi Zhang	Florida Institute of Technology, USA

External Reviewers

David Espes	Yechen Qiao
Matthias Hummer	Daniel Ricardo Dos Santos
Peter Kieseberg	Ruben Rios
Michael Kunz	Rolf Schillinger
Giovanni Livraga	Ethan Sprissler
Tobias Mueller	Riccardo Traverso
Sebastian Neuner	Cory Thoma
Ana Nieto	Artemios Voyiatzis
Panagiotis Papadopoulos	Gaoyao Xiao
Thanasis Petsas	Eunjung Yoon
Olgierd Pieczul	Ye Zhang

Contents

Information Flow and Inference

Data Anonymization and Computation

MR-RBAT: Anonymizing Large Transaction Datasets Using MapReduce

Neelam Memon[(✉)] and Jianhua Shao

School of Computer Science and Informatics, Cardiff University, Cardiff, UK
{MemonNG,ShaoJ}@cardiff.ac.uk

Abstract. Privacy is a concern when publishing transaction data for applications such as marketing research and biomedical studies. While methods for anonymizing transaction data exist, they are designed to run on a single machine, hence not scalable to large datasets. Recently, MapReduce has emerged as a highly scalable platform for data-intensive applications. In the paper, we consider how MapReduce may be used to provide scalability in transaction anonymization. More specifically, we consider how RBAT may be parallelized using MapReduce. RBAT is a sequential method that has some desirable features for transaction anonymization, but its highly iterative nature makes its parallelization challenging. A direct implementation of RBAT on MapReduce using data partitioning alone can result in significant overhead, which can offset the gains from parallel processing. We propose MR-RBAT that employs two parameters to control parallelization overhead. Our experimental results show that MR-RBAT can scale linearly to large datasets and can retain good data utility.

1 Introduction

Publishing transaction data is important to applications such as personalized web search or understanding purchasing trends. A transaction is a set of items associated with an individual, e.g. search query logs, diagnosis codes or shopping cart items. Such data often contain person-specific sensitive information which may be disclosed in the process. De-identification (i.e. removing personal identifiers) may not provide sufficient protection for individuals' privacy [3,14], and attack on de-identified data can still lead to two forms of disclosure: *identity disclosure* where an individual can uniquely be linked to their transactions in the dataset and *sensitive item disclosure* where sensitive information about an individual is learnt with or without identifying their transactions.

One approach to protecting privacy is anonymization [10]. Various methods have been proposed [5,11,13,15,17,19], and RBAT [13] is one of them that has some desirable features. RBAT is able to deal with both types of disclosure, and can retain high data utility by allowing fine-grained privacy requirements to be specified. However, RBAT is designed to work in a centralized setting and requires the whole dataset to be memory-resident, on a single machine throughout the anonymization process. This makes RBAT un-scalable to large datasets.

© IFIP International Federation for Information Processing 2015
P. Samarati (Ed.): DBSec 2015, LNCS 9149, pp. 3–18, 2015.
DOI: 10.1007/978-3-319-20810-7_1

For instance, Walmart [18] handles more than one million customers every hour, collecting an estimated 2.5 petabytes of transaction data in the process. RBAT is unable to handle datasets of this scale.

Recently, MapReduce [7] has emerged as a scalable and cost-effective data-processing platform for data-intensive applications. In this paper, we study how MapReduce may be used to improve RBAT's scalability. This is not straightforward due to the highly iterative tasks that RBAT performs. MapReduce does not support iterative processing well [4,12], and computation in each iteration must be configured separately. This can generate a significant overhead which, if not managed, can offset the gains from parallel processing. To achieve high scalability while ensuring reasonable response time, we propose MR-RBAT, a MapReduce version of RBAT, which implements the key operations of RBAT in parallel and employs two parameters to control the overhead generated by MapReduce. Our experimental results show that MR-RBAT can scale linearly to large datasets and can retain good data utility.

The rest of the paper is organized as follows. Section 2 discusses the related work. In Sect. 3, we introduce some notations and give an overview of RBAT. Section 4 describes MR-RBAT that we propose in this paper. The experimental results are given in Sect. 5. Finally, Sect. 6 concludes the paper.

2   Related Work

Different privacy models have been proposed to guard transaction datasets against disclosure attacks, for example, k^m-anonymity [15,17], l^m-diversity [16], complete k-anonymity [11], ρ-uncertainty [5], (h,k,p)-Coherence [19] and PS-rules [13]. These models differ in terms of how they assume that the data may be attacked, e.g. k^m-anonymity assumes that an attacker knows up to m items in a transaction and ρ-uncertainty does not distinguish between public and sensitive items, but their sanitization approach is largely similar, relying on some form of data distortion. In this paper, we do not propose yet another privacy model, but instead we focus on the parallelization of the data sanitization method adopted by RBAT.

Recently, there has been a considerable interest in MapReduce as a scalable platform for data intensive applications. One issue that has received much attention is how to handle iterations efficiently in MapReduce. One approach is to extend the standard MapReduce framework itself. Ekanayake et al. [8] and Bu et al. [4], for example, proposed to avoid reading unnecessary data repeatedly from distributed storage, by identifying invariant data and keeping them locally over iterations. However, such methods can only be levered when most of the data remain static between iterations. Iterations of RBAT do not satisfy this requirement. Furthermore, they need to limit some features of the standard MapReduce framework, for example, forcing the data to remain locally means that tasks involving such data cannot be scheduled to be processed on multiple computing nodes. Such limitations can result in poor performance, especially over heterogeneous clusters.

Other works have proposed to deal with iterative computations in MapReduce algorithmically. Chierichetti et al. [6] implemented an existing greedy Max-k-cover algorithm using MapReduce efficiently and achieved provably approximation to sequential results. Bahmani et al. [2] obtained a parallel implementation of K-means++ [1] and empirically showed to have achieved similar results in a constant number of rounds. MapReduce solutions have also been proposed for anonymization [20–22], but were limited to achieving k-anonymity for relational data only. Our work is similar to these works in that we also address the iteration issue algorithmically, but the existing methods, including those designed to achieve k-anonymity, cannot trivially be adopted to parallelize the operations performed by RBAT.

3   Background

In this section, we first present some basic notations and concepts necessary to understand our proposed solution, then give a brief overview of RBAT.

3.1   Preliminaries

Let D be a collection of transactions. Each transaction $t \in D$ is a non-empty subset of $I = \{i_1, \cdots, i_n\}$ where each $i_j \in I$, $1 \leq j \leq n$ is called an item. Any $\lambda \subseteq I$ is called an itemset.

Definition 1 (Support). *Given an itemset λ, its support in D, denoted by $\sigma_D(\lambda)$, is the number of transactions containing λ, that is, $\sigma_D(\lambda) = |\{t \in D \wedge \lambda \subseteq t\}|$.*

We partition I into two disjoint subsets P and S such that $P \cup S = I$ and $P \cap S = \varnothing$. S contains items that are sensitive about the associated individuals and P contains all other items called public items. We assume that S needs to be published intact and that an attacker may have knowledge about individuals in the form of P.

When a set of transactions is released in its original form, certain combinations of public items may not appear frequently enough. This allows an adversary to link an individual to a small set of transactions, thereby breaching privacy. To protect this, PS-rules may be specified [13].

Definition 2 (PS-rule). *Given two itemsets $p \subseteq P$ and $s \subseteq S$, a PS-rule is an implication of the form $p \rightarrow s$.*

Each PS-rule captures an association between a public and a sensitive itemset. The antecedent and consequent of each rule can consist of any public and sensitive items respectively and many PS-rules can be specified by data publishers to capture detailed privacy requirements. A published transaction dataset is deemed to be protected if the specified PS-rules are protected.

Definition 3 (Protection of PS-rule). *Given a dataset D, the parameters $k \in [2, |D|]$ and $c \in [0, 1]$, a PS-rule $p \rightarrow s$ is protected in D if (1) $\sigma_D(p) \geq k$ and (2) $Conf(p \rightarrow s) \leq c$ where $Conf$ is defined as $\frac{\sigma_D(p \cup s)}{\sigma_D(p)}$.*

Condition 1 protects data against identity disclosure by ensuring that the probability of associating an individual to his or her transaction in D using the antecedent of any PS-rule is no more than $1/k$. Condition 2 prevents sensitive item disclosure by ensuring that the probability of linking an individual to a set of sensitive items specified by the consequent of a PS-rule is at most c, given that the probability of associating an individual to his or her transaction using the rule's antecedent is no more than $1/k$.

Given a set of transactions D and a set of PS-rules Θ, if any rule in Θ is not protected, then D must be sanitized. One sanitization approach is set-based generalization which attempts to hide an original item by replacing it with a set of items. It has been shown that set-based generalization retains data utility better than other generalization methods [13]. Consider D given in Table 1, for example. Suppose that we require $k = 3$ and $c = 0.6$. PS-rule $ac \rightarrow h$ is not protected in D as ac has a support of 1 only. But $ac \rightarrow h$ is protected in $\tilde{D}$ given in Table 2 where items a, b and f are replaced by (a, b, f) and c, d and e by (c, d, e) following the generalization, since ac is now supported by 4 transactions and $Conf(ac \rightarrow h) = 0.5$.

Table 1. Original dataset D

Diagnosis Codes
b, c, e, **g, h**
a, c, d, i, j
a, f, l
b, e, **g, h**
d, f, l

Table 2. Anonymized dataset $\tilde{D}$

Diagnosis Codes
(a,b,f), (c,d,e), **g, h**
(a,b,f), (c,d,e), i, j
(a,b,f), l
(a,b,f), (c,d,e), **g, h**
(c,d,e), (a,b,f), l

It is easy to see that there can be many possible generalizations of a dataset to protect a set of PS-rules. The one that incurs least distortion (or has a minimum loss of information) is preferred. RBAT uses the following measure to capture the loss of information as a result of generalization.

Definition 4 (Utility Loss). *Given a generalized dataset $\tilde{D}$, the utility loss of a single generalized item $\tilde{i}$ is given by $UL(\tilde{i}) = \frac{2^{|\tilde{i}|} - 1}{2^{|P|} - 1} \times w(\tilde{i}) \times \sigma_{\tilde{D}}(\tilde{i})$. The utility loss of the whole dataset $\tilde{D}$ is calculated as $\sum_{\forall \tilde{i} \in \tilde{P}} UL(\tilde{i})$, where $\tilde{P}$ is a set of all generalized items in $\tilde{D}$.*

The UL measure given in Definition 4 captures the loss of information in terms of the size of the generalized itemset, its significance (weight) and its support in $\tilde{D}$. The more items are generalized together, the more uncertain we are about its original representation, hence more utility loss. $w(\tilde{i})$ assigns some penalty based on the importance of the items in $\tilde{i}$. The support of the generalized item also affects the utility of anonymized data. The more frequently the generalized item occurs in $\tilde{D}$, the more distortion to the whole dataset is.

3.2 The RBAT Algorithm

RBAT [13] is a heuristic method for anonymizing transaction data. It is based on the PS-rule privacy model and uses set-based generalization in data sanitization. The key steps of RBAT are given in Algorithm 1.

Algorithm 1. RBAT $(D, \Theta, \tilde{i}, k, c)$

Input: Original dataset D, a set of PS-rules Θ, the most generalized item $\tilde{i}$, minimum support k and maximum confidence c.
Output: Anonymized dataset $\tilde{D}$
1: Q.enqueue($\tilde{i}$), $\tilde{D} \leftarrow$ GENERALIZE($D, \tilde{i}$)
2: **while** $|Q| > 0$ **do**
3:    $\tilde{i} \leftarrow Q$.dequeue()
4:    $\{\tilde{i}_l, \tilde{i}_r\} \leftarrow$ SPLIT($\tilde{i}$)
5:    $D' \leftarrow$ UPDATE($\tilde{i}_l, \tilde{i}_r, \tilde{i}, \tilde{D}, D$)
6:    **if** CHECK(D', Θ, k, c) = true **then**
7:       Q.enqueue($\tilde{i}_l$), Q.enqueue($\tilde{i}_r$), $\tilde{D} \leftarrow D'$
8:    **end if**
9: **end while**
10: **return** $\tilde{D}$

RBAT is iterative and works in a top-down fashion. Starting with all public items mapped to a single most generalized item $\tilde{i}$ and D generalized to $\tilde{D}$ according to $\tilde{i}$ (step 1), each iteration involves replacing a generalized item $\tilde{i}$ with two less generalized items $\tilde{i}_l$ and $\tilde{i}_r$. RBAT does this greedily by using a two-step split phase (step 4). The first step finds a pair of items from $\tilde{i}$ incurring maximum UL when generalized together. The second step uses the pair as seeds to split $\tilde{i}$ into two disjoint subsets $\tilde{i}_l$ and $\tilde{i}_r$.

To ensure that the anonymized data after replacing $\tilde{i}$ with $\tilde{i}_l$ and $\tilde{i}_r$ still offers the required privacy protection, each split is followed by an update (step 5) and check phase (step 6–8). The update step creates a temporary dataset D' by copying $\tilde{D}$ and replacing $\tilde{i}$ with $\tilde{i}_l$ and $\tilde{i}_r$. D' is then checked to see if Θ is still protected. If it is, D' becomes new $\tilde{D}$ and $\tilde{i}_l, \tilde{i}_r$ are queued for further split. The split-update-check is repeated until $|Q| = 0$, in which case $\tilde{D}$ is returned as the result. This top-down specialization process effectively constructs a binary *Split Tree* with the root representing the most generalized item and set of all leaf nodes forming a *Split Cut* representing the final generalization.

4 MR-RBAT

In this section, we describe MR-RBAT. We assume that there are sufficient processing nodes to store all of the data across them and to run all map and reduce tasks in parallel. Algorithm 2 shows the overall structure of MR-RBAT, which mirrors RBAT (to retain its useful properties), but performs its key computations in parallel (to address scalability). Algorithm 2 is performed on a single processing node as a control, but the functions indicated by an $\mathcal{MR}$ subscript are performed in parallel using MapReduce. In the following sections, we explain the key steps of MR-RBAT.

Algorithm 2. MR-RBAT $(D, \Theta, \tilde{i}, k, c)$

Input: Original dataset D, a set of PS-rules Θ, the most generalized item $\tilde{i}$, minimum support k and maximum confidence c.
Output: Anonymized dataset $\tilde{D}$

1: $\tilde{P} \leftarrow \text{COMPUTEUL}_{\mathcal{MR}}(P, D)$
2: $\tilde{D} \leftarrow \text{GENERALIZE}_{\mathcal{MR}}(D, \tilde{i})$
3: $Q.\text{enqueue}(\tilde{i})$
4: **while** $|Q| > 0$ **do**
5:      $\tilde{i} \leftarrow Q.\text{dequeue}()$
6:      $\{\tilde{i_l}, \tilde{i_r}\} \leftarrow \text{SPLIT}_{\mathcal{MR}}(\tilde{i}, \tilde{P}, \tilde{D})$
7:      $D' \leftarrow \text{UPDATE}_{\mathcal{MR}}(\tilde{i_l}, \tilde{i_r}, \tilde{i}, \tilde{D}, D)$
8:      **if** $\text{CHECK}_{\mathcal{MR}}(D', \Theta, k, c) = \text{true}$ **then**
9:          $Q.\text{enqueue}(\tilde{i_l})$, $Q.\text{enqueue}(\tilde{i_r})$, $\tilde{D} \leftarrow D'$
10:     **end if**
11: **end while**
12: **return** $\tilde{D}$

4.1 Data Partitioning and Preparation

We partition D among M mappers equally using a horizontal file-based data partitioning strategy. That is, first n transactions of D are assigned to the first mapper, the next n to the second mapper, and so on, where $n = \lceil |D|/M \rceil$. This strategy has been shown to be more efficient than other methods [9]. Note that our partitioning method is based on the number of transactions only and does not take into account mappers' memory usage. However, this can be trivially accounted for.

For efficiency, we prepare two datasets, $\tilde{P}$ and $\tilde{D}$, before anonymizing D. We first compute $\tilde{P}$ to contain pairwise ULs of all public items in P (step 1) and then generalize D into $\tilde{D}$ according to the most generalized item $\tilde{i}$. Both are performed using a single MapReduce round and are straightforward, so we will not discuss them further. The benefit of having these computed beforehand will become evident when we discuss the split and update functions later.

4.2 Split$_{\mathcal{MR}}$

This corresponds to the split phase of RBAT (step 4 of Algorithm 1) and is carried out in two steps. The first step uses a single MapReduce round with M mappers and a single reducer to find a pair which when generalized together incurs maximum UL (Algorithm 3). Each mapper reads a subset of $\mathcal{P}$ from the distributed file system (DFS), finds the pair with maximum UL locally, and sends it to a single reducer (steps 2–3) which finds the pair $\langle i_x, i_y \rangle$ with maximum UL globally (step 5).

Algorithm 3. FINDMAXPAIR $(\tilde{i})$

Input: A generalized item $\tilde{i}$ to split.
Output: A pair $i_x, i_y \in \tilde{i}$ such that $UL(i_x, i_y)$ is maximum.

1: **Map**$(m, \mathcal{P}_m)$
2:     $\mathcal{P}_m \leftarrow$ Load the m-th $\tilde{P}$ from DFS
3:     EMIT$(\varnothing, \langle i_a, i_b \rangle)$ such that $UL(i_a, i_b)$ is maximum in $\mathcal{P}_m$
4: **Reduce**$(\varnothing, [\langle i_{a_1}, i_{b_1} \rangle, \langle i_{a_2}, i_{b_2} \rangle, \ldots, \langle i_{a_M}, i_{b_M} \rangle])$
5:     $\langle i_x, i_y \rangle \leftarrow \langle i_{a_j}, i_{b_j} \rangle$ such that $UL(i_{a_j}, i_{b_j})$ is maximum, $1 \leq j \leq M$
6:     EMIT$(\varnothing, \langle i_x, i_y \rangle)$

The second step uses $\langle i_x, i_y \rangle$ to split $\tilde{i}$ into two less generalized items $\tilde{i}_l$ and $\tilde{i}_r$. RBAT does this by assigning i_x and i_y to I_l and I_r first, then considering each item $i_q \in \tilde{i} - \{i_x, i_y\}^1$ in turn and assigning it to either I_l or I_r based on $UL(I_l \cup i_q)$ and $UL(I_r \cup i_q)$. A direct parallelization of this heuristic will require $|\tilde{i}| - 2$ MapReduce rounds, as the assignment of each item is recursively dependent on the assignment of the items preceding it. In the worse case when the most generalized item is split to single items, one per iteration, it will require a total of $O(|P|^2)$ MapReduce rounds. This will result in a significant setup and data loading overhead.

Alternatively, one may split $\tilde{i}$ based on seeds only. That is, we decide whether an item $i_q \in \tilde{i}$ should be assigned to I_l or I_r based on $UL(i_q, i_x)$ and $UL(i_q, i_y)$. This would then require only a single MapReduce round to split $\tilde{i}$. While this can cut the number of MapReduce rounds significantly, it may cause substantial data utility loss. Consider an extreme case where $\tilde{i} = \{i_1, \ldots, i_{|P|}\}$ is the most generalized item, i_1 and $i_{|P|}$ are the seeds, $\sigma_D(i_j) < k/4, j < |P|$ and $k/2 < \sigma_D(i_{|P|}) < k$. Assuming that a uniform weight of 1 is used in UL calculation, then it is easy to see that using this strategy all the items will be generalized with i_1, resulting in $\tilde{i}_l = (i_1, \cdots, i_{(|P|-1)})$ and $\tilde{i}_r = (i_{|P|})$. As $\sigma_D(i_{|P|}) < k$, $\tilde{i}$ cannot be split, and the data has to be generalized using the most generalized item $\tilde{i}$, incurring a substantial utility loss.

Splitting $\tilde{i}$ by seeds or by preceding items in fact represent two *extreme* strategies for parallelizing split: one has the potential to retain utility better and the other incurs least parallelization overhead. We propose a control that allows a specified number of MapReduce rounds to be run, thereby balancing efficiency and utility retention.

Definition 5 (α-Split). *Given a generalized item $\tilde{i}$ and a pair of seeds i_x and i_y, α-split, $1 \leq \alpha \leq |\tilde{i}| - 2$, partitions $\tilde{i}$ into α buckets and splits $\tilde{i}$ in α iterations.*

---

[1] In the rest of this paper, when the context is clear, we shall simply use $\tilde{i}$ instead of $\tilde{i} - \{i_x, i_y\}$ to refer to the set of items in $\tilde{i}$ to be split.

Items in each bucket are split based on seeds only, and the splits obtained from the previous iterations are used as the seeds in the current iteration.

Algorithm 4 shows how α-Split works. $\tilde{i}$ is partitioned into α disjoint buckets (step 2), and α MapReduce rounds are used to split $\tilde{i}$ (step 3). Within each round, each mapper reads a copy of I_l, I_r, bucket $\tilde{i}_h$ and a subset of D, computes the partial support of $I_l \cup i_q$ and $I_r \cup i_q$ for each item $i_q \in \tilde{i}_h$ locally, and then shuffles the results to the reducers (steps 4–9). Each reducer aggregates the partial supports for i_q, assigns i_q to I_l or I_r based on their UL values, and emits updated I_l and I_r as seeds for the next iteration (steps 11–16). Note that currently $\tilde{i}$ is partitioned randomly, i.e. the first $\frac{|\tilde{i}|-2}{\alpha}$ items form the first bucket, the next $\frac{|\tilde{i}|-2}{\alpha}$ items form the second bucket, and so on. Exploring how to best assign items to buckets is beyond the scope of this paper.

Algorithm 4. α-Split $(\tilde{i}, i_x, i_y, \alpha)$

Input: Two seeds i_x, i_y, a generalized item $\tilde{i}$ to split, and split threshold α.
Output: Less generalized items $\tilde{i}_l$ and $\tilde{i}_r$

1:   $I_l \leftarrow i_x, I_r \leftarrow i_y$
2:   $\{\tilde{i}_1, \tilde{i}_2, \ldots, \tilde{i}_\alpha\} \leftarrow \text{PARTITION}(\tilde{i} - \{i_x, i_y\})$
3:   **for** $h = 1$ to α **do**
4:      **Map**$(m_i, \langle I_l, I_r, \tilde{i}_h, D_m \rangle)$
5:        $\mathcal{D}_m \leftarrow$ Load the m-th partition of D from DFS
6:        **for** each $i_q \in \tilde{i}_h$ **do**
7:          $\tilde{i}_l \leftarrow I_l \cup \{i_q\}, \tilde{i}_r \leftarrow I_r \cup \{i_q\}$
8:          $\text{EMIT}(i_q, \langle \sigma_{D_m}(\tilde{i}_l), \sigma_{D_m}(\tilde{i}_r) \rangle)$
9:        **end for**
10:   **Reduce**$(i_q, [\langle \sigma_{D_1}(\tilde{i}_l), \sigma_{D_1}(\tilde{i}_r) \rangle, \langle \sigma_{D_2}(\tilde{i}_l), \sigma_{D_2}(\tilde{i}_r) \rangle, \ldots, \langle \sigma_{D_M}(\tilde{i}_l), \sigma_{D_M}(\tilde{i}_r) \rangle])$
11:      **if** $UL(\tilde{i}_l) > UL(\tilde{i}_r)$ **then**
12:        $I_l \leftarrow I_l \cup \{i_q\}$
13:      **else**
14:        $I_r \leftarrow I_r \cup \{i_q\}$
15:      **end if**
16:      $\text{EMIT}(r, \langle I_l, I_r \rangle)$
17: **end for**
18: **return** $\langle \tilde{i}_l = I_l, \tilde{i}_r = I_r \rangle$

It is easy to see that α-Split is a generalization of RBAT Split: when $\alpha = |\tilde{i}|$, α-Split becomes RBAT Split. Any other settings of α represent a tradeoff between efficiency and potential utility loss. This gives us a control to balance between performance and quality in anonymizing large transaction datasets, as we will show in Sect. 5.

We now analyse the overhead cost associated with $\text{SPLIT}_{\mathcal{MR}}$. Let $\tilde{i}$ be the item to be split, $s_m(M)$ and $s_r(R)$ be the cost of setting up M mappers and R reducers, ω be the average time that it takes to read a transaction (of average size in D) from the distributed file system. The overall map cost t_M of a single MapReduce round is given by

$$t_M = s_m(M) + \frac{|D|}{M} \cdot \omega \tag{1}$$

Assume that each mapper has enough parallel connections to send data across the network to R reducers in parallel, the shuffle cost t_S of a single MapReduce round is as follows, where ξ is a network efficiency constant.

$$t_S = \frac{|\tilde{i}| - 2}{\alpha \times min(R, \frac{|\tilde{i}|-2}{\alpha})} \cdot \xi \tag{2}$$

Note that map output with the same key must be sent to the same reducer, so the number of reducers needed is determined by $min(R, \frac{|\tilde{i}|-2}{\alpha})$ in (2). The reduce cost t_R of a single MapReduce round is dominated by the cost of setting up the reducers and reading the shuffled data sent by the mappers:

$$t_R = s_r(R) + \frac{M \times (|\tilde{i}| - 2)}{\alpha \cdot min(R, \frac{|\tilde{i}|-2}{\alpha})} \cdot \omega \tag{3}$$

The overall cost of SPLIT$_{\mathcal{MR}}$ using α iterations to split $\tilde{i}$ is therefore

$$T_{total} = \alpha \times \left[s_m(M) + s_r(R) + \frac{|D|}{M} \cdot \omega + \frac{|\tilde{i}| - 2}{\alpha \times min(R, \frac{|\tilde{i}|-2}{\alpha})} \cdot (\xi + M \cdot \omega) \right] \tag{4}$$

Clearly, a large α, which a direct parallelization of RBAT would imply, can result in a significant overhead cost due to the setup and data loading requirements. We will show in Sect. 5 that it is possible to use a small α in split to control overhead while retaining good data utility.

4.3 Check$_{\mathcal{MR}}$

Once $\tilde{i}$ is split and $\tilde{D}$ is updated (using a single MapReduce round), Θ must be checked to see if it is still protected. Parallelizing rule-checking while keeping overhead low is another issue to address. RBAT checks all PS-rules in sequence and stops if any rule is found unprotected. Implementing this directly in MapReduce could incur the cost of setting up $O(|\Theta|)$ rounds. We observe that when every rule in Θ is protected, it is more efficient to use a single MapReduce round: mappers check every rule locally and reducers check the overall protection. But when not every rule is protected, this is not efficient. For example, if the first rule in Θ is not protected, then no other rules need to be checked. However, the MapReduce architecture does not allow the nodes to communicate with each other until the whole round is finished, effectively requiring all rules to be checked. This increases the network cost of shuffling partial supports and will incur extra, but unnecessary, computation of checking all the rules.

Again, we observe that checking all rules or one rule only in a single MapReduce round are two extremes of optimisation: checking one rule per round will avoid checking unnecessary rules but can incur severe parallelization overhead, whereas checking all rules in a single round will minimise parallelization overhead but can perform a large amount of unnecessary computation. To balance this, we propose another parameter γ to control the number of MapReduce rounds used to check rules.

Definition 6 (γ-Check). *Given a set of PS-rules Θ, γ-Check, $1 \le \gamma \le |\Theta|$, checks Θ in γ iterations. Each iteration checks $\frac{|\Theta|}{\gamma}$ PS-rules in Θ.*

Algorithm 5 shows how γ-Check works. It checks $|\Theta|$ in γ MapReduce rounds, each round checking $\frac{|\Theta|}{\gamma}$ rules. Each mapper checks every rule $p \rightarrow s \in \Theta_j$ in a single round, by computing the partial support of $\tilde{p}$ and $\tilde{p} \cup s$ (steps 5–8, where $\phi(p) = \tilde{p}$ generalizes p). The reducers aggregate the partial supports pertaining to each rule and check the protection conditions (steps 9–13). The algorithm will not undergo any subsequent rounds, if any rule is found unprotected in the current round. Hence, γ-Check at maximum checks ($\frac{|\Theta|}{\gamma} - 1$) more rules than RBAT does, but would require a maximum of γ MapReduce rounds only.

Algorithm 5. γ-Check (D', Θ, k, c, γ)

Input: Temporarily anonymized dataset D', PS-rules Θ, Minimum support k, Maximum confidence c, Check threshold γ.
Output: True if each protected PS-rule and False otherwise.

1: $\{\Theta_1, \Theta_2, \dots, \Theta_\gamma\} \leftarrow$ PARTITION(Θ)
2: **for** $j \leftarrow 1$ to γ **do**
3:     **Map**(m, $\langle D'_m, \Theta_j \rangle$)
4:         $D'_m \leftarrow$ Load the m-th partition of D' from DFS
5:         **for** each rule $p \rightarrow s \in \Theta_j$ **do**
6:             $\tilde{p} \leftarrow \phi(p)$
7:             EMIT ($p \rightarrow s$, $\langle \sigma_{D'_m}(\tilde{p}), \sigma_{D'_m}(\tilde{p} \cup s) \rangle$)
8:         **end for**
9:     **Reduce**($p \rightarrow s$, $[\langle \sigma_{D'_j}(\tilde{p}), \sigma_{D'_j}(\tilde{p} \cup s) \rangle, 1 \le j \le M]$)
10:         $\sigma_{D'}(\tilde{p}) = \Sigma_{j=1}^{M} \sigma_{D'_j}(\tilde{p}), \quad \sigma_{D'}(\tilde{p} \cup s) = \Sigma_{j=1}^{M} \sigma_{D'_j}(\tilde{p} \cup s)$
11:         **if** $\sigma_{D'}(\tilde{p}) < k$ or $\frac{\sigma_{D'}(\tilde{p} \cup s)}{\sigma_{D'}(\tilde{p})} > c$ **then**
12:             EMIT(r, False)
13:         **end if**
14: **end for**

The cost analysis of CHECK$_{\mathcal{MR}}$ mirrors that of SPLIT$_{\mathcal{MR}}$. That is, Eqs. (1–4) apply to CHECK$_{\mathcal{MR}}$ if we replace α by γ and $|\tilde{i}| - 2$ by Θ, So no further analysis is given here. It is useful to note that γ-Check is a generalization of RBAT Check: when $\gamma = 1$, it becomes RBAT Check. However, unlike the α control, using any γ value in rule checking will not affect the quality of anonymization, but only the performance.

5   Experimental Evaluation

This section describes our experiments. The default settings of parameters are given in Sect. 5.1 and experimental results are analysed in Sect. 5.2.

5.1   Setup

All experiments were performed using the Apache Hadoop[2], an open-source implementation of MapReduce. We conducted the experiments over a cloud of thirteen computing nodes, physically located within the same building and inter-connected by 100 Mbps ethernet connection. One of the machines was allocated to run the MR-RBAT master program (Algorithm 2). All client machines were homogenous in configuration containing 2 GB memory and 2 physical cores. Each machine was set to use one core only and was assigned to run a single mapper or reducer instance.

We used a real-world dataset BMS-POS [23] as D, containing several years of point-of-sale transaction records. We have $|D| = 515597$ and $|I| = 1657$ with the maximum and average transaction size being 164 and 6.5, respectively. The larger datasets were constructed by random selection of transactions from D, and we refer to these datasets as nX, where $n \in [0.5, 16]$ is a blow up factor. $|S|$ was set to $0.1 \times |I|$. We used ARE (average relative error) [13] to quantify the utility of anonymized data. We used a workload of 1000 randomly generated queries, each consisting of a pair of public items and a single sensitive item. Default settings of parameters used in the experiments are given in Table 3.

Table 3. Default parameter settings

Parameter	Default Value
$|D|$	4X
$|\Theta|$	4000
k	5
c	0.9
α	4
γ	4

5.2   Scalability and Performance

Figure 1(a) shows how MR-RBAT performed w.r.t. varying data sizes. For smaller datasets, it performed no better than RBAT due to the overwhelm-ing parallelization overhead. However, the run-time of MR-RBAT grows much

---

[2] http://hadoop.apache.org/.

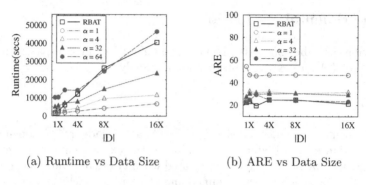

(a) Runtime vs Data Size   (b) ARE vs Data Size

Fig. 1. Runtime and ARE of MR-RBAT

more slowly than RBAT does, especially when α is small. This demonstrates its scalability to large datasets. It is interesting to observe the run-time for $\alpha = 64$. At this setting, MR-RBAT and RBAT achieved almost the same performance. This suggests the severity of overhead caused by iteration using MapReduce: the gains from parallel processing has almost been exhausted entirely by the overhead. It is also interesting to observe ARE results in these experiments. It is expected that setting a smaller α would help performance, but could potentially affect utility. However, Fig. 1(b) shows that almost identical utility can be achieved when $\alpha = 64$. This confirms the feasibility and effectiveness of using α in the split phase of MR-RBAT to balance performance and utility retention.

We also evaluated the scalability of MR-RBAT by varying cluster size. Figure 2(a) and (b) shows the runtime and speedup, respectively. The speedup is measured as the ratio of the runtime of a 1-node cluster to that of the cluster tested. MR-RBAT achieved a near linear speedup when a smaller cluster (relative to data size) was used. This is because MR-RBAT uses one reducer only in the first step of SPLIT$_{\mathcal{MR}}$, and others are used as mappers. Increasing the number of mappers causes more transactions to be fetched and processed by the single reducer, thereby degrading the speedup. Furthermore, we used a dataset of $4X$ in these experiments. With this data size and when cluster size increased, the computation performed by each mapper became lighter, and the effect of overhead on runtime became more significant. So adopting a suitable ratio of data size to cluster size is important to achieving a good speedup.

We then tested the effect of α on runtime and on data utility. As can be seen from Fig. 3(a), runtime scales largely linearly w.r.t. α. This suggests that dividing $\tilde{i}$ into different sizes of buckets had little impact on the outcome of split in each iteration. This is further confirmed by the ARE results in Fig. 3(b). When α is very small, many items of $\tilde{i}$ are put into one bucket and assigned to I_l or I_r based on seeds only. This caused items with high ULs to be generalized together. But once α is large enough, i.e. buckets are smaller enough, the α value only affected runtime, not ARE. This shows that the performance of splitting $\tilde{i}$ can be significantly improved by using a relatively small α without compromising data utility.

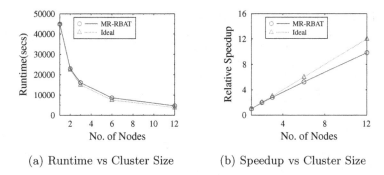

(a) Runtime vs Cluster Size   (b) Speedup vs Cluster Size

Fig. 2. Scalability of MR-RBAT

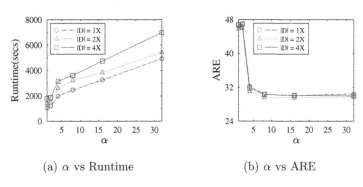

(a) α vs Runtime   (b) α vs ARE

Fig. 3. Effect of α

We also observed a relationship between α and split skewness during these experiments. Let S_α be the split tree constructed by MR-RBAT based on some α, and $\tilde{i}$ be a non-leaf node of S_α with $\tilde{i}_l$ and $\tilde{i}_r$ as its left and right children respectively. We measure split skewness $\xi(S_\alpha)$ as

$$\xi(S_\alpha) = \sum_{\tilde{i} \in S_\alpha} || \, |\tilde{i}_l| - |\tilde{i}_r| \, || \tag{5}$$

It was observed that split skewness decreased as α was increased. This is because when α is small, a large bucket of items will be split in a single round based on the seeds only. If data distribution is such that generalizing most of items in the bucket with one of the seeds produces a larger UL than the other seed does, then most of the items will be generalized with one seed, resulting in a skewed split. Skewed splits are more likely to make Θ unprotected, resulting in an early stop in split and a higher ARE. This is confirmed by Fig. 3(b). Very small α values are therefore to be avoided.

Next, we varied domain size to see its effect on runtime. As shown in Fig. 4(a) and (b), MR-RBAT's runtime was more stable and grew much more slowly than RBAT did as the domain size increased. On the other hand, the difference in ARE between RBAT and MR-RBAT increased slightly as the domain size was increased. This is because MR-RBAT uses a fixed number of MapReduce rounds in split. Increasing domain size causes more items to be put in one bucket and generalized in one round. This contributed to an increased ARE.

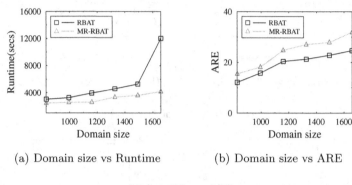

(a) Domain size vs Runtime   (b) Domain size vs ARE

Fig. 4. Effect of $|I|$

Finally, we tested the effect of γ on runtime. Note that a γ setting will only affect runtime, not ARE, so only the runtime results are reported in Fig. 5. Observe that initially the runtime was decreased when we increased γ (see Fig. 5(a)). This is because when γ is small, the inefficiency introduced by CHECK$_{\mathcal{MR}}$ is mainly from the need to check extra, but unnecessary rules. As γ increases, the number of unnecessary rules to check decreases, resulting in a better runtime. However, as we further increase γ, reduction through checking fewer unnecessary rules decreases, but the cost of setting up more iterations increases, making an increase in the overall runtime.

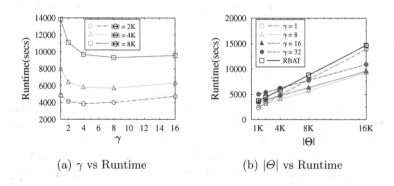

(a) γ vs Runtime   (b) $|\Theta|$ vs Runtime

Fig. 5. Effect of γ

Increasing the number of rules also caused the runtime of MR-RBAT to increase, but much more slowly than RBAT did, except for $\gamma = 1$, as shown in

Fig. 5(b). When $\gamma = 1$, MR-RBAT checks every rule in Θ and is not efficient for the reason we gave above. All other settings of γ have resulted better runtime and scalability w.r.t the number of rules to be enforced in anonymization.

6 Conclusions

In this paper, we have studied how RBAT may be made scalable using MapReduce. This is important to a range of transaction data anonymization solutions as most of them, like RBAT, are designed for a centralized setting and involve some iterative data distortion operations in data sanitization. We have shown that parallelizing RBAT in MapReduce by some straightforward data partitioning can incur an overwhelmingly high parallelization cost due to the iterative operations to be performed. We proposed MR-RBAT which employ two controls to limit the maximum number of MapReduce rounds to be used during data generalization, thereby reducing the overhead and computational cost. We have empirically studied the effect of different settings of these controls and have found that MR-RBAT can scale nearly linear w.r.t. the size of data and can efficiently anonymize datasets consisting of millions of transactions, while retaining good data utility.

References

1. Arthur, D., Vassilvitskii, S.: k-means++: the advantages of careful seeding. In: Proceedings of the Eighteenth Annual ACM-SIAM Symposium on Discrete Algorithms, pp. 1027–1035. Society for Industrial and Applied Mathematics (2007)
2. Bahmani, B., Moseley, B., Vattani, A., Kumar, R., Vassilvitskii, S.: Scalable k-means++. Proc. VLDB Endow. **5**(7), 622–633 (2012)
3. Barbaro, M., Zeller, T., Hansell, S.: A face is exposed for aol searcher no. 4417749. New York Times **9**, 2008 (2006). 8For
4. Bu, Y., Howe, B., Balazinska, M., Ernst, M.D.: Haloop: efficient iterative data processing on large clusters. Proc. VLDB Endow. **3**(1–2), 285–296 (2010)
5. Cao, J., Karras, P., Raïssi, C., Tan, K.-L.: ρ-uncertainty: inference-proof transaction anonymization. Proc. VLDB Endow. **3**(1–2), 1033–1044 (2010)
6. Chierichetti, F., Kumar, R., Tomkins, A.: Max-cover in map-reduce. In: Proceedings of the 19th International Conference on World Wide Web. WWW 2010, pp. 231–240. ACM, New York (2010)
7. Dean, J., Ghemawat, S.: Mapreduce: simplified data processing on large clusters. Commun. ACM **51**(1), 107–113 (2008)
8. Ekanayake, J., Li, H., Zhang, B., Gunarathne, T., Bae, S.-H., Qiu, J., Fox, G.: Twister: a runtime for iterative mapreduce. In: Proceedings of the 19th ACM International Symposium on High Performance Distributed Computing, pp. 810–818. ACM (2010)
9. Cordeiro, R.L.F., Traina Jr., C., Traina, A.J.M., López, J., Kang, U., Faloutsos, C.: Clustering very large multi-dimensional datasets with mapreduce. In: Proceedings of the 17th ACM SIGKDD International Conference on Knowledge Discovery and Data Mining. KDD 2011, pp. 690–698. ACM, New York (2011)

10. Fung, B.C.M., Wang, K., Chen, R., Yu, P.S.: Privacy-preserving data publishing: a survey of recent developments. ACM Comput. Surv. **42**(4), 14:1–14:53 (2010)
11. He, Y., Naughton, J.F.: Anonymization of set-valued data via top-down, local generalization. Proc. VLDB Endow. **2**(1), 934–945 (2009)
12. Lee, K.-H., Lee, Y.-J., Choi, H., Chung, Y.D., Moon, B.: Parallel data processing with mapreduce: a survey. SIGMOD Rec. **40**(4), 11–20 (2012)
13. Loukides, G., Gkoulalas-Divanis, A., Shao, J.: Anonymizing transaction data to eliminate sensitive inferences. In: Bringas, P.G., Hameurlain, A., Quirchmayr, G. (eds.) DEXA 2010, Part I. LNCS, vol. 6261, pp. 400–415. Springer, Heidelberg (2010)
14. Narayanan, A., Shmatikov, V.: How to break anonymity of the netflix prize dataset. CoRR abs/cs/0610105 (2006)
15. Terrovitis, M., Mamoulis, N., Kalnis, P.: Privacy-preserving anonymization of set-valued data. Proc. VLDB Endow. **1**(1), 115–125 (2008)
16. Terrovitis, M., Mamoulis, N., Kalnis, P.: Local and global recoding methods for anonymizing set-valued data. VLDB J. **20**(1), 83–106 (2011)
17. Terrovitis, M., Mamoulis, N., Liagouris, J., Skiadopoulos, S.: Privacy preservation by disassociation. Proc. VLDB Endow. **5**(10), 944–955 (2012)
18. The Economist: A special report on managing information: data, data everywhere. The Economist, February 2010
19. Xu, Y., Wang, K., Fu, A.W.-C., Yu, P.S.: Anonymizing transaction databases for publication. In: Proceedings of the 14th ACM SIGKDD International Conference on Knowledge Discovery and Data Mining. KDD 2008, pp. 767–775. ACM, New York (2008)
20. Zhang, X., Liu, C., Nepal, S., Yang, C., Dou, W., Chen, J.: Combining top-down and bottom-up: scalable sub-tree anonymization over big data using mapreduce on cloud. In: 2013 12th IEEE International Conference on Trust, Security and Privacy in Computing and Communications (TrustCom), pp. 501–508, July 2013
21. Zhang, X., Liu, C., Nepal, S., Yang, C., Dou, W., Chen, J.: A hybrid approach for scalable sub-tree anonymization over big data using mapreduce on cloud. J. Comput. Syst. Sci. **80**(5), 1008–1020 (2014). Special Issue on Dependable and Secure Computing The 9th IEEE International Conference on Dependable, Autonomic and Secure Computing
22. Zhang, X., Yang, L., Liu, C., Chen, J.: A scalable two-phase top-down specialization approach for data anonymization using mapreduce on cloud. IEEE Trans. Parallel Distrib. Syst. **25**(2), 363–373 (2014)
23. Zheng, Z., Kohavi, R., Mason, L.: Real world performance of association rule algorithms. In: Proceedings of the Seventh ACM SIGKDD International Conference on Knowledge Discovery and Data Mining. KDD 2001, pp. 401–406. ACM, New York (2001)

Towards Collaborative Query Planning in Multi-party Database Networks

Mingyi Zhao[1](✉), Peng Liu[1], and Jorge Lobo[2]

[1] Pennsylvania State University, State College, USA
{muz127,pliu}@ist.psu.edu
[2] ICREA-Universitat Pompeu Fabra, Barcelona, Spain
jorge.lobo@upf.edu

Abstract. Multi-party distributed database networks require secure and decentralized query planning services. In this work, we propose the collaborative query planning (CQP) service that enables multiple parties to jointly plan queries and controls sensitive information disclosure at the same time. We conduct several simulated experiments to evaluate the performance characteristics of our approach compared to other planning schemes, and also study the trade-off between information confidentiality and query plan efficiency. The evaluation shows that when sharing more than 30% of query planning information between coalition parties, the CQP service is able to generate reasonably efficient query plans. We also outline potential improvements of the CQP service at the end.

Keywords: Information confidentiality · Multi-party database network · Optimization

1 Introduction

Many organizations today form coalitions to facilitate information sharing and processing for a common mission. In a typical coalition, multiple parties may connect their database severs with each other to form a federated database and enable querying over the network. Such federation of multiple database servers can be supported by products like IBM GaianDB [1].

Since coalition networks are formed by independent parties with different level of trust among each other, information confidentiality becomes an important concern. Significant effort has been made to protect data confidentiality in mutli-party database networks by enforcing data authorization policies [3,8,9,14]. Previous work has also proposed new query engines that consider query information confidentiality during collaborative query execution [4–6].

A common assumption behind most of previous work is the existence of a fully trusted central query planning server. This query planning server will enforce data authorizations to protect confidentiality while finding the optimal execution plan for a query. Therefore, the planner needs to know query planning information, such as metadata of relations, query information, data authorizations, etc., from all coalition parties. However, this assumption limits the usage

© IFIP International Federation for Information Processing 2015
P. Samarati (Ed.): DBSec 2015, LNCS 9149, pp. 19–34, 2015.
DOI: 10.1007/978-3-319-20810-7_2

of federated databases for most coalition scenarios for mainly two reasons. First, in a coalition network, it is very rare that a party can be fully trusted by all other parties. Thus, building a central authority server which all trust will be difficult. Second, the central planning server becomes a single point of failure in this multi-party database network. This is particularly worrisome in ad hoc and dynamic situations where nodes may enter and leave the network anytime. Some existing systems such as the GaianDB avoid using this central planning design, and only use the basic data shipping plan as the query execution strategy where all required data is sent to the querying node and the query is processed locally, hence losing all the performance benefits from distributed query processing.

We cannot directly apply existing decentralized query planning frameworks [11–13] to multi-party scenarios, since they are designed for scenarios where servers can trust each other (e.g., all servers belong to a single organization). More specifically, the interaction process between servers in these frameworks could leak sensitive information in multi-party scenarios.

Our first contribution in this work is a new decentralized query planning service, called collaborative query planning (CQP), for multi-party database networks. This service allows coalition parties to collaboratively plan queries while at the same time control information disclosure among collaborating parties. A premise of our work is that coalitions are formed because there is some willingness among the parties to collaborate and hence some level of trust. Therefore, we assume that coalition parties share certain query planning information with other parties in order to facilitate the common mission. Given a query, different coalition parties might be able to do part of the query planning based on the amount of information they know. The querying party can thus assemble these partial results to generate a final plan. Our second contribution is to empirically evaluate the performance characteristics of our approach compared to other planning schemes in different scenarios. We are particularly interested in how the level of information sharing between coalition parties influences the decentralized query planning. That is, we study and measure the trade-off between information confidentiality and query plan efficiency.

2   Background

2.1   Query Planning in Database Networks

We briefly describe key concepts of query planning in database networks based on a simple example. In Fig. 1, four companies formed an information sharing coalition on top of a database network. A is a target advertising company who analyzes data from various sources and creates targeted advertisements for Internet users. E is an E-commerce company that maintains a large online sale data in relation R_E. S is a search engine company that stores search log in R_S. Finally, N is an online social network company that owns user profile information as relation R_N. Each party has a server and the topology of this database

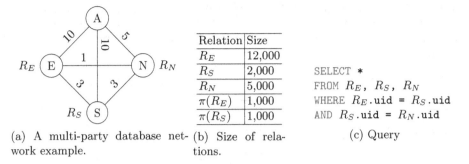

Relation	Size
R_E	12,000
R_S	2,000
R_N	5,000
$\pi(R_E)$	1,000
$\pi(R_S)$	1,000

```
SELECT *
FROM R_E, R_S, R_N
WHERE R_E.uid = R_S.uid
AND R_S.uid = R_N.uid
```

(a) A multi-party database network example.

(b) Size of rela-
tions.

(c) Query

Fig. 1. The setting of a simple multi-party database network.

network is shown in Fig. 1a. The number on each link is the communication cost of using that link. Now, A wants to retrieve the data of all customers who have bought products from E and have also used services provided by S and N. So A formulates the query $R_E \bowtie R_S \bowtie R_N$ shown in Fig. 1c.

The query needs to be translated into an executable *query plan*, which is defined as a multi-graph $< V, E >$, where V is the set of vertices in the graph. Each vertex refers to a database server and describes operations to be performed on that server. E is the set of edges. Each edge is represented by (S_i, S_j, D) and it means that server S_i will send data D, which will be the result of the operations executed in S_i, to server S_j. Figure 2 gives two possible query plans for the example query. In Fig. 2a, the querier A first retrieve data from remote servers and the process the data locally. In Fig. 2b, party N helps A to process the query and then sends the result to A.

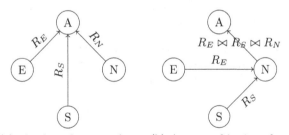

(a) The data shipping plan.   (b) A query shipping plan.

Fig. 2. Two final plans for the query.

The process of translating a query into a query plan is called *query planning*. Since usually a query can be translated into a large number of possible execution plans, the query planner will aim to find the minimal cost plan using algorithms such as dynamic programming [7,10]. In this work, we consider a basic cost model, which estimates the cost of a query plan only based on data transmissions.

Table 1. Size of join results. π represents the projection operation in the semijoin [10].

Relation	Size
$\pi(R_E) \bowtie R_S$	500
$\pi(R_S) \bowtie R_E$	1,000
$R_S \bowtie R_E$	2,000
$R_S \bowtie R_E \bowtie R_N$	5,000

Table 2. Information sharing policies defined in this coalition network. We assign an id for each authorization for easy reference. Q' is $R_E \bowtie R_S$.

Creator	Data auth.	Query auth.	Auth. sharing
A	-	7.$A \xrightarrow{Q'} E$ 8.$A \xrightarrow{Q} S$	$A \xrightarrow{A_7} S \; A \xrightarrow{A_8'} E$
E	1.$E \xrightarrow{R_E} A$ 2.$E \xrightarrow{R_E} S$	-	$E \xrightarrow{A_1} S$
S	3.$S \xrightarrow{R_S} A$ 4.$S \xrightarrow{R_S} E$	-	$S \xrightarrow{A_3} E \; S \xrightarrow{A_4} A$
N	5.$N \xrightarrow{R_N} A$ 6.$N \xrightarrow{R_N} S$	-	$N \xrightarrow{A_5} S$

We denote the cost of sending a unit data from S_i to S_j as $cost(S_i, S_j)$. Then the cost of a query plan QP is defined as:

$$cost(QP) = \sum_{\forall (S_i, S_j, D) \in QP} |D| \times cost(S_i, S_j) \tag{1}$$

To estimate the cost of query plan candidates, the query planner also needs to estimate the size of join results based on metadata including the statistics of join operands. We have listed the estimation results of our example in Table 1. The cost model and the join result size estimation show that the cost of the data shipping plan is 165,000, while the cost of the query shipping plan is only 43,000, because the server of N is closer to data sources than the server of A.

2.2 Information Confidentiality Requirements in Multi-party Database Networks

The example shows that *collaborative query execution* can significantly reduce the cost of processing queries. That is, instead of having the querier to retrieve all base relations from remote servers and process the data locally, the querier now delegates sub queries to collaborating parties, which can process the sub queries more efficiently. However, collaborative query execution might disclose sensitive information, such as data tuples [3,14] and query information [4]. To protect information confidentiality, coalition parties create polices to share selected information with others. The query planner, knowing all information sharing policies, will enforce these policies during the generation of query plans. In this work, we consider the following three types of information confidentiality.

Data Confidentiality. For a party in a multi-party database network, not all data can be shared. Instead, the party wants to selectively share certain data with other parties. A party P_i can authorize another party P_j to access relation R using a *data authorization* $P_i \xrightarrow{R} P_j$. We call P_i the *owner* and P_j the *consumer*. We have created data authorizations for the above example in Table 2.

The query planner shall make sure that the final query plan is compliant with all data authorizations. The plan in Fig. 2a is legal because A is authorized to access R_E, R_S and R_N. However, the plan in Fig. 2b is illegal because N is neither authorized to access R_E nor R_S. In a special case, P_i can only authorize P_j to access metadata of R, including its schema and statistics, in order to let P_j be able to help with planning queries related to R, as we shall discuss later. This metadata sharing policy is defined as $P_i \xrightarrow{M(R)} P_j$.

Query Confidentiality. A query Q is considered sensitive information because it contains the intent of the querier [4]. The execution of non-data shipping plans can disclose information of the query to other parties. For example, in Fig. 2b, the party N who executes the query from A, will also learn the content of the query, which might not be desirable for A. A party P_i can share a sub query $Q' \subseteq Q$ with another party P_j using *query authorization* $P_i \xrightarrow{Q'} P_j$. We list some example query authorizations in Table 2. Specifically, A shares the full query with S but only shares a partial query with E. The planner then guarantees that the final query plan is compliant with query authorizations [5].

Authorization Confidentiality. The data authorizations and query authorizations defined between coalition parties are also sensitive, for they contain information regarding the collaboration relationships between different parties. For instance, in the example of Fig. 1, party E authorizes A to access R_E. However, E might not want N to know this policy $E \xrightarrow{R_E} A$ due to business secret concerns. A party P_i can share an authorization with P_j using *authorization sharing policy* $P_i \xrightarrow{A} P_j$, where A is an authorization and P_i is the owner of A. Examples of authorization sharing policies can be found in Table 2.

The query planning server needs to know metadata, queries and authorizations in order to generate query plans. So we call these three types of information *query planning information*. There are other types of information required for query planning, such as the network topology of the database network. In this work, we assume these types of information are known to all parties.

2.3 Discussions

A central query planning service needs to know all query planning information from every coalition party in order to find the optimal plan. However, as we have discussed in Sect. 1, this assumption usually does not hold for multi-party database networks.

Our Goal. In this work, we propose a new decentralized query planning service that only uses information shared explicitly between parties to generate executable query plans. This query planning service enforces the information sharing policies to ensure that the query planning process only disclose information allowed by policies to collaborators.

Threat Model. We assume a curious-but-honest model. That is, each party will follow the steps in the service but might passively learn information that might be disclosed during query planning and query execution. The rationale behind this threat model is that certain level of trust is the pre-condition of establishing a coalition network. Therefore, parties that maliciously attack other parties should be excluded from the coalition in the first place.

3   Collaborative Query Planning

3.1   Overview

The basic idea of our collaborative query planning (CQP) service is that the querier first delegates sub queries[1] to collaborating parties under query authorizations. Then the collaborating parties generate query plans for the received sub queries, and report their findings back to the querier. Finally, the querier assembles the final query plan. Using this service, the querier can utilize information known to collaborating parties to generate an efficient query plan. Figure 3 provides an overview of the CQP. We assume that each party has a planning server, which plans its owner's queries and offers planning service to other parties. We also assume that before executing any query, all parties have created information sharing policies according to its needs.

The CQP service is similar to previous decentralized query planning frameworks [11–13] that attempt to address the problem of missing query planning information in a distributed database setting. However, the cause of insufficient information in previous scenarios was the difficulty in obtaining planning information, rather than information sharing policies. We will discuss more about the differences between these frameworks and our design in Sect. 6.

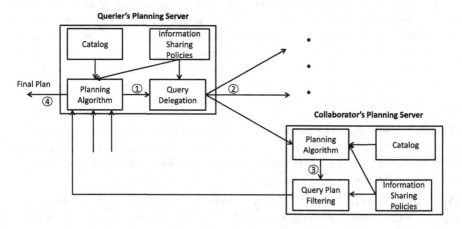

Fig. 3. Overview of the CQP service. The four main steps are labeled.

---

[1] For simplicity, the term sub query also refers to the full query.

In general, we can consider four query planning frameworks in the potential design space of query planning services for multi-party distributed database: (1) if there is no query planning information sharing at all, then all queries have to be executed using data shipping plans. However, the cost of data shipping plans are usually high; (2) if there is certain level of query planning information sharing but no planning collaboration between coalition parties, then we call it *local planning*, since the querier relies on its own limited knowledge of the whole database network to plan the query; (3) if there is certain level of query planning information sharing and planning collaboration between parties, we have a collaborative query planning framework and our design of CQP is one instance of it; (4) if we increase the level of query planning information sharing to the point that one party knows all query planning information, then we actually have the central query planning framework. We will next present the CQP service, and then compare it with other designs in the spectrum in Sect. 4.

3.2   The CQP Service

In this section, we explain the details of the CQP service.

1. Initiation. Given a query, the querier first runs a local planning solely based on information it knows and obtains the locally generated optimal plan QP_l, and the data shipping plan QP_d. Given a fixed *delegation threshold* T_c defined by the querying party, if $\frac{cost(QP_l)}{cost(QP_d)} < T_c$, the querier will directly execute QP_l and no further query planning is required. Otherwise, the querier will initiate collaborative query planning in order to obtain a more efficient query plan. $T_c = 0.5$ means that collaborative query planning will only happen if the locally generated plan cannot reduce at least 50 % of the cost of the data-shipping plan.

Example. Let's revisit the example in Fig. 1. The querier A first runs a local planning. However, it can only generate the data shipping plan QP_d (Fig. 2a) due to the lack of planning information. More specifically, A almost knows nothing about authorizations between other parties, so it cannot generate a plan utilizing other parties' servers. Therefore, we have $QP_l = QP_d$. The cost of the data shipping plan QP_d is $12,000 \times 10 + 2,000 \times 10 + 5,000 \times 5 = 165,000$. If we set $T_c = 0.5$, then we have $\frac{cost(QP_l)}{cost(QP_d)} = 1 > T_c$, so A will initiate the CQP to find a cheaper plan.

2. Delegation. The querier next decides which portion of the query will be delegated to which collaborating party. We currently consider a simple process in which the querier tries to maximize the delegation in order to get as much help as possible from others, constrained by its own query authorizations. We will discuss potential improvements of the delegation strategy in Sect. 5. The pseudo code of the delegation process is shown in Algorithm 1. Given a query Q and information sharing policies defined by the querier, this algorithm generates a set of delegation tasks. A delegation task $(collaborator, subquery)$ asks the *collaborator* to plan the *subquery*. Line 5 checks whether party P is allowed to know sub query Q' based on information sharing policies. Lines 7–9 remove delegation tasks for which sub queries are contained by other tasks.

Algorithm 1: Collaborative query planning delegation task generation.

input : Query Q and information sharing policies of the querier
output: Delegation tasks for Q

```
1 tasks = {};
2 foreach P in parties do
3 │   for i in 2 to n do
4 │   │   foreach subquery Q' with length i do
5 │   │   │   if allows(P, Q') then
6 │   │   │   │   tasks.addNew(P, Q');
7 │   │   │   │   foreach t in tasks and t.Q'' ⊂ Q' do
8 │   │   │   │   │   tasks.remove(t);
9 return tasks;
```

Example. Based on the information sharing policies defined in Table 2, A generates the following two delegations:

- $(E,\ R_E \bowtie R_S)$
- $(S,\ R_E \bowtie R_S \bowtie R_N)$.

3. Optimization. Each collaborating party tries to find the optimal plan of delegated sub queries based on query planning information known to that party. This process is based on the classic dynamic programming algorithm [7], with enforcement of information sharing policies [5,14]. We will not describe the algorithm in this paper. The result is a triple $(collaborator, subquery, plan)$ in which the *plan* is the best plan found by this collaborator, or null if the collaborator fails to find any plan. Note that this query plan has to be filtered by the collaborator before sending it to the querier. This is because the query plan could contain sensitive information of data authorization that is not supposed to be known by the querier. The filtering algorithm is shown in Algorithm 2. In line 3, $L_{DA}(v)$ returns data authorization information associated with the vertex v in the query plan graph. As long as there is one data authorization that the querier is not allowed to see, the algorithm will replace this vertex with its cost and remove all associated edges in Lines 4–5. $v.succ$ returns the successor of this vertex in the query plan graph. $v.preds$ returns a list of predecessors of the vertex.

Example. E and S now plan the sub queries delegated to them. For $R_E \bowtie R_S$, E has found a semi-join based query plan QP_E in Fig. 4a. For $R_E \bowtie R_S \bowtie R_N$, S has found the plan QP_S shown in Fig. 4b. We calculate the cost of these two query plans as follows: $cost(QP_E) = 1000 \times 3 + 500 \times 3 + 2000 \times 10 = 24,500$ and $cost(QP_S) = 1000 \times 3 + 1000 \times 3 + 5000 \times 3 + 3000 \times 10 = 51,000$. Both plans are filtered based on authorization sharing policies in Table 2.

Algorithm 2: Query plan filtering.

---

input : Query plan QP and authorization sharing policies of the collaborator
output: Filtered query plan QP'
1 $QP' \leftarrow QP$;
2 **foreach** v *in* $QP.V$ **do**
3   **if** $!allows(querier, L_{DA}(v))$ **then**
4   v.succ.preds[v] $\leftarrow$ cost(v);
5   QP.remove(v.edges);
6 **return** QP';

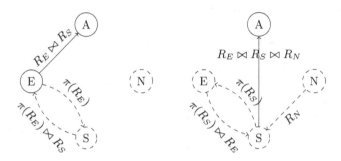

(a) Plan QP_E generated by E.   (b) Plan QP_S generated by S.

Fig. 4. Query plans generated by collaborating parties. Dashed components are not disclosed to the querier A.

4. Synthesis. The querier synthesizes sub query plans from collaborating parties and creates the final plan by running the query planning algorithm again. Different from the first run, this time some sub queries already have candidate plans available from collaborating parties. These candidate plans might be building blocks for an efficient final plan. The querier might not know the content of these plans due to the filtering in step 3. However, the cost information is enough for the querier to do optimization. It is also possible that none of the collaborating parties have provided a valid plan. In this case, the querier has to use the initial local planning result.

Example. Since A is not allowed to view the content of QP_E and QP_S based on policies, A will only receive the cost of each query plan:

- $(E, R_E \bowtie R_S, \text{24,500})$
- $(S, R_E \bowtie R_S \bowtie R_N, \text{51,000})$.

The querier A will run the query planning algorithm again and take QP_E as one candidate for executing $R_E \bowtie R_S$, and take QP_S as one candidate for executing the whole query $R_E \bowtie R_S \bowtie R_N$. Figure 5a shows the final optimal plan QP_A. This plan incorporates QP_E and costs 49,500, less than the cost of QP_S. Also, compared with the data-shipping plan QP_d, QP_A saves 70% of the query execution cost.

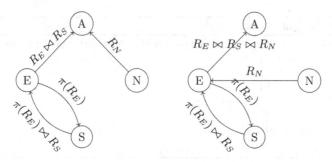

(a) Final optimal plan QP_A.   (b) A cheaper final query plan.

Fig. 5. Two final plans for the query.

There are actually query plans cheaper than QP_A that are also compliant with all policies. For example, the plan in Fig. 5b only costs 39,500. However, this plan cannot be generated in CQP because of limited information sharing and limitations of the collaboration process. In a centralized scenario, the central planner with all planning information available can discover it. We will evaluate the performance gap between CQP and central planning at different levels of information sharing in the next section.

Summary. In this section, we have presented the design of the CQP service. However, this design is only the first step towards secure decentralized query planning for multi-party database network. We will discuss potential improvements in Sect. 5. Next section, we will evaluate the CQP service's performance by comparing it with the central planning and the local planning.

4   Evaluation

The goal of the evaluation is threefold. First, we want to compare the CQP with the central planning, which always returns the minimum cost plan. The query planning under the CQP will only perform equal or worse than the central planning, and the goal of our evaluation is to measure this difference quantitatively. The second goal is to compare the CQP with local planning in order to see the benefit of introducing collaboration into query planning. The third goal is to study the trade-off between information sharing and query planning effectiveness under the CQP. Sharing more information can definitely give more chances of finding an efficient plan, and we want to quantitatively measure this trade-off.

4.1   Settings

We have created a multi-party database network simulator whose parameters are listed in Table 3.[2] The simulator will randomly generate information sharing

---

[2] For simplicity, we ignore the sharing of query authorizations. That means whenever P_i shares a sub query with another party P_j, P_i shares all query authorizations of that sub query with P_j as well.

Table 3. Simulation parameters.

Parameters	Values	Explanation
N_P	9	Number of parties
N_S	7	Number of database servers each party has. There are $N_P \times N_S = 63$ servers in the simulated database network
N_R	15	Number of relations each party has. There are $N_P \times N_R = 135$ relations in total
N_A	[3, 10]	Number of attributes a relation has
$N_t(R)$	[100, 50000]	Number of tuples in relation R
$C(s_i, s_j)$	[1, 50]	The communication cost between server s_i and s_j. We used the Erdös-Renyi model to connect two servers at a probability of 0.1. Then the communication cost between any two servers is the cost of the shortest path between them
T_c	0	The CQP initiation threshold described in Sect. 3.2. $T_c = 0$ forces CQP to be initiated for every query
$authProb$	0.5	Data authorization generation probability, which is the probability that a party is authorized to view a relation
ρ_{DA}	[0,1]	Data authorization sharing probability
ρ_Q	[0,1]	Query sharing probability
ρ_M	[0,1]	Metadata sharing probability

policies between coalition parties based on probability values ρ_{DA}, ρ_Q and ρ_M shown in the table. The process of generating those polices is described in Algorithm 3. Basically, the algorithm goes through each pair of (*info*, *party*) and shares *info* to *party* with the corresponding probability.

Algorithm 3: Information Sharing Policy Generation

    input : Settings of the database network $\mathcal{N}$
    output: A set of information sharing policies
1 policies = {};
2 infoSet = genPlanInfoSet($\mathcal{N}$);
3 **foreach** P_j *in parties* **do**
4   **foreach** *info in infoSet* **do**
5   P_i = owner(*info*) ;
6   rand = random(P_j);
7   ρ = getShareProb(getType(*info*)) ;
8   **if** *rand* < ρ **then**
9   policies.addNew($P_i \xrightarrow{info} P_j$) ;
10 **return** polices;

4.2 Results

We conduct 11 query planning experiments with different information sharing probability values $\rho = \rho_{DA} = \rho_Q = \rho_M$ from 0.0, 0.1, ... 1.0. In each experiment, we use CQP, central planning and local planning to plan 10,000 simulated queries. We use the average query cost of central planning as the reference to normalize the average query plan cost for CQP and local query planning. So the cost values shown below are the relative costs compared to the central planning.

The result is shown in Fig. 6a, which leads to several observations: **(O1)** a small amount of information sharing can significantly reduce the query plan cost of both CQP and local planning. We can see that when ρ is increased from 0 (no sharing at all) to 0.3, the relative cost drops from 3.5 to 2.2. **(O2)** when the level of information sharing is low ($\rho \in [0, 0.3]$), the CQP and local planning have the same performance. This is because collaborating parties in the CQP do not have enough information to offer help. **(O3)** when there is enough information sharing between parties ($\rho \in [0.4, 0.8]$), CQP will outperform local planning in a narrow margin, since the collaborating parties can now utilize their knowledge

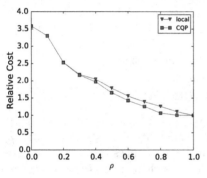

(a) Compare local planning and CQP under different ρ.

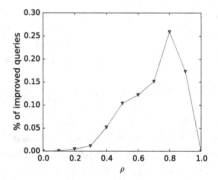

(b) Percentage of CQP-improved queries under different ρ.

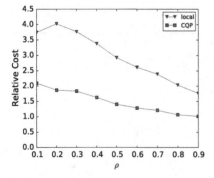

(c) Compare local planning and CQP for CQP-improved queries.

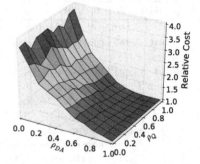

(d) Relation between ρ_{DA}, ρ_Q and the relative cost.

Fig. 6. Evaluation results.

to help the querier. The narrow margin between CQP and local planning can possibly be explained by two reasons. First, the tested queries are generated from uniform distributions. Therefore, the improvements for certain queries are diluted by other queries. We will investigate this hypothesis further in the next evaluation. The second reason is that the current CQP has certain limitations, so the potential of collaborative query planning has not been fully exploited yet. We will discuss potential improvements in Sect. 5. (**O4**) as coalition parties further share more information by increasing ρ from 0.8 to 1.0, the gain of CQP is negligible. The cost curves of CQP and local planning converge to the central planning (relative cost is 1) when $\rho = 1$ (all information is shared).

To examine the hypothesis raised in O3, we show the percentages of queries for which CQP outperforms local planning in Fig. 6b. We found that (**O5**) as we increase the level of information sharing, the planning result more queries will be improved by CQP. However, after certain threshold ($\rho = 0.8$ in our evaluation), the advantage of CQP over local planning quickly drops to none, which is consistent with O4. We further compare the relative cost of CQP and local planning for CQP-improved queries only in Fig. 6c. The result shows that (**O6**) CQP outperforms local planning for certain queries by a large margin. This supports the hypothesis raised in O3. We will further discuss the implication of this observation in Sect. 5.

Next, we examine the impact of different information sharing parameters. We record the relative cost of CQP under different data authorization sharing probabilities (ρ_{DA}) and query information sharing probabilities (ρ_Q) for 10,000 simulated queries, and show the result in Fig. 6d[3]. We see that (**O7**) although increasing ρ_{DA} alone can reduce the cost of query plans (through local planning), the cost reduction is faster if coalition parties share both data authorization information and query information, and utilize CQP.

5 Discussion

Our CQP service is only a first step towards a secure decentralized query planning system for multi-party database networks, and there are potential improvements for the service.

Query Delegation. The current query delegation component (Algorithm 1) in CQP can be improved when we consider it as a decision making process. Basically, the querier needs to estimate the potential gain (e.g. whether the collaborator has enough information, the size of the data, etc.) and lost (e.g. the risk of disclosing a query information to a collaborator) of a potential delegation, and then make a decision based on the trade-off between them. Existing risk-based access control methods could be useful in this scenario [2].

Synthesis. It is also possible that a collaborator fails to find the query plan for the delegated sub query. In our current implementation, the collaborator will return a null plan. However, it is possible that the collaborator obtains some

---

[3] We set the metadata sharing probability $\rho_M = 1$ for simplicity.

partial results which might still be helpful for the querier. It would be good if the querier can synthesize these partial results as well.

Information Sharing. Our evaluation only considers different levels of information sharing. However, based on observation O5, it seems that certain pieces of query planning information are more important for the queries than others, particularly when the queries are not generated uniformly. In other words, the planning service of CQP can perform better under the same level of information sharing, if information shared is aligned with the query workload. Therefore, an important future work is to create a decision making mechanism to guide coalition parties sharing information in such a way that the risk of information disclosure is low while the performance gain of CQP is high.

6   Related Work

Most existing distributed database systems have a central query planner which uses dynamic programming [7,10] to find the optimal query plan. A few pieces of work have also built decentralized query planning services [11–13], whose common motivation is that in a distributed scenario, accurate information of remote sites is hard to obtain, so query planning cannot be done by a central planner. Papadimos and Maier have proposed the Mutant Query Plan (MQP) [11], in which a query plan is sent to different servers and each server will try to plan and process a part of it. Farnan et al. proposed the harden MQP to encrypt certain parts of a query plan in order to protect query information [6]. This is similar to the query plan filtering step in our CQP service. Mariposa [13] and the query trading framework [12] apply ideas from Economy to the problem of decentralized query planning. In the query trading framework, the querier makes sub query planning requests to collaborating parties, who then do query planning and make offers to the querier. The querier combines different offers into the final plan, and pay for it. The querier-collaborator interaction process in the CQP is similar to and also simpler than the query trading framework, which also supports iterative negotiation, nested delegation, etc. However, CQP protects information confidentiality during a collaborative query planning process.

Another line of related work focuses on protecting the confidentiality of sensitive information in multi-party database network. Vimercati et al. proposed a new data authorization that enables authorizing the join result of several tables to a party based on the concept of join path [3]. Qiang et al. applied pairwise authorizations to enforce horizontal access control of relation data between coalition parties [14]. Farnan et al. studied the query information protection problem in distributed database network, and then extended the SQL syntax to enable query privacy constraints for distributed query execution [4].

7   Conclusion

In this work, we present CQP, a decentralized query planning service that allows multiple parties to jointly plan queries based on limited information shared between them. Our evaluation shows that CQP performs better than local planning when 30 %–90 % information are shared between parties. We have also measured the trade-off between information sharing and query planning effectiveness. Potential enhancements of CQP have been discussed in Sect. 5.

Acknowledgment. We would like to thank Dr. Alessandra Russo and the anonymous reviewers for their valuable comments and suggestions. This research was sponsored by the U.S. Army Research Laboratory and the U.K. Ministry of Defence and was accomplished under Agreement Number W911NF-06-3-0001. The views and conclusions contained in this document are those of the author(s) and should not be interpreted as representing the official policies, either expressed or implied, of the U.S. Army Research Laboratory, the U.S. Government, the U.K. Ministry of Defence or the U.K. Government. The U.S. and U.K. Governments are authorized to reproduce and distribute reprints for Government purposes notwithstanding any copyright notation hereon.

References

1. Bent, G., Dantressangle, P., Vyvyan, D., Mowshowitz, A., Mitsou, V.: A dynamic distributed federated database. In: Second Annual Conference of ITA, Imperial College, London (2008)
2. Cheng, P.-C., Rohatgi, P., Keser, C., Karger, P.A., Wagner, G.M., Reninger, A.S.: Fuzzy multi-level security: an experiment on quantified risk-adaptive access control. In: 2007 IEEE Symposium on Security and Privacy, SP 2007, pp. 222–230. IEEE (2007)
3. De Capitani di Vimercati, S., Foresti, S., Jajodia, S., Paraboschi, S., Samarati, P.: Authorization enforcement in distributed query evaluation. J. Comput. Secur. **19**(4), 751–794 (2011)
4. Farnan, N.L., Lee, A.J., Chrysanthis, P.K., Yu, T.: Don't reveal my intension: protecting user privacy using declarative preferences during distributed query processing. In: Atluri, V., Diaz, C. (eds.) ESORICS 2011. LNCS, vol. 6879, pp. 628–647. Springer, Heidelberg (2011)
5. Farnan, N.L., Lee, A.J., Chrysanthis, P.K., Yu, T.: Paqo: preference-aware query optimization for decentralized database systems. In: IEEE 30th International Conference on Data Engineering (ICDE) (2014)
6. Farnan, N.L., Lee, A.J., Yu, T.: Investigating privacy-aware distributed query evaluation. In: Proceedings of the 9th Annual ACM Workshop on Privacy in the Electronic Society, pp. 43–52. ACM (2010)
7. Kossmann, D.: The state of the art in distributed query processing. ACM Comput. Surv. (CSUR) **32**(4), 422–469 (2000)
8. Le, M., Kant, K., Jajodia, S.: Rule enforcement with third parties in secure cooperative data access. In: Wang, L., Shafiq, B. (eds.) DBSec 2013. LNCS, vol. 7964, pp. 282–288. Springer, Heidelberg (2013)
9. Le, M., Kant, K., Jajodia, S.: Consistent query plan generation in secure cooperative data access. In: Atluri, V., Pernul, G. (eds.) DBSec 2014. LNCS, vol. 8566, pp. 227–242. Springer, Heidelberg (2014)
10. Özsu, M.T., Valduriez, P.: Principles of Distributed Database Systems. Springer, New York (2011)
11. Papadimos, V., Maier, D.: Distributed queries without distributed state. In: Proceedings of WebDB 2002, pp. 95–100 (2002)

12. Pentaris, F., Ioannidis, Y.: Query optimization in distributed networks of autonomous database systems. ACM Trans. Database Syst. (TODS) **31**(2), 537–583 (2006)
13. Stonebraker, M., Devine, R., Kornacker, M., Litwin, W., Pfeffer, A., Sah, A., Staelin, C.: An economic paradigm for query processing and data migration in mariposa. In: 1994 Proceedings of the Third International Conference on Parallel and Distributed Information Systems, pp. 58–67. IEEE (1994)
14. Zeng, Q., Zhao, M., Liu, P., Yadav, P., Calo, S., Lobo, J.: Enforcement of autonomous authorizations in collaborative distributed query evaluation. IEEE Trans. Knowl. Data Eng. **27**, 979–992 (2014)

Privacy-Preserving Range Queries from Keyword Queries

Giovanni Di Crescenzo$^{(\boxtimes)}$ and Abhrajit Ghosh

Applied Communication Sciences, Basking Ridge, NJ, USA
{gdicrescenzo,aghosh}@appcomsci.com

Abstract. We consider the problem of a client performing privacy-preserving *range queries* to a server's database. We propose a cryptographic model for the study of such protocols, by expanding previous well-studied models of keyword search and private information retrieval to the range query type and to incorporate a multiple-occurrence attribute column in the database table.

Our first two results are 2-party privacy-preserving range query protocols, where either (a) the value domain is linear in the number of database records and the database size is only increased by a small constant factor; or (b) the value domain is exponential (thus, essentially of arbitrarily large size) in the number of database records and the database size is increased by a factor logarithmic in the value domain size. Like all previous work in private information retrieval and keyword search, this protocol still satisfies server time complexity linear in the number of database payloads.

We discuss how to adapt these results to a 3-party model where encrypted data is outsourced to a third party (i.e., a cloud server). The result is a private database retrieval protocol satisfying a highly desirable tradeoff of privacy and efficiency properties; most notably: (1) *no unintended information* is leaked to clients or servers, and the information leaked to the third party is characterized as 'access pattern' on encrypted data; (2) for each query, all parties run in time *only logarithmic* in the number of database records and linear in the answer size; (3) the protocol's query runtime is practical for real-life applications.

1 Introduction

The recent computing trend of outsourcing big data in the cloud for simplified and efficient application deployment is being embraced in government, as well as other areas, including finance, information technology, etc. In government, large databases are needed in many contexts (e.g., no-fly lists, metadata of communication records, etc.). In finance, banks and other financial institutions need to store huge data volumes and compute over them on a daily basis. In information technology, web and social networks collect huge data from computer users, which is then made available for different uses and computations. To facilitate and guarantee success for all of these applications, databases are very useful data management tools, and cloud storage and computing provide tremendous efficiency

© IFIP International Federation for Information Processing 2015
P. Samarati (Ed.): DBSec 2015, LNCS 9149, pp. 35–50, 2015.
DOI: 10.1007/978-3-319-20810-7_3

and utility for users, as exemplified by the increasingly successful database-as-a-services application paradigm (see, e.g., [13]). On the other hand, cloud storage and computing paradigms are also accompanied by privacy risks (see, e.g., [21]). To mitigate these risks, database-management systems can use *privacy-preserving database retrieval protocols* that allow users to submit queries and receive results in a way that clients learn nothing about the contents of a database except the results of their queries, and servers do not learn which queries are submitted. The research literature has attempted to address these issues, by studying private database retrieval protocols in limited database and query models and with limited efficiency properties. In this paper we partially address some of these limitations, by using a practical database model, and proposing protocols in both a client-server model and a 3-party model, where servers can outsource data to a third party (in encrypted form). In these models, practical and privacy-preserving database retrieval protocols for basic query types such as keyword queries, have been recently shown to be possible. In this paper, we attempt to show that practical and privacy-preserving database retrieval protocols are possible for a more complex query type: *range queries*.

Previous Work. The security and cryptography literature contains a significant amount of research in the private information retrieval (PIR) [6,18,20] and keyword search (KS) [3,5,10] areas. Both areas consider rather theoretical data models, as we now discuss. In PIR, a database is modeled as a string of n bits, and the query value is an index $i \in \{1, \ldots, n\}$. In KS, early data models were also somewhat restrictive; for instance, [10] only admitted a single matching record per query. The inefficiency of the server runtime in PIR and KS protocols has been well documented (see, e.g., [24]). Some results attempted to use a third party and make the PIR query subprotocol more efficient but require a practically inefficient preprocessing phase [8]. Recently, however, some results on provably privacy-preserving and practical keyword queries in a practical database model and in an outsourced-data scenario were concurrently shown by [7,17], where significant efficiency is achieved by provably limiting the privacy loss to encrypted data "access-pattern" information, only leaked to the cloud server.

The literature also contains a significant amount of work on range queries or range computations on encrypted data. Some papers (starting with [4,22]) focus on encrypting messages, on which one can later perform range query computations. These approaches offer interesting provable security properties but make heavy use of asymmetric cryptography techniques and seem hard to translate into practical protocols for databases. Promising approaches to achieve at least some limited amount of privacy (with tradeoffs against efficiency) on range queries in an outsourced database setting have also been shown (see, e.g., [14] and follow-up work), typically based on variants of "bucketization" approaches. The primitive of order-preserving encryption gives rise to elegant and efficient range query protocols in the "database-as-a-service" model (see, e.g., [1] and follow-up work), but constructions of order-preserving encryption are still not very efficient and especially come with static leakage on the encrypted data to the server holding it [2]. Overall, the question of designing provably privacy-preserving range queries in a practical data model, even in the outsourced-data scenario, seems to still deserve more attention from the security community.

Our Contribution. We study range queries in a more practical (outsourced or not) database model, capturing record payloads, possibly equal attribute values across different database records, and multiple answers to a given query. In this model, we define suitable correctness, privacy and efficiency requirements.

We then design two range query protocols in the 2-party model, which satisfy desired privacy properties (i.e., the server learns no information about the query range other than the number of matching records, and the client learns no information about the database other than matching database records) in our data model. Our first protocol works for linear-size value domains by only increasing database size by a small constant, and our second protocol works for exponential-size (thus, essentially arbitrary-size) value domains while increasing database size by a factor logarithmic in the value domain size. These protocols are constructed directly from any KS protocol and, like previous PIR and KS protocols, have server time complexity linear in the database size, a drawback dealt with in our next result.

Our third protocol transforms any of our 2-party range query protocols into a 3-party protocol, where the third party can be a cloud server, based on any 3-party KS protocol (like the one in [7], only based on any pseudo-random function, implemented as a block cipher). In this protocol, both server and third party *run queries in logarithmic time* and the following privacy properties provably hold: the server learns nothing about the query range, the client learns nothing about the database in addition to the matching database records, and the third party learns nothing about the query range or the database content, other than the repeating of queries from the client and repeated access to the encrypted data structures received by the server at initialization. This solves the problem of achieving provable privacy (against a semi-honest adversary) and efficient server runtime at the cost of a 'third-party'-server and some leakage to the third party characterized as 'access-pattern' to encrypted data. We stress that this protocol has efficient running time not only in an asymptotic sense, but in a sense that makes it ready for real-life applications (where such form of leakage to the third party is tolerable). In our implementation of a computationally similar protocol, we reached our main performance goal of achieving response time to be *less than 1 order of magnitude* slower than commercial non-private protocols like MySQL. Our protocol solves a number of technical challenges using simple and practical techniques, including a reduction step via an intermediate rank database and a 'lazy' database value shifting approach. The privacy loss traded for such a practicality property was already studied in [15,16], who also proposed simple techniques to mitigate leakage to the cloud server in the form of 'access-pattern' to encrypted data, at least in the case of keyword queries. (Here, note that in the presence of such leakage, neither the client nor the server learn anything new, and the cloud server does not statically learn anything about the plain database content). We believe that one appropriate mitigation technique needed for such solutions could be based on Oblivious RAM (an active area started in [12]), and it is plausible that dedicated Oblivious RAM techniques in the 3-party model may nullify or mitigate any such leakage based on 'access-pattern' over encrypted data. This is indeed a promising direction as, while years ago Oblivious RAM was considered inefficient, recent advances (see, e.g., [23]) have made it significantly less inefficient. In all our protocols, we only consider privacy against a semi-honest adversary corrupting at most one party (i.e., an adversary that follows the protocol and then attempts to violate the privacy of one of the parties).

2   Models and Requirements

Data and Query Models. We model a *database* as an n-row, 2-column matrix $D = (A_1, A_2)$, where each column is associated with an *attribute*, denoted as A_j, for $j = 1, 2$, and each *entry* is denoted as $A_j(i)$. The first column is a *value attribute*, where entries are values in a *domain Dom* with a total order $\leq$, and the last column A_2, is a *payload attribute*, where entries can be arbitrary binary strings. The database *schema*, assumed to be publicly known to all parties, includes parameter n, the security parameter, and the description of the attribute value domain. A database row is also called *record*, and is assumed to have the same length ℓ_r (if data is not already in this form, techniques from [9] are used to efficiently achieve this property), where ℓ_r is constant with respect to n.

A *query* q is modeled to contain one or more *query values* from the relative attribute domains. We mainly consider Range queries, defined as:

SELECT * FROM *main* WHERE attribute_name $\in [v_0, v_1]$,

where v_0, v_1 are the query values. A *valid response (to a range query)* consists of all payloads $A_2(i)$, for $i \in [1, n]$, such that $A_1(i) \in [v_0, v_1]$, and we say that these payloads (or records) *match* the query. We also discuss KS queries, defined as:

SELECT * FROM *main* WHERE attribute_name $= v$,

where v is the query value. A *valid response (to a keyword query)* consists of all payloads $A_2(i)$, for $i \in [1, n]$, such that $A_1(i) = v$.

Participant Models. We consider the following *efficient* (i.e., running in probabilistic polynomial-time in a common security parameter 1^σ) participants. The *client* is the party, denoted as C, that is interested in retrieving data from the database. The *server* is the party, denoted as S, holding the database (in the clear), and is interested in allowing clients to retrieve data. The *third party*, denoted as TP, helps the client to carry out the database retrieval functionality and the server to satisfy efficiency requirements during the associated protocol. By *2-party model* we denote the participant model that includes C, S and no third party. By *3-party model* we denote the participant model that includes C, S, and TP. (See Figs. 1 and 2 for a comparison of the two participant models.)

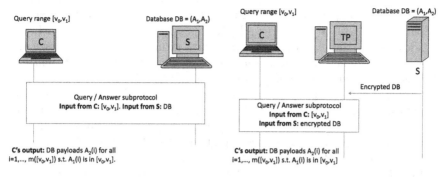

Fig. 1. Structure of our 2-party RQ protocol

Fig. 2. Structure of our 3-party RQ protocol

Range Query Protocols. In the above data, query, and participant models, we consider a *(static-data) range query* (briefly, RQ) protocol that extends the KS protocol, as defined in [10] (in turn, an evolution of the PIR protocol, as defined in [18]), in that it considers range queries instead of keyword queries, and it allows the attribute column to have multiple occurrences of the same value. (We can also extend the model so to incorporate databases that contain multiple attributes). Specifically, we define an RQ protocol as a pair (Init, Query) of subprotocols, as follows. The initialization subprotocol Init is used to set up data structures and cryptographic keys before C's queries are executed. The query subprotocol Query allows C to make a single query to retrieve (possibly multiple) matching database records. We also define an *RQ protocol execution* as a sequence of executions of subprotocols (Init, $Query_1, \ldots, Query_q$), for some q polynomial in the security parameter, and all subprotocols are run on inputs provided by the involved parties (i.e., a database from S and query values from C). We would like to build RQ protocols that satisfy the following (informal) list of *requirements*:

1. *Correctness*: the RQ protocol allows a client to obtain all payloads from the current database associated with records that match its issued query; more specifically, for any RQ protocol execution, and any inputs provided by the participants, in any execution of a Query subprotocol, the probability that C obtains all records in the current database that match C's query value input to this subprotocol, is 1.

2. *Privacy*: informally speaking, the RQ protocol preserves privacy of database content and query values, ideally only revealing what is leaked by system parameters known to all parties and by the intended functionality output (i.e., all payloads in matching records to C); more specifically, we require the subprotocols in an RQ protocol execution to not leak information beyond the following

- Init: all system parameters, including the database schema and a security parameter, will be known to all participants; in the 3-party model, an additional string eds (for encrypted data structures) will be known to TP, will be encrypted under one or more keys unknown to TP and its length is known from quantities in the database schema;
- Query, based on query range $qr = [v_0, v_1]$ and the database D: all payloads $\{p(i) : i = i(1), \ldots, i(m(qr))\}$ such that $A_1(i) \in [v_0, v_1]$, for $i = i(1), \ldots, i(m(qr))$, will be obtained by C, as a consequence of the correctness requirement; in the 2-party model, the value $m(qr)$ will be known to S; in the 3-party model, the value $m(qr)$, all bits in eds read by TP according to the instructions in the Query protocol, and which previous executions of Query used the same query value v, will be known to TP.
3. *Efficiency*: the protocol should have low time, communication and round complexity, as a function of system parameters, including the number n of database records.

Given the characterization of intended leakage in the above privacy definition, a formal privacy definition can be derived using known definition techniques from simulation-based security and composable security frameworks often used in the cryptography literature.

Similarly as noted for keyword queries in [7], we observe that the communication exchanged in each execution of any subprotocol Query has to leak an upper bound on the value $m(qr)$, i.e., the number of matching records, to S in the 2-party model, and to the coalition of TP and S in the 3-party model. Accordingly, we target the design of protocols that may leak $m(qr)$ to S in the 2-party model. In the 3-party model, different RQ protocols could leak $m(qr)$ only to S, or only to TP, or somehow split this leakage between S and TP. Having to choose between one of these options, we made the practical consideration that privacy against S (i.e., the data owner) is typically of greater interest than privacy against TP (i.e., the cloud server helping C retrieve data from S) in many applications, and therefore we focused in this paper on seeking protocols that leak $m(qr)$ to TP and nothing at all to S. Moreover, in the 3-party model, we made a definitional choice of leaking patterns of repeated access to encrypted data to TP; this is not due to a theoretical limitation, but seems a well-characterized privacy leakage, which, depending on the application at hand, either is a small price to pay towards achieving very efficient time-complexity requirements on S and TP, or can be reduced by using separate techniques.

With respect to efficiency, although we design protocols with low time, round and communication complexity, we focus our discussions on the communication complexity of the query subprotocols, and on the running time of S in the 2-party model and of S and TP in the 3-party model.

Background: Keyword Search Protocols. A *random function R* is a function that is chosen with distribution uniform across all possible functions with some pre-defined input and output domains. A keyed function $F(k, \cdot)$ is a *pseudorandom function* (PRF, first defined in [11]) if, after key k is randomly chosen, no efficient algorithm allowed to query an oracle function O can distinguish whether O is $F(k, \cdot)$ or O is a random function R (over the same input and output domain), with probability greater than $1/2$ plus a negligible quantity. A *KS protocol* is a protocol between two parties A, having as input a keyword $v \in \{1, \ldots, n\}$, and B, having as input a 2-column database represented as $D = (A_1, A_2)$. The protocol consists in a private retrieval of the value(s) $A_2(i)$ such that $A_1(i) = v$, returned to A (thus, without revealing any information about i to B or about $A_2(1), \ldots, A_2(i-1), A_2(i+1), \ldots, A_2(n)$ to A). Several KS protocols have been presented in the cryptographic literature, starting with [18], using number-theoretic hardness assumptions (see also [5,7,10]).

3   Range Queries in the Two-Party Model

We describe two RQ protocols for range queries in this model: the first protocol, presented in Sect. 3.1, works for ranges with elements in any linear-size domain; the second protocol, presented in Sect. 3.2, works for ranges with elements in any exponential-size (in practice, arbitrarily large) domain.

3.1   A Range Query Protocol for Linear-Size Domains

Our first 2-party RQ protocol considers range values in linear-size domains (that is, where the domain size is equal to the number of database records). This protocol follows the general structure outlined in Fig. 1 and satisfies the following

Theorem 1. Consider a database with n records and domain $Dom = [0, n-1]$. Assuming the existence of a 2-party privacy-preserving KS protocol $\pi_0 = (\mathsf{Init}_0, \mathsf{Query}_0)$, there exists (constructively) a 2-party privacy-preserving RQ protocol $\pi_1 = (\mathsf{Init}_1, \mathsf{Query}_1)$ for such a database, satisfying:

1. correctness
2. privacy against C (i.e., it only leaks the matching records to C);
3. privacy against S (i.e., it only leaks the number of matching records to S);
4. communication complexity of Query_1 on a queried range qr is $O(m(qr))$ times the communication complexity of Query_0;
5. the S-time complexity in Query_1 on a queried range qr is $O(m(qr))$ times the S-time complexity in Query_0 plus $O(n)$.

We prove Theorem 1 by describing RQ protocol π_1 and its properties.

The RQ Protocol π_1: Basic Definitions. Let Dom be a value domain with a total order $\leq$ defined on it. We say that Dom is a *linear-size domain* if it holds that $|Dom| \leq n$. Given a list U of (not necessarily distinct) values $u_1, \ldots, u_n \in Dom$, we say that a value $v \in Dom$ has *lower U-rank r*, also denoted as $Lrank(U, v) = r$, if there are r values strictly smaller than v. We say that a value $v \in Dom$ has *upper U-rank r*, also denoted as $Urank(U, v) = r$, if there are $n - r$ values in U strictly larger than v. Let $sU = (u_{h(0)}, \ldots, u_{h(n-1)})$ denote the list obtained from U by sorting its n elements. These definitions directly imply the following:

Fact 1. Given values $v_0, v_1 \in Dom$ such that $v_0 \leq v_1$, it holds that

1. $U \cap [v_0, v_1] = \emptyset$ if and only if $Lrank(U, v_0) \geq Urank(U, v_1)$.
2. $U \cap [v_0, v_1] \neq \emptyset$ if and only if $u_{h(a)}, \ldots, u_{h(b)} \in [v_0, v_1]$, for $a = Lrank(U, v_0)$ and $b = Urank(U, v_1) - 1$.

The RQ Protocol π_1: An Informal Description. A first approach in our protocol goes as follows. At initialization S splits database D into two databases: a rank database rD and a payload database pD. At query time, C asks S for the lower rank of v_0 and the upper rank of v_1, where $[v_0, v_1]$ denotes the range queried by C. Because in this protocol we consider only linear-size value domains, S can store at initialization the lower rank and the upper rank of each value in the domain in rD; thus, it suffices C to perform a keyword query to rD to retrieve the two upper and lower rank values. Given these retrieved values, C can compute how many attribute values (if any) are in $[v_0, v_1]$ (i.e., the upper rank minus the lower rank), and then perform as many keyword queries in pD to retrieve the records matching the queried range. As written so far, the protocol satisfies our desired correctness and efficiency properties, but not the privacy property, as C learns the two rank values associated with the queried range's endpoints. We fix this problem by requiring S to randomize the rank values by a random shift of the attribute values, a variation of an idea first used in [8] to improve the efficiency of keyword queries in a 3-party model. Thus, the ranks received by C will be randomly distributed, conditioned by the fact that the difference between them remains the same, and C is entitled to know this difference because of the correctness requirement.

The RQ Protocol π_1: A Formal Description. Protocol π_1 uses a KS protocol $\pi_0 = (\mathsf{Init}_0, \mathsf{Query}_0)$ for a 2-column database, which can be obtained from protocol π_1 in [7] or protocol 2 in [10]. Both these protocols use the KS protocol in [5], which in turn is based on any semi-private PIR protocol (e.g., [18]).

Init_1. On input database $D = (A_1, A_2)$, S sets U as the list $(A_1(1), \ldots, A_1(n))$, and builds an associated rank database $rD = (rA_1, rA_2)$ and an associated payload database $pD = (pA_1, pA_2)$, computed as follows.
For each $i = 1, \ldots, n$,

1. $rA_1(i) = i$,
2. $rA_2(i) = (Lrank(U, i)), Urank(U, i))$, and

for each $i = 0, \ldots, n$,

1. $pA_1(i) = i$, and
2. $pA_2(i) = A_2(j)$ where $j \in \{1, \ldots, n\}$ satisfies $Lrank(U, A_1(j)) = i$.

Query_1. Let $\gg_n$ denote the operation 'right shift modulo n'. On input query range $qr = [v_0, v_1]$, where $v_0, v_1 \in Dom$, from C, and all quantities computed during Init_1, the following steps are run:

1. If $v_0 > v_1$ then C sends failure symbol $\perp$ to S and halts;
2. S randomly chooses value $s \in \{0, \ldots, n-1\}$

3. for $i = 1, \ldots, n$,
   S sets $Lr'(U, i) = Lrank(U, i) \gg_n s$, $Ur'(U, i) = Urank(U, i) \gg_n s$;
   S sets $rA_2'(i) = (Lr'(U, i), Ur'(U, i))$
4. S runs Init_0 on input 2-column database $rD = (rA_1, rA_2')$
5. for $j = 0, 1$: C and S run Query_0, where C uses v_j as query value and S provides (rA_1, rA_2') as a 2-column database; at the end of the protocol, C computes the payload $rA_2'(i(j)) = (Lr'(U, i(j)), Ur'(U, i(j)))$ such that $rA_1(i(j)) = v_j$;
6. if $Lr'(U, i(0)) = Ur'(U, i(1))$ then
   C sends failure symbol $\perp$ to S and halts.
7. for $i = 0, \ldots, n$,
   S sets $pA_1'(i) = pA_1(i) \gg_n s$;
8. S runs Init_0 on input 2-column database $pD = (pA_1', pA_2)$
9. for $j = Lr'(U, i(0)), \ldots, Ur'(U, i(1)) - 1$, possibly cycling from $n - 1$ to 0: C and S run Query_0, where C uses j as query value and S provides (pA_1', pA_2) as a 2-column database; at the end of the protocol, C computes the payload $pA_2(i(j))$ such that $pA_1'(i(j)) = j$.

Properties of π_1. We now show that π_1 satisfies the correctness, privacy and efficiency properties defined in the 2-party model.

Correctness. First of all, note that by the test in step 1, we can assume that $v_0 \leq v_1$, which implies that $Lrank(U, i(0)) \leq Urank(U, i(1))$.

By the correctness property of the KS protocol π_0, at the end of step 5 of Query_1, C can compute the shifted lower rank $Lr'(U, i(0))$ of v_0 and the shifted upper rank $Ur'(U, i(1))$ of v_1. As both values are obtained as a shift, by the same random number s, of $Lrank(U, i(0))$ and $Urank(U, i(1))$, respectively, it holds that $Lr'(U, i(0)) = Ur'(U, i(1))$ if and only if $Lrank(U, i(0)) = Urank(U, i(1))$. Using item 1 of Fact 1, this implies that if $U \cap [v_0, v_1] = \emptyset$, it will hold that $Lrank(U, i(0)) = Urank(U, i(1))$ and thus $Lr'(U, i(0)) = Ur'(U, i(1))$, and then C will halt in step 6 of Query_1, without receiving any payload from S. On the other hand, if $U \cap [v_0, v_1] \neq \emptyset$, at the end of step 9 of Query_1, by the correctness property of the KS protocol π_0, C computes the payload $pA_2(i(j))$ such that $pA_1'(i(j)) = j$, for all $j = Lr'(U, i(0)), \ldots, Ur'(U, i(1)) - 1$, possibly cycling from $n - 1$ to 0. Using item 2 of Fact 1, this implies that S receives all payloads corresponding to values $A_1(i)$ in the range $[v_0, v_1]$.

Privacy. We show that π_1 satisfies our privacy requirement when the adversary corrupts any one among S or C.

When the adversary corrupts S, privacy (i.e., corrupting S does not provide the adversary any new information about C's range query $[v_0, v_1]$ other than system parameters and the number of matching payloads) can be proved by using the analogue privacy property of the KS protocol π_0. First of all, we observe that Query_1 in protocol π_1 consists of 1 execution of Query_0 followed by either no further execution of Query_0 (resulting in no payload received by C) or by $m(qr) = Urank(U, v_1) - Lrank(U, v_0)$ additional executions of Query_0 (resulting in $m(qr) > 0$ payloads received by C). Thus, given the number $m(qr) \geq 0$ of payloads received by C, an efficient simulator for the view obtained by S is obtained by suitably calling the efficient simulator for the view by S in the KS protocol π_0.

When the adversary corrupts C, privacy (i.e., corrupting C does not provide the adversary with any information about S's database D other than system parameters and what intended by the correctness requirement) can be proved by using the analogue privacy property of protocol π_0. Here, the proof is similar to the previous case: given the number $m(qr) \geq 0$ of payloads received by C, a simulator for C's view is obtained by suitably calling the simulator for C's view in the KS protocol π_0.

Efficiency. As Query_1 essentially consists of running $m(qr) + 1$ times Query_0, the communication complexity (resp., S-time complexity) of Query_1 is $O(m(qr))$ times the communication complexity (resp., S-time complexity) of Query_0. Thus, the communication complexity is desirably linear in the number of matching records (and can be sub-linear in the number n of total database records). Analogously, the S-time complexity of Query_1 is $O(m(qr))$ times the S-time complexity of Query_0 plus $O(n)$. Here, note that the S-time complexity of Query_1 is linear in n already for small values of $m(qr)$ as so is the S-time complexity of Query_0. This inefficiency is a major and known drawback of all 2-party model solutions for protocols like PIR, KS, and therefore, of protocols π_0 and π_1. Indeed, this motivated our study of RQ protocols in the 3-party model in Sect. 4.

3.2   A Range Query Protocol for Exponential-Size Domains

Our second 2-party RQ protocol considers range values in exponential-size (which means, practically speaking, arbitrarily large) domains. This protocol follows the general structure outlined in Fig. 1 and satisfies the following

Theorem 2. Consider a database with n records and domain $Dom = [0, 2^d - 1]$, for some d polynomial in n. Assuming the existence of a 2-party privacy-preserving KS protocol $\pi_0 = (\mathsf{Init}_0, \mathsf{Query}_0)$, there exists (constructively) a 2-party privacy-preserving RQ protocol $\pi_2 = (\mathsf{Init}_2, \mathsf{Query}_2)$ for such a database, satisfying:

1. correctness
2. privacy against C (i.e., it only leaks the matching records to C);
3. privacy against S (i.e., it only leaks the number of matching records to S);
4. communication complexity of Query_1 on a queried range qr is $O(m(qr))$ times the communication complexity of Query_0;
5. the S-time complexity in Query_1 on a queried range qr is $O(m(qr))$ times the S-time complexity in Query_0 plus $O(dn)$.

We prove Theorem 2 by describing RQ protocol π_2 and its properties.

The RQ Protocol π_2: Basic Definitions. Let Dom be a value domain with a total order $\leq$ defined on it. We say that Dom is an *exponential-size domain* if it holds that $|Dom| \leq 2^d \leq 2^{p(n)}$, for some polynomial p. For simplicity, we restrict to the case Dom is the d-*dimensional hypercube*, i.e. $Dom = [0, 2^d - 1]$, but note that our results can be extended to any exponential-size domain.

We define the *set $cI(Dom)$ of canonical intervals* for Dom by the following recursion: first, add Dom into $cI(Dom)$; then, split Dom into Dom_0, containing the first half of its elements, and Dom_1 containing the second half; then, for $i = 0, 1$, generate $cI(Dom_0)$, the set of canonical intervals for Dom_i; finally, add $cI(Dom_0), cI(Dom_1)$ to $cI(Dom)$.

An interval $[a, b] \subseteq Dom$ is a *border interval in Dom* if there exists an interval $I \in cI(Dom)$ such that either a is the first element in I or b is the last element in I. The following fact directly follows by the above definitions of border and canonical intervals.

Fact 2. For every interval $[a, b] \subseteq Dom$, either $[a, b]$ is a border interval in Dom, or there exists c such that $[a, c]$ and $[c + 1, b]$ are border intervals in Dom.

For any interval $[a, b] \subseteq Dom$, intervals $[a, c_1], [c_1 + 1, c_2], \ldots, [c_t, b]$ are said to *cover* $[a, b]$. We note that a border interval is covered by at most $d - 1$ canonical intervals. This, together with Fact 2, implies the following

Fact 3. For every interval $[a, b] \subseteq Dom$, there exists a set of $\leq 2(d-1)$ canonical intervals covering $[a, b]$.

We note that results similar to Fact 3 have already been studied in other papers (see, e.g., [19]), but we could not find range query protocols based on them with provable privacy properties.

The RQ Protocol π_2. We would like to construct $\pi_2 = (\mathsf{Init}_2, \mathsf{Query}_2)$ as an extension of $\pi_1 = (\mathsf{Init}_1, \mathsf{Query}_1)$, based on the above notions of canonical intervals, and interval covering.

At initialization S again splits database D into two databases: a rank database rD and a payload database pD. This time, however, since we consider exponential-size value domains (as opposed to linear-size value domains used for π_1), S cannot store at initialization the lower rank and the upper rank of each domain value in rD. Then, instead of storing all domain elements in rD, we store all attribute values $u_1, \ldots, u_n$ in D and, for each interval $[u_{i-1} + 1, u_i - 1]$, we consider the set of canonical intervals covering it, as guaranteed by Fact 3, and store each one of these intervals in rD. Note that in each of these latter intervals, each domain value has the same lower and upper ranks, so we only need to store a single copy of these two values in rD as well. Thus, in $rD = (rD_1, rD_2)$, the column rD_1 contains the following

1. the attribute values $u_1, \ldots, u_n$ in D;
2. each one of the canonical intervals covering every interval $[u_{i-1} + 1, u_i - 1]$, where $u_1, \ldots, u_n$ are the attribute values in D.

After this modification, the remaining computations in Init_2, including of the lower/upper ranks, continue as in π_1. Because of Fact 3, this modified initialization at most increases the size of rD by a multiplicative factor of $2(d - 1)$.

At query time, denoting as $[v_0, v_1]$ the range queried by C, the computation of the shifted lower/upper ranks continue as in Query_1. However, C not only asks S for the lower rank of v_0 and the upper rank of v_1 by 2 KS queries as in π_1, but also makes KS queries on input all canonical intervals that contain v_0 and all canonical intervals that contain v_1. Here, note that if v_0 (resp., v_1) is different from all attribute values, then exactly one of the canonical intervals containing v_0 (resp., v_1) was included in rD during initialization. Thus, only one of the KS queries associated with v_0 and only one of the KS queries associated with v_1 will be successfully completed, returning to C ranks for either an attribute value u_i or a canonical interval containing the query range value. From now on, protocol Query_2 continues exactly as Query_1. That is, C can use the obtained ranks to generate the $m(qr)$ keyword queries to database pD, and obtain $m(qr)$ matching records.

Properties of π_2. The proofs that π_2 satisfies the correctness, privacy and efficiency properties defined in the 2-party model are obtained by extending the analogue proofs for π_1, using the properties of the KS protocol π_0. In particular, the correctness property of π_2 is showed by additionally using Facts 2 and 3. The privacy and the communication complexity properties are not significantly affected by the modifications in π_2 with respect to π_1. The S-time complexity changes by observing that rD is larger in π_2 by a multiplicative factor of d.

4   Range Queries in the Three-Party Model

We show a 3-party RQ protocol by extending the 2-party protocol in Sect. 3.1. Our protocol follows the general structure outlined in Fig. 2 and satisfies the following

Theorem 3. Consider a database with n records and domain $Dom = [0, n-1]$. Assuming the existence of a pseudo-random function, there exists (constructively) a 3-party privacy-preserving RQ protocol $\pi_3 = (\mathsf{Init}_3, \mathsf{Query}_3)$ for such a database, satisfying:

1. correctness
2. privacy against C (i.e., it only leaks the matching records to C);
3. privacy against S (i.e., it does not leak anything to S);
4. privacy against TP (i.e., it only leaks number of matching records, the repetition of query values and the repeated access to initialization encrypted data structures);
5. communication complexity of Query_3 on a queried range qr is $O(m(qr))$;
6. the TP-time complexity in Query_3 on a queried range qr is $O(m(qr) \log n)$.

Remark: on Exponential-Size Domains. We stated Theorem 3 for linear-size value domains, and established it by transforming the 2-party protocol π_1 into the 3-party model. By a very similar transformation, we can adapt the 2-party protocol π_2 into the 3-party model, and obtain a similar result for exponential-size value domains.

Our RQ Protocol in the 3-Party Model: An Informal Description.
Briefly speaking, our protocol π_3 is obtained by performing the following two main modifications in the 3-party model to protocol π_1 (which was designed in the 2-party model): (1) the KS protocol in the 2-party model is replaced by a KS protocol in the 3-party model [7], that was constructed starting from any pseudo-random function; and (2) the shifts performed to the entire databases rD_2 and pD_1 in protocol π_1 are now replaced by a 'lazy shifting' technique, according to which shifts are performed only to database entries which are used in the protocol. We note that the first modification replaces the use of asymmetric cryptography protocols with only symmetric cryptography techniques, and the second modification eliminates linear-time computations from S during the query subprotocol.

In fact, we can use the following simplified version of the KS protocol in the 3-party model from [7], by assuming that each keyword query will have at most 1 matching record (which was shown to be the case in π_1). First of all, S encrypts both the attribute column and the payload column in its database, where the attribute column is encrypted using deterministic encryption, via a pseudo-random permutation (which can be built from any pseudo-random function). As a result, the encrypted attribute column is searchable by TP using a conventional search data structure (i.e., a binary search tree). Later, S sends the encrypted database to TP and C sends its query values encrypted using the same pseudo-random permutation used by S (with key unknown to TP). Finally, TP can search such value in the search data structure over the encrypted attribute values and return the matching record to C.

Given the above 3-party KS protocol, our 3-party RQ protocol π_3 works as follows. The following high-level structure of π_1 remains in π_3: specifically, S constructs a rank database rD and a payload database pD, and C will perform keyword queries first based on rD and later based on pD. In π_3, however, S sends encrypted versions of rD and pD to TP, and from then on, C only performs keyword queries to TP. Specifically, while the payload columns of rD and pD are encrypted using conventional probabilistic encryption, the attribute columns of rD and pD are encrypted using deterministic encryption, based on a pseudo-random permutation, which makes attribute column values searchable by TP. To encrypt an attribute value $v \in Dom$, S randomly chooses v_0 and an *initial shift* s such that $v_0 + is = v \bmod n$, and returns ciphertext $(f_k(v_0), is)$, where f is the pseudo-random permutation, and k is a key known to C and S but not to TP. An interesting property of such ciphertexts is that TP can compute a 'lazy shift' of v over its encryption and by any random *next shift ns*, by returning $(f_k(v_0), cs)$, where the *current shift cs* is $= is + ns \bmod n$. Such ciphertexts will be used by S to encrypt lower and upper ranks in rD before sending them to TP. Then, after C's keyword query to (the encrypted version of) database rD held by TP, such encrypted ranks will not be directly returned to C (or otherwise this may leak some information to C across multiple queries). Instead, TP and C will run a 2-party secure function evaluation (using Yao's protocol [25]), where C provides key k as input, TP provides the encrypted ranks and the current shift cs as input and the output returned to TP will be the encrypted queries for (the encrypted version of) database pD. Then, by using the current shift as input to the secure function evaluation protocol, TP obtains encrypted keyword queries, each of them being used to search across the first ciphertext component of all encrypted attribute values in pD, exactly as done in the above 3-party KS protocol.

Practical Performance of Our 3-Party Protocol. In our implementation, the S and TP processes and an instance of MySQL server version 5.5.28 were running on a Dell PowerEdge R710 server with two Intel Xeon X5650 2.66 Ghz processors, 48 GB of memory, 64-bit Ubuntu 12.04.1 operating system, and connected to a Dell PowerVault MD1200 disk array with 12 2 TB 7.2K RPM SAS RQives in RAID6 configuration. The C process was running on a Dell PowerEdge R810 server with two Intel Xeon E7-4870 2.40 GHz processors, 64 GB of memory, 64-bit Red Hat Enterprise Linux Server release 6.3 operating system, and connected to the Dell PowerEdge R710 server via switched Gigabit Ethernet.

The 3-party protocol that we implemented was somewhat different than the ones discussed in this paper, because it was developed under more complex and specific project requirements. However, by protocol analysis, we have noted that these differences are not expected to significantly affect practical performance of the protocols. Accordingly, we briefly report on the performance of our implemented protocols, as a useful indication on the performance of the protocols described here.

In our implementation, we have noted practical efficiency and scalability of our 3-party protocols, and were able to achieve query latency performance of no more than 1 order of magnitude slower than a comparable non-private protocol for the same task (specifically, a mySQL protocol for range queries over same-size value domains and database size). This result was achieved, with minor differences, over both linear-size and exponential-size value domains. A similar performance result was presented in [7] in the same implementation environment for keyword queries. In achieving such a result for range queries, our approach of constructing range query protocols from keyword query protocols was critical. This is especially the case when considering that the dominating performance factor in all our range query protocols is given by the performance of one keyword query for each of the records matching the range query. Performance numbers (where time is measured in milliseconds and communication in bytes) for range queries matching 1 % of the database records, are captured in Figs. 3 and 4.

The most challenging aspect in our performance analysis was the scalability of the initialization procedure, where we observed the following results: the initialization of the 3-party protocol for linear-size value domains, based on a transformation of the 2-party protocol π_1, does achieve satisfactory scalability properties; however, the initalization phase of the 3-party protocol for exponential-size value domains, based on a transformation of the 2-party protocol π_2, does not achieve satisfactory scalability properties, especially as the logarithm of the domain size grows. Although the initialization procedure is typically a one-time procedure, we still consider the following an interesting open problem: designing a 3-party privacy-preserving range query protocol that achieves scalable performance on both query latency and initialization.

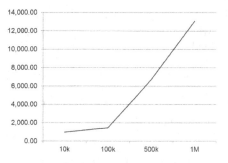

DB Size	Bytes Sent	Bytes Received	Response Time
10k	12,927	48,891	978.00
100k	99,327	486,291	1,445.75
500k	483,327	2,430,303	6,712.50
1M	963,327	4,860,321	13,066.25

Fig. 3. Time and communication performance for different database sizes.

Fig. 4. Time performance as a function of database size.

Acknowledgments. Many thanks to Euthimios Panagos and Aditya Naidu for helping on performance evaluation. Most of this work was supported by the Intelligence Advanced Research Projects Activity (IARPA) via Department of Interior National Business Center (DoI/NBC) contract number D13PC00003. The U.S. Government is authorized to reproduce and distribute reprints for Governmental purposes notwithstanding any copyright annotation hereon. Disclaimer: The views and conclusions contained herein are those of the authors and should not be interpreted as necessarily representing the official policies or endorsements, either expressed or implied, of IARPA, DoI/NBC, or the U.S. Government.

References

1. Agrawal, R., Kiernan, J., Srikant, R., Xu, Y.: Order-preserving encryption for numeric data. In: Proceedings of the ACM SIGMOD International Conference on Management of Data, Paris, France, June 13–18, pp. 563–574 (2004)
2. Boldyreva, A., Chenette, N., O'Neill, A.: Order-preserving encryption revisited: improved security analysis and alternative solutions. In: Rogaway, P. (ed.) CRYPTO 2011. LNCS, vol. 6841, pp. 578–595. Springer, Heidelberg (2011)
3. Boneh, D., Di Crescenzo, G., Ostrovsky, R., Persiano, G.: Public key encryption with keyword search. In: Cachin, C., Camenisch, J.L. (eds.) EUROCRYPT 2004. LNCS, vol. 3027, pp. 506–522. Springer, Heidelberg (2004)
4. Boneh, D., Waters, B.: Conjunctive, subset, and range queries on encrypted data. In: Vadhan, S.P. (ed.) TCC 2007. LNCS, vol. 4392, pp. 535–554. Springer, Heidelberg (2007)
5. Chor, B., Gilboa, N., Naor, M.: Private information retrieval by keywords. IACR Cryptology ePrint Archive (1998)
6. Chor, B., Kushilevitz, E., Goldreich, O., Sudan, M.: Private information retrieval. J. ACM **45**(6), 965–981 (1998)
7. Di Crescenzo, G., Cook, D., McIntosh, A., Panagos, E.: Practical private information retrieval from a time-varying, multi-attribute, and multiple-occurrence database. In: Atluri, V., Pernul, G. (eds.) DBSec 2014. LNCS, vol. 8566, pp. 339–355. Springer, Heidelberg (2014)
8. Di Crescenzo, G., Ishai, Y., Ostrovsky, R.: Universal service-providers for private information retrieval. J. Cryptology **14**(1), 37–74 (2001)

9. Di Crescenzo, G., Shallcross, D.: On minimizing the size of encrypted databases. In: Atluri, V., Pernul, G. (eds.) DBSec 2014. LNCS, vol. 8566, pp. 364–372. Springer, Heidelberg (2014)

10. Freedman, M.J., Ishai, Y., Pinkas, B., Reingold, O.: Keyword search and oblivious pseudorandom functions. In: Kilian, J. (ed.) TCC 2005. LNCS, vol. 3378, pp. 303–324. Springer, Heidelberg (2005)

11. Goldreich, O., Goldwasser, S., Micali, S.: How to construct random functions. J. ACM **33**(4), 792–807 (1986)

12. Goldreich, O., Ostrovsky, R.: Software protection and simulation on oblivious RAMs. J. ACM **43**(3), 431–473 (1996)

13. Hacigümüs, H., Iyer, B.R., Li, C., Mehrotra, S.: Executing SQL over encrypted data in the database-service-provider model. In: SIGMOD Conference, pp. 216–227 (2002)

14. Hore, B., Mehrotra, S., Tsudik, G.: A privacy-preserving index for range queries. In: (e)Proceedings of the Thirtieth International Conference on Very Large Data Bases, Toronto, Canada, August 31 – September 3, pp. 720–731 (2004)

15. Islam, M.S., Kuzu, M., Kantarcioglu, M.: Access pattern disclosure on searchable encryption: ramification, attack and mitigation. In: NDSS (2012)

16. Islam, M.S., Kuzu, M., Kantarcioglu, M.: Inference attack against encrypted range queries on outsourced databases. In: Fourth ACM Conference on Data and Application Security and Privacy, CODASPY'14, San Antonio, TX, USA, March 03–05, pp. 235–246 (2014)

17. Jarecki, S., Jutla, C.S., Krawczyk, H., Rosu, M.-C., Steiner, M.: Outsourced symmetric private information retrieval. In: ACM Conference on Computer and Communications Security, pp. 875–888 (2013)

18. Kushilevitz, E., Ostrovsky, R.: Replication is not needed: single database, computationally-private information retrieval. In: FOCS, pp. 364–373 (1997)

19. Li, J., Omiecinski, E.R.: Efficiency and security trade-off in supporting range queries on encrypted databases. In: Jajodia, S., Wijesekera, D. (eds.) Data and Applications Security 2005. LNCS, vol. 3654, pp. 69–83. Springer, Heidelberg (2005)

20. Ostrovsky, R., Skeith III, W.E.: A survey of single-database private information retrieval: techniques and applications. In: Okamoto, T., Wang, X. (eds.) PKC 2007. LNCS, vol. 4450, pp. 393–411. Springer, Heidelberg (2007)

21. Samarati, P., De Capitani di Vimercati, S.: Data protection in outsourcing scenarios: issues and directions. In: Proceedings of the 5th ACM Symposium on Information, Computer and Communications Security, ASIACCS 2010, Beijing, China, April 13–16, pp. 1–14 (2010)

22. Shi, E., Bethencourt, J., Chan, H.T., Song, D.X., Perrig, A.: Multi-dimensional range query over encrypted data. In: 2007 IEEE Symposium on Security and Privacy (S&P 2007), 20–23 May 2007, Oakland, California, USA, pp. 350–364 (2007)

23. Stefanov, E., van Dijk, M., Shi, E., Fletcher, C.W., Ren, L., Yu, X., Devadas, S.: Path ORAM: an extremely simple oblivious RAM protocol. In: 2013 ACM SIGSAC Conference on Computer and Communications Security, CCS 2013, Berlin, Germany, November 4–8, pp. 299–310 (2013)

24. Wang, S., Ding, X., Deng, R.H., Bao, F.: Private information retrieval using trusted hardware. In: Gollmann, D., Meier, J., Sabelfeld, A. (eds.) ESORICS 2006. LNCS, vol. 4189, pp. 49–64. Springer, Heidelberg (2006)

25. Yao, A.C.-C.: How to generate and exchange secrets (extended abstract). In: FOCS, pp. 162–167 (1986)

Access Control and Authorization

An Administrative Model
for Relationship-Based Access Control

Scott D. Stoller[(⊠)]

Department of Computer Science, Stony Brook University,
Stony Brook, USA
`stoller@cs.stonybrook.edu`

Abstract. Relationship-based access control (ReBAC) originated in the context of social network systems and recently is being generalized to be suitable for general computing systems. This paper defines a ReBAC model, based on Crampton and Sellwood's RPPM model, designed to be suitable for general computing systems. Our ReBAC model includes a comprehensive administrative model. The administrative model is comprehensive in the sense that it allows and controls changes to all aspects of the ReBAC policy. To the best of our knowledge, it is the first comprehensive administrative model for a ReBAC model suitable for general computing systems. The model is illustrated with parts of a sample access control policy for electronic health records in a healthcare network.

1 Introduction

Gates introduced the term relationship-based access control (ReBAC) to describe access control policies expressed in terms of interpersonal relationships in social network systems (SNSs) [8]. While much of the work on ReBAC retains this focus on SNSs, there is a movement to generalize ReBAC to be suitable for general computing systems, by extending it to consider relationships involving all kinds of entities and by increasing the expressiveness of the policy language. The motivation for a general ReBAC framework is that ABAC is not well suited to express policies that depend on relationships involving entities beyond the subject (user) and target (resource) of the access request, especially when those additional entities are identified by following chains of relationships and attribute dereferences.

This paper defines a ReBAC model based on Crampton and Sellwood's RPPM model for ReBAC [3,4]. RPPM is designed to be suitable for general computing systems. It combines ideas from the UNIX access control model, ReBAC, and role-based access control (RBAC).

This material is based upon work supported in part by NSF under Grants CNS-1421893, CNS-0831298, CCF-1248184, and CCF-1414078. Any opinions, findings, and conclusions or recommendations expressed in this material are those of the author and do not necessarily reflect the views of NSF.

P. Samarati (Ed.): DBSec 2015, LNCS 9149, pp. 53–68, 2015.
DOI: 10.1007/978-3-319-20810-7_4

The most distinguishing feature of our ReBAC model is that it includes a comprehensive administrative model. The administrative model is *comprehensive* in the sense that it allows and controls changes to all aspects of the ReBAC policy. To the best of our knowledge, it is the first comprehensive administrative model for a ReBAC model suitable for general computing systems. Although the details of our administrative model are specific to our RPPM-based ReBAC model, a similar approach can be used to develop comprehensive administrative models for other ReBAC models. For example, a similar approach can be used to develop a comprehensive administrative model for ReBAC models that use modal logic [5,7], instead of path conditions [4], to characterize composite relationships between entities in the system graph.

A central principle underlying the design of our administrative framework is *economy of mechanism*. Saltzer and Schroeder advocate this principle in their classic paper on design of secure information systems [14]. Li and Mao followed this principle in their design of UARBAC, an administrative framework for RBAC. They note that, in that context, this principle means "Use RBAC to administer RBAC" [12]. In our context, it means "Use ReBAC to administer ReBAC". However, RPPM is not sufficiently powerful to support self-administration. We propose a more expressive version of RPPM, which we call "RPPM Modified", abbreviated $RPPM^2$, that supports self-administration. $RPPM^2$ also includes some extensions, such as parameters for relationship labels, not required for self-administration but required to express the complex policies in some application domains, including our running example of electronic health records in a healthcare network.

The most challenging aspect of the design of the administrative model is authorization of actions that add or remove authorization rules. The challenge arises from the tension between giving administrators the flexibility to introduce a variety of customized authorization rules and limiting administrators to ensure that they cannot introduce rules that violate desired safety or availability properties. Our approach is to define a strictness order on authorization rules and specify in the policy the least strict rules that each subject is allowed to add or remove.

2 Background: RPPM Model

The RPPM model is defined as follows [4]. The name "RPPM" reflects that the model is based on relationships, paths, and principal-matching.

System Model. A *system model* comprises a set of types T (also called *entity types*), a set of relationship labels R, a set of symmetric relationship labels $S \subseteq R$ and a permissible relationship graph $G_{PR} = (V_{PR}, E_{PR})$, where $V_{PR} = T$ and $E_{PR} \subseteq T \times T \times R$.

System Instance. Given a system model (T, R, S, G_{PR}), a *system instance* is defined by a system graph $G = (V, E)$ and a type function $\tau : V \to T$, where V is the set of entities and $E \subseteq V \times V \times R$. We say G is *well-formed* if for each entity v in V, $\tau(v) \in T$, and for every edge $(v, v', r) \in E$, $(\tau(v), \tau(v'), r) \in E_{PR}$.

Path Condition. Path conditions are defined recursively: $\diamond$ is a path condition; r is a path condition, for all $r \in R$; if π and π' are path conditions, then $\pi_1; \pi_2$, π^+, and $\overline{\pi}$ are path conditions. Informally, $\diamond$ represents the empty path; r represents a path containing exactly one edge, labeled with r; $\pi_1; \pi_2$ represents the concatenation of paths; π^+ represents one or more occurrences, in sequence, of π; and $\overline{\pi}$ represents π reversed. A path condition of the form r or $\overline{r}$ is called an *edge condition*. Every path condition can be rewritten as a *simple path condition*, in which the reversal operator appears only in edge conditions. We assume hereafter that all path conditions are simple.

Request and Principal-Matching Policy. A *request* has the form (s, o, a), where s (the "subject") is an entity requesting to perform action a on entity o (the "object", *i.e.*, target).

A *principal-matching rule* has the form (π, p), where p is an authorization principal and π is either a path condition defined on R or the special symbol $\top$. A principal-matching rule (π, p) matches a request (s, o, a) if (1) π is $\top$, or (2) π is a path condition, and the system graph contains a path from subject s to object o that satisfies π.

A *principal-matching policy* is a list of principal-matching rules. It may contain at most one rule containing $\top$, and that rule, if present, must appear last. A *principal-matching strategy* defines how the principals in matched rules should be combined to obtain the set of principals that match a request. For example, the AllMatch strategy includes in the set the principals from all matched rules in the policy.

Authorization Rule and Authorization Policy. An *authorization rule* has the form $(p, \star, a, d)$ or (p, o, a, d), where p is a principal, o is an entity (the "object", *i.e.*, target), a is an action, and $d \in \{0, 1\}$ is the decision ($0 = \text{deny}$, $1 = \text{permit}$). We call "$\star$" the *wildcard*. The rule $(p, \star, a, d)$ says that decision d is a possible decision when principal p requests to perform action a on any object. The rule (p, o, a, d) says that decision d is a possible decision when principal p requests to perform action a on object o. A *permit rule* is an authorization rule whose decision is 1 (permit). A *deny rule* is an authorization rule whose decision is 0 (deny).

An *authorization policy* is a list of authorization rules. A *conflict resolution strategy* determines the decision when rules with different possible decisions match a request; as in XACML [16], the strategies include DenyOverride, First-Match, and PermitOverride.

Defaults. The policy must specify a system-wide default decision, which is used when no rules and no other defaults apply. The policy may optionally specify a default decision for each subject and a default decision for each object.

Authorization Algorithm. The algorithm for determining whether a request is authorized has two main stages. First, the request (s, o, a) is matched against the rules in the principal-matching policy, and the principal-matching strategy is applied to obtain a set of matching principals. Second, if the set of matching principals is non-empty, a list of possible decisions is obtained from the authorization rules with principal p, action a, and object o or $\star$. If the list contains only 0 s or only 1s, then that value is the decision. If it contains 0 s and 1s, the conflict resolution strategy is applied to obtain a decision. If the list is empty, the default decision for the object is used, if it was specified, otherwise the system-wide default decision is used. If the set of matching principals is empty, then the default decision for the subject is used, if it was specified, otherwise the default decision for the object is used, if it was specified, otherwise the system-wide default decision is used.

3   RPPM^2 Model

This section presents our variant of the RPPM model, which we refer to as "RPPM Modified", abbreviated RPPM^2. Our administrative model, presented in the next section, is for RPPM^2.

System Model and System Instance. The definitions of system model and system instance are unchanged, except that system models are extended to include a set T_{ne} of non-entity types, and relationship labels may have typed parameters. These extensions are not required for our administrative framework. They are introduced to provide the expressiveness needed for our sample policy for a healthcare network, described in Sect. 4. For example, a patient might consent to treatment by a clinician at a particular healthcare facility (possibly also limited to a particular time period or medical episode). This would be reflected in the system model by including the facility as a parameter of the relationship label, *e.g.*, an edge from type Patient to type Clinician labeled with consent-ToTreatmentAt(Facility), or, for brevity, consent(Facility), where Facility is the type of the parameter.

Request. In RPPM, every request involves exactly two entities, the subject and a single target object. This is insufficient for policy administration, because many administrative actions involve multiple target entities. For example, adding an edge to the system graph involves two equally important target entities, namely, the source and destination nodes of the edge. Therefore, we generalize the definition of actions to allow actions to have any number of parameters, including entities and non-entities, and we do not distinguish any parameter as *the* target. In RPPM^2, a request has the form $(s, op(v_1, ..., v_n))$ where s is the subject (*i.e.*, the entity attempting the operation), op is the operation, and the v_i are arguments. Each operation has a type signature, specifying the type of each parameter.

Path Condition and Path Expression. A *path expression* is defined in the same way as a path condition in RPPM, except, for convenience, we also allow π^*. We change the terminology from "path condition" to "path expression" because, in our framework, a path expression cannot be evaluated to a truth value until the source and target nodes are specified. Each argument of an edge label in a path expression is a wildcard, a constant of the appropriate type, or, if the parameter has an entity type, a variable. A *path condition* in RPPM^2 has the form $e_1 \cdot \pi \cdot e_2$, where each e_i is an entity constant or a variable, and π is a path condition. A path condition $e_1 \cdot \pi \cdot e_2$ holds if there exists a substitution θ mapping the variables (if any) in the path condition to values such that the system graph contains a path from $e_1\theta$ to $e_2\theta$ that matches $\pi\theta$, where $t\theta$ denotes the result of applying substitution θ to term t.

Principal-Matching Policy. In RPPM, a principal name serves as a shorthand for a path expression expressing a relationship between subject and target. This eliminates the need to repeat that path expression, if it is used in multiple rules. In RPPM^2, because there is not a single distinguished target entity, and because we use path expressions to express relationships between the subject and target entities and between target entities, we replace the notion of principal-matching policy with a simpler and more flexible *path-expression naming* mechanism that simply allows names to be given to path expressions. These names can be used in authorization rules (described below) wherever a path expression is called for. Furthermore, a name can be defined to represent multiple path expressions; a rule in which that name is used expands to multiple rules, one for each path expression associated with the name.

For simplicity, we do not consider path-expression names to be a collectively managed part of the ReBAC policy. Instead, each entity authorized to add authorization rules has its own library of definitions of path-expression names; some might be copied from trusted (e.g., centralized organization-approved) sources, and some might be developed independently. When an authorization rule is added to the policy, the current definitions of path-expression names used in it are stored together with the rule. This allows the rule to be displayed as written (for readability) or in expanded form. The expanded form is used when authorizing the action that adds the authorization rule and when enforcing the authorization rule. If desired, path-expression name definitions can be made a shared and collectively managed part of the ReBAC policy, by defining administrative operations for them and introducing authorization rules for those operations.

Authorization Rule and Authorization Policy. An *authorization rule* has the form $(s, op(a_1, ..., a_n), c, d)$ where:

- the *subject* s is a variable or an entity constant;
- the *action* is an operation op with arguments a_i; each argument with entity type is an entity constant, the wildcard, or a variable; each argument with non-entity type is a constant or a wildcard;
- the *condition* c is a conjunction of path conditions; and
- the *decision* d is 0 (deny) or 1 (permit).

This rule says that decision d is a possible decision when principal p requests to perform action $op(a_1, ..., a_n)$ and the conditions in c are satisfied. Variables that appear in the condition but not in the subject or action are, implicitly, existentially quantified.

As in RPPM, an *authorization policy* is a list of authorization rules, and a *conflict resolution strategy* determines the decision when rules with different possible decisions match a request.

Notation. We adopt several notational conventions for readability and brevity. We write authorization rules as itemized lists of components instead of tuples. We elide the decision when it is 1 (permit). We allow disjunction as a top-level connective in conditions; this is shorthand for a set of rules, one for each disjunct. We use identifiers that start with upper case for types and variables, and identifiers that start with lower case for relationship labels and constants.

4   Example: Healthcare Network

We illustrate our framework with a sample policy for electronic health records at a healthcare network. It is based partly on the sample policy in [9,10]. The permissible relationship graph appears in Fig. 1. The figure also shows the entity types and the relationship labels with their parameter types. Some edges have multiple relationship labels; this is equivalent to putting those relationship labels on separate edges with the same source and target. The figure shows all of the relationship labels in our case study, even though some relationship labels are not used in the sample authorization rules presented in this paper. "humRes-Mgr" abbreviates "human resources manager". "policyOfcr" abbreviates "policy officer".

The healthcare network consists of multiple facilities, such as hospitals and substance-abuse facilities. We assume that the healthcare network maintains a centralized database of health records; separate health records at each facility could easily be modeled. An health record is composed of hierarchically structured items. The "consent" relation indicates that a patient has given consent to treatment by a clinician or workgroup (abbreviated "wkgroup"). A patient's consent to treatment by a clinician may be limited to specified healthcare facilities in the network, so the consent relationship between them is parameterized by facility. Such parameterization is not needed for the consent relation between

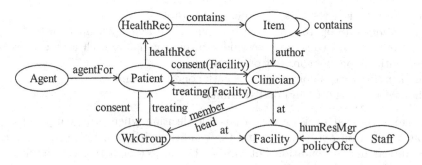

Fig. 1. Permissible relationship graph for the healthcare network example.

patients and workgroups, because a workgroup exists at a single facility. Similarly, the "treating" relationship between clinicians and patients is parameterized by the facility, while the "treating" relationship between workgroups and patients does not need this parameterization. We assume that a patient's agent may represent the patient at any facility in the healthcare network, so the agent-For relation is not parameterized by facility, but this parameter could easily be added if desired.

The following sample authorization rule expresses that a clinician can read an item in a patient's health record if the clinician is treating the patient, is a member of a workgroup treating the patient, or is the item's author.

Subject: Clinician
Action: read(Clinician, Item)
Condition: Clinician · treating($\star$); healthRec; contains$^+$ · Item
　　　　　　　$\vee$ Clinician · $\overline{\text{member}}$; treating($\star$); healthRec; contains$^+$ · Item
　　　　　　　$\vee$ Clinician · $\overline{\text{author}}$ · Item

The common sub-expression in the first two path conditions could be factored out with a path-expression name definition, *e.g.*, itemOfTreatedPatient = treating($\star$); healthRec; contains$^+$.

For an example of a rule that can be expressed more conveniently in RPPM^2 than ABAC, consider an extension of the system model that includes types of organizational units in the healthcare network, a type for documents such as budgets, a relationship label "orgHrchy" for edges in the organizational hierarchy, a relationship label "manages" to express that a user manages an organizational unit, and a relationship label "budget" to express that a document is an organizational unit's budget. For example, the system graph might contain an entity representing the entire healthcare network with child entities representing facilities with child entities representing centers (e.g., cancer center, heart center) with child entities representing departments (e.g., radiation oncology, surgical oncology) with child entities representing wards. The following rule concisely expresses that the manager of an organizational unit can read the budgets of that organizational unit and its descendants in the organizational hierarchy. This policy cannot be expressed so concisely in traditional role-based access control (RBAC) or attribute-based access control (ABAC) frameworks.

Subject: Manager
Action: read(Manager, Budget)
Condition: Manager · manages; orgHrchy*; budget · Budget

5   Authorization Checking Algorithm

We sketch an authorization checking algorithm for RPPM^2, based on Crampton and Sellwood's authorization checking algorithm for RPPM [4]. The heart of their authorization checking algorithm is an algorithm, called MatchPrincipal, that, given a system graph, a path expression, a source node, and a target node, performs a modified bread-first search (BFS) to determine whether the graph contains a path from the source node to the target node that matches the path expression.

Two main extensions to their authorization checking algorithm are needed to obtain an algorithm for determining whether a RPPM[2] authorization rule applies to a given request. First, MatchPrincipal needs to be extended to match parameters in relationship labels as it traverses edges. This requires maintaining a substitution that maps the existentially-quantified variables to values. The algorithm adds and removes bindings from this substitution as it traverses edges and backtracks across them, respectively.

Second, the overall authorization checking algorithm needs to be extended to check all of the path conditions in the condition c of a given authorization rule. Let pc_i denote the path condition in the i'th conjunct of c. For each i, starting with $i = 1$, a BFS for pc_i is initiated, using the substitution obtained from the BFS for pc_{i-1} as the initial substitution (as a special case, when $i = 1$, the empty substitution is used as the initial substitution). When a path and associated substitution satisfying pc_i is found, a BFS for pc_{i+1} is initiated, in the same manner. If the BFSs for all path conditions succeed, the overall algorithm terminates with the result that the authorization rule applies to the given request. If the BFS for pc_i fails, then the BFS for pc_{i-1} resumes until it finds a satisfying path with a different associated substitution, at which point a new BFS for pc_i is initiated. This process iterates until either the BFSs for all path conditions succeed, yielding the result mentioned above, or the BFS for some path condition pc_i terminates, in which case there are no more ways to try to satisfy pc_i, and the overall algorithm terminates with the result that the authorization rule does not apply to the given request.

One issue glossed over above is that, when a BFS for some pc_i is initiated, the source node for the BFS could be an unbound variable. In principle, this can easily be handled by adding a loop that considers every node in the system graph as a potential source node. In practice, this would be unacceptably inefficient, and the authorization rule should probably be rejected if this iteration cannot be avoided; this can be determined with a simple static analysis, so the authorization rule can be rejected before it is added to the policy. We expect that this will rarely occur in practice. Even if the source node in some path condition pc_i is an existentially quantified variable V, two techniques can be used to try to avoid this iteration: (1) if the target node for pc_i is known (*i.e.*, is not an unbound variable), reverse the path expression, and swap the source and target nodes; (2) change the order in which the path conditions in c are considered (in effect, permute the conjuncts of c), so that some path condition that has a known source or target node and that contains V (hence will generate a binding for V) is considered before pc_i.

6 Administrative Model

There are administrative operations to add and delete entities, edges, and authorization rules, plus three administrative actions to set defaults. We discuss administrative policy for each of them in turn. As discussed in Sect. 1, administrative policies are expressed in the same way as non-administrative policies, using authorization rules, as defined above. Any desired authorization rules may be used to control these administrative operations. However, authorization rules for actions that add or delete rules are given special interpretations, as discussed in detail below. We refer to authorization rules for administrative actions as *administrative rules* or *administrative policy*. Our administrative model is comprehensive: even the administrative policy can be modified dynamically, using the same administrative operations.

We sometimes refer to entities authorized to perform one or more administrative actions as *administrators*. These entities are not special in any other way; for example, they may also have non-administrative permissions.

Add Edge and Delete Edge. The action addEdge(e_1, e_2, r) adds an edge from e_1 to e_2 labeled r. If the edge already exists, the action has no effect. For example, the following authorization rule expresses that a clinician who is a member of a workgroup WG can create a treating relationship between WG and a patient, if the patient has given consent to treatment by WG.

> **Subject:** Clinician
> **Action:** addEdge(WG, Patient, treating)
> **Condition:** Clinician · member · WG ∧ Patient · consent · WG

The action deleteEdge(e_1, e_2, r) deletes an edge from e_1 to e_2 labeled r. If the edge does not exist, the action has no effect. For example, the following authorization rule expresses that a human resources manager for a facility can remove a clinician's association with the facility.

> **Subject:** HumResMgr
> **Action:** deleteEdge(Clinician, Facility, at)
> **Condition:** HumResMgr · humResMgr · Facility

Add Entity and Delete Entity. We require that, when a new entity is added, an edge relating it to an existing entity is also added. This provides a reference point to determine permissions. For example, a typical pattern is to add an "owner" edge between the subject and the new entity. This requirement is analogous to the requirement in ARBAC97 that, when a new role is added, it must be attached to the existing role hierarchy [15]. When such a reference is not needed (*e.g.*, a user is authorized to add new entities of a given type anywhere in the system graph), the new entity can be related to a dummy entity.

The action addEntity(T, e_1, e_2, r) adds a new entity e_1 of type T, and adds an edge labeled r from e_1 to existing entity e_2. If e_1 already exists, the action has no effect. For example, the following authorization rule expresses that a human resources manager for a facility can add new clinicians at the facility.

> **Subject:** HumResMgr
> **Action:** addEntity(Clinician, NewClinician, Facility, at)
> **Condition:** HumResMgr · humResMgr · Facility

The action deleteEntity(e_1) deletes entity e_1 and all edges incident on e_1. This action is permitted only if the subject is authorized to delete e_1 and to delete all edges currently incident on e_1. For example, the following authorization rule expresses that the human resources manager for a facility can remove workgroups at that facility. This action is permitted only if the workgroup is not currently treating any patients, because human resources managers are not authorized to delete treating relationships between workgroups and patients. The Facility variable in this rule does not appear in the subject or action and hence is existentially quantified.

> **Subject:** HumResMgr
> **Action:** deleteEntity(WG)
> **Condition:** HumResMgr · humResMgr · Facility ∧ WG · at · Facility

Add Authorization Rule. The action addRule($s, op(a_1, ..., a_n), c, d$) adds the specified authorization rule to the authorization policy.

We could authorize such actions in exactly the same way as other actions, using authorization rules with addRule actions, without any special treatment, but this would be undesirably limiting, because each administrator would only be able to select from a finite, fixed set of rules that he or she is permitted to add. In practice, more flexible administrative policies are usually desired, that allow an administrator to add authorization rules selected from a large or unbounded set of authorization rules that are consistent with the administrator's scope of authority and with desired safety and availability properties. Safety properties require that, under specified conditions, specified entities do not have specified permissions. Availability properties require that, under specified conditions, specified entities have specified permissions. Note that these properties depend on the administrative policy as a whole, not only the policies for adding and removing rules. Support for verifiable enforcement of such properties is an important design principle for our administrative model, although details of specification and verification of such properties are left for future work.

Based on this consideration, one might design an administrative policy for addRule actions that directly specifies the set of authorizations that each entity is permitted to grant by adding permit rules, and the set of authorizations that each entity is permitted to revoke by adding deny rules. An *authorization* is a pair consisting of an entity and an action, representing permission for that entity to perform that action. In this approach, an addRule action for a permit rule is allowed if the proposed rule grants a subset of the specified authorizations in the current state, *i.e.*, with respect to the current system graph. Similarly, an addRule action for a deny rule is allowed if the proposed deny rule revokes a subset of those authorizations in the current state.

This approach allows a wider variety of rules to be added, but it is brittle and potentially insecure: the authorization check for addRule actions is too dependent on the current state, and added rules might have undesired consequences in other states, *e.g.*, after the system graph changes. This is true regardless of whether the two aforementioned sets of authorizations are specified explicitly by enumeration or implicitly using formulas (*e.g.*, using a combination of first-order predicate logic and path conditions). For example, an administrator could circumvent the intended administrative policy by first adding a permit rule that grants dangerous authorizations only if a certain relationship exists in the system graph, and later adding that relationship.

Our approach is based on using logical implication to compare a proposed authorization rule to specified authorization rules that represent the "loosest" (least strict) authorization rules that the subject is allowed to add. A key feature of this approach is that the authorization test for an addRule action is independent of the current state and hence can ensure that the meaning of a proposed rule is acceptable in all states. We introduce a partial order on authorization rules, called *strictness order*. Informally, rule ρ_1 is at least as strict as rule ρ_2, denoted $\rho_1 \leq_{\text{rule}} \rho_2$, if they have the same action and the same decision, and the condition in ρ_1 entails (*i.e.*, implies) the condition in ρ_2. The strictness order is designed to provide the guarantee: if $\rho_1 \leq_{\text{rule}} \rho_2$, then in every state, ρ_1 grants (or denies) a subset of the authorizations that ρ_2 grants (or denies).

An addRule(ρ_1) action by a subject s is allowed if there exists an authorization rule ρ_2 such that (1) the authorization rules imply s can add ρ_2 and (2) ρ_1 is at least as strict as ρ_2.

Roughly speaking, a rule ρ_1 is at least as strict as a rule ρ_2 if ρ_1 can be obtained from ρ_2 by renaming variables, instantiating variables with constants, adding conjuncts to the condition, and replacing path expressions in the condition with stricter path expressions. A formal definition of the strictness order follows.

A substitution θ is a mapping from variables to variables and constants. Recall that $t\theta$ denotes the result of applying substitution θ to term t.

Authorization rule $\rho_1 = (s_1, a_1, c_1, 1)$ is *at least as strict as* authorization rule $\rho_2 = (s_2, a_2, c_2, 1)$, denoted $\rho_1 \leq_{\text{rule}} \rho_2$, if there exists a substitution θ such that $s_1 = s_2\theta$ and $a_1 = a_2\theta$ and, for each conjunct $e_2 \cdot \pi_2 \cdot e_2'$ in condition $c_2\theta$, there is a conjunct $e_1 \cdot \pi_1 \cdot e_1'$ in condition c_1 such that $e_1 = e_2$, $e_1' = e_2'$, and $\pi_1 \leq_{\text{pe}} \pi_2$.

The strictness order $\leq_{\text{pe}}$ on path expressions is designed to provide the guarantee: if $\pi_1 \leq_{\text{pe}} \pi_2$, then in every system graph, every path satisfying π_1 also satisfies π_2. Informally, a path expression π_1 is at least as strict as a path expression π_2, denoted $\pi_1 \leq_{\text{pe}} \pi_2$, if π_1 can be obtained from π_2 by replacing path expressions involving transitive closure with path expressions denoting paths with the same or more constrained labels and the same or more constrained lengths (*e.g.*, replacing π^+ with $\pi;\pi$). A formal definition of $\leq_{pe}$ follows. It is unnecessary (although safe) to allow instantiation of variables with constants in this definition, because the instantiation can be done by the substitution applied to c_2 in the definition of $\leq_{rule}$.

Path expression π_1 is *at least as strict as* path expression π_2, denoted $\pi_1 \leq_{pe} \pi_2$, if any of the following conditions hold: (1) $\pi_1 = \pi_2$; (2) π_2 has the form π^+ and π_1 either (a) has the form $\pi_{1,0}$ or $\pi_{1,0}^+$ with $\pi_{1,0} \leq_{pe} \pi$, or (b) is a sequential composition $\pi_{1,1};\pi_{1,2}$ such that, for $i = 1..2$, $\pi_{1,i}$ has the form $\pi_{1,i,0}$, $\pi_{1,i,0}^+$, or $\pi_{1,i,0}^*$ with $\pi_{1,i,0} \leq_{pe} \pi$, and such that $\pi_{1,1}$ and $\pi_{1,2}$ do not both have $*$ as the top-level operator; (3) π_2 has the form π^* and either π_1 satisfies the conditions in case (2) or π_1 is $\diamond$; (4) π_2 has the form $\pi_{2,1}^*;\pi_{2,2}$ or $\pi_{2,2};\pi_{2,1}^*$ and π_1 satisfies $\pi_1 \leq \pi_{2,2}$; (5) π_2 has the form $\pi_{2,1};\cdots;\pi_{2,n}$ and π_1 has the form $\pi_{1,1};\cdots;\pi_{1,m}$ and there exist i and j such that $1 < i < m$ and $1 < j < n$ and $\pi_{1,1};\cdots;\pi_{1,i} \leq_{pe} \pi_{2,1};\cdots;\pi_{2,j}$ and $\pi_{1,i+1};\cdots;\pi_{1,m} \leq_{pe} \pi_{2,j+1};\cdots;\pi_{2,n}$. Case (5) reflects the associativity of sequential composition.

For example, the following authorization rule expresses that the policy officer for a facility can add rules allowing a member of a workgroup to establish a treating relationship with a patient if the patient has consented to that relationship.

> **Subject:** PolicyOfcr
> **Action:** addRule(**Subject:** Clinician
> > **Action:** addEdge(WG, Patient, treating)
> > **Condition:** Clinician · member · WG
> > $\wedge$ Patient · consent · WG)
>
> **Condition:** PolicyOfcr · policyOfcr · Facility

Note that the authorization rule in the addRule action is the example authorization rule for addEdge given above. This authorization rule for addRule allows a policy officer at a facility to add either the authorization rule as given here, meeting the minimal safety requirements imposed by the healthcare network, or a stricter version imposing additional facility-specific requirements, *e.g.*, that only the head of a workgroup can establish a treating relationship between the workgroup and a patient.

Delete Authorization Rule. The action deleteRule(s, $op(a_1, ..., a_n)$, c, d) deletes the specified authorization rule from the authorization policy. Authorization rules for deleteRule actions are interpreted in the same was as authorization rules for addRule actions. This implies that, if the policy contains an authorization rule for addRule and an authorization rule for deleteRule with the same subject, the same condition, and the same authorization rule in the actions, then each user has symmetric permissions, *i.e.*, the set of authorization rules that can be added by a user equals the set of authorization rules that can be removed by that user.

Set System-Wide Default and Set Conflict-Resolution Strategy. The action setSystemDefaultDecision(d) sets the system-wide default decision to d. The action setConflictResolutionStrategy(s) sets the conflict-resolution strategy to s. The system-wide default decision and the conflict resolution strategy may be fixed in many systems, in which case no authorization rules for these actions are needed. For systems in which, for example, a system security officer can change the system-wide default decision, the system graph might contain an entity named "sso", corresponding to the system security officer role, and the policy might contain the authorization rule

> **Subject:** SSO
> **Action:** setSystemDefaultDecision(Default)
> **Condition:** SSO · member · sso

Set Per-Subject and Per-Object Defaults. setSubjectDefaultDecision(s, d) sets the default decision for subject s to d. setObjectDefaultDecision(o, d) sets the default decision for object o to d. For example, a policy with ownership-based authorization for setting per-object defaults might contain the authorization rule

> **Subject:** Owner
> **Action:** setObjectDefaultDecision(Obj, Default)
> **Condition:** Owner · owner · Obj

If objects are organized in a hierarchy (*e.g.*, in folders) represented by the "contains" relation, and ownership propagates down the hierarchy, then the rule might be

> **Subject:** Owner
> **Action:** setObjectDefaultDecision(Obj, Default)
> **Condition:** Owner · owner ; contains* · Obj

7 Related Work

Related Work on ReBAC. Several ReBAC frameworks have been proposed, by Fong [5], Carminati, Ferrari, and Perego [1], Cheng, Park, and Sandhu [2], Hu, Ahn, and Jorgensen [11], and others. We chose RPPM [3,4] as the basis for our work, because, as Crampton and Sellwood discuss [4], it is designed to be suitable for general computing systems, in contrast to other ReBAC models designed primarily with social network systems in mind.

Our RPPM^2 model extends the generality and expressiveness of RPPM in several ways, in addition to providing a comprehensive administrative model.

RPPM² allows relationship labels to have parameters. It allows actions to involve multiple entities and other parameters rather than only one object. It allows authorization rules to depend on relationships between all pairs of entities involved in a request, and to depend on multiple relationships between each such pair of entities. It allows entity constants as the source or target of path conditions; in RPPM, the source and target of the path condition must be the subject and object of the request, respectively.

In [5], Fong introduces the concept of *context* in a ReBAC model for social network systems. Contexts are scopes in which relationships (*i.e.*, edges in the social network graph) exist. Contexts are hierarchically organized, and the creation and destruction of contexts follow a stack discipline. The usefulness of contexts is illustrated in [5] in a sample policy for electronic health records (without considering administration of that policy). For example, a treating relationship between a clinician and a patient can be limited to a context corresponding to a healthcare facility or a medical case. We achieve a similar effect by allowing relationship labels to have parameters. Parameters can be used to indicate the scope of a relationship, among other things. Relationship labels are less structured than the contexts in [5] but more flexible; for example, they do not impose a strictly hierarchical organization on scopes or a stack discipline on the management of the scopes.

Related Work on Administration of ReBAC. Crampton and Sellwood [3,4] do not consider administration of RPPM.

Fong [5] defines transitions that push and pop contexts and a transition that adds and removes edges in the social network, but does not discuss authorization of those transitions, except for the comment that "In principle, the transitions can be considered resources and thus protected by the same protection system". Furthermore, Fong assumes in [5] that access control policies "remain constant throughout system lifetime", and he does not define operations for changing access control policies or consider authorization of such operations.

Fong, Anwar, and Zhao [6] define a ReBAC model for Facebook-style social network systems (SNSs), including administrative operations that allow each user to set policies for access to his/her own profile and items within it, and policies for communication (e.g., messaging). That model has some SNS-specific features not included in our model, *e.g.*, communication policies. However, that model is developed with SNSs in mind and is less applicable to general computing systems than RPPM and our model. Policy administration in that model is much simpler, because each user sets only policy for access to his/her own resources, and because the model does not use path conditions, modal logic, or any similarly expressive formalism to characterize paths in the graph.

Hu, Ahn, and Jorgensen [11] consider multiparty access control (MPAC) in the context of online social networks. MPAC allows multiple users to jointly determine the access control policy for a resource, e.g., a photo of a group of users. The core of their approach is a flexible voting-based conflict-resolution scheme to handle situations in which the resource's owner and other relevant users, called *stakeholders*, have different access control preferences for a resource. Our model does not support voting-based MPAC but could be extended to do so.

Related Work on Administration of ABAC. Gupta, Stoller, and Xu define an ABAC model with a comprehensive administrative model [9,10]. Specifically, they define a policy language with Datalog-like authorization rules, and an administrative model based on operations that add and remove facts and rules in the policy. They define a strictness order on authorization rules, and they interpret authorization rules for addition or deletion of authorization rules to allow addition or deletion, respectively, of rules that are at least as strict as the specified rules. We adopt this approach in the design of RPPM^2. They also present an abductive policy analysis algorithm, specifically, a semi-decision procedure for determining whether a specified set of users can together change the policy to grant a specified authorization.

8 Conclusion

This paper presents an expressive ReBAC model that includes a comprehensive administrative model. There are many directions for future work. One direction is to develop a similar comprehensive administrative model for a ReBAC model that uses modal logic [5,7], instead of path conditions [4], to characterize composite relationships between entities in the system graph. A second direction is to optimize the authorization checking algorithm sketched in Sect. 5, using techniques such as: pre-computation and caching, which are discussed for RPPM in [3]; more aggressive exploitation of constraints from multiple path conditions in a rule to prune the search for a path satisfying the overall condition; and elimination of redundant computations for policies in which path conditions in the same or different authorization rules contain common subexpressions. Another approach to developing an efficient authorization checking algorithm is to try to adapt Liu and Stoller's approach to efficient implementation of complex graph queries [13]. A third direction for future work is to develop policy analysis algorithms, to help policy developers understand the full implications of proposed administrative policies. We plan to explore an abductive policy analysis for RPPM^2 along the lines of Gupta, Stoller, and Xu's abductive policy analysis for ACAR [9,10].

References

1. Carminati, B., Ferrari, E., Perego, A.: Enforcing access control in Web-based social networks. ACM Trans. Inf. Syst. Secur. **13**(1), 1–38 (2009)
2. Cheng, Y., Park, J., Sandhu, R.: A user-to-user relationship-based access control model for online social networks. In: Cuppens-Boulahia, N., Cuppens, F., Garcia-Alfaro, J. (eds.) DBSec 2012. LNCS, vol. 7371, pp. 8–24. Springer, Heidelberg (2012)
3. Crampton, J., Sellwood, J.: Caching and auditing in the RPPM model. In: Mauw, S., Jensen, C.D. (eds.) STM 2014. LNCS, vol. 8743, pp. 49–64. Springer, Heidelberg (2014)

4. Crampton, J., Sellwood, J.: Path conditions and principal matching: a new approach to access control. In: Proceedings of the 19th ACM Symposium on Access Control Models and Technologies (SACMAT), pp. 187–198. ACM (2014)

5. Fong, P.W.L.: Relationship-based access control: protection model and policy language. In: Proceedings of the First ACM Conference on Data and Application Security and Privacy (CODASPY), pp. 191–202. ACM (2011)

6. Fong, P.W.L., Anwar, M., Zhao, Z.: A privacy preservation model for Facebook-style social network systems. In: Backes, M., Ning, P. (eds.) ESORICS 2009. LNCS, vol. 5789, pp. 303–320. Springer, Heidelberg (2009)

7. Fong, P.W.L., Siahaan, I.: Relationship-based access control policies and their policy languages. In: Proceedings of the 16th ACM Symposium on Access Control Models and Technologies (SACMAT), pp. 51–60. ACM, June 2011

8. Gates, C.E.: Access control requirements for Web 2.0 security and privacy. In: IEEE Web 2.0 Security & Privacy Workshop (W2SP 2007), May 2007

9. Gupta, P.: Verification of security policy administration and enforcement in enterprise systems. Ph.D. thesis, Stony Brook University, December 2011. https://dspace.sunyconnect.suny.edu/handle/1951/59677

10. Gupta, P., Stoller, S.D., Xu, Z.: Abductive analysis of administrative policies in rule-based access control. IEEE Trans. Dependable Secure Comput. 11(5), 412–424 (2014)

11. Hu, H., Ahn, G.J., Jorgensen, J.: Multiparty access control for online social networks: model and mechanisms. IEEE Trans. Knowl. Data Eng. 25(7), 1614–1627 (2013)

12. Li, N., Mao, Z.: Administration in role based access control. In: Proceedings of the 2nd ACM Symposium on InformAtion, Computer and Communications Security (ASIACCS), pp. 127–138. ACM, March 2007

13. Liu, Y.A., Stoller, S.D.: Querying complex graphs. In: Van Hentenryck, P. (ed.) PADL 2006. LNCS, vol. 3819, pp. 199–214. Springer, Heidelberg (2005)

14. Saltzer, J.H., Schroeder, M.D.: The protection of information in computer systems. Commun. ACM 17(7), 388–402 (1974)

15. Sandhu, R., Bhamidipati, V., Munawer, Q.: The ARBAC97 model for role-based administration of roles. ACM Trans. Inf. Syst. Secur. 2(1), 105–135 (1999)

16. eXtensible Access Control Markup Language (XACML). http://www.oasis-open.org/committees/xacml/

Migrating from DAC to RBAC

Emre Uzun[1]([✉]), David Lorenzi[1], Vijayalakshmi Atluri[1],
Jaideep Vaidya[1], and Shamik Sural[2]

[1] MSIS Department, Rutgers Business School, Newark, USA
{emreu,dlorenzi,atluri,jsvaidya}@cimic.rutgers.edu
[2] School of Information Technology, IIT Kharagpur, Kharagpur, India
shamik@sit.iitkgp.ernet.in

Abstract. Role Based Access Control (RBAC) is one of the most popular means for enforcing access control. One of the main reasons for this is that it is perceived as the least expensive configuration with respect to security administration. In this paper, we demonstrate that security administration is not always cheaper under RBAC when compared to the traditional Discretionary Access Control (DAC). If RBAC proves to be beneficial, organizations may choose to migrate from DAC to RBAC. There have been many algorithms developed to generate RBAC configurations from DAC configuration. Although these algorithms provide an RBAC configuration, the *quality* of the generated RBAC configuration could vary among different algorithms and DAC configurations. In this paper, we propose a decision support framework, which provides a basis for comparison among different potential RBAC derivations from DAC to determine the most desirable outcome with respect to the cost of security administration.

1 Introduction

Access control facilitates controlled sharing and protection of resources in an enterprise. While there exist a variety of formal authorization models to meet a variety of organizational requirements in specifying their access control policies, most of today's commercial software including operating systems, database systems, enterprise resource planning and workflow systems offer either Discretionary Access Control (DAC) or Role Based Access Control (RBAC) as their primary mechanism to enforce security. Typically, under DAC, users are directly assigned permissions to access resources, called User Permission Assignment (UPA).

In contrast to DAC where users are directly assigned to permissions, in RBAC, users are assigned to roles (user role assignment, UA), and roles in turn are groups of permissions (permission role assignment PA). It is assumed that this additional layer facilitates easier administration when users and their access permissions change. This is simply because the total number of assignments that the administrator has to manage under RBAC ($|UA| + |PA|$) is typically lower than that of DAC ($|UPA|$), since typically the number of roles is expected to be much smaller than the number of permissions.

© IFIP International Federation for Information Processing 2015
P. Samarati (Ed.): DBSec 2015, LNCS 9149, pp. 69–84, 2015.
DOI: 10.1007/978-3-319-20810-7_5

Because of the ease of administration as well as its flexibility and intuitiveness, RBAC is one of the most preferred access control models used in computer systems. As a result, many organizations are attempting to migrate from their existing access control model, which is usually DAC, to RBAC in order to enjoy its benefits.

The process of discovering roles from DAC configuration has received significant attention recently. This process, called role mining, is a bottom-up approach that utilizes the existing permission assignments (UPA) of DAC and groups these permissions to obtain roles. There also exist top-down approaches for role discovery, that examine all of the job functions to determine the permissions required to pursue the tasks assigned to them. Although this approach generates meaningful roles that represent various job functions, the overall process of forming roles could be tedious and labor intensive [3,8]. Moreover, in the presence of certain exceptional cases in permission assignments where a user that belongs to a job function needs an additional permission that none of the other users of the same job function has, there would be problems forming roles that are as generic as possible, while preserving each user's permission requirements. Nevertheless, there is a case study that has results in favor of a top down approach implemented in a bank [15].

The advantage of the bottom-up approach is that it is an unsupervised approach and therefore is a more automated process as opposed to the manual top-down approach and also has the additional benefit of taking care of the exceptional cases discussed above while forming roles. However, in this approach, the existing business processes are ignored and the roles obtained as a result might not represent meaningful job functions. The automated process of obtaining an RBAC configuration with the bottom-up approach is useful for many organizations as they would like to migrate to RBAC to realize its benefits without a huge investment of time and money as in the case of top-down approach. Therefore, in this paper, we take the path of the bottom-up approach to migrate from DAC to RBAC.

However, we argue in this paper that migrating from DAC to RBAC may not always be beneficial with respect to reducing the administrative load. Therefore, before one jumps on to such a decision to migrate from DAC to RBAC, some key questions should be asked at that point:

1. *Is migrating to RBAC from an existing DAC configuration a wise option?* In this paper, we demonstrate that, while RBAC eases the burden of security administration for certain access control configurations, DAC may be more beneficial for other configurations. Towards this end, we present a decision support model to help with this analysis.
2. *If migrating to RBAC is more beneficial, what is the best suitable approach for a given DAC configuration to help with this migration from DAC to RBAC?* In this paper, we study a number of such approaches and present our experimental results. These approaches include three previously proposed algorithms – FastMiner [21], MBC [3] and ORCA [16], as well as one new algorithm, called DEMiner, proposed in this paper.

Towards this end, in this paper, we make the following major contributions: First, we propose a framework that can be utilized in three different ways: (1) Determining whether migrating to RBAC from an existing DAC configuration is beneficial, (2) Comparing alternative RBAC derivations of the same DAC configuration to pick the most desirable one in terms of administrative load, and (3) Comparing the results of different role mining algorithms.

Our framework can serve as a *Decision Support System* to aid organizations to make an informed decision about whether it is desirable to switch to an RBAC configuration. Using our framework, organizations will be able to determine if they really need to implement RBAC, and if so which alternative configuration provides the best "fit" to its specific policies. Our framework comprises a number of different cost metrics derived from the UPA and the corresponding RBAC derivation from a role mining approach to determine if it is worth migrating.

Second, we propose a new and pragmatic role mining algorithm, called DEMiner, which does not necessarily produce optimal roles, but is quite simple, since it produces disjoint roles.

The paper is organized as follows: In Sect. 2, we elaborate with examples on the key questions discussed above. In Sect. 3, we discuss our proposed cost metrics that will aid in distinguishing the performance of different role mining algorithms in terms of ease in administration, along with the main framework for comparison. In Sect. 4 we review different role mining algorithms and also present a new role mining algorithm. Finally, in Sect. 5 we provide experimental results of our proposed decision support framework for four different role mining algorithms to give an insight about the administrative load of the RBAC decompositions they produce.

2   Key Questions

Now let us turn our attention to each of the questions we raised in the previous section.

2.1   Is DAC to RBAC Migration Beneficial at All?

In the following, we show with examples that it is beneficial to migrate from DAC to RBAC for certain DAC configurations and not so for other configurations.

Consider the two example UPAs given in Tables 1 and 4. Essentially, A permission is of the form (resource, access mode). For example a permission $p_1 = $ (File A, read) indicates the read access to File A. In the User-Permission Assignment (UPA) matrix, 1 indicates that a particular user has access to a specific resource in the system. For example, the presence of 1 in the first cell of Table 1 indicates that Alice has permission p_1.

Now, deriving RBAC from DAC is simply to decompose UPA into two matrices, UA and PA. Assume that UPA in Table 1 is decomposed into an RBAC configuration with the minimal number of edges [19]. The decomposition is given in Tables 2 and 3. This decomposition has $|UA| + |PA| = 12$ assignments, whereas

Table 1. Example UPA 1

	p_1	p_2	p_3	p_4
Alice	1	1	1	1
Bob		1	1	
Cathy			1	1
David		1		

Table 2. UA for Example UPA 1

	r_1	r_2	r_3	r_4
Alice	1	1	1	
Bob	1			1
Cathy		1		
David	1			

Table 3. PA for Example UPA 1

	p_1	p_2	p_3	p_4
r_1		1		
r_2			1	1
r_3	1			
r_4			1	

the UPA has only 9 assignments ($|UPA| < |UA| + |PA|$). It is clear that, this optimal RBAC decomposition has more administrative cost than that of DAC.

On the other hand, consider the DAC configuration given in Table 4. The optimal RBAC decomposition with minimum number of edges is given in Tables 5 and 6. This RBAC configuration has $|UA| + |PA| = 9$ assignments. However, the DAC configuration has 10 assignments, hence making the RBAC configuration better than the DAC in terms of administrative cost ($|UPA| > |UA| + |PA|$).

Table 4. Example UPA 2

	p_1	p_2	p_3	p_4
Alice	1	1	1	1
Bob	1	1		
Cathy	1	1		
David			1	1

Table 5. UA for Example UPA 2

	r_1	r_2
Alice	1	1
Bob	1	
Cathy	1	
David		1

Table 6. PA for Example UPA 2

	p_1	p_2	p_3	p_4
r_1	1	1		
r_2			1	1

The above examples clearly demonstrate that for certain DAC configurations, migrating to RBAC will reduce the administrative load, whereas for certain other DAC configurations migrating to RBAC will indeed increase the administrative load. Therefore, blindly switching to RBAC without first evaluating its benefits is not a good idea.

2.2 What Is the Best DAC to RBAC Configuration that Minimizes the Administrative Burden?

A poor RBAC decomposition, regardless of how fast it is obtained, could degrade the usefulness of RBAC up to the very extreme point where the corresponding DAC is significantly better in terms of its average effort of administration. For example, consider two alternative decompositions to the UPA given in Table 1. The first one is obtained by minimizing the number of roles (given in Tables 7 and 8) and the second one is an arbitrary decomposition – no specific optimization performed (given in Tables 9 and 10).

Although the first decomposition is an optimal decomposition for the UPA, is clear that this decomposition creates redundancy, since the permission-role assignment relation actually is the same as the UPA itself, and the user-role

Table 7. Alternative UA 1 for Example UPA 1

	r_1	r_2	r_3	r_4
Alice	1			
Bob		1		
Cathy			1	
David				1

Table 8. Alternative PA 1 for Example UPA 1

	p_1	p_2	p_3	p_4
r_1	1	1	1	1
r_2		1	1	
r_3			1	1
r_4	1			

Table 9. Alternative UA 2 for Example UPA 1

	r_1	r_2	r_3	r_4	r_5
Alice	1		1	1	1
Bob		1			
Cathy				1	1
David			1		

Table 10. Alternative PA 2 for Example UPA 2

	p_1	p_2	p_3	p_4
r_1	1			
r_2		1	1	
r_3		1		
r_4			1	
r_5				1

assignment relation is simply an identity matrix. Also, the total number of assignments is 13, which is more than that of the DAC configuration. The other decomposition also has a higher administrative cost, since not only is there more assignments in total ($|UA| + |PA| = 14$), but also there is one additional role than the previous decomposition. Considering the three decompositions given the UPA in Table 1 (Tables 2, 3, 7, 8, 9 and 10), the one that has the least administrative cost is given in Tables 2 and 3.

There are many different algorithms proposed to construct an RBAC configuration from a DAC configuration. The very first algorithms aim to find a decomposition to a given UPA matrix. CompleteMiner [21], FastMiner [21] and ORCA [16] are some of these algorithms used to perform this process. After the formalization of the role mining problem (RMP) and its variants by Vaidya et al. [19], many different new algorithms that are capable of handling the new objectives are proposed. Many of these new algorithms are basically an adaptation of the solution procedures of an existing problem. Some examples are: Utilizing Minimum Database Tiling Problem, Discrete Basis Problem, Minimum Biclique Cover Problem and Graph Optimization [3,19,26]. There is also a study to mine temporal roles when the role assignments are dependent on temporal constraints [11]. While providing the same level of security as long as the resulting RBAC configuration is an exact decomposition of the DAC, each of these algorithms could perform differently, among which some could be superior.

In order make an analytical comparison, Molloy et al. [14] propose a method where, the metric for comparison is a weighted sum of the number of roles, user-role assignments, permission-role assignments, role-role assignments and user-permission assignments that is obtained via a role mining algorithm. Although these components provide crucial information about the decomposition, they do not provide a comparison perspective with respect to the marginal gain of using a particular decomposition.

3 Cost Metrics for Comparing Alternative RBAC Decompositions

Role Mining is a dataset dependent process in addition to being algorithm dependent. A role mining algorithm can output a satisfactory result on one dataset, yet may perform worse on another. Moreover, expectations on the resulting RBAC decomposition could vary in different applications. For example, a startup company would expect to get a flexible role distribution – more likely with a higher number of roles – to quickly adapt to potential new positions without defining new roles from scratch each time. On the other hand, a more mature company would wish to have a more compact set of roles that precisely define its job functions. Therefore, in order to cover as many different objectives as possible, while remaining as generic as possible, we develop certain cost metrics that are applicable to any dataset for various purposes.

We base our metrics to capture the basic principle of why RBAC should perform better. RBAC imposes the *role* layer to the UPA in order to *group* permissions to reduce *redundancy* in the permission assignments. If there is less redundancy, the administration of the access control system would get better. So, if a specific RBAC decomposition does not address this *redundancy* or if the UPA does not have any *redundancy*, then RBAC will not provide substantial benefits in terms of its ease in administration. This issue could be of many different types, such as having roles with only a single permission, having more roles than the number of permissions, or even having a decomposition that has more assignments than the UPA. Towards this end, in the following, we present our proposed cost metrics that are used to determine the amount of benefits realized from a transition from DAC to RBAC. We develop some of these metrics on the End-User Benefits of the NIST study related to RBAC [17].

Let the sets U, R, $PRMS$ denote users, roles and permissions, respectively. $UA \subseteq U \times R$ and $PA \subseteq PRMS \times R$ denote user to role and permission to role relations, respectively. We define $UPA \subseteq U \times PRMS$ as the user to permission relation for DAC. Before we present our cost metrics, we provide definitions for some statistical measures that we obtain from DAC and RBAC configurations.

Definition 1. *Average Number of Users per Role (AUR):* *Let $(u,r) \in UA$ be a user-role assignment tuple. Number of user assignments for role r is denoted as $UR_r = |\{(u,r) : (u,r) \in UA\}|$. Then $AUR = \sum_{r \in R} UR_r / |R|$ is the average number of users that a role has in a given configuration.*

Definition 2. *Average Number of Roles per User (ARU):* *Let $(u,r) \in UA$ be a user-role assignment tuple. Number of role assignments for user u is denoted as $RU_u = |\{(u,r) : (u,r) \in UA\}|$. Then $ARU \sum_{u \in U} RU_u / |U|$ is the average number of roles that a user has in a given configuration.*

Definition 3. Average Number of Permissions per Role (APR): Let $(p, r) \in PA$ be a permission-role assignment tuple. Number of permission assignments for role r is denoted as $PR_r = |\{(p, r) : (p, r) \in PA\}|$. Then $APR = \sum_{r \in R} PR_r / |R|$ is the average number of permissions that a role has in a given configuration.

Definition 4. Average Number of Permissions per User (APU): Let $(u, p) \in UPA$ be a user-permission assignment tuple. Number of permission assignments for user u is denoted as $PU_u = |\{(u, p) : (u, p) \in UPA\}|$. Then $APU = \sum_{u \in U} PU_u / |U|$ is the average number of permissions that a user has in a given configuration.

Under these definitions, we present four different cost metrics that we utilize in our decision support framework:

Amount of Generic Roles (GEN): First, we define exclusive roles (EXC). A role is said to be *exclusive* if that role is assigned to only a *few* users to reflect exceptional situations. Usually, they are assigned to a single user to provide access to an exclusive task that is not covered by any other roles. For example, the roles r_1, r_3 and r_4 in the example decomposition given in Table 3 are said to be exclusive roles. A high number of exclusive roles is considered undesirable from a management perspective. For this metric, we utilize AUR and APR to determine for a specific role $r \in R$, how different the values of UR_r and PR_r are from AUR and APR. A role $r \in R$ is said to be exclusive if

$$\frac{AUR - UR_r}{AUR} > \epsilon_1 \text{ and } \frac{APR - PR_r}{APR} > \epsilon_2$$

where $\epsilon_1 \in [0, 1]$ and $\epsilon_2 \in [0, 1]$ are threshold values that statistically distinguish an exclusive role. Any role r that satisfies the above relations is in $r \in R_x \subseteq R$. Then, $EXL = \frac{|R_x|}{|R|}$, where R_x is the set of exclusive roles. Any role that is not exclusive is said to be a generic role, hence, the amount of generic roles, GEN, is calculated as $GEN = 1 - EXL$.

Amount of Assignments (ASN): The number of user-permission, user-role and permission-role assignments provide a basis for comparison to determine whether RBAC provides a better configuration as opposed to DAC in terms of both usability and security. A high number of total assignments would not only increase the amount of time required to perform assignments but also it makes the system more prone to potential security violations due to misconfiguration. Hence we will compare $|UPA|$ with $|UA| + |PA|$ to determine the amount of reduction in the number of assignments. The amount of assignments, ASN, is the percentage deviation of the total number of user-role and permission-role assignments in RBAC with respect to user-permission assignments in DAC. More formally, the amount of assignments, ASN, is determined by

$$ASN = max(0, \frac{|UPA| - (|UA| + |PA|)}{|UPA|})$$

Although the metric itself can never be negative, the component $\frac{|UPA|-(|UA|+|PA|)}{|UPA|}$ can have negative values, which means there is a need for more user-role and permission-role assignments in RBAC to represent the associated DAC configuration. Therefore, when $ASN = 0$, it means that the DAC configuration is better in terms of amount of assignments.

Average Cost of an Administrative Operation (ADM): The cost of an administrative operation is the amount of changes in the number of user-permission, user-role and permission-role assignments. In RBAC, user-role assignments are modified more often. Permission-role assignments, however, would not usually be altered unless a new role is created. Following the NIST study [17], we base our calculations on ARU as it shows an estimate of how many role assignments are required per user on average. So, the average cost of an administrative operation is

$$ADM = max(0, \frac{APU - ARU}{APU})$$

Sizes of the Decomposed Matrices (SIZ): This metric is basically the percentage difference of the total size of the RBAC decomposition with respect to its DAC counterpart. Essentially, it is directly dependent on the number of roles $|R|$ in the decomposition. In a majority of the cases where number of roles is far less than the number of permissions, RBAC is preferable. But the configurations given in the example decompositions in Sect. 1 would make this decision less obvious, as there is just a small difference between the number of user-permission assignments in DAC and user-role and role-permission assignments in RBAC. We calculate the sizes of the decomposed matrices, SIZ, using

$$SIZ = max(0, \frac{|U||PRMS| - (|U||R| + |PRMS||R|)}{|U||PRMS|})$$

This metric also has a similar type of output as ASN. Although SIZ can never be negative, $\frac{|U||PRMS|-(|U||R|+|PRMS||R|)}{|U||PRMS|}$ can get negative values. This means that the decomposed matrices are larger in size than the original user-permission assignment matrix. From an administrative perspective, there will be more possibilities for assignment – since there are more *cells* in the decomposed matrices to *flip* while making updates in role and permission assignments. So, this makes the decomposition more error-prone due to misconfiguration. Also, since the RBAC matrix sizes are greater than the DAC configuration, the decomposition is likely to be sparser than the original configuration which is also undesirable in terms of memory requirements.

Our decision support framework is a function that outputs a percentage value denoting how favorable an RBAC configuration is with respect to the

DAC configuration that it is generated from. The function is basically a linear combination of the four cost metrics defined in Sect. 3.

Definition 5. *Decision Support Function: The function given by* $f = w_1$ $(GEN) + w_2(ASN) + w_3(ADM) + w_4(SIZ)$, *where* w_1, w_2, w_3 *and* w_4 *are non-negative weights for the corresponding cost component* $(\sum_{i=1}^{4} w_i = 1)$, *denotes the percentage benefit of a given RBAC decomposition with respect to a DAC that is used to generate it.*

We note that, each metric we define in this section could be used individually to determine if an RBAC decomposition is favorable. It is better to have higher values for each metric, as this would imply migrating RBAC is favorable. The decision support function combines these metrics to obtain a more compact framework where the weights are picked based on the preferences of the system administrator or the management that governs the RBAC migration. As discussed previously in this section, a startup company where a handful of employees work, the administrative cost would not so significant, hence w_3 could be set to a low value, whereas in a more mature company with a large number of employees would like to reduce the administrative cost so they should set w_3 a higher value. Similarly, it is more beneficial for a mature company to reduce the number of assignments as much as possible, so the value of w_2 should also be higher. More discussion on the effects of the weights is provided in Sect. 5.

4   Role Mining Algorithms

In this section, we briefly discuss the role mining algorithms that we use in our experiments.

4.1   FastMiner

FastMiner is proposed by Vaidya et al. [21] and it is the simplified version of CompleteMiner, which is a subset enumeration based role mining algorithm. CompleteMiner has three major steps:

1. Identification of Initial Set of Roles: The algorithm starts with an initial set of roles populated by each user's permissions. So, all users who have the exact same set of permissions are grouped together. These form the initial set of roles, say *InitRoles*.
2. Subset Enumeration: In this phase, all of the potentially interesting roles are discovered by computing all possible intersection sets of all the roles created in the identification step and each unique intersection is placed in the set *GenRoles*.
3. User Count Computation: In this phase, for each generated role in *GenRoles*, the number of users who have the permissions associated with that role is counted.

CompleteMiner has exponential time complexity in terms of the size of the *InitRoles*. However, FastMiner only considers pairwise intersections, hence reducing the time complexity to $O(|U|^2|PRMS|)$.

4.2   MBC

Role Mining using Minimum Biclique Cover is proposed by Ene et al. [3]. They map the UPA into a bipartite graph where there are two sets, users U and permissions $PRMS$ and the assignments in UPA are mapped as edges in the graph, such that if $(u, p) \in UPA$, then there exists an edge between the user u and the permission p in the graph. The users and permissions that are included in a role create a biclique on this graph. Hence, this mapping allows algorithms to solve minimum biclique cover problem to be applied for role minimization problem.

4.3   ORCA

ORCA is proposed by Schlegelmilch and Steffens [16] and is a clustering based role mining algorithm. The clusters are formed using permissions and the users that are assigned to those permissions. The algorithm, then, merges these clusters based on the maximum overlap between the users.

Specifically, the ORCA algorithm begins with a cluster set with one cluster c_r for every permission. The permissions in a cluster are represented by $permissions(c_r)$ and the users associated with the permissions within a cluster are represented by $members(c_r)$. The algorithm starts with a partially ordered set of clusters ($\prec$), as the cluster hierarchy, which is initially set to be an empty set. Then, pairs of clusters with maximal overlap among the users are first merged and placed in the $\prec$. More formally, for every pair of clusters $\langle c_i, c_j \rangle$, $members(\langle c_i, c_j \rangle) = members(c_i) \cap members(c_j)$ and $permissions(\langle c_i, c_j \rangle) = permissions(c_i) \cup permissions(c_j)$. Among the pairs, the one with the highest number of common users and highest number of permissions is selected. The ties are broken randomly. The newly generated cluster (c_n) becomes a super cluster to its child-clusters (c_i, c_j) in the hierarchy. c_i and c_j are no longer considered in the algorithm. The algorithm continues in this fashion until there remains no clusters to merge. ORCA has a time complexity of $O(|PRMS|^2|U|)$.

4.4   DEMiner: A Simple Role Mining Algorithm

In this section, we present a new and simple role mining algorithm, called DEMiner, which is focused on obtaining a decomposition with roles as compact as possible while maintaining them disjoint among each other. This will achieve three important outcomes: (1) It provides an upper bound to $|R| \leq |PRMS|$, which is significant in terms of scalability. (2) Implementing Dynamic Separation of Duty constraints becomes easier especially when permission level SoD constraints are defined (3) Administration becomes much easier especially when a role with a specific permission is sought for – there will not be more than one alternative role to determine which one suits the best.

At each iteration the DEMiner algorithm generates a candidate role to be intersected with the existing roles in R. In particular, each candidate role is simply the collection of permissions of a user already assigned in the UPA.

The algorithm begins with two roles, $R = \{\{p : (u_1, p) \in UPA\}, \{p : (u_1, p) \notin UPA\}\}$, namely the permissions of the first user and the remaining permissions. Then, at each iteration the new candidate role is intersected with the roles in R. The UA assignments are performed at each iteration to reflect the updates in R. The algorithm runs until the users set is traced completely. The complete pseudocode for the DEMiner algorithm is shown in Algorithm 1.

Algorithm 1. DEMiner Algorithm
___

Input UPA
Initialize and set $R = \{\{p : (u_1, p) \in UPA\}, \{p : (u_1, p) \notin UPA\}\}$
for all Users $u \in U \backslash \{u_1\}$ **do**
    Create a candidate role $r^* = \{p : (u, p) \in UPA\}$
    for all $r \in R$ **do**
      $R = R \backslash r$
      Set $R = R \cup \{\{r^* \cap r\}, \{r^* \backslash r\}, \{r \backslash r^*\}\}$
    end for
end for
for all Roles $r \in R$ **do**
    for all Permissions $p \in r$ **do**
      for all Users $u \in U$ **do**
        if $(u, p) \in UPA$ **then**
          $UA = UA \cup \{(u, r)\}$
        end if
      end for
    end for
end for
Output UA, R.

The DEMiner generate UA given in Table 12 and PA given in Table 13 for the UPA given in Table 11.

Table 11. Example UPA

	p_1	p_2	p_3	p_4
Alice	1	1	1	1
Bob		1	1	1
Cathy			1	1
David		1		

Table 12. UA obtained by DEMiner

	r_1	r_2	r_3
Alice	1	1	1
Bob		1	1
Cathy			1
David		1	

Table 13. PA obtained by DEMiner

	p_1	p_2	p_3	p_4
r_1	1			
r_2		1		
r_3			1	1

Proposition 1. *The average number of roles created at an arbitrary iteration is bounded by* $|PRMS|/|U|$.

Proof. It is trivial from the output of the algorithm that since all of the roles are disjoint, $|R| \leq |PRMS|$, i.e., one role for each permission. Since there is one iteration per user, there will be at most $|PRMS|/|U|$ roles that can be generated per iteration on the average.

5   Experimental Results

We perform our experiments using various sized real world data sets obtained from HP Labs [3]. We use FastMiner [21], MBC [3], ORCA [16] and DEMiner as the algorithms. We show how different algorithms can provide different decompositions – as seen through the outputs of our cost component metrics – on the same dataset, so that our framework facilitates an informed decision about whether to switch to a particular RBAC decomposition or not. In the experiments, we set $\epsilon_1 = \epsilon_2 = 0.80$ and all weights equal ($w_i = 0.25$), but specific precedence could be given to the desired metric to obtain customized results.

In Table 14, we report the percentage benefits of the RBAC decompositions. In column "Size", we report the size of the UPA in terms of number of users and number of permissions. The columns "GEN", "ASN", "ADM" and "SIZ" denote the specific value of each cost metric that a dataset and its RBAC decomposition produce for each role mining algorithm. RBAC provides more benefit as these values approach to 1. Conversely, if any of these values are 0, then RBAC configuration will not provide any benefit in terms of administration. For example, the RBAC decomposition for Domino obtained by FastMiner has 81 % generic roles and improves the administrative operations by 79 %. Also the size of the decomposition is improved by 61 %. However, RBAC decomposition has more assignments than the DAC. On the other hand, for Emea, FastMiner produces a decomposition that has 70 % generic roles and improves the administrative operations by 99 %. But, both the decomposition size and the amount of assignments for RBAC configuration are greater than that of the DAC, making this RBAC decomposition not favorable in terms of these cost metrics. Finally, the column "Total" shows the value obtained from the Decision Support Function.

Figure 1 provides a graphical comparison with respect to total percentage improvements. The decompositions obtained for Firewall 1, Firewall 2, Americas Small and Americas Large outperform the other datasets, regardless of the role mining algorithm. Especially for Firewall 2, there will be a 97 % total improvement

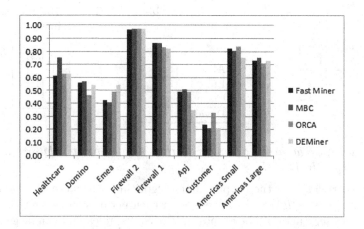

Fig. 1. Comparison of total percentage benefits

Table 14. Values of the Cost Metrics for Different Role Mining Algorithms and Datasets

Dataset	Size Users	Perms.	Fast Miner GEN	ASN	ADM	SIZ	Total
Healthcare	46	46	1.00	0.45	0.74	0.26	0.61
Domino	79	231	0.81	0.00	0.79	0.64	0.56
Emea	35	3046	0.70	0.00	0.99	0.00	0.42
Firewall 2	325	590	1.00	0.95	0.98	0.95	0.97
Firewall 1	365	709	0.99	0.83	0.93	0.73	0.87
Apj	2044	1164	0.93	0.13	0.50	0.37	0.49
Customer	10961	284	0.97	0.00	0.00	0.00	0.24
Americas Small	3477	1587	0.76	0.80	0.90	0.82	0.82
Americas Large	3485	10127	0.86	0.32	0.97	0.78	0.73
	Size Users	Perms.	MBC GEN	ASN	ADM	SIZ	Total
Healthcare	46	46	1.00	0.74	0.91	0.35	0.75
Domino	79	231	0.85	0.00	0.76	0.66	0.57
Emea	35	3046	0.62	0.00	1.00	0.02	0.41
Firewall 2	325	590	1.00	0.95	0.98	0.95	0.97
Firewall 1	365	709	0.97	0.84	0.94	0.71	0.87
Apj	2044	1164	0.89	0.22	0.54	0.39	0.51
Customer	10961	284	0.84	0.00	0.00	0.00	0.21
Americas Small	3477	1587	0.72	0.80	0.89	0.80	0.81
Americas Large	3485	10127	0.76	0.50	0.98	0.84	0.75
	Size Users	Perms.	ORCA GEN	ASN	ADM	SIZ	Total
Healthcare	46	46	0.79	0.78	0.94	0.00	0.63
Domino	79	231	0.81	0.00	0.00	0.20	0.46
Emea	35	3046	0.98	0.04	0.95	0.00	0.49
Firewall 2	325	590	1.00	0.96	0.99	0.93	0.97
Firewall 1	365	709	0.90	0.91	0.97	0.54	0.83
Apj	2044	1164	0.84	0.35	0.61	0.16	0.49
Customer	10961	284	0.90	0.20	0.22	0.00	0.33
Americas Small	3477	1587	0.89	0.90	0.95	0.61	0.84
Americas Large	3485	10127	0.80	0.75	0.96	0.35	0.71
	Size Users	Perms.	DEMiner GEN	ASN	ADM	SIZ	Total
Healthcare	46	46	0.95	0.68	0.71	0.17	0.63
Domino	79	231	0.82	0.34	0.66	0.35	0.54
Emea	35	3046	0.94	0.40	0.82	0.00	0.54
Firewall 2	325	590	1.00	0.95	0.97	0.95	0.97
Firewall 1	365	709	0.92	0.86	0.88	0.64	0.82
Apj	2044	1164	0.69	0.16	0.33	0.22	0.35
Customer	10961	284	0.84	0.00	0.00	0.00	0.21
Americas Small	3477	1587	0.79	0.77	0.78	0.68	0.75
Americas Large	3485	10127	0.85	0.78	0.83	0.45	0.73

with respect to the DAC configuration. For these datasets, RBAC is likely to improve administration. On the other hand, the decompositions for Customer dataset is the worst in terms of the percentage benefits with an average of 25 % total improvement. The other datasets have around 50 % improvement, which could be treated as satisfactory.

When we compare the configurations obtained from different role mining algorithms, we see that they perform close to each other with the exception of the Healthcare and Customer datasets. In Healthcare, MBC and in Customer, ORCA provide a much better decomposition than the other algorithms. Finally, we point out some interesting facts in the details of the Customer dataset. Notice that the cost metrics ASN, ADM and SIZ are all 0 % for FastMiner, MBC and DEMiner. This shows that the resulting RBAC decompositions actually have more assignments, and the size of the RBAC decomposition is greater than that of the original DAC configuration and the average administrative operation takes longer amount of time. Configurations like these show that there could be cases where one should retain the original DAC configuration in order not to increase the complexity needlessly.

The selection of the weights is important in the analysis and could yield a totally different result for the same role mining algorithm and for the same dataset. Consider the output of FastMiner on Emea. Suppose that emphasis is given on the size of the decomposition and the number of assignments (hence w_2 and w_4 are set to 0.50 and w_1 and w_3 are set to 0.00) then the decision support system will output 0.00 % total improvement since the ASN and SIZ are all 0.00 implying that the RBAC decompositions have more roles than permissions and more assignments. On the other hand, if the emphasis is given on the ease in administrative time (ADM), therefore setting $w_3 = 1.00$, the decision support system will output 99 % improvement. So, the selection of weights has significant importance on the output.

Finally, we compare the performance of DEMiner with the other algorithms. For Emea, DEMiner performs better (6 % or more) than all other algorithms. For Firewall 2, all algorithms perform the same. DEMiner also outperforms ORCA for Domino and Americas Large datasets. Overall, the DEMiner outperforms at least one algorithm in nine datasets and despite being a simple algorithm DEMiner performs within 2 % range to the other algorithms on the average over all datasets.

6   Related Work

Role mining is the process of obtaining an RBAC decomposition from a DAC configuration. There are various different algorithms proposed in the literature. CompleteMiner and FastMiner are proposed by Vaidya et al. [21,22] for generating a set of candidate roles from an input UPA using subset enumeration. Clustering based algorithm, ORCA, is proposed by [16]. There are also approaches focused on role mining complexity [1,25], on role hierarchies [12,13], mining semantically meaningful roles based either on optimization of policy quality metrics [24], consideration of user attributes and use of entitlements [13] or consideration of business information [2]. Reference [23] proposes an approach that deals with scalability issues.

Vaidya et al. propose the problem of deriving an optimal RBAC configuration from a UPA as the role mining problem. Such an optimal configuration consists of a set of roles, a user assignment relation UA, a permission assignment relation PA and optionally a role hierarchy RH. Optimality can be achieved by minimizing one or more metrics. Basic-RMP [19,20] is the problem of minimizing the number of roles from a given UPA and it has been shown to be NP-complete. Vaidya et al. [19] have mapped it to the Minimum Tiling Problem of databases. Ene et al. [3] show the equivalence between Basic-RMP and the Minimum Biclique Cover (MBC) problem and propose a greedy algorithm to solve Basic-RMP. Huang et al. [6,7] propose an alternative approach to Basic-RMP using Set Cover Problem. Several variants of Basic-RMP have also been proposed. δ-approx RMP [19,20], MinNoise RMP [19], Edge-RMP [10] and Extended Role Mining [18] and User-Oriented Exact RMP [9]. Zhang et al. [26] propose a variant of Edge-RMP where the sum of the sizes of the derived role set, UA and PA is minimized. There are also some extensions that focus on the role hierarchy [4,5,13], and mining roles on Temporal RBAC [11].

7 Conclusions

Although the RBAC model is perceived to incur lower security administration cost, in certain security policy configurations, DAC may indeed have lower administration cost than that of RBAC. Moreover, the different role mining algorithms that facilitate migration from DAC to RBAC should be carefully examined to determine if the resulting RBAC decomposition provides sufficient improvement with respect to the DAC so that it makes administrative sense to migrate to that particular decomposition. The decision support framework proposed in this paper is a tool that could be utilized by organizations to perform the comparison between different RBAC decompositions to figure out the one that would provide them with the greatest benefit.

Acknowledgments. This work is supported in part by NSF under grant number 1018414.

References

1. Colantonio, A., Di Pietro, R., Ocello, A., Verde, N.V.: Taming role mining complexity in RBAC. Comput. Secur. 29(5), 548–564 (2010)
2. Colantonio, A., Di Pietro, R., Verde, N.V.: A business-driven decomposition methodology for role mining. Comput. Secur. 31(7), 844–855 (2012)
3. Ene, A., Horne, W., Milosavljevic, N., Rao, P., Schreiber, R., Tarjan, R.E.: Fast exact and heuristic methods for role minimization problems. In: SACMAT, pp. 1–10 (2008)

4. Frank, M., Buhman, J.M., Basin, D.: Role mining with probabilistic models. ACM Trans. Inf. Syst. Secur. (TISSEC) 15(4), 15 (2013)
5. Guo, Q., Vaidya, J., Atluri, V.: The role hierarchy mining problem: Discovery of optimal role hierarchies. In: ACSAC, pp. 237–246. IEEE (2008)
6. Huang, H., Shang, F., Liu, J., Du, H.: Handling least privilege problem and role mining in RBAC. J. Comb. Optim. 1–24 (2013). doi:10.1007/s10878-013-9633-9
7. Huang, H., Shang, F., Zhang, J.: Approximation algorithms for minimizing the number of roles and administrative assignments in RBAC. In: COMPSACW, pp. 427–432. IEEE (2012)
8. Kuhlmann, M., Shohat, D., Schimpf, G.: Role mining - revealing business roles for security administration using data mining technology. In: SACMAT (2003)
9. Lu, H., Hong, Y., Yang, Y., Duan, L., Badar, N.: Towards user-oriented RBAC model. In: Wang, L., Shafiq, B. (eds.) DBSec 2013. LNCS, vol. 7964, pp. 81–96. Springer, Heidelberg (2013)
10. Lu, H., Vaidya, J., Atluri, V.: Optimal boolean matrix decomposition: application to role engineering. In: ICDE, pp. 297–306 (2008)
11. Mitra, B., Sural, S., Atluri, V., Vaidya, J.: Toward mining of temporal roles. In: Wang, L., Shafiq, B. (eds.) DBSec 2013. LNCS, vol. 7964, pp. 65–80. Springer, Heidelberg (2013)
12. Molloy, I., Chen, H., Li, T., Wang, Q., Li, N., Bertino, E., Calo, S., Lobo, J.: Mining roles with semantic meanings. In: SACMAT, pp. 21–30. ACM (2008)
13. Molloy, I., Chen, H., Li, T., Wang, Q., Li, N., Bertino, E., Calo, S., Lobo, J.: Mining roles with multiple objectives. TISSEC 13(4), 36 (2010)
14. Molloy, I., Li, N., Li, T., Mao, Z., Wang, Q., Lobo, J.: Evaluating role mining algorithms. In: SACMAT (2009)
15. Schaad, A., Moffett, J., Jacob, J.: The role-based access control system of a european bank: a case study and discussion. In: SACMAT, pp. 3–9 (2001)
16. Schlegelmilch, J., Steffens, U.: Role mining with orca. In: SACMAT (2005)
17. Tassey, G., Gallaher, M.P., OConnor, A.C., Kropp, B.: The economic impact of role-based access control. Econ. Anal. (2002)
18. Uzun, E., Atluri, V., Lu, H., Vaidya, J.: An optimization model for the extended role mining problem. In: Li, Y. (ed.) DBSec. LNCS, vol. 6818, pp. 76–89. Springer, Heidelberg (2011)
19. Vaidya, J., Atluri, V., Guo, Q.: The role mining problem: Finding a minimal descriptive set of roles. In: SACMAT, pp. 175–184 (2007)
20. Vaidya, J., Atluri, V., Guo, Q.: The role mining problem: a formal perspective. ACM Trans. Inf. Syst. Secur. (TISSEC) 13(3), 27 (2010)
21. Vaidya, J., Atluri, V., Warner, J.: Roleminer: mining roles using subset enumeration. In: CCS, pp. 144–153 (2006)
22. Vaidya, J., Atluri, V., Warner, J., Guo, Q.: Role engineering via prioritized subset enumeration. TDSC 7(3), 300–314 (2010)
23. Verde, N.V., Vaidya, J., Atluri, V., Colantonio, A.: Role engineering: from theory to practice. In: DBSec, pp. 181–192. ACM (2012)
24. Xu, Z., Stoller, S.D.: Algorithms for mining meaningful roles. In: SACMAT, pp. 57–66. ACM (2012)
25. Zhang, D., Ramamohanarao, K., Versteeg, S., Zhang, R.: Graph based strategies to role engineering. In: CSIIRW, p. 25. ACM (2010)
26. Zhang, D., Ramamohanrao, K., Ebringer, T.: Role engineering using graph optimisation. In: SACMAT, pp. 139–144 (2007)

Assisting the Deployment of Security-Sensitive Workflows by Finding Execution Scenarios

Daniel R. dos Santos[1,2,3]([✉]), Silvio Ranise[1], Luca Compagna[2], and Serena E. Ponta[2]

[1] Fondazione Bruno Kessler (FBK), Trento, Italy
dossantos@fbk.eu
[2] SAP Labs France, Mougins, France
[3] University of Trento, Trento, Italy

Abstract. To support the re-use of business process models, an emerging trend in Business Process Management, it is crucial to assist customers during deployment. We study how to do this for an important class of business processes, called security-sensitive workflows, in which execution constraints on the tasks are complemented with authorization constraints (e.g., Separation of Duty) and authorization policies (constraining which users can execute which tasks). We identify the capability of solving Scenario Finding Problems (SFPs), i.e. finding concrete execution scenarios, as crucial in supporting the re-use of security-sensitive workflows. Solutions of SFPs provide evidence that the business process model can be successfully executed under the policy adopted by the customer. We present a technique for solving two SFPs and validate it on real-world business process models taken from an on-line library.

1 Introduction

Organizations rely on Business Process Management (BPM) [22] to achieve certain business objectives by orchestrating workflows, which are collections of sequences of tasks executed by human or software agents. An increasingly important class of workflows is that of *security-sensitive workflows* [1], in which task execution constraints are complemented with an authorization policy (defining which users can execute which tasks) and a set of authorization constraints (further restricting which users can execute some sub-sets of the tasks).

Example 1 (Trip Request Workflow (TRW)). A typical example of a security-sensitive workflow has the goal of requesting trips for employees in an organization. It is composed of five tasks: Trip request ($t1$), Car rental ($t2$), Hotel booking ($t3$), Flight reservation ($t4$), and Trip validation ($t5$). The execution of the tasks is constrained as follows: $t1$ must be executed first, then $t2$, $t3$ and $t4$ can be executed in any order, and when all have been performed, $t5$ can be executed. Overall, there are six possible task execution sequences in which the

---

This work has been partly supported by the EU under grant 317387 SECENTIS (FP7-PEOPLE-2012-ITN).

P. Samarati (Ed.): DBSec 2015, LNCS 9149, pp. 85–100, 2015.
DOI: 10.1007/978-3-319-20810-7_6

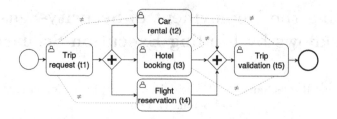

Fig. 1. TRW in (extended) BPM notation

first is always task $t1$, the last is always task $t5$, and—in between—there is any one of the six permutations of $t2$, $t3$ and $t4$.

It is also required that each task is executed under the responsibility of a user who has the right to execute it according to some authorization policy. To prevent frauds, five authorization constraints—called Separation of Duty (SoD) in the literature; see, e.g., [8]—must also be enforced: each one of the following pairs of tasks must be executed by distinct users in any sequence of task executions of the workflow: $(t1, t2)$, $(t1, t4)$, $(t2, t3)$, $(t2, t5)$, and $(t3, t5)$.

This workflow can be modeled in a graphical notation such as BPMN [15] as shown in Fig. 1: the circle on the left represents the start event (triggering the execution of the workflow), whereas that on the right the end event (terminating the execution of the workflow), tasks are depicted by labeled boxes, the constraints on the execution of tasks are shown as solid arrows (for sequence flows) and diamonds labeled by + (for parallel flows), the fact that a task must be executed under the responsibility of a user is indicated by the man icon inside a box, and the SoD constraints as dashed lines labeled by $\neq$.   □

One of the most important problems for security-sensitive workflows is the Workflow Satisfiability Problem (WSP) [8], which consists of checking if there exists an assignment of users to tasks such that at least one task execution sequence in a workflow successfully terminates while satisfying all authorization constraints and the authorization policy. Several papers (see, e.g., [8–10,21]) have provided solutions to the WSP, which are becoming less and less satisfactory because of the recent trend in BPM of collecting and re-using large numbers of business process models [11,19,23]. For instance, the SAP HANA Workflow[1] is a BPMN-based solution that allows for the creation of business process models (templates) that can be deployed and operated in different contexts. At deployment time, what is crucial for customers re-using a template from the library is to understand whether it can be successfully instantiated with the authorization policy adopted by their organization. This means that customers want to scrutinize concrete *execution scenarios* showing the termination of the instantiated business process model by giving evidence that some of the employees can successfully execute the various tasks in the workflow.

Example 2. A simple situation in which the TRW in Example 1 can be deployed is a tiny organization with a set $U = \{a, b, c\}$ of three users and the following

---

[1] http://help.sap.com/saphelp_hana_opint/SAP_OPInt_Developers_Guide.pdf.

authorization policy $TA = \{(a, t1), (b, t1), (a, t2), (b, t2), (c, t2), (a, t3), (b, t3),$ $(c, t3), (a, t4), (a, t5), (b, t5), (c, t5)\}$, where $(u, t) \in TA$ means that user u is entitled to execute task t. The organization would then like to know if there is an execution scenario that allows the process to terminate according to TA. Indeed, this is the case as shown by the following sequence of task-user pairs: $\eta = t1(b), t3(c), t4(a), t2(a), t5(b)$ where $t(u)$ means that user u has executed task t and the position in the sequence corresponds to the order in which the tasks have been executed (i.e. $t1$ has been executed first, $t5$ last, $t3$ after $t1$ but before $t4$, $t2$, and $t5$, etc.). It is easy to check that the tasks in η are executed so that the ordering constraints on task execution are satisfied, each user u in each pair $t(u)$ of η is authorized to execute t since $(u, t) \in TA$, and each SoD constraint is satisfied (e.g., tasks $t1$ and $t2$ are executed by the distinct users b and a, respectively).□

Among all possible scenarios permitting a workflow to terminate, customers may be particularly interested in those that can be executed by a smallest possible set of users, called minimal user base in the literature [10]. This knowledge would enable organizations to assess the likelihood of emergencies or extraordinary situations due to, e.g., employee absences.

We call *Scenario Finding Problems (SFPs)* this kind of problems. Techniques for solving the WSP can also be used to solve SFPs; unfortunately, this has a very high computational cost because they are not able to exploit the fact that execution and authorization constraints are fixed and only the authorization policy changes at deployment time. (WSP is NP-hard already in the presence of one SoD constraint [21].)

The **main contributions** of this paper are three. First, we give precise statements of two SFPs together with a discussion of their relationships with the WSP (Sect. 2). Second, we describe techniques to solve them by adapting the technique for the synthesis of run-time monitors for the WSP developed in [5] (Sect. 3). Third, we validate our solutions on real-world examples from a library of re-usable business process models (Sect. 4). We use the TRW in Example 1 as a running example to illustrate the main notions in the paper.

2 From the WSP to SFPs

Let T be a finite set of tasks and U a finite set of users. An *execution scenario* (or, simply, a *scenario*) is a finite sequence of pairs of the form (t, u), written as $t(u)$, where $t \in T$ and $u \in U$. The intuitive meaning of a scenario $\eta = t_1(u_1), ..., t_n(u_n)$ is that task t_i is executed before task t_j for $1 \leq i < j \leq n$ and that task t_k is executed by user u_k for $k = 1, ..., n$. A *workflow* $W(T, U)$ is a set of scenarios. Among the scenarios in a workflow, we are interested in those that describe successfully terminating executions in which users execute tasks satisfying the authorization constraints and the authorization policy. Since the notion of successful termination depends on the definition of the workflow (e.g., in case of a conditional choice, we will have two acceptable execution sequences according to the Boolean value of the condition), in the following we focus only on the authorization policy and the authorization constraints while assuming that all the scenarios in the workflow characterize successfully terminating behaviors.

Given a workflow $W(T, U)$, an *authorization relation* TA is a sub-set of $U \times T$. Intuitively, $(u, t) \in TA$ means that u is authorized to execute task t. We say that a scenario η of a workflow $W(T, U)$ is *authorized* according to TA iff (u, t) is in TA for each $t(u)$ in η. An *authorization constraint* over a workflow $W(T, U)$ is a tuple (t_1, t_2, ρ) where $t_1, t_2 \in T$ and ρ is a sub-set of $U \times U$. (It is possible to generalize authorization constraints to the form (T_1, T_2, ρ) where T_1, T_2 are sets of tasks as done in, e.g., [9]. We do not do this here for the sake of simplicity.) For instance, a SoD constraint between tasks t and t' can be formalized as $(t, t', \neq)$ with $\neq$ being the relation $\{(u, u') | u, u' \in U$ and $u \neq u'\}$. A scenario η of $W(T, U)$ *satisfies* the authorization constraint (t_1, t_2, ρ) over $W(T, U)$ iff there exist $t_1(u_1)$ and $t_2(u_2)$ in η such that $(u_1, u_2) \in \rho$. Let C be a (finite) set of authorization constraints, a scenario η satisfies C iff η satisfies c, for each c in C. A scenario η of a workflow $W(T, U)$ is *eligible according to a set C of authorization constraints* iff η satisfies C.

A workflow $W(T, U)$ is *security-sensitive* according to an authorization relation TA and a (finite) set C of authorization constraints iff every scenario η in $W(T, U)$ is both authorized and eligible. There are various ways to specify security-sensitive workflows. For instance, [9] introduces the notion of "constrained workflow authorization schema" as a tuple $(T, U, \leq, TA, C)$, where $\leq$ is a partial order over T and the other components are as above. Then, it defines an "execution schedule" as a tuple $(t_1, ..., t_k)$ of tasks such that $\{t_1, ..., t_k\} = T$ and $t_j \not\leq t_i$ for each $1 \leq i < j \leq k$ and a "valid plan" π as a mapping from T to U such that $(t, \pi(t)) \in TA$ and $(\pi(t_1), \pi(t_2)) \in \rho$ for each constraint (t_1, t_2, ρ) in C. Given an execution schedule and $(t_1, ..., t_k)$ and a valid plan π of a constrained workflow authorization schema $(T, U, \leq, TA, C)$, it is easy to derive an authorized and eligible scenario $t_1(\pi(t_1)), ..., t_k(\pi(t_k))$ of the security-sensitive workflow $W(T, U)$ according to TA and C.

Definition 1 (Workflow Satisfiability Problem (WSP)). Given a workflow $W(T, U)$, an authorization relation TA, and a set C of authorization constraints, return (if possible) a scenario η which is authorized according to TA and eligible according to C.

Recall Example 2 in Sect. 1 for an instance of this problem and a solution.

2.1 Scenario Finding Problems

In the context of business process reuse, it is possible to compute—once and for all—the set E of eligible scenarios associated to a security-sensitive workflow in a library (we will describe how to compute and compactly represent this set in Sect. 3 below). The problem is then to look for those scenarios in E with some properties when an authorization policy becomes available.

Definition 2 (Basic Scenario Finding Problem (B-SFP)). Given the finite set E of eligible scenarios according to a set C of authorization constraints in a workflow $W(T, U)$, return (if possible) a scenario $\eta \in E$ which is authorized according to a given authorization relation TA.

Example 3. Let us consider the TRW. If $U = \{$ *Alice, Bob, Charlie, Dave, Erin, Frank* $\}$ is the set of users, then the set E of eligible scenarios contains, among many others, the following elements:

$$\eta_1 = t_1(\textit{Alice}), t_2(\textit{Bob}), t_3(\textit{Charlie}), t_4(\textit{Dave}), t_5(\textit{Erin})$$
$$\eta_2 = t_1(\textit{Bob}), t_2(\textit{Alice}), t_3(\textit{Charlie}), t_4(\textit{Alice}), t_5(\textit{Bob})$$
$$\eta_3 = t_1(\textit{Bob}), t_4(\textit{Charlie}), t_2(\textit{Alice}), t_3(\textit{Dave}), t_5(\textit{Bob})$$

Now, let $TA = \{(\textit{Alice}, t_1), (\textit{Bob}, t_1), (\textit{Alice}, t_2), (\textit{Bob}, t_2), (\textit{Charlie}, t_3), (\textit{Alice}, t_4),$ $(\textit{Dave}, t_4), (\textit{Bob}, t_5), (\textit{Erin}, t_5)\}$ be the authorization relation, then η_1 and η_2 are solutions to the B-SFP, while η_3 is not because $(\textit{Dave}, t_3) \notin TA$. □

A scenario η solving the B-SFP is also a solution of the WSP and vice versa. So, in principle, to solve the B-SFP for a workflow $W(U, T)$, a set C of authorization constraints, an authorization policy TA, and $\eta_e = t(u), t'(u'), \dots$ an eligible scenario in E, we can re-use an algorithm $\mathcal{A}$ returning answers to the WSP as follows. Initially, we consider the task-user pair $t(u)$ in η_e and create a new authorization relation $TA_1 = TA|_{(u,t)}$ derived from TA by deleting all pairs $(x, t) \in TA$ with $x \neq u$. We invoke $\mathcal{A}$ on the WSP for $W(U, T)$, C, and TA_1: if $\mathcal{A}$ returns a scenario, this must have the form $t(u), \eta$ where η is some sequence of task-user pairs (notice that $t(u), \eta$ and η_e are guaranteed to have only $t(u)$ as a common prefix). Afterwards, we move to the task-user pair $t'(u')$ in η_e and run $\mathcal{A}$ on the WSP for $W(U, T)$, C, and $TA_2 = TA_1|_{(u',t')}$. If $\mathcal{A}$ returns a scenario, this must have the form $t(u), t'(u'), \eta'$ where η' is some sequence of task-user pairs (notice that $t(u), t'(u'), \eta'$ and η_e are guaranteed to have only $t(u), t'(u')$ as a common prefix). By repeating this process for each η_e in E, until all tasks in η_e are executed, we can check if it is also authorized according to TA (besides being eligible as η_e is in E). Overall, there are at most $O(\ell_{max} \cdot |E|)$ invocations to $\mathcal{A}$, where ℓ_{max} is the longest (in terms of number of task-user pairs occurring in it) scenario of E. Indeed, this is very expensive from a computational point of view since the WSP is NP-hard already in presence of one SoD constraint [21] and, most importantly, we do not exploit the fact that the scenarios in E are eligible.

A better approach to solve the B-SFP is to consider each eligible scenario η_e in E and check if all task-user pairs in η_e are authorized according to TA. This means that there are at most $O(\ell_{max} \cdot |E|)$ invocations to the algorithm for checking membership of a user-task pair to TA. The complexity of such an algorithm depends on how TA has been specified. Policy languages are designed to make such a check very efficient (e.g., linear or polynomial); this is in sharp contrast to the heavy computational cost of running $\mathcal{A}$. Below, we assume authorization policies to be specified in Datalog so that checking membership to TA is equivalent to answering a Datalog query, which is well-known to have polynomial-time (data) complexity [6]. Even though checking for membership to TA is efficiently performed, the overall computational complexity may be problematic since such a check must be repeated $O(\ell_{max} \cdot |E|)$ and $|E|$ may be very large. For instance, as we will show below, already for the simple TRW with $|U| = 6$ (as in Example 3), the cardinality of E is 19,080. Intuitively, the larger the set U of users, the higher the cardinality of E. It is thus important to design a suitable data structure to represent the available set E of eligible scenarios which permits to design an efficient strategy to search through all scenarios and identify one that is authorized. We will see this in Sect. 3.1.

A refinement of B-SFP is to search for (eligible and) authorized scenarios in which a "minimal" set of users occurs. Formally, let η be a scenario in a workflow $W(T, U)$, the set of users occurring in η is $usr(\eta) = \{u|t(u) \in \eta\}$. Following [10], we define a *minimal user base* of a workflow $W(T, U)$ to be a sub-set U' of the set U of users such that there exists a scenario η in $W(T, U)$ in which $usr(\eta) = U'$ and there is no scenario η' in $W(T, U)$ in which $usr(\eta')$ is a strict sub-set of U'.

Definition 3 (Minimal User-Base Scenario Finding Problem (MUB-SFP)). Given the set E of eligible scenarios according to a set C of authorization constraints in a workflow $W(T, U)$, return (if possible) a scenario $\eta \in E$ which is authorized according to a given relation TA and such that the set $usr(\eta)$ of users occurring in η is a minimal user base.

Example 4. Let us consider again the TRW together with the set U of users, the set E of eligible scenarios, and the authorization relation TA of Example 3. A solution to the MUB-SFP is $\eta_M = t_1(Bob), t_2(Alice), t_3(Charlie), t_4(Alice), t_5(Bob)$ and a minimal user base is $usr(\eta_M) = \{Alice, Bob, Charlie\}$.   □

An approach derived from that solving the B-SFP can also solve the MUB-SFP. We consider each eligible scenario η_e in E and check if all task-user pairs in η_e are authorized according to TA. We also maintain a variable η_M storing an eligible scenario in E such that η_M is authorized (according to TA) and $usr(\eta_M)$ is a candidate minimal user base. Initially, η_M is set to the empty sequence ϵ. If the eligible scenario η_e under consideration is authorized and $\eta_M \neq \epsilon$, then we compare the cardinalities of $usr(\eta_e)$ and $usr(\eta_M)$: if $|usr(\eta_e)| < |usr(\eta_M)|$, then $\eta_M \leftarrow \eta_e$; otherwise η_M is left unchanged. When $\eta_M = \epsilon$, we do not perform the comparison between the cardinalities of $usr(\eta_e)$ and $usr(\eta_M)$ and simply set η_M to η_e. Indeed, when all eligible scenarios in E have been considered, $usr(\eta_M)$ stores a minimal user base. This process requires that there are $O(\ell_{max} \cdot |E|)$ invocations to the algorithm for checking membership of a user-task pair to TA. Although the complexity bounds of solving the B-SFP and the MUB-SFP are identical, the bound for the latter is tighter than the former. This is so because we always need to consider all eligible scenarios in E for the MUB-SFP whereas we can stop as soon as we find an authorized scenario for the B-SFP. This is confirmed by our experimental evaluation in Sect. 4 (compare the timings for solving SFPs with those for MUB-SFPs in Table 2).

3   From Solving the WSP to Solving SFPs

We now briefly recall the technique in [5] to synthesize run-time monitors solving the WSP. This is important as it provides us with a compact data structure to represent the set of all eligible scenarios in a workflow, which is crucial for the design of an efficient solution to SFPs. It takes as input the specification of a security-sensitive workflow (e.g., the BPMN in Fig. 1 for the TRW with the specification of an authorization policy, such as the relation TA of Example 2) and consists of two steps.

Off-line step. A symbolic transition system S is automatically derived (in a way similar to that described in [20]) from the task execution constraints of a workflow $W(T, U)$ and the set C of authorization constraints (notice that TA is not yet taken into consideration). S is used to compute a *symbolic reachability graph RG*, i.e. a directed graph whose edges are labeled by task-user pairs in which users are symbolically represented by variables (called *user variables*) and whose nodes are labeled by a symbolic representation (namely, a formula of first-order logic) of the set of states from which it is possible to reach a state in which the workflow successfully terminates (for the TRW, this is the set of states in which all five tasks have been executed). A sequence $\eta_s = t_1(v_{j_1}), ..., t_n(v_{j_n})$ of task-user pairs is a *symbolic execution scenario* where v_{j_i} is a user variable with $1 \leq j_i \leq n$ and $i = 1, ..., n$. A *well-formed* path in RG is a path starting with a node without an incoming edge and ending with a node without an outgoing edge. The crucial property of RG is that the symbolic execution scenario $\eta_s = t_1(v_{j_1}), ..., t_n(v_{j_n})$ collected while traversing one of its well-formed paths corresponds to an eligible (according to C) execution scenario $\eta_c = \mu(\eta_s) = t_1(\mu(v_{j_1})), ..., t_n(\mu(v_{j_n}))$ for μ an injective function from the set $\Upsilon = \{v_{j_1}, ..., v_{j_n}\}$ of user variables (also called *symbolic users*) to the given set U of users of $W(T, U)$. Three observations are in order. First, μ is extended to symbolic execution scenarios in the obvious way, i.e. by applying it to each user variable occurring in them. Second, since j_i can be equal to $j_{i'}$ for $1 \leq i \neq i' \leq n$, the cardinality of Υ is at most equal to the number n of tasks in the symbolic execution scenario. Third, since μ is injective, distinct user variables are never mapped to the same user.

Example 5. An excerpt of the symbolic reachability graph for the TRW is depicted in Fig. 2 where a task-user pair $t(v_k)$ labeling an edge is abbreviated by $t(k)$ for the sake of compactness.

For instance, the symbolic execution scenario $\eta_s = t1(v_3), t3(v_3), t4(v_2),$ $t2(v_2), t5(v_1)$ (cf. the well-formed path identified by the blue nodes in Fig. 2) represents all those execution scenarios in which a symbolic user identified by v_3 first performs task $t1$ followed by t_3, then a symbolic user identified by v_2 performs $t4$ and $t2$ in this order, and finally a symbolic user identified by v_1 executes $t5$. If we apply an injective function μ from the set $\Upsilon = \{v_1, v_2, v_3\}$ of user variables to any finite set U of users (of cardinality at least three), the corresponding execution scenario $\eta_c = \mu(\eta_s)$ is eligible according to the set C of SoD constraints shown in Fig. 1.   □

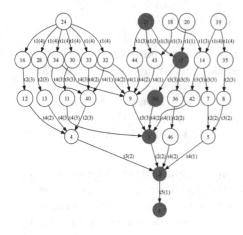

Fig. 2. An excerpt of the symbolic reachability graph for the TRW

Table 1. A run of the monitor program for the TRW

#	History	Query	Answer
0	∅	$can\_do(a,t1)$	deny
1	-	$can\_do(b,t1)$	grant
2	$h(t1,b)$	$can\_do(c,t3)$	grant
3	$h(t3,c)$	$can\_do(a,t4)$	grant
4	$h(t4,a)$	$can\_do(b,t2)$	deny
5	-	$can\_do(a,t2)$	grant
6	$h(t2,a)$	$can\_do(b,t5)$	grant
7	$h(t5,b)$	-	-

On-line Step. A non-recursive Datalog program M with negation is derived from the symbolic reachability graph RG by building a clause of the form $can\_do(v,t) \leftarrow \beta_v$ where β_v is the formula labeling node v in RG. (For more details on how M is built, the interested reader is pointed to [5]). The formula β_v contains invocations to the binary predicates $auth$ and h. The former is the interface to the authorization policy and such that $auth(u,t)$ holds iff $(u,t) \in TA$ while the latter keeps track of which user has executed which task, i.e. $h(t,u)$ means that t has been executed by u. Following an established tradition (see, e.g., [13]) claiming that (variants of) Datalog are adequate to express a wide range of access control policy idioms, we assume $auth$ to be defined by a Datalog program P. Instead, the predicate h is dynamic and defined by a set H of (ground) facts which is updated after each task execution. Thus, if the query $can\_do(u,t)$ can be derived from M, P, H (in symbols, $M, P, H \vdash can\_do(u,t)$), then user u can execute task t and the workflow can terminate while satisfying the authorization policy and the authorization constraints.

Example 6. For the TRW, let us consider again the set of users and the authorization policy discussed in Example 2. The relation TA can be specified after the Role Base Access Control (RBAC) model [17] by the Datalog program P:

$$ua(a,r1).\ ua(a,r2).\ ua(a,r3).\ ua(b,r2).\ ua(b,r3).\ ua(c,r2).$$
$$pa(r3,t1).\ pa(r2,t2).\ pa(r2,t3).\ pa(r1,t4).\ pa(r2,t5).$$
$$auth(v,\tau) \leftarrow ua(v,\rho) \wedge pa(\rho,\tau).$$

where $r1$, $r2$, and $r3$ are roles, ua is the user-role assignment (cf. first line of facts), pa is the role-task assignment (cf. second line of facts), v is a user variable, τ is a variable ranging over tasks, and $auth$ is defined as the join of the relations ua and pa (cf. Datalog clause in the last line). Recall the definition of TA in Example 2 and notice that $P \vdash auth(u,t)$ iff $(u,t) \in TA$ for user u and task t.

An example run of the monitor derived from the symbolic reachability graph in Fig. 2 combined with the RBAC policy above is shown in Table 1: column 'History' shows which facts are added to the set H and column 'Answer' reports grant (deny, respectively) when the query in column 'Query' can (cannot, respectively) be derived from M, P, H. For instance, there are two denied requests: in line 0, user a requests to execute task $t1$ but this is not possible since a is the only user authorized to execute $t4$, and if a executes $t1$, he/she will no more be allowed to execute $t4$ because of the SoD constraint between $t1$ and $t4$ (see Fig. 1); in line 4, user b requests to execute task $t2$ but again this is not possible since b has already executed task $t1$ and this would violate the SoD constraint between $t1$ and $t2$. All other requests are granted, as they violate neither task execution nor authorization constraints. The scenario resulting from this run of the monitor is $t1(b), t3(c), t4(a), t2(a), t5(b)$, which is derived from the symbolic execution scenario $t1(v_1), t3(v_3), t4(v_2), t2(v_2), t5(v_1)$ in the graph of Fig. 2 (cf. the path with the blue nodes; see also Example 5) by applying the injective function μ mapping v_1 to b, v_2 to a, and v_3 to c.   □

3.1 Solving the SFPs

In order to solve B-SFPs and MUB-SFPs (recall Definitions 2 and 3), we need to decide how the set E of eligible scenarios and the authorization policy TA are specified as input to the algorithm solving the problems. For TA, we have already assumed (see paragraph **On-line step** in previous section) the availability of a Datalog program P defining the binary predicate $auth$. For E, we define the *set $E(RG, U)$ of eligible scenarios induced by a symbolic reachability graph RG and a set U of users* as the collection of all the scenarios of the form $\mu(t_1(v_{j_1}), ..., t_n(v_{j_n}))$ where $v_0 \xrightarrow{t_1(v_{j_1})} \cdots \xrightarrow{t_n(v_{j_n})} v_{n+1}$ is a well-formed path in RG and μ is an injective function from $\Upsilon = \{v_{j_1}, ..., v_{j_n}\}$ to U. Two observations are important. First, there are several different sets $E(RG^*, U)$ induced by a fixed symbolic reachability graph RG^* and a varying set U of users. Second, a symbolic reachability graph—once a set of users is fixed—provides an implicit and compact representation of the set of eligible scenarios. This is due to two reasons: one is the sharing of common sub-sequences of task-user pairs in execution scenarios and the other is the symbolic representation of several execution scenarios by means of a single symbolic execution scenario. This is best illustrated through an example.

Example 7. Let us consider the TRW with a set U of 6 users. The graph in Fig. 2 is, for the sake of readability, an excerpt of the full symbolic reachability graph showing only a small sub-set of all well-formed paths. The full graph has 46 nodes, 81 edges, and 61 well-formed paths of which 21, 34, and 6 contain 3, 4, and 5, respectively, symbolic users. For instance, notice how the sub-sequence $t3(v_2), t5(v_1)$ is shared by 6 distinct (symbolic) execution scenarios induced by the well-formed paths whose initial node is 24 (left of figure). Additionally, observe that, from the definition of $E(RG, U)$ above, in order to establish the number of all eligible paths when $|U| = n$, we just need to calculate how many injective functions there are from a set of cardinality k to a set of cardinality n—which is known to be $J(n, k) = n(n - 1)(n - 2) \cdots (n - k + 1)$—for $n = 6$, $k = 3, 4, 5$, and take their sum. Thus, the set of all eligible paths in our case is $21 \cdot J(6, 3) + 34 \cdot J(6, 4) + 6 \cdot J(6, 5) = 19,080$. Compare this, with the number of well-formed paths in the symbolic reachability graph which is only 61: the blow-up factor is more than 300. Indeed, the increase is even more dramatic for larger sets of users.   □

We are now ready to describe our technique, depicted in Algorithm 1, to solve the B-SFP. For the time being, let us ignore the additional input set Γ (by setting it to $\emptyset$); it will be explained later. The main idea underlying the algorithm is to adapt a standard Depth-First Search (DFS) algorithm to explore all well-formed paths in the reachability graph RG while checking that the scenario associated to the path is indeed authorized by using the run-time monitor, synthesized in the on-line phase of the technique in [5]. Lines 1–2 are the standard initialization phase of a DFS algorithm in which all nodes in RG (returned by the function Nodes) are marked as not yet visited. Lines 3–6 invoke the (modified) DFS algorithm on each node without an incoming edge in RG (returned by the function NoIncoming) until either all such nodes have been considered (this allows us to consider all well-formed paths) or an authorized scenario (if any) has been found (line 7). Lines 8–19 show the (modified) DFS recursive function which takes as input a node v and extends a sequence η of task-user pairs to an authorized execution scenario (if possible). Line 9 marks as visited the node v under consideration and computes its set OE of outgoing edges (returned by the function OutGoing). Line 10 checks whether the set of outgoing edges of v is empty: if this is the case, then we have considered all task-user pairs in a well-formed path and the sequence η containing them is an authorized execution scenario. If this is not the case, we have not yet considered all task-user pairs in a well-formed path of RG and thus we need to consider the possible continuations in OE. This is done in the loop at lines 12-16: an edge $v \xrightarrow{t(v)} w$ in OE is selected (line 12), it is checked if the node w is not yet visited and if the run-time monitor combined with the authorization policy P can find a user u capable of executing the task t in label of the edge in OE under consideration (line 13). The second check (namely, $M, P, H \vdash^{v \mapsto u} can\_do(t, v)$) is done by asking a Datalog engine to find a user u in U to which the user variable v can be mapped (cf. superscript of $\vdash$) without violating the execution and the authorization constraints together with the authorization policy specified by P. If the test at line 13 is successful, line 14 is executed whereby a recursive call to the DFS function is performed in which the new node to consider is w, the sequence η of task-user pairs is extended with $t(u)$ (by invoking the function append), and the set H of facts keeping track of the tasks executed so far is also extended by $h(t, u)$. In case all edges in OE have been considered but none of them makes the check at line 13 successful, the empty sequence is returned (line 18). Notice that at line 13, instead of enumerating all suitable users in U to which v can be mapped, we exploit the capability of the Datalog engine to find the right user. This permits us to exploit well-engineered implementations of Datalog engines instead of designing

---

Algorithm 1. Solving the B-SFP

Input: RG symbolic reachability graph, U set of users,
$\qquad$ P Datalog program defining $auth$, Γ set of facts
Output: η authorized execution scenario
 1: **for all** $v \in \mathsf{Nodes}(RG)$ **do** $visited[v] \leftarrow \mathtt{false}$;
 2: **end for**
 3: $\eta \leftarrow \epsilon$; $NI \leftarrow \mathsf{NoIncoming}(RG)$;
 4: **while** $(v \in NI$ **and** $\eta = \epsilon)$ **do**
 5: $\qquad \eta \leftarrow \mathrm{DFS}v, \epsilon, \Gamma$; $NI \leftarrow NI \setminus \{v\}$;
 6: **end while**
 7: **return** η
 8: **function** $\mathrm{DFS}(v, \eta, H)$
 9: $\qquad visited[v] \leftarrow \mathtt{true}$; $OE \leftarrow \mathsf{OutGoing}(v)$;
10: $\qquad$ **if** $OE = \emptyset$ **then return** η
11: $\qquad$ **else**
12: $\qquad\qquad$ **for all** $v \xrightarrow{t(v)} w \in OE$ **do**
13: $\qquad\qquad\qquad$ **if** (**not** $visited[w]$ **and** $M, P, H \vdash^{v \mapsto u} can\_do(t, v)$) **then**
14: $\qquad\qquad\qquad\qquad$ **return** $\mathrm{DFS}(w, \mathsf{append}(\eta, t(u)), H \cup \{h(t, u)\}$
15: $\qquad\qquad\qquad$ **end if**
16: $\qquad\qquad$ **end for**
17: $\qquad$ **end if**
18: $\qquad$ **return** ϵ
19: **end function**

---

and implementing new heuristics to reduce the time taken to enumerate the users in U. This concludes the description of the algorithm solving the B-SFP.

An interesting extension of the algorithm is provided by considering a set Γ of facts, which can be used to drive the search for a scenario with particular characteristics. For instance, one can be interested in authorized scenarios in which a certain user only, say u^*, executes a given task, say t^*. It is possible to steer the search towards such scenarios by setting Γ to the singleton containing the fact $h(t^*, u^*)$. Another use of Γ is guiding the search towards scenarios in which the tests of certain conditionals are either true or false. Again, it is possible to add the facts encoding the truth or falsity of the condition to Γ in order to drive the algorithm and find scenarios with such conditions. The flexibility provided by Γ is illustrated in Sect. 4 below.

It is possible to modify Algorithm 1 following the idea discussed after Example 4 in order to solve the MUB-SFP. This requires to avoid returning the authorized scenario as soon as we find one (line 10) so that all well-formed paths in RG are considered. Moreover, a global variable η_M is maintained in which a candidate scenario with a minimal user base is stored and updated according to the strategy discussed above comparing the users occurring in η_M and those in the currently considered scenario. Also the search of this modified algorithm can be driven by a set Γ of facts as it was the case for the algorithm solving B-SFP.

The complexity of both algorithms can be derived from that of the standard DFS algorithm, which is $O(n+m)$ for n the number of nodes and m the number of

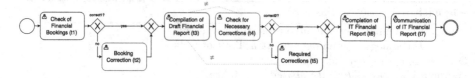

Fig. 3. ITIL 2011—IT Financial Reporting (abbreviated ITIL)

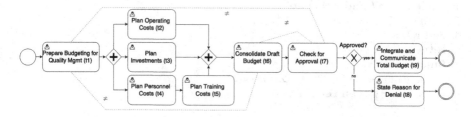

Fig. 4. ISO9000—Budgeting for Quality Management (abbreviated ISO)

edges, when using an adjacency list to represent the graph. Notice that the most computationally intensive operation is the invocation of the Datalog engine at line 13, which takes polynomial time as the only part that changes over time is the set H of facts whereas the Datalog programs M and P are fixed; cf. the results on data complexity of Datalog programs in [6]. It is easy to see that we invoke $O(n + m)$ times the Datalog engine (at most) in line 13 for both the Algorithm 1 and its modified version described above for solving the MUB-SFP. This is much better than the upper bounds discussed in Sect. 3.1. To see this, consider the situation in Example 7: $\ell_{max} = 5$ and $|E| = 19,080$ so that the check for authorization (modulo constant factors) is invoked at most $95,400$ times whereas in Algorithm 1 (or its modified version for the MUB-SFP) the same check is invoked at most $n + m = 46 + 81 = 127$ times.

4   Validation of the Technique

We consider two real-world examples, shown in Figs. 3 and 4, derived from business processes available in an on-line library provided by Signavio,[2] which contains more than 120 models inspired by the ISO9000 standard for quality management and the ITIL 2011 set of best practices for IT service management.

ITIL. The goal of this workflow is to report costs and revenues of an IT Service. It is composed of 7 tasks and 2 SoD constraints. Tasks $t1$, $t2$, $t3$, $t6$ and $t7$ are for the checking and correction of bookings, compilation of the financial report, and its communication; tasks $t4$ and $t5$ are for checking and defining corrections. The execution of tasks $t2$ and $t5$ depends on the conditions associated to two exclusive gateways: *correct1?* (abbreviated with $c1$) and *correct2?* (abbreviated

---

[2] Available at http://www.signavio.com/reference-models/.

with $c2$), respectively. The SoD constraints forbid that the same user compiles a draft report and checks for errors $(t3, t4, \neq)$ or compiles the draft and defines the corrections $(t3, t5, \neq)$.

ISO. The goal of this workflow is to plan for enough financial resources to fulfill quality requirements. It is composed of 9 tasks and 3 SoD constraints. Tasks $t1$, $t2$, ..., $t6$ involve the detailed preparation and consolidation of a draft budget, whereas tasks $t7$, $t8$ and $t9$ are for the approval of the previous activities, the integration into the total budget, and the communication of the results. The execution of tasks $t8$ or $t9$ depends on the exclusive gateway *approved?* (abbreviated with *appr*). The SoD constraints forbid that the same user prepare and consolidate a budget $(t1, t6, \neq)$, prepare and approve a budget $(t1, t7, \neq)$, or consolidate and approve a budget $(t6, t7, \neq)$.

Although none of the workflows comes with an authorization policy, swimlanes (not shown in Figs. 3 and 4) suggest that a controlling manager executes tasks $t1$, $t2$, $t3$, $t6$ and $t7$ while a financial manager executes tasks $t4$ and $t5$ for ITIL and that a quality manager executes tasks $t1$, ..., $t6$ and a controlling manager executes tasks $t7$, $t8$ and $t9$ for ISO. These indications are taken into consideration for designing the authorization policies (based on the RBAC model and encoded in Datalog) in various scenarios with a fixed set $U = \{u1, ..., u9\}$ of users. For the TRW, we consider two policies P_0 and P_1: the former is that in Example 6 and the latter is derived from the former in such a way that no user is authorized to execute $t1$ (thus no authorized scenario should be found). For ITIL, we have policies P_2 and P_3, each one with 3 users as financial managers, 3 users as controlling managers, and 3 with both roles; P_3 is derived from P_2 by preventing users to be able to execute task $t6$. For ISO, we consider policies P_4 and P_5, each one with 3 users assigned to the role of quality manager, 3 users as controlling managers, and 3 users assigned to both roles; P_5 is derived from P_4 by preventing users to be able to execute task $t3$.

Before executing our techniques for solving SFPs, we need to build the symbolic reachability graph (and the run-time monitor) for each example. We did this by running the implementation of the off-line step (described in Sect. 3) from [5]. For the TRW, the symbolic reachability graph is computed in around a second and contains 46 nodes with 81 edges. For the ITIL, the graph is computed in around 3.5 s and has 78 nodes with 72 edges. For the ISO, graph building takes around 10.5 s and has 171 nodes with 669 edges. These timings, as well as all those that follow below, have been obtained by using a MacBook Air 2014 with Mac OS X v10.10.2. The time for deriving the monitor M from the symbolic reachability graph of each example is negligible and thus omitted.

We have implemented Algorithm 1 for solving B-SFPs and its modification for solving MUB-SFPs (described towards the end of Sect. 3.1) in Python v2.7.9. The invocation to the Datalog engine at line 13 in Algorithm 1 is implemented with the Datalog engine pyDatalog v0.15.2. Table 2 shows the findings of our experiments.

Each entry in column 'Instance,' describing the input to Algorithm 1 (or its modification to solve the MUB-SFP), is of the form $W + P_i$ where W is the

Table 2. Experiments

#	Instance	Γ	Solution Scenario	Time
B-SFP				
0	TRW+P_0	∅	$t1(b), t2(a), t4(a), t3(c), t5(b)$	0.288
1	ITIL+P_2	$\{c1, c2\}$	$t1(u3), t3(u9), t4(u8), t6(u9), t7(u9)$	4.267
2	ITIL+P_2	$\{c1, \textbf{not } c2\}$	$t1(u3), t3(u3), t4(u7), t5(u8), t6(u3), t7(u7)$	4.454
3	ITIL+P_2	$\{\textbf{not } c1, c2\}$	$t1(u3), t2(u1), t3(u9), t4(u8), t6(u9), t7(u9)$	4.374
4	ITIL+P_2	$\{\textbf{not } c1, \textbf{not } c2\}$	$t1(u3), t2(u1), t3(u3), t4(u7), t5(u8), t6(u3), t7(u7)$	4.561
5	ISO+P_4	$\{appr\}$	$t1(u3), t4(u7), t5(u8), t2(u3), t3(u7), t6(u9), t7(u7), t9(u8)$	6.581
6	ISO+P_4	$\{notappr\}$	$t1(u3), t4(u7), t5(u8), t2(u3), t3(u7), t6(u7), t7(u8), t8(u6)$	6.637
7	TRW+P_1	∅	ϵ	0.407
8	TRW+P_0	$\{t2(b)\}$	ϵ	1.554
9	ITIL+P_3	∅	ϵ	9.562
10	ISO+P_5	∅	ϵ	44.076
MUB-SFP				
11	TRW+P_0	∅	$t1(b), t2(c), t3(b), t4(a), t5(a)$	2.385
12	ITIL+P_2	$\{c1, c2\}$	$t1(u1), t3(u1), t4(u7), t6(u1), t7(u1)$	108.819
13	ITIL+P_2	$\{c1, \textbf{not } c2\}$	$t1(u3), t3(u3), t4(u7), t5(u7), t6(u3), t7(u3)$	116.525
14	ITIL+P_2	$\{\textbf{not } c1, c2\}$	$t1(u1), t2(u1), t3(u1), t4(u7), t6(u1), t7(u1)$	108.827
15	ITIL+P_2	$\{\textbf{not } c1, \textbf{not } c2\}$	$t1(u3), t2(u3), t3(u3), t4(u7), t5(u7), t6(u3), t7(u3)$	116.533
16	ISO+P_4	$\{appr\}$	$t1(u5), t3(u5), t2(u5), t4(u5), t5(u5), t6(u3), t7(u7), t9(u7)$	166.632
17	ISO+P_4	$\{\textbf{not } appr\}$	$t1(u5), t3(u5), t2(u5), t4(u5), t5(u5), t6(u9), t7(u6), t8(u9)$	166.644

identifier of one of the three security-sensitive workflows and P_i is one of the authorization policies described above. Column 'Γ' shows the facts in the set Γ that can be used to drive the search of execution scenarios with particular properties. For instance, ITIL contains two exclusive gateways labeled with conditions $c1$ and $c2$: we may be interested in those scenarios in which $c1$ and $c2$ take some particular truth values (see lines 1–4 and 12–15 of the table). Another use of the set Γ is shown at line 8: we are interested in finding authorized scenarios of TRW under the authorization policy P_0 in which task $t2$ is always executed by user b. There is no such scenario (the 'Solution Scenario' column reports the empty sequence) since when b performs $t2$, a must perform $t1$—because of the SoD constraint $(t1, t2, \neq)$—but if a performs $t1$, no user can perform $t4$—because of the other SoD constraint $(t1, t4, \neq)$. Column 'Time' reports the running time (in seconds) taken to find a scenario (if any).

Discussion. Our experiments indicate that the SFPs introduced in this paper together with Algorithm 1 (and its modification for the MUB-SFP) fit well with emerging BPM practices for re-use. Whenever a customer wants to deploy a business process by re-using a workflow template, some SFP is solved (if possible) to provide him/her with an authorized scenario showing that a template business process can be successfully instantiated by his/her authorization policy. The efficiency of the proposed approach exploits the fact that the eligible scenarios (resulting from execution and authorization constraints) can be computed once and re-used with every authorization policy. In this way, multiple changes to a policy, which are well-known to be costly [14], become much less problematic to handle and customers can even explore and evaluate the suitability of variants of a policy. This is in sharp contrast to the approach discussed in Sect. 2.1 (after Example 3) that consists of re-invoking an available algorithm for solving the WSP on every task-user pair in a scenario. To illustrate, consider the instance at line 4 of Table 2. Recall that the off-line step for ITIL takes around 3.5 s and observe that this is computed once and for all. If, instead, we use the technique to solve the WSP in [5] as a black-box (i.e. without being able to retrieve the symbolic reachability graph computed during the off-line phase), which is common to almost all techniques available in the literature, solving the same B-SFP would require almost 30 s resulting from re-computing 7 times (corresponding to the 7 task-user pairs in the returned scenario) the same symbolic reachability graph (compare this with the timing of 4.561 s reported in the table). This is a significant performance gain despite the small size of the example.

5   Conclusions

We have introduced two SFPs, discussed their relationships with the WSP, and argued that solving them supports the deployment of business processes in the activity of model reuse. We have also described algorithms to solve two SFPs, based on a previously proposed technique [5] for the WSP. An experimental evaluation on two real-world examples shows that our techniques can be used in practice at deployment time since they perform the computationally heaviest part (namely, computing the set of eligible scenarios) once and for all when the workflow is added to a library and re-use it for any possible authorization policy.
Related work. Bertino et al. [4] were the first to present, among many other contributions, a method capable of computing execution scenarios by using logic programming techniques. The practical feasibility of the approach is not assessed as we do for our technique in Sect. 4. Kohler and Schaad [12] introduces the notion of policy deadlocks (corresponding to situations in which the WSP is unsolvable) and propose a graph-based technique to compute minimal user bases to help policy designers avoid such situations. There are some similarities with our approach (e.g., the use of symbolic users) but our work is not limited to RBAC policies as theirs and focuses on business process reuse, which is not considered in [12]. Solworth [18] uses an approvability graph to describe sequences of actions defining the termination of a workflow. His technique focus on linear workflows whereas we support constructs for parallel executions and conditionals. Many works [2,3,7–10,14,16,21] study the WSP. As discussed above, most of them cannot be used to solve the SFPs without an unacceptable decrease in performances because they are not able to pre-compute the set of eligible scenarios. The works in [2,7] separate between an off-line and on-line phase as done in [5] and here but do not exploit it for business process reuse as we do.
Future work. We intend to study the notion of resiliency [21] in SFPs and how to automatically suggest changes to authorization policies so that solutions of an SFP are optimal with respect to some criteria, e.g., least privilege.

References

1. Armando, A., Ponta, S.E.: Model checking of security-sensitive business processes. In: Degano, P., Guttman, J.D. (eds.) FAST 2009. LNCS, vol. 5983, pp. 66–80. Springer, Heidelberg (2010)
2. Basin, D., Burri, S.J., Karjoth, G.: Obstruction-free authorization enforcement: aligning security with business objectives. In: CSF 2011, pp. 99–113. IEEE (2011)
3. Basin, D., Burri, S.J., Karjoth, G.: Optimal workflow-aware authorizations. In: Proceedings of SACMAT 2012, pp. 93–102. ACM, New York (2012)
4. Bertino, E., Ferrari, E., Atluri, V.: The specification and enforcement of authorization constraints in workflow management systems. TISSeC 2, 65–104 (1999)
5. Bertolissi, C., dos Santos, D.R., Ranise, S.: Automated synthesis of run-time monitors to enforce authorization policies in business processes. In: ASIACCS 2015. ACM, USA (2015)
6. Ceri, S., Gottlob, G., Tanca, L.: What you always wanted to know about datalog (and never dared to ask). IEEE TKDE 1(1), 146–166 (1989)
7. Cohen, D., Crampton, J., Gagarin, A., Gutin, G., Jones, M.: Iterative plan construction for the workflow satisfiability problem. JAIR 51, 555–577 (2014)
8. Crampton, J.: A reference monitor for workflow systems with constrained task execution. In: 10th ACM SACMAT, pp. 38–47. ACM (2005)
9. Crampton, J., Gutin, G., Yeo, A.: On the parameterized complexity of the workflow satisfiability problem. In: CCS 2012, pp. 857–868. ACM (2012)
10. Crampton, J., Huth, M., Kuo, J.: Authorized workflow schemas: deciding realizability through LTL(F) model checking. STTT 16(1), 31–48 (2014)
11. Dijkman, R., La Rosa, M., Reijers, H.A.: Editorial: managing large collections of business process models-current techniques and challenges. CI 63(2), 91–97 (2012)
12. Kohler, M., Schaad, A.: Avoiding policy-based deadlocks in business processes. In: ARES 2008, pp. 709–716. IEEE (2008)
13. Li, N., Mitchell, J.C.: DATALOG with constraints: a foundation for trust management languages. In: Dahl, V. (ed.) PADL 2003. LNCS, vol. 2562, pp. 58–73. Springer, Heidelberg (2002)
14. Lu, H., Hong, Y., Yang, Y., Fang, Y., Duan, L.: Dynamic workflow adjustment with security constraints. In: Atluri, V., Pernul, G. (eds.) DBSec 2014. LNCS, vol. 8566, pp. 211–226. Springer, Heidelberg (2014)
15. OMG. Business process model and notation (BPMN), Version 2.0. Technical report, Object Management Group (2011)
16. Ray, I., Yang, P., Xie, X., Lu, S.: Satisfiability analysis of workflows with control-flow patterns and authorization constraints. IEEE TSC PP(99), 1–14 (2013)
17. Sandhu, R., Coyne, E., Feinstein, H., Youmann, C.: Role-based access control models. IEEE Comput. 2(29), 38–47 (1996)
18. Solworth, J.A.: Approvability. In: Proceedings of ASIACCS 2006, pp. 231–242. ACM, New York (2006)
19. van der Aalst, W.M.P.: Business process management: a comprehensive survey. ISRN Softw. Eng. 2013, 1–37 (2013)
20. van der Aalst, W.M.P., Ter Hofstede, A.H.M.: Yawl: yet another workflow language. Inf. Sys. 30, 245–275 (2003)
21. Wang, Q., Li, N.: Satisfiability and resiliency in workflow authorization systems. TISSeC 13, 40:1–40:35 (2010)
22. Weske, M.: Business Process Management: Concepts, Languages, Architectures. Springer-Verlag New York Inc., Secaucus (2007)
23. Zaaboub Haddar, N., Makni, L., Ben Abdallah, H.: Literature review of reuse in business process modeling. Softw. Syst. Model. 13(3), 975–989 (2014)

User Privacy

Privacy Preserving Record Matching Using Automated Semi-trusted Broker

Ibrahim Lazrig[1]([⊠]), Tarik Moataz[1,2], Indrajit Ray[1], Indrakshi Ray[1],
Toan Ong[3], Michael Kahn[3], Frédéric Cuppens[2], and Nora Cuppens[2]

[1] Department of Computer Science, Colorado State University,
Ford Collins, CO, USA
{lazrig,tmoataz,indrajit,iray}@cs.colostate.edu
[2] Institut Mines-Télécom, Télécom Bretagne, Cesson Sévigné, France
{frederic.cuppens,nora.cuppens}@telecom-bretagne.eu
[3] Anschutz Medical Campus, University of Colorado, Denver, USA
{Toan.Ong,Michael.Kahn}@ucdenver.edu

Abstract. In this paper, we present a novel scheme that allows multiple data publishers that continuously generate new data and periodically update existing data, to share sensitive individual records with multiple data subscribers while protecting the privacy of their clients. An example of such sharing is that of health care providers sharing patients' records with clinical researchers. Traditionally, such sharing is performed by sanitizing personally identifying information from individual records. However, removing identifying information prevents any updates to the source information to be easily propagated to the sanitized records, or sanitized records belonging to the same client to be linked together. We solve this problem by utilizing the services of a third party, which is of very limited capabilities in terms of its abilities to keep a secret, secret, and by encrypting the identification part used to link individual records with different keys. The scheme is based on strong security primitives that do not require shared encryption keys.

1 Introduction

Many applications exist where a group of data sources (publishers) continuously generate sensitive data, periodically update the same, and share the data with another group of data analyzers (subscribers). To protect the privacy of the clients of the publishers, the data sharing needs to occur in a privacy-preserving manner, which in its simplest form is enabled by removing identifying information from the data. An example of such data sharing is observed in the so-called clinical data-sharing networks. Different health care providers (e.g., medical clinics, laboratories, hospitals and pharmacies) are the publishers of the data for the networks while clinical researchers are the subscribers of the data. Unlike the traditional privacy-preserving data publishing domain, the data in such clinical data-sharing networks are not static but are updated every time a patient interacts with a data publisher.

© IFIP International Federation for Information Processing 2015
P. Samarati (Ed.): DBSec 2015, LNCS 9149, pp. 103–118, 2015.
DOI: 10.1007/978-3-319-20810-7_7

Owing to the updatable nature of the data, a unique and challenging situation occurs in such applications that is not observed in traditional privacy preserved data publishing setups. Any updates to a record on the publisher side must be pushed to the corresponding record on the subscriber side even though these two records have been delinked via sanitization algorithms. Consider the clinical data-sharing example. Assume that a clinical researcher needs data related to a specific demography. In this case, patients' identification information (such as SSN, driver's license number, date of birth, etc.) are typically removed when the medical information is shared with the researcher. To provide the most relevant and current data, patients' progress under treatment regimens would need to be propagated to the clinical researcher. Similarly, the researcher should also be able to pull updates from the publisher or at a minimum be able to query the publisher for updates. To allow such sharing of information, records at the publisher need to be somehow linked back to corresponding sanitized records at the subscriber in a privacy preserving manner.

Things become more challenging if this sharing needs to be carried out between multiple publishers and multiple subscribers. Publishers are often business competitors and unwilling to reveal to each other that they might be sharing clients between themselves. In such cases, two publishers should not know that they have a common group of clients. (Sharing such information under explicit directives from a client is allowed and is not considered here). For privacy reasons, two subscribers should not be able to determine that they have clients in common; they should not be able to link or trace two sanitized records to the same client. When a publisher has more than one record for the same client, the same number of sanitized records should be available at the subscriber and be updated as needed. This occurs, for example, when a patient has repeated visits to the doctor for treatment.

Not much work has been done in this area of privacy preserving record linkage in dynamic setting. Some existing techniques that partially address the problem require encryption of linkage information using a shared key between data publishers to find if matched individuals' data exist across multiple sites. However, this technique works for small communities; it is expensive to deploy in large heterogeneous setups. In addition, shared keys among a large number of entities increase the chances of key leakage. An alternative technique that is used in the medical community is to utilize the services of a trusted third party, HB, called the Honest Broker. The third party maintains the linking information between the subscriber data and the publisher data in a de-identified manner. The problem with this approach is that the Honest Broker has all information, which makes it a lucrative target for attackers. If the Honest Broker is compromised it will cause a catastrophic damage to both data publishers as well as to individual clients.

In this work, we address this problem of privacy preserving record linkage by proposing a secure scheme based on partially homomorphic encryption and a third party. The third party is responsible just for automatically and blindly perform record matching. It is honest in the sense that it follows the protocol correctly but is not trusted to keep a secret, secret. It is curious about the sensitive information contained in individual records and can act accordingly.

However, our protocol ensures that it is prevented from getting such information without colluding with publishers. The third party knows that two publishers or subscribers have clients in common; however, it does not know the identities of these clients.

The main idea behind our protocol is as follows. Each data publisher creates a "key converter" in collaboration with other data publishers. Each key converter is then given to the third party (henceforth referred to simply as the broker). Each data publisher encrypts critical identification information of its data using it own secret key. Later, the broker uses the "key converters" to blindly transform all publisher-encrypted identification information to an alternate encrypted form under some other key that is not known to any party including the broker itself. The broker needs to collude with at least one of the publishers to find that key. Once the linkage information is encrypted under the same key, the broker can easily determine matching records. The broker can also keep track of the individuals found at different sites for retrospective update queries purposes. Since the data is encrypted at the source with different keys that the broker does not have access to, the risk of privacy breach in case of the broker getting compromised is limited.

The rest of the paper is organized as follows: In Sect. 2, we walk through previous works related to the underlined problem. Section 3 gives some background information about primitives used to construct the scheme. In Sect. 4, we detail our construction. In Sect. 5, we provide a brief complexity and security analysis. Finally, Sect. 6 concludes the paper.

2   Related Work

Privacy preserving data sharing has been a well studied problem, particularly in the context of sharing information from databases controlled by multiple parties. The participating parties in a privacy preserving database querying system are: the *data owner*, variously called the data source or publisher of the data, who provides access to its data to others, the *data querier* who generates query against the publisher's data and receives the results, and the *host* who (potentially) stores the publisher's data, and executes the query by performing relevant computations.

In our setting, we respectively denote by publisher, subscriber and broker the data owner, data querier and the host. The challenging scenario addressed in this work considers many competitor publishers that do not want to reveal any information about their data to each other but would like to anonymously and securely share some information with the subscriber. In addition, the subscriber is not only interested in querying their data separately, but jointly in order to find connected records across the databases. Furthermore, the subscriber wants to be able to retrieve updates about some previously queried entities.

If the querier is the owner of the data itself, and the host is an untrusted outsourced third party, searchable encryption schemes or Oblivious RAM (ORAM) are used to protect the data and maintain the owner privacy. Considerable amount of research has been done towards this problem that resulted in very efficient and expressive schemes [1–6]. However, in searchable encryption schemes, the data to be joined must be encrypted under the same key that has been shared among the owners. So searchable encryption schemes cannot directly be applied for our scenario.

In some settings, there are at least two parties each hosting their own data and either one or both of them wants to query other's data against his data. Each of them is considered the adversary to the other and ideally should not learn any thing beyond the query result. For such cases, private set intersection [7,8] and multi-party computation are potential solutions [9]. For instance, Agrawal et al. [10] propose a set of operations on private databases between two parties where nothing is learned by the parties rather than the results of the operations. De Cristofaro et al. [11] make also use of set intersection techniques, yet using a certification authority (CA) to authorize queries and leverage client and server privacy. However, these solutions although appealing from a security perspective are not very efficient for large settings.

Solutions proposed in [12,13] introduce a third party (Honest Broker) who will work as a mediator between the querier and the owners. This solution is impractical and not secure. In fact, although these solutions could be easy to deploy, non-cryptographic hash usage makes unauthorized users able to compute the hash; if the domain of the information is small or well known then it is possible to find the original information or at least to verify if some value exists or not. If pseudo-random functions are used instead, then a shared secret key must be used, which is undesirable in our setup because of the competition between different publishers. In addition, owing to the significant amount of trust required on the Honest Broker it becomes an appealing target for the attackers and malicious insiders [14,15].

Yin and Yau [16] propose a privacy preserving repository for data integration across data sharing services that allows owners to specify integration requirements and data sharing services to safeguard their privacy. The owners determine who and how their data can be used. The authors presented what they call context aware data sharing to help data services to share data with the repository. However, the matching process between records is done using the hash value of their identification information, which is not secure and does not preserve privacy. This scheme suffers from the same underlying problems of the previous construction, namely, a mandatory secret sharing between competing parties. Carbunar and Sion [17] introduce a mechanism for executing a general binary join operation on an outsourced relational database with low overhead using predefined binary finite match predicates for computed match set. However they assume that the keys of both columns used in the join are known to the data owner. If the data belongs to two different owners, this key must be shared beforehand – essentially the same problem as earlier.

Chow et al. [18] propose a model for performing privacy preserving operations in a distributed database environment. The model, called Two-Party Query computation, comprises a randomizer and computing engine that do not reveal any information between themselves. The model in essence emulates a central party with the functions split into two entities. In order to guarantee that the randomizer and the computing engine do not collude, the authors proposes to use key agreement protocol among the participating entities. This protocol has limited applicability to our scenario since it doesn't not support the retrospective queries.

Finally, a solution presented by Tassa et al. [19] targets gathering data between horizontally or vertically divided dataset while preserving sensitive information. The computation is over sanitized data set using k-anonymity or l-diversity sanitizing techniques. Their main focus is on anonymization of distributed databases in such a way that each party locally anonymizes its data without revealing its original content to others. While the ideas and techniques of this work are suitable for distributed data mining problems, since our requirements are quite different Tassa et al.ś work cannot be easily used to serve our needs.

3   Background

In the following, we recapitulate some important concepts that we use to build our protocols.

3.1   ElGamal Cryptosystem

ElGamal public-key cryptosystem [20] is defined over finite field $\mathbb{F}_q$ of a prime order q. The public key pk equals (G, q, g, h), where G is a cyclic group of order q with g as a generator, and $h = g^x$. The private key sk equals $x \xleftarrow{R} \{1, \cdots, q-1\}$.

The encryption of a message m using the public key is (c_1, c_2) and computed such that $(c_1, c_2) = \mathsf{Enc}_{\mathsf{pk}}(m) = (g^r, m \cdot h^r)$, where $r \xleftarrow{R} \{0, \ldots, q-1\}$. To decrypt the ciphertext (c_1, c_2) and retrieve $m = \mathsf{Dec}_{\mathsf{sk}}(c_1, c_2)$, the private key is needed as follows: first compute $s = c_1^{\mathsf{sk}} = (g^r)^x$. The decrypted message m equals $m = c_2 \cdot s^{-1} = m \cdot h^r \cdot g^{-rx} = m \cdot (g^x)^r \cdot g^{-rx} = m$.

3.2   Elliptic Curve Cryptography and the Discrete Logarithm Problem (ECDLP)

An Elliptic Curve [21] E over a finite field $\mathbb{F}_q$ of prime order q, is a set of points with coordinates from that field defined by an equation of the form $y^2 + a_1 xy + a_3 y = x^3 + a_2 x^2 + a_4 x + a_6$ for all $a_i \in \mathbb{F}_q$, or of the simpler form $y^2 = x^3 + ax + b$, with $a, b \in \mathbb{F}_q$ for finite fields of order different from 2 or 3. The coefficients define the shape of the curve and are the parameters of the curve. The set of points together with a special point called the point at infinity $\mathcal{O}$, form a group under the addition of points operation. Multiplication of points is not defined; however, multiplying a point P by a scalar u is defined as the addition of the point P u number times, i.e. $uP = \underbrace{P + P + \cdots + P}_{u \ times}$. The cyclic subgroup $E(\mathbb{F}_q)$ is defined by its generator (base point) P with order n, which is the smallest positive integer such that $nP = \mathcal{O}$. This subgroup $E(\mathbb{F}_q) = \{\mathcal{O}, P, 2P, \ldots, (n-1)P\}$ is denoted by its domain parameters (q, a, b, P, n).

Given an Elliptic Curve $E(\mathbb{F}_q)$ over a finite field and two points $P, Q \in E$, it is hard to find an integer $x \in \mathbb{Z}_q$ such that $Q = xP$. This is known as the Elliptic Curve Discrete Logarithm Problem (ECDLP). ECDLP is believed to be harder than finding Discrete Logarithms for finite fields, which is why many public key cryptosystems uses Elliptic Curves (EC) as the underlying group. For our purposes, the ElGamal cryptosystem and its variations are defined using EC as follows.

First, the communicating parties agree on the EC parameters and the corresponding field, i.e., $E(\mathbb{F}_q)$, the generator point G, and its order n. From these parameters each party generates its private key as $\mathsf{sk}_i = x, x \xleftarrow{R} \{1, \cdots, n-1\}$, and its public key as the point $\mathsf{pk}_i = xG$. The messages to be encrypted must be encoded as points on the curve in order to apply the group addition, or the messages must be integer scalars in the range $\{1, \cdots, n-1\}$ to use multiplications of points by scalars. The encryption of encoded message M is then performed by the sender A using the recipient B's public key sk_B as $C_1 = r \cdot G$, and $C_2 = r \cdot \mathsf{pk}_B + M$, where $r \xleftarrow{R} \{1, \cdots, n-1\}$. The decryption at the receiver side B is done using its private key sk_B as $M = C_2 - \mathsf{sk}_B \cdot C_1 = r \cdot \mathsf{pk}_B + M - \mathsf{sk}_B \cdot r \cdot G = r \cdot k \cdot G - k \cdot r \cdot G + M = M$.

3.3 Homomorphic Encryption

Homomorphic encryption allows arithmetic operations to be carried out on ciphertext in such a way that the decrypted result matches the result of the operations when performed on the plaintext. *Partially* Homomorphic Encryption system (PHE) allows either addition or multiplication but not both. In this work, we focus only on the multiplicative property.

The homomorphic property of ElGamal cryptosystem over a finite field ensures that the product of two encrypted messages $\mathsf{Enc}_{\mathsf{pk}}(m_1)$ and $\mathsf{Enc}_{\mathsf{pk}}(m_2)$ will decrypt to the product of their corresponding plaintext messages $m_1 \cdot m_2$,

$$
\begin{aligned}
\mathsf{Enc}_{\mathsf{pk}}(m_1) \cdot \mathsf{Enc}_{\mathsf{pk}}(m_2) &= (g^{r_1}, m_1 \cdot h^{r_1}) \cdot (g^{r_2}, m_2 \cdot h^{r_2}) \\
&= (g^{r_1+r_2}, (m_1 \cdot m_2)h^{r_1+r_2}) \\
&= \mathsf{Enc}_{\mathsf{pk}}(m_1 \cdot m_2).
\end{aligned}
$$

If $s = c_1^{\mathsf{sk}} = g^{(r_1+r_2)x}$ then $s^{-1} = g^{-(r_1+r_2)x}$ and the decryption will result in

$$
\begin{aligned}
\mathsf{Dec}_{\mathsf{sk}}(\mathsf{Enc}_{\mathsf{pk}}(m_1) \cdot \mathsf{Enc}_{\mathsf{pk}}(m_2)) &= \mathsf{Dec}_{\mathsf{sk}}(\mathsf{Enc}_{\mathsf{pk}}(m_1 \cdot m_2)) \\
&= \mathsf{Dec}_{\mathsf{sk}}(g^{r_1+r_2}, (m_1 \cdot m_2)h^{r_1+r_2}) \\
&= (m_1 \cdot m_2) \cdot g^{(r_1+r_2)x} \cdot s^{-1} \\
&= (m_1 \cdot m_2) \cdot g^{(r_1+r_2)x} \cdot g^{-(r_1+r_2)x} \\
&= m_1 \cdot m_2
\end{aligned}
$$

4   Scheme Construction

Our scheme works in three phases: the *setup* phase, the *encryption of query results* phase, and the *secure record matching* phase. The setup phase is executed only once by the data publishers to create the so-called publishers' "key converters". It utilizes properties of homomorphic encryption to create these "key converters". The encryption of query results phase occurs at the publisher side whenever it executes a query, to encrypt the identifying part of the query results. This encryption is performed using the publisher's secret non-shared key before sending the results to the broker. The secure record matching phase occurs at the broker side to determine the linkages between the records coming from the publishers after executing the queries.

We begin by discussing the adversarial model and privacy requirements, then we explain each phase in details.

4.1   Adversary Model and Privacy Requirements

Data publishers are considered competitors who do not want to share data with each other. Each publisher tries to determine information about the clients of competitor publisher, or at a minimum, tries to determine if any one of its clients is also a client of its competitor. However, publishers are also honest in the execution of the protocol steps and willing to share information with subscribers *privately*, that is, without revealing real identities, and *securely*, that is, without any leakage of information to other data publishers, and without revealing the publisher identity to the subscribers.

A data subscriber, on the other hand, needs to determine if any information that came from different publishers belong to the same individual so they could be grouped together as such and treated accordingly. For example, if a researcher is looking for the side effects of a new drug used for skin treatment on patients who has kidneys problems, then he has to match patients from the (Dermatology) and (kidney diseases) departments to find patients under these conditions. We need to allow such grouping at the subscriber side.

Further more, the subscriber is allowed to issue *retrospective* queries regarding some individual client, for example, update queries regarding the progress of treatment of certain patients. Subscribers (researchers) are considered curious in the sense they will try to determine the real identities of the individuals. Some information about individual identities might be leaked from their non-identification information (i.e. eye color, age, weight, etc.) using statistical inference techniques. This is a separate problem that needs to be addressed with anonymization (i.e. k-anonymity) or other sanitization methods, and is not considered in this work.

The broker is honest in the sense that it will not collude with any of the parties, but is curious and not trusted to keep a secret, secret. The broker will work as a mediator between the data publishers and the subscribers by honestly performing the following tasks:

- Hide the source of information (publishers and clients' identities) from the subscribers.
- Blindly determine record linkages among the encrypted publishers' records and assign alternate random identifiers to the linked records before sharing them with the subscribers. The broker will just know the linkages without knowing the real identifiers.

4.2   Setup Phase

In order to create its key converter, each publisher is required to initially interact with other publishers participating in the sharing system, keeping in mind that other publishers are competitors. Every publisher needs to go through the setup protocol once at the beginning of the system instantiation when it joins the sharing system. An existing publisher also needs to embark upon the setup phase if a refreshing of keys is required when new publishers join the system. These key converters will be delegated to the third party (broker) and will be used to convert records encrypted under different keys of different publishers, to records encrypted under a common key. This common key is such that it cannot not be re-constructed by any of the parties, namely, individual publishers, broker and subscribers. This means that the encrypted data is safe if there is no collusion between any of the publishers and the broker at the instantiation time. In this scheme, we propose a secure protocol to create the key converters among the publishers using ElGamal homomorphic cryptosystem that supports product operation over the encrypted keys. At the end of this phase, every publisher is associated with a special key converter that allows the broker to perform the matching process.

Each publisher from the set of N publishers $D = \{d_i\}_{i \in [N]}$ has its secret key sk_i, and the broker which has a public key pk and private key sk pair. The setup phase is illustrated in Fig. 1 and works as follows.

- **Step 1**: The broker broadcasts its public key $\mathsf{pk} = (G, q, g, g^{\mathsf{sk}})$ for ElGamal homomorphic encryption to all publishers.
- **Step 2**: Each publisher d_i generates an initial random secret $r_i \xleftarrow{R} \{1, \cdots, q-1\}$, where q is the order of G, encrypts it using the master key pk. Let $t_{i \to j}$ denote the temporary encrypted key converter of publisher i when being processed by publisher j, and $t_{i \to final}$ the final converter when it gets back to the publisher i after being processed by all parties. Publisher d_i generates the initial temporary encrypted key converter $t_{i \to i} = \mathsf{Enc}_{\mathsf{pk}}(r_i^{-1})$, then forwards it to the next publisher $d_{(i \bmod (N))+1}$.
- **Step 3**: Each publisher d_j receives a value $t_{i \to j}$ from its upstream neighbor d_i ($i \neq j$), securely multiplies it using ElGamal homomorphic cryptosystem with its secret key sk_j encrypted under the broker's public key pk as follows:

$$t_{i \to i+1} = t_{i \to i} \cdot \mathsf{Enc}_{\mathsf{pk}}(\mathsf{sk}_{i+1})$$
$$= \mathsf{Enc}_{\mathsf{pk}}(r_i^{-1} \cdot \mathsf{sk}_{i+1})$$

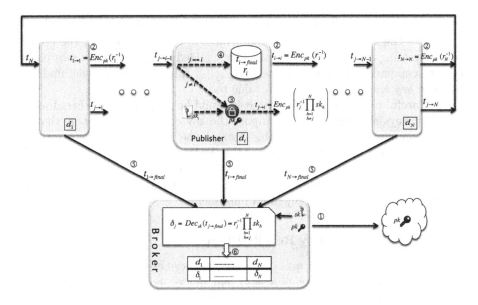

Fig. 1. High level setup phase illustration

This operation is repeated through $N - 1$ publishers. The temporary value of publisher d_i generated by the jth publisher equals:

$t_{i \to j} = \mathsf{Enc}_{\mathsf{pk}}(r_i^{-1} \cdot \prod_{c=i+1}^{j} \mathsf{sk}_c)$

- **Step 4**: After $N - 1$ transitions, the initials publisher receives the final key converter $t_{i \to final}$ as

$$t_{i \to final} = \mathsf{Enc}_{\mathsf{pk}} \left(r_i^{-1} \prod_{\substack{j=1 \\ j \neq i}}^{N} \mathsf{sk}_j \right)$$

- **Step 5**: After each publisher is able to generate its key converter value after being processed by all other publishers, the publisher d_i sends its $t_{i \to final}$ value to the broker, and saves a copy of it for future updates in case new publishers joined the system.

- **Step 6**: For each $t_{i \to final}$, the broker extracts the key conversion factor δ_i such that: $\delta_i = \mathsf{Dec}_{\mathsf{sk}}(t_{i \to final}) = r_i^{-1} \prod_{\substack{j=1 \\ j \neq i}}^{N} sk_j$

Key Converter Refresh: If a new publisher d_{N+1} joins the system, then it follows the previous steps to create its own key converter t_{N+1}, while other publishers just need to update their own key converters. To accommodate the key of the new publisher, old publishers send their previously created $t_{i \to final}$ values to the new one, which in turn securely adds its secret key sk_{N+1} to this value $t_{i \to final}$ to get $t'_{i \to final}$, and sends it back to the source. Each publisher d_i

then refreshes its $t'_{i \to final}$ with a new random value r'_i and sends the updated $t'_{i \to final}$ to the broker. This new random value r'_i is used to prevent the broker from extracting information about the newly added secret key of the new party d_{N+1} by comparing the new with the old $t_{i \to final}$ values. Each publisher updates its secret key with this new random value too.

Note: Careful readers might think that it would be simpler if publishers broadcast their keys and then locally compute the key converters. It is true that in term of communication overhead, this method also involves $O(n^2)$ interactions, however, in term of information shared, it leaks more. In this solution, each publisher submits its key encrypted with the public key of the broker. If the broker can somehow eavesdrops the communication between the publishers, it can decrypt and obtains the key of all publishers.

4.3 Encryption of Query Results Phase

This phase is triggered by a query sent by a subscriber requesting information from publishers. This represents a *data pull* model; however, our scheme can be also used in a *data push* mode where publishers send data directly to the broker which redirects it to the corresponding subscribers. After executing the received query, each publisher encrypts the identifying parts of the query results using any cryptosystem that relies on DDH (Decisional Diffie-Hellman) or DL (Discrete Logarithm) hardness assumptions, such as ElGamal cryptosystem. For performance reasons, our construction uses Elliptic Curves (EC) instead of Finite Groups of large primes as the underlying group for the used cryptosystem.

Each publisher has the publicly known ElGamal EC parameters, i.e., the curve parameters $E(\mathbb{F}_q)$ and the point on the curve P of prime order n. The public/private key pair will be $(r_i \cdot \mathsf{sk}_i \cdot P, r_i \cdot \mathsf{sk}_i)$ and both of th keys are kept secret. The message to be encrypted, id, in our multiplicative scheme needs to be a scalar. We denote by $\mathsf{E}(.)$ the encryption of ElGamal based on EC.

The publisher first hashes the identifying part of every record in the result set using a universal hash function H. The result set is the data outputted by executing the subscriber query. The publisher uses its secret key multiplied by the corresponding random value, $(r_i \cdot \mathsf{sk}_i)$, to encrypt the resulting hash. That is, the encryption of any identifier id will be:

$$\mathsf{E}_{(r_i \cdot \mathsf{sk}_i)}(H(id)) = H(id) \cdot r_i \cdot \mathsf{sk}_i \cdot P$$

Finally, the publisher substitutes the real identifying part, id, by $\mathsf{E}_{(r_i \cdot \mathsf{sk}_i)}(H(id))$ for all records in the result set. Finally, each record is composed of the encrypted identification part, plus, the other client's information. The data in plaintext in each record will be sanitized if necessary, according to the publisher's policy, before being sent to the broker. Sanitizing techniques details are out of scope of this work.

Publishers can avoid having the broker store the key converter $(\delta_i)_{i \in [N]}$. For this purpose, each publisher encrypts the identifiers of the query results with a new random value r_i, updates the key converter $t_{i \to final}$, then sends these results to the broker accompanied with the new key converter. This solution adds negligible communication overhead, but ensures a zero-key stored on the broker side.

4.4 Secure Record Matching Phase

The broker receives the encrypted identifiers with different keys from different publishers. The broker's job is to merge similar clients' records from different publishers such that they will map to the same newly generated identifier. The broker will use the key converters δ_i to change the encryption key in such a way that similar data will be deterministically encrypted with the same key without requiring any decryption to be performed along the way.

The broker uses the δ_i values to convert any identifier id encrypted by publisher d_i under its secret key $(r_i \cdot \mathsf{sk}_i)$, to a value encrypted under a different secret key Δ, i.e., $\mathsf{E}_\Delta(H(id))$. The key $\Delta = \prod_{i=1}^N \mathsf{sk}_i$ is resulting from the product of all the secret keys of all publishers. In order to perform the secure record matching, the broker re-encrypts the encrypted identifying parts of the records coming from the publisher d_i using the corresponding key converter δ_i as:

$$\mathsf{E}_{\delta_i}\left(\mathsf{E}_{(r_i \cdot \mathsf{sk}_i)}(H(id))\right) = \mathsf{E}_\Delta(H(id))$$

That this process does indeed perform correct matching is shown by the fact that:

$$\mathsf{E}_{\delta_i}\left(\mathsf{E}_{(r_i \cdot \mathsf{sk}_i)}(H(id))\right) = \mathsf{E}_{\delta_i}\left(H(id) \cdot r_i \cdot \mathsf{sk}_i \cdot P\right)$$
$$= H(id) \cdot r_i \cdot \mathsf{sk}_i \cdot P \cdot r_i^{-1} \prod_{j=1, j\neq i}^N \mathsf{sk}_j$$
$$= H(id) \cdot \prod_{j=1}^N \mathsf{sk}_j \cdot P$$
$$= H(id) \cdot \Delta \cdot P = \mathsf{E}_\Delta(H(id))$$

In order to maintain the linkages between publishers' data records and the randomly generated identifiers for subscribers, the broker keeps track of the processed identifiers for both flows, i.e., from publishers to subscribers and vice versa. The aim of this mapping is two folds: first we do not want to give the ability to the subscribers to know whether they share the same client and second give the ability to the broker to map back these random values to the same client. For this purpose, the broker builds two secure inverted indexes, one to map the encrypted identifiers after conversion (i.e. $\mathsf{E}_\Delta(H(id))$) to their corresponding subscriber identifiers such that for each we generate a random value rid concatenated to the subscriber identifier sid. The second maps $rid\|sid$ to the set of corresponding encrypted clients' identifiers concatenated with their publisher id such that $\mathsf{E}_{r_i \cdot \mathsf{sk}_i}(H(id))\|d_i$, for $i \in [N]$, see Table. 1. These secure inverted indexes can be constructed following searchable encryption data structure instantiation, see [1,2].

Table 1. Conceptual representation of secure inverted indexes

$E_\Delta(H(id))$	$rid\|sid$
0xAB4542..24	0x354AE2..16 || 1, 0xF14598..24 || 5
0xC2C6A5..59	0x413F56..AE || 2
....	..

$rid\|sid$	$E_{r_i \cdot sk_i}(H(id))\|d_i$
0x354AE2..16 || 1	0x6547A..6A || 2, 0x45CA4..B2 || 5
0x413F56..AE || 2	0x48F53..12 || 11
..	....

4.5 Matching Phase Walk-Through

We now summarize all the interactions between the three parties, namely, publishers, subscribers and the broker to describe how privacy preserving record matching system works to serve the subscriber's needs. These interactions schematically shown in Fig. 2, with each of following steps corresponding to the numbers shown in the figure.

1. The subscriber sends a query Q to the broker.
2. The broker sanitizes the query if necessary, and checks if this query Q is a query that seeks information about new clients or a retrospective query (requesting more information about an individual whose data has been seen before). If it is a new query, it forwards the query to publishers and wait for the answers.
3. If the query Q is a retrospective query, the broker first looks up the $rid\|sid$ in the inverted index for the corresponding encrypted identifiers and their associated publisher identities, i.e. $E_{r_i \cdot sk_i}(H(id))\|d_i$. The broker then replaces $rid\|sid$ with the corresponding $E_{r_i \cdot sk_i}(H(id))$ and finally forwards the query Q only to their associated publishers d_i.
4. For each query Q it receives, the publisher d_i checks if it is a new query or a retrospective query. If it is a retrospective query, the publisher can directly look up the matching records while for a new query a search has to be done to find the corresponding clients. In either case, the publisher applies its local sanitizing policies to the results, encrypts the identification part using its secret key $(r_i \cdot sk_i)$, and finally sends the results to the broker.
5. Upon receiving the results of the forwarded query from the publishers, the broker further sanitizes the results according to the general sharing policies and regulations. Then it performs the secure record matching process, and updates its inverted indexes as follows:
   - Using the first inverted index, and for each distinct $E_{r_i \cdot sk_i}(H(id))$ in the query result, apply the key converters to get $E_\Delta(H(id))$. If a match is found then this identifier has been sent before (it might be from a different publisher though). So the broker retrieves the corresponding $\{rid\|sid\}$, and updates the second inverted index with the encrypted id

$\mathsf{E}_{r_i \cdot \mathsf{sk}_i}(H(id))\|d_i$ in case it has been previously sent from a different publisher.

- If the converted encrypted $\mathsf{E}_\Delta(H(id))$ is not found, then it means that this identifier has not been sent before by any publisher. The broker adds this converted value to the first inverted index, with a new subscriber and random identifier $rid\|sid$. The second inverted index is updated accordingly.
- The encrypted identifier $\mathsf{E}_{r_i \cdot \mathsf{sk}_i}(H(id))$ in each record in the results is then replaced with its corresponding $rid\|sid$ before being sent to the corresponding subscribers.

As we have mentioned earlier, these inverted indexes are encrypted under the broker's secret keys, and all the searching and update operations are performed on encrypted data using any adaptive secure searchable encryption scheme data structures.

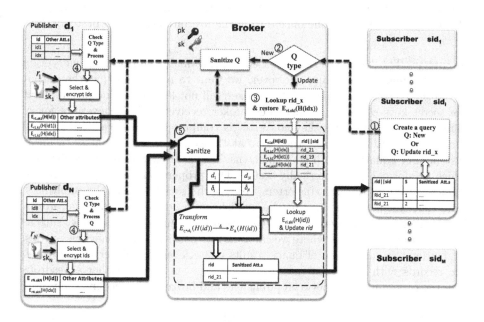

Fig. 2. Matching phase walk-through illustration

5   Complexity and Security Analysis

Complexity: Our scheme is practicable and can be efficiently implemented in real scenarios. The construction is composed of three main steps, the setup, the encryption of query results and the secure record matching phase. The setup phase depends on the number of publishers N. The entire setup phase results in a total communication overhead which is $O(N^2)$. To generate *one* key converter, the publishers needs to transfer one message each, while the computation is constant per each transfer. The total communication and computation overhead per publisher is in $O(N)$. The setup phase is performed just once and is done in an off-line manner. The encryption of query results overhead depends on the matching set and the data structure that the publisher is using for its own data storage. The search complexity depends on the query sent by the subscriber through the broker. Also the complexity of this phase greatly depends on the size of the database of the publishers and the sanitizing protocols used as well. For this reason, we consider only the communication overhead for this phase. For the last phase performed by the broker, given all identifiers that match the query, the goal consists of retrieving all subscribers identifiers as well as the randomized identifiers. Using SSE, the search is optimal and similar to plaintext data. Given an identifier, the search complexity will be in the number of matching results.

To sum up, the construction does not induce any overhead during the matching phase more than the one expected on plaintext data. The linear construction of the key converters is done once during the instantiation of the protocol.

Security: The key converter is based on ElGamal homomorphic encryption which is semantically secure. However, we want to make sure that the output of the key converter received by the broker will not leak any information about the secret keys of any publisher. The broker receives N key converters for N different publishers. Every key converter is composed of $N - 1$ secret key and a random value. The broker then has, at the end of the setup phase, a linear system of N equations with $2N$ unknowns. This is an under-determined system which is information theoretically secure. This property ensures that the broker cannot, based on the key converters, recover the secret keys of the publishers. Note that this is true as long as the publishers do not collude with the broker. We can enhance this key converter generation with much secure schemes such as multi-party computation where we can take into consideration malicious parties.

During the encryption of query results phase, every publisher is encrypting the records with a different secret key. Thus, even if a publisher eavesdrops over the communication between publishers and broker, it cannot infer anything about the clients identity.

For the storage of the encrypted identifiers at the broker side, a conversion of the encryption is necessary. The broker therefore knows that this encrypted identifier (whatever be the identifier) is linked to the same client in different publishers. This feature is very important for the scheme correctness since it enables the broker to aggregate the exact subscriber query results. From a security perspective, we want to hide not only the association between encrypted identifiers and subscribers but also the mapping between the publisher identifiers and the encrypted identifiers. For this purpose, we use a symmetric searchable encryption inverted index that enables to store securely these mappings. Consequently, even if the data at the broker is somehow leaked, the entire inverted indexes are encrypted and the mapping will not be disclosed.

6   Conclusions and Future Work

We have presented a novel scheme to allow multiple data publishers, who encrypt their data with their private non-shared key, to share their clients' records with subscribers while protecting the identities of their clients. The scheme is based on partially homomorphic encryption to create "key converters" that allow a third party with limited trust (broker), to perform privacy preserving record matching. The role of the broker is to determine the linkages without identifying the real identities of the publishers' clients but also to hide from the subscriber which publisher generated the information. Our construction is achieved by allowing each publisher to use his own secret key to guarantee the security of its data, and the broker, with the help of the key converters, to convert encrypted data of each publisher under different keys to data encrypted under the same key. Both the key converter and data conversion are implemented using ElGamal cryptosystem. Future work aims to provide an experimental evaluation with real-world clinical data and a practical implementation of this system for the clinical data-sharing network called CHORDS (Colorado Health Outcome Research Data Services).

Acknowledgments. This work was partially supported by the U.S. National Science Foundation under Grant No. 0905232, and by Colorado State University under an internal research grant.

References

1. Chase, M., Kamara, S.: Structured encryption and controlled disclosure. In: Abe, M. (ed.) ASIACRYPT 2010. LNCS, vol. 6477, pp. 577–594. Springer, Heidelberg (2010)
2. Curtmola, R., Garay, J.A., Kamara, S., Ostrovsky, R.: Searchable symmetric encryption: improved definitions and efficient constructions. In: Proceedings of the 13th ACM Conference on Computer and Communications Security, Alexandria, VA, USA. pp. 79–88 (2006)
3. Moataz, T., Shikfa, A.: Boolean symmetric searchable encryption. In: Proceedings of the 8th ACM Symposium on Information, Computer and Communications Security, Hangzhou, China. pp. 265–276 (2013)
4. Cash, D., Jarecki, S., Jutla, C., Krawczyk, H., Roşu, M.-C., Steiner, M.: Highly-scalable searchable symmetric encryption with support for boolean queries. In: Canetti, R., Garay, J.A. (eds.) CRYPTO 2013, Part I. LNCS, vol. 8042, pp. 353–373. Springer, Heidelberg (2013)
5. Stefanov, E., van Dijk, M., Shi, E., Fletcher, C.W., Ren, L., Yu, X., Devadas, S.: Path ORAM: an extremely simple oblivious RAM protocol. In: Proceedings of ACM Conference on Computer and Communications Security, Berlin, Germany. 299–310 (2013)
6. Strizhov, M., Ray, I.: Multi-keyword similarity search over encrypted cloud data. In: Cuppens-Boulahia, N., Cuppens, F., Jajodia, S., Abou El Kalam, A., Sans, T. (eds.) SEC 2014. IFIP AICT, vol. 428, pp. 52–65. Springer, Heidelberg (2014)
7. Dachman-Soled, D., Malkin, T., Raykova, M., Yung, M.: Efficient robust private set intersection. Int. J. Appl. Crypt. **2**, 289–303 (2012)

8. Kamara, S., Mohassel, P., Raykova, M., Sadeghian, S.: Scaling private set intersection to billion-element sets. In: Christin, N., Safavi-Naini, R. (eds.) FC 2014. LNCS, vol. 8437, pp. 193–213. Springer, Heidelberg (2014)
9. Goldreich, O.: Secure multi-party computation. Manuscript. Preliminary version (1998). http://citeseerx.ist.psu.edu. Accessed on 30 April 2015
10. Agrawal, R., Evfimievski, A., Srikant, R.: Information sharing across private databases. In: Proceedings of the 2003 ACM SIGMOD International Conference on Management of Data, San Diego, CA, USA. pp. 86–97 (2003)
11. De Cristofaro, E., Lu, Y., Tsudik, G.: Efficient techniques for privacy-preserving sharing of sensitive information. In: McCune, J.M., Balacheff, B., Perrig, A., Sadeghi, A.-R., Sasse, A., Beres, Y. (eds.) Trust 2011. LNCS, vol. 6740, pp. 239–253. Springer, Heidelberg (2011)
12. Boyd, A.D., Saxman, P.R., Hunscher, D.A., Smith, K.A., Morris, T.D., Kaston, M., Bayoff, F., Rogers, B., Hayes, P., Rajeev, N., Kline-Rogers, E., Eagle, K., Clauw, D., Greden, J.F., Green, L.A., Athey, B.D.: The University of Michigan honest broker: a web-based service for clinical and translational research and practice. J. Am. Med. Inform. Assoc. : JAMIA **16**, 784–791 (2009)
13. Dhir, R., Patel, A.A., Winters, S., Bisceglia, M., Swanson, D., Aamodt, R., Becich, M.J.: A multidisciplinary approach to honest broker services for tissue banks and clinical data. Cancer **113**, 1705–1715 (2008)
14. Jefferies, N., Mitchell, C.J., Walker, M.: A proposed architecture for trusted third party services. In: Proceedings of the International Conference on Cryptography: Policy and Algorithms, Brisbane, Queensland, Australia. pp. 98–104 (1995)
15. Ajmani, S., Morris, R., Liskov, B.: A trusted third-party computation service (2001). http://www.pmg.lcs.mit.edu/~ajmani/papers/tep.ps. Accessed on 30 April 2015
16. Yau, S., Yin, Y.: A privacy preserving repository for data integration across data sharing services. IEEE Trans. Serv. Comput. **1**, 130–140 (2008)
17. Carbunar, B., Sion, R.: Toward private joins on outsourced data. IEEE Trans. Knowl. Data Eng. **24**, 1699–1710 (2012)
18. Chow, S.S., Lee, J.H., Subramanian, L.: Two-party computation model for privacy-preserving queries over distributed databases. In: Proceedings of the 2009 Network and Distributed System Security Symposium, San Diego, CA, USA (2009)
19. Tassa, T., Gudes, E.: Secure distributed computation of anonymized views of shared databases. ACM Trans. Database Syst. (TODS) **37**, 11 (2012)
20. El Gamal, T.: A public key cryptosystem and a signature scheme based on discrete logarithms. In: Blakely, G.R., Chaum, D. (eds.) CRYPTO 1984. LNCS, vol. 196, pp. 10–18. Springer, Heidelberg (1985)
21. Koblitz, N.: Elliptic curve cryptosystems. Math. Comput. **48**, 203–209 (1987)

Outsourceable Privacy-Preserving Power Usage Control in a Smart Grid

Hu Chun[1], Kui Ren[2], and Wei Jiang[1]($^\boxtimes$)

[1] Department of Computer Science, Missouri University of Science and Technology,
Rolla, MO, USA
{wjiang,chwrc}@mst.edu
[2] Department of Computer Science and Engineering, SUNY Buffalo,
Buffalo, NY, USA
kuiren@buffalo.edu

Abstract. The smart grid systems, in replace of the traditional power grid systems, have been widely used among some well-known telecommunication, IT and power industries. These systems have multiple advantages such as energy efficiency, reliability and self-monitoring. To prevent power outage, threshold based power usage control (PUC) in a smart grid considers a situation where the utility company sets a threshold to control the total power usage of a neighborhood. If the total power usage exceeds the threshold, certain households need to reduce their power consumption. In PUC, the utility company needs to frequently collect power usage data from smart meters. It has been well documented that these power usage data can reveal a person's daily activity and violate personal privacy. To avoid the privacy concern, privacy-preserving power usage control (P-PUC) protocols have been introduced. However, the existing P-PUC protocols are not very efficient and the computations cannot be outsourced to a cloud server. Thus, the utility company cannot take advantage of the cloud computing paradigm to potentially reduce its operational cost. The goal of this paper is to develop a P-PUC protocol whose computation/execution is outsourceable to a cloud. In addition, the proposed protocol is much more efficient than the existing P-PUC protocols. We will provide extensive empirical study to show the practicality of our proposed protocol.

Keywords: Smart grid · Privacy-preserving · Power usage control

1 Introduction

A smart grid can improve the efficiency, reliability, economics, and sustainability of a utility company to produce and distribute electricity. In a smart grid, smart meters can collect the power usage data of each household in a neighborhood to help a utility company self-monitor the power supply of the neighborhood to prevent power outage. For example, when the total power usage is extremely high, physical components in a smart grid could be overloaded. In order to

© IFIP International Federation for Information Processing 2015
P. Samarati (Ed.): DBSec 2015, LNCS 9149, pp. 119–134, 2015.
DOI: 10.1007/978-3-319-20810-7_8

prevent the failures of these physical components (consequently the power outage of the entire system), the power consumption of some households needs to be reduced (e.g., by setting the temperature of an AC a little bit higher without affecting a person's well-being).

In general, a utility company can set a power usage threshold beyond which the physical components of a smart grid may work dangerously above their expected capacities. Then the threshold can be compared with the total power usage of a neighborhood at a particular time that can be computed based on the power usage readings from the smart meters of individual households. When the total power usage exceeds the threshold, the energy consumptions of certain households need to be reduced. To achieve this kind of threshold based power usage control (PUC), a utility company needs to collect power usage data frequently from the smart meters of individual households. However, it has be shown that by analyzing 15-minute interval household energy consumption data (even in an aggregated form), the usage patterns of most major home appliances can be determined [8,21].

From these usage patterns, a malicious party can infer activities of daily livings (ADL) information [1] and can potentially initiate any malicious acts toward a particular household. Therefore, it is in the best interest of the utility company not to collect each household's power usage data. In addition, the threshold set by the utility company can reveal its operational capacity and the number of its customers in a neighborhood. To preserve competitive advantage, any information regarding the threshold values should not be disclosed to the public. Now the question becomes: can a utility company perform any PUC tasks without the company disclosing its threshold values and individual households disclosing their power usage data? Such a problem is termed as privacy-preserving power usage control (P-PUC).

Secure protocols have been proposed to solve the P-PUC problem [11,26] under different power adjusting strategies. However, those protocols are executed directly between a utility company and its household customers. It is hard to see how to implement the existing protocols effectively in practice since they require each household to actively participate in online computations. To summarize, the exiting work has at least one of the following limitations:

- Not very efficient when the threshold values are from a large domain.
- Leak certain intermediate information that can be used to infer knowledge about the private power usage data of individual households and the threshold values set by the utility companies.
- Incur heavy computations between the households and the utility company.

To eliminate the above problems, in this paper, we develop a novel P-PUC protocol which allows computations to be completely outsourced to cloud servers. Recently, cloud computing has emerged as cost efficiency and operational flexibility approach for entities to outsource their data and computations for on-demand services. Because the power usage data can be very large in quantity (especially when these data are collected with high frequency), it is beneficial for a utility company to outsource the data and the computations related to P-PUC protocols to a cloud.

As discussed before, the power usage data and the threshold values are sensitive information, so these data should not be disclosed to the cloud. Thus, before outsourcing, the data need to be encrypted, and the cloud only stores and processes the encrypted data. When the data are encrypted with fully homomorphic encryption schemes, the cloud can perform any arbitrary computations over the encrypted data without ever decrypting them. Nevertheless, fully homomorphic encryption schemes have yet to be practical due to their extremely high computational cost. As a result, we adopt a multi-server framework to securely and efficiently implement the proposed protocol.

1.1 Problem Definition

Suppose a neighborhood has n households $P_1, \ldots, P_n$. For $1 \leq i \leq n$, let a_i denote the average power consumption of P_i at a specific time interval and t be a threshold designated by the utility company for the neighborhood. We use a to denote the power usage aggregation of the neighborhood where $a = \sum_{i=1}^{n} a_i$. If $a > t$, each P_i is required to reduce its power consumptions by δ_i to prevent the possibility of power outage in the neighborhood. The value δ_i is determined by the following equation:

$$\delta_i = \frac{a_i}{a} * (a - t) = a_i * \left(1 - \frac{t}{a}\right) \tag{1}$$

Here δ_i is a lower bound on the amount of power usage the user P_i should cut. After each round of power reduction, the total average power usage of the neighborhood will be at a safe level (e.g., $a < t$). This is the common strategy adopted by the existing P-PUC protocols [11].

In our problem setting, the input values $a_1, \ldots, a_n$ and t should be hidden from the cloud servers. That is, before outsourcing, these values need to be either encrypted or secretly shared. In the proposed protocols, we adopt additive secret sharing scheme to hide the original values. The proposed outsourceable privacy-preserving power usage control (OP-PUC) protocol can be formulated as follows:

$$\langle P_1, \delta_1 \rangle, \ldots, \langle P_n, \delta_n \rangle \leftarrow \text{OP-PUC}(\langle P_1, a_1 \rangle, \ldots, \langle P_n, a_n \rangle, S_1, S_2, \langle U, t \rangle) \tag{2}$$

According to the above formulation, there are three types of participating entities: n households, two cloud service providers S_1 and S_2, and a utility company U. The input for each household or customer P_i is its average power consumption a_i within a specific period of time, and the input of U is a threshold t. The two cloud servers perform the necessary computations, and there are no explicit inputs for the two servers. After the execution of the OP-PUC protocol, each P_i receives a value denoted by δ_i, the minimum amount of the energy consumption that needs to be reduced by P_i. The other participating entities do not receive any outputs. (A max-usage based control strategy is discussed in Sect. 3).

Privacy and Security Guarantee. During the execution of the OP-PUC protocol, a_i is private to P_i, and it should not be disclosed to the other households. In addition, a_i should not be known to the two cloud servers and the utility company. Since t is private to the utility company U, t should not be known to the other participating entities.

- a_i is only known to P_i, for $1 \leq i \leq n$, and
- t is only known to U.

Threat Model. In the paper, we adopt the commonly accepted security definition of secure multiparty computation (SMC). More specifically, we assume the participating entities are semi-honest; that is, the entities follow the prescribed procedures of the protocol. Under the semi-honest model, it is implicit that the participating entities do not collude. Another adversary model of SMC is the malicious model. Under the malicious model, the entities can behave arbitrarily. Most efficient SMC-protocols are secure under the semi-honest model since less number of steps are needed to enforce honest behaviors. We have the following motivations to adopt the semi-honest model:

- The OP-PUC protocol needs to be sufficiently efficient. Between the semi-honest model and the malicious model, the semi-honest model always leads to much more efficient protocol.
- Smart meters can be made temper proof, so we can assume the households cannot modify the readings from smart meters and the messages sent from the smart meters to the two cloud servers. Thus, the semi-honest model fits our problem domain well regarding the households.
- The cloud service providers and the utility company are legitimate business. It is hard to see they collude and initiate any malicious act to discover the private smart meter readings. For well-known and reputable cloud servers (e.g., Amazon and Google), it makes sense to assume they follow the protocol and behave semi-honestly.

1.2 Our Contribution

In this paper, we develop an efficient OP-PUC protocol that incurs almost no computations on the households since the computations are completely outsourced to the cloud servers. The proposed protocol is secure under the semi-honest model and satisfies all the security requirements discussed in Sect. 3. Due to the fact that all computations are outsourced to the cloud servers and the computations are only performed on encrypted data, the existing P-PUC protocols cannot be applied to our problem setting. Plus, our proposed protocol is more efficient because it takes advantage of both secret sharing based secure computation and Yao's Garbled Circuit [29].

The proposed protocol consists of three stages: (1) data collection and integration, (2) comparing a and t, and (3) computing the δ_i values. At the first stage, the two cloud servers collect the average power consumption data a_i from each household P_i, and the threshold value t from the utility company. This stage utilizes additive secret sharing which is extremely efficient to securely combine the data together to generate secret shares of the total power consumption a of the neighborhood. The second stage determines the comparison result between a and t. The third stage computes the δ values using the garbled circuit. The key functionality involved in this stage is secure division. The existing secure division protocols are very inefficient, and our work provides a new and more efficient implementation of secure division. Details regarding our proposed protocol is given in Sect. 3.

The rest of the paper is organized as follows: Sect. 2 discusses the work most related to the proposed problem domain. Section 3 provides the detailed implementation of the proposed OP-PUC protocol. Section 4 presents empirical results to show the practicality of OP-PUC. Section 5 summarizes the paper and points out some important future research directions.

2   Related Work and Background

In this section, we provide an overview of the existing work related to our proposed problem including privacy issues related to energy consumption data in a smart grid and the current P-PUC protocols. In addition, we present some background information on secure division and Yao's garbed circuit.

2.1   Privacy Issues in Smart Grids

The use of smart grid infrastructure is growing rapidly; however, there exist potential privacy and security risks during the process of collecting power usage of data [1,13,16]. It is shown in [22] that data collected over a reasonable time interval (e.g., 15 or 30-minute) can be used to identify most household appliances. Another work [21] also shows that power consumption data collected in every 15-minute time interval can be used to uniquely identify home appliances with 90 % accuracy. From these data, various information about a person's daily activities can be inferred such as how many people are home, sleeping schedule, laundry and cooking routines [15,19,24]. If these data are in the wrong hand, the safety of a household will be at a very high risk. Therefore, power consumption data are considered private, and it is necessary to build privacy-preserving protocols to preserve user's privacy in smart grids.

2.2   Privacy-Preserving Protocols in Smart Grids

Most privacy-preserving protocols in smart grids [14,17,23,25,27] are not focusing on the P-PUC problem. To our knowledge, the protocols presented in [11,26] are the only existing work closely related to the proposed problem. The first two P-PUC protocols are proposed in [11] built based on two strategies. The protocols leak the total energy consumption to one of the households, and the maximum

Table 1. Common notations

SMC	Secure Multi-Party Computation
P-PUC	Threshold-Based Power Usage Control
OP-PUC	Outsourceable P-PUC
a_i	Power consumption of user P_i within specific period
a_i' and a_i''	Secret shares of a_i between two parties
t	Threshold value provided by a utility company
t' and t''	Secret shares of t between two parties
S_1 and S_2	Two independent cloud servers
U	The utility company
P_i	One user in a neighborhood, $i = 1,\ldots,n$

energy consumption among the households is also revealed. In addition, they utilize a secure division protocol among several proposed protocols in [2]. Its secret sharing based secure division protocol requires at least three parties, and it is not applicable in our problem setting where we assume two independent cloud servers perform all necessary secure computations. Although there is an efficient two-party secure division protocol [2], one party needs to perform division operations between randomized values to obtain the final division result. However, the division result is known to the party which is not allowed in our problem domain. Also, we are not certain how to modify it to hide the final division result securely and efficiently.

In [26], another P-PUC protocol is developed to address the security issues of the earlier P-PUC protocols. However, the protocol is still not very efficient in that the individual households and the utility company involve in heavy computations. More importantly, all the exiting P-PUC protocols are not applicable in our problem domain where the computations are completely outsourced to the cloud which results in a more practical P-PUC protocol from the perspectives of individual households and utility companies.

2.3   Secure Division and Yao's Garbled Circuit

In [11], the authors utilize a secure division protocol based on homomorphic encryption, but the protocol is not secure and efficient. Although the secure division protocol in [26] is secure, the protocol is efficient for very small domains. Also, one of the inputs of this secure division protocol is not encrypted. In our case, all input values are encrypted. To implement an efficient secure division protocol under the proposed problem domain. We adopt the garbled circuit approach introduced by Yao [29]. Recently, an intermediate language for describing and executing garbled circuits - the GCParser [18] has been proposed. This framework can implement any optimizations at both the high level and the low level, and it has already been applied to optimizing free XOR-gates and pipelin-

---

Algorithm 1. Secure_Split(α) $\rightarrow$ (α', α'')

Require: P has α and N where $\alpha < N$
1: P:

    (a) $\alpha' \leftarrow \alpha + r \bmod N$, where $r \in_R \mathbb{Z}_N$
    (b) $\alpha'' \leftarrow N - r$
    (c) Send α' to S_1 and send α'' to S_2

2: S_1 and S_2:

    (a) Receive α' and α'' respectively

---

ing circuit generation and execution. We adopt this framework to build a garbled circuit for secure division.

3 The Proposed OP-PUC Protocol

In this section, we adopt the same notations from the previous sections summarized in Table 1. The same as the existing work, the proposed OP-PUC protocol adopts the following two power usage control strategies when $a > t$: (1) reducing the power usage for the user who used the maximum amount of energy among all users, and (2) providing the specific power reduction amount each individual users in a particular neighborhood.

3.1 The First Stage of OP-PUC

In our problem settings, the cloud servers first need to gather the needed data from power customers and the utility company, then compare the total power consumption of those customers a with the threshold given by utility company t. If $a > t$, users need to reduce their power usage for the next period. The first stage of OP-PUC is data collection.

During the first stage, we emphasize that data must be hidden before outsourced. In the previous P-PUC protocols, homomorphic encryptions are utilized to encrypt the power usage data. However, if we extend the homomorphic encryption approach in this outsourced environment, huge computations would be incurred on the cloud servers. Therefore, to have a more efficient protocol, we adopt secret sharing approach for the data collection stage.

To get shared inputs, we use the Secure_Split protocol presented in Algorithm 1 where we assume N is a large number. In this protocol, P split its input value α to two random values α' and α'' so that $\alpha' + \alpha'' = \alpha \bmod N$, and send them to S_1 and S_2 respectively. At the end, S_1 holds α', and S_2 holds α''. They do not know anything about α except for N.

Algorithm 2 gives the main steps for the data collection stage of OP-PUC. For each user P_i, the power consumption value a_i is split into a'_i and a''_i and sent to servers S_1 and S_2 by using Secure_Split. At the same time, the utility company

Algorithm 2. Data_Collection$\rightarrow \{(a_1', a_1''), \ldots, (a_n', a_n''), (a', a''), (t', t'')\}$

Require: P_i has a_i where $1 \leq i \leq n$, U has t, and N is publicly known
  1: P_i: Secure_Split(a_i)
  2: U: Secure_Split(t)
  3: S_1: $a' = \sum_{i=1}^{n} a_i'$
  4: S_2: $a'' = \sum_{i=1}^{n} a_i''$

U also uses Secure_Split to send the secret shares of t to the two cloud servers. At the end, S_1 and S_2 compute $a' = \sum_{i=1}^{n} a_i'$ and $a'' = \sum_{i=1}^{n} a_i''$ separately. It is easy to see $a = a' + a'' \mod N$ is the total power usage at a specific period. Since each server has one secret share of each value, they do not know anything about the original values.

3.2 The Second Stage of OP-PUC

The main task for the second stage of the proposed protocol is to securely determine whether $a > t$ or not; thus, we need a secure comparison protocol to compare a and t with secret shares of each value as inputs. We consider to use garbled circuit to securely perform the comparison task because the existing secure comparison protocols [3,6,7,9,20] are not directly applicable in our problem domain. These protocols require that the inputs need to be the actual values. In addition, garbled circuit is known for its efficiency to securely evaluate simple functionalities such as secure comparison. A garbled circuit has only one round of communication. Details about constructing and evaluating a garbled circuit are given in [12]. In this paper, we assume that the secure comparison protocol built by a garbled circuit is denoted by Secure_Comparison$(a', a'', t', t'') \rightarrow b$. The protocol is performed by S_1 and S_2, where a' and t' are the inputs of S_1, and a'' and t'' are the inputs of S_2. The protocol returns a bit b to the servers. If $b = 1$, the total power usage exceeds the threshold, and the OP-PUC protocol will proceed to the next stage.

3.3 The Third Stage of OP-PUC Based on Strategy 1

For strategy 1, the user with the most power consumption is selected and ordered to reduce his power usage. During the process, the cloud servers are not allowed to know which user is chosen. Basically, in this stage, a Secure_Maximum protocol is used to securely pick out the maximum value among n shared values. We utilize garbled circuit approach to implement Secure_Maximum. The key steps can be found in [11]. At the end, the maximum value will be known to each user. The user had the maximum energy consumption will reduce its power consumption. As stated in the existing work, how much energy consumption needs to be reduced is hard to decide. Thus, the second strategy is more practical.

Algorithm 3. Division$(t, a) \rightarrow q$

Require: Bit representation of t is $t_0, \ldots, t_{l-1}$ and bit representation of a is $a_0, \ldots, a_{m-1}$ from the least to the most significant bits. Expand dividend t with m bits and set $t_i = 0$ where $l \leq i < l + m$ and expand another bit $t_{l+m} = 0$ as sign bit of dividend.

1: **for** $1 \leq i \leq m$:

    (a) Shift left t for 1 bit

    (b) **if** $t_{l+m} = 0$ subtract $\overline{t_{l+m-1} \ldots t_l}$ with a

    (c) **else** add $\overline{t_{l+m-1} \ldots t_l}$ with a

2: $q \leftarrow \overline{t_{l-1} \ldots t_0}$

3.4 The Third Stage of OP-PUC Based on Strategy 2

When the total energy consumption exceeds the threshold t, each user needs to reduce his or her power usage. How to decide a reasonable power reduction for everybody is really important. Here we adopt the function from the prior work which has been shown in Eq. 1. By using this equation, every user P_i will reduce at least δ_i power which is decided by a_i weighted in a. Since party P_i has his or her power consumption value a_i the, $\frac{t}{a}$ needs to be calculated at the servers.

To securely compute $\frac{t}{a}$, two secure division protocols using additive homomorphic encryption schemes were introduced in [4,26]. However, we believe that a garbled circuit approach should be more efficient. The reason is that in the outsourced environment, inputs to the secure protocols are hidden from the cloud servers. Thus, it is not easy to extend the prior solutions to fit our problem domain. In particular, when both t and a are hidden, to compute division between two encrypted values under homomorphic encryption is very expensive. Whereas in the garbled circuit approach, we can directly use the secret shares of t and a as inputs to the circuits.

We build the division circuit based on the "shift and subtract" non-restoring method. Algorithm 3 gives a detail of this method. In general, if we want to calculate the quotient of l-bit number t and m-bit number a, first we need to expand t with $m + 1$ bits and perform an iterative algorithm. In each loop, t makes a left shift and subtract or add a from the lth bit to the $(l + m - 1)^{th}$ bit based on the value of t_{l+m}: if $t_{l+m} = 0$ then subtraction, otherwise addition. After m rounds, the latest t_0 to t_{l-1} store the quotient q.

Here we provide an example of how this method works. If we want to calculate the quotient of 11 (e.g., 1011 in binary format) divided by 3 (i.e., 0011 in binary format), first we expand 1011 to 000001011 and shift left of this number. Then we get $00001011x_1$, using the left most $l + m - 1 = 5$ bits to subtract 0011, we have $11110011x_1$. Now the first bit is 1, so we set $x_1 = 0$ and shift left again. We then use the most 5 bits of $11100110x_2$ to add 0011 since $x_1 = 0$. We get $11111110x_2$, and set $x_2 = 0$. Shift and add again for $x_2 = 0$, this round we get $00010100x_3$, $x_3 = 1$ because the most significant is 0. For next and last round

---

Algorithm 4. OP-PUC-Stage-3$(a_i, t', t'', a', a'') \rightarrow \delta_i$

Require: S_1 has a' and t', S_2 has a'' and t'', P_i has a_i for $1 \leq i \leq n$, N is public
1: S_1 and S_2:

  (a) **do** Secure_Division$(t', t'', a', a'') \rightarrow (q', q'')$
  (b) Send q' and q'' to every power users

2: P_i:

  (a) Calculate $\delta_i = a_i * (1 - \frac{t}{a})$ and reduce at least δ_i power usages

---

we need to shift and subtract, finally we get result of $00010001x_4$, $x_4 = 1$. Thus the quotient of this example is 3 (i.e., 0011 in binary format).

Our garbled division circuit follows the basic rules of "shift and subtract" non-restoring method, and it is denoted by Secure_Division$(t', t'', a', a'') \rightarrow (q', q'')$. The inputs of the circuit are secret shares of t and a from S_1 and S_2. The outputs are secret shares of q so that S_1 and S_2 cannot infer anything about a and t. At the end, every power user will get $q = q' + q''$ mod N so as to compute δ_i by Eq. 1. Algorithm 4 summarizes the main steps of the third stage of the OP-PUC protocol.

3.5   Complexity Analysis

In this section we analyze both computation and communication complexities of proposed OP-PUC protocol. First, we analyze the computation complexity for different sub-protocols at each stage. At the first stage, each user P_i and P perform the Secure_Split protocol, which just has two addition operations. Servers S_1 and S_2 perform summations of n values, so the computation complexity of the first stage is bounded by O(n) summations.

For the second stage, we need to consider the secure comparison protocol. For the garbled circuit approach, the inputs are two random shares with size bounded by N, so O$(\log N)$ gates are needed in the initial phase of the garbled circuit to add the shares. This step will result in much smaller values than N, so the total number of gates for the comparison circuit is bounded by O$(\log N)$.

Protocols under two strategies become different at the third stage. For strategy 1, the maximum value among the n values needs to be found. This is achieved by a number of secure comparison circuits. Thus, there are at least O$(n \log N)$ gates in the initial stage. Since the numbers involved are much less than N, the total number of gates is bounded by O$(n \log N)$. Each gate of the garbled circuit is encrypted by AES encryption. Therefore, the computation complexity of stage 2 and stage 3 under strategy 1 is bounded by O$(n \log N)$ AES encryptions. The total computation complexity of OP-PUC under strategy 1 is bounded by O(n) summations plus O$(n \log N)$ AES encryptions.

Under strategy 2 of stage 3, the secure division circuit needs to be built and evaluated. As before, the computation complexity of initial stage is also bound by $O(\log N)$. Since the bit lengths of dividend and divisor are much less than N, the computation complexity of the division circuit is also bound by $O(\log N)$. Each gate of the garbled circuit is encrypted by AES encryption. Therefore, the computation complexity of stage 2 and stage 3 is bounded by $O(\log N)$ AES encryptions. The total computation complexity of OP-PUC under strategy 2 is bounded by $O(n)$ summations plus $O(\log N)$ AES encryptions.

To analyze the communication complexity, we need to know the size of the secret shares. Since the value of each share is bounded by N, we need $\log N$ bits to represent each share. Thus, at the first stage, the total communication complexity is bounded by $O(n \cdot \log N)$ bits. Because the AES key size is a constant value varying from 128 to 256, the communication complexity for both stage 2 and stage 3 is bounded by $O(\log N)$ bits and $O(n \cdot \log N)$ bits under strategy 1 and strategy 2 respectively. Therefore, regardless the strategies, the total communication complexity of OP-PUC is bounded by $O(n \cdot \log N)$ bits.

3.6 Security Analysis

The security proof of the proposed protocols is straightforward. Here we only provide a high level discussion. In the second stage and third stage, comparison and division garbled circuit are used which is proved secure under the semi-honest model [12]. Since all the intermediate outputs of these protocols are random shares, Based on the sequential Composition Theorem [10], the OP-PUC protocols are also secure under the semi-honest model.

4 Experimental Results

In this section, we discuss the performance of the OP-PUC protocols in details under different parameter settings. Then, we evaluate the computation costs of the existing methods [11] and compare them with our proposed protocols.

In the OP-PUC protocols, each P_i and U only interact with the cloud servers for one round: sending their inputs and receiving the final outputs. Between the two cloud servers S_1 and S_2, a garbled circuit can be evaluated in about two rounds of communication. Therefore, regardless of different strategies and stages, the total number of interactions between the two cloud servers are constant or just several rounds.

Since the communication complexity of the proposed protocol is very small, and the communications between the individual users and the cloud servers at the first stage are parallelizable. Here we ignore the communication complexity. We simulate the computation complexity on a Linux machine with an Intel® Xeon® Six-Core™ CPU 3.07 GHz processor and 12GB RAM running Ubuntu 12.04 LTS. Since the main part of the protocol is based on the garbled circuits method, we implement the protocol on top of FastGC [12], a Java-based framework that allows users to define Boolean circuits. After the circuits are constructed, the framework encrypts the circuits, performs oblivious transfer, and evaluates the garbled/encrypted circuits. We also fix the size of inputs for

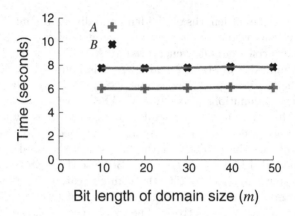

Fig. 1. Complexity of OP_PUC for $n = 50$

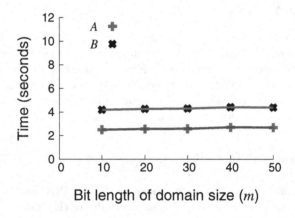

Fig. 2. Complexity of OP_PUC^2 for $n = 50$

cloud servers to a 1024-bit modulus. In our experiments, we randomly generate the values of a_i's and t such that $a > t$ and $1 \leq a, t \leq 2^m$, where m is an upper bound bit length of the domain size.

4.1 Performance of OP_PUC and OP_PUC^2

Let OP_PUC^2 denote the proposed protocol based on the second strategy. We first compute the computation costs of different parties involved in the OP_PUC protocol for $n = 50$ and varying m. That is, the running time of cloud servers A and B (or S_1 and S_2) is analyzed for one iteration (the same as the existing work). We do not consider the costs of individual users and the power company, since almost all the computations are outsourced to the cloud servers. As shown in Fig. 1, the computation costs of A and B are 6.043 and 7.767 s respectively for $m = 10$. Although the computation times of A and B are increasing with m, the portion of increasing is very small in comparison with the expansion of the domain size. For example, even when $m = 50$, the computation costs of A and B are 6.123 and 7.854 s respectively, and they are pretty close to what they were when $m = 10$. This is due to the inner structure of maximum circuit: with the domain size expanding, many new *xor* gates are plotted which are free for evaluation, whereas the number of costly *and* gates does not increase significantly.

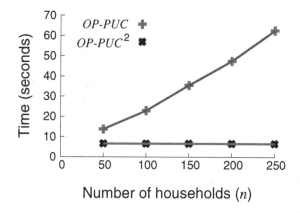

Fig. 3. Complexity: OP_PUC Vs. OP_PUC^2

In a similar manner, the computation costs of A and B in the OP_PUC^2 protocol is analyzed for varying m and with $n = 50$ and $\theta = 10$, where θ is the bit length of a scalar factor. Note that the output of the division circuit is an integer, and a and t might be very close, so we need a scalar factor to come up with more accurate quotient. Therefore, the inputs of the division circuit are one $m + \theta$-bit dividend and one m-bit divisor. The computation costs of different parties in OP_PUC^2 are shown in Fig. 2. The same as OP_PUC, the computation costs of individual users and the power company are negligible and not counted. On the other hand, for $m = 10$, the computation costs of A and B are 2.497 and 4.195 s respectively. Similarly, the costs of A and B grow slightly with the increasing of m. For instance, the computation time of A is 2.688 s when $m = 50$, and it is only increased by 0.191 second with a 40-bit size expansion.

We now compare the total computation costs of cloud providers A and B in OP_PUC (for one iteration) and OP_PUC^2 for $m = 10$ and varying n, where n denotes the number of households from a given neighborhood. As shown in Fig. 3, the total running time of OP_PUC varies from 13.81 to 62.635 s when n is changed from 50 to 250. On the other hand, the total running time of OP_PUC^2 remains to be nearly constant at 6.692 s in average since t is independent of n. Following from Fig. 3, it is clear that the total run time of OP_PUC (even for one iteration) is always greater than that of OP_PUC^2. According to the above analyses, we conclude that the proposed protocols are very practical especially for OP_PUC^2. Besides, there is nearly no computation costs for the individual users and the utility company.

4.2 Performance Comparison with the Existing Work

Finally, we compare the computation costs of our protocols with the existing work [11]. For $n = 50$ and $m = 10$ (note that when $m = 10$, the domain size is $2^{10} = 1024$ already slightly bigger than $l = 1000$ in previous paper), the performance of OP_PUC is close to the STPUC$_{max}$, which is roughly 13–15 s. We notice that the running time of OP_PUC increases quickly when number of households increases. However, according to the domain size, OP_PUC is more scalable: the running time is nearly stable e.g., even when domain size is increased by a factor of 10^4 with the size of the neighborhood fixed to 50, the running time of OP_PUC just increases less than 1 second. Note that in STPUC$_{max}$, execution time is significantly increased with the increase of the domain size. Experiments showed that when domain size changes from 1024 to 4096, and fix the number of neighborhood to 50 users, the running time of STPUC$_{max}$ increases from 11.02 s to 33.75 s. Also OP_PUC^2 is more efficient and scalable than STPUC$_{div}$. For example, when the domain size is 5000, OP_PUC^2 is faster than STPUC$_{div}$ by a factor of 3 to 4. Besides, although the problem definition of our work is different from the existing work, our protocols achieve the same power usage control in a more efficient way.

5   Conclusion

In this paper, we developed outsourceable, privacy-preserving power usage control (OP-PUC) protocols. Comparing to the existing work, the proposed protocols are more efficient and as secure. More importantly, the computation costs for the users and the utility company are negligible. As a future research direction, we will develop OP-PUC protocols secure under the malicious model and utilize more than two cloud servers to further improve the computation costs.

If there are at least three cloud servers, all secure computations can be performed on secure shares. Secret sharing based secure computations can be more efficient than the garbled circuit. we will investigate if the efficiency of the OP-PUC protocols can be improved under the secret sharing model. To develop OP-PUC protocols secure under the malicious model, we may adopt threshold homomorphic encryption [5] or Shamir secret sharing [28]. We will investigate the pros and cons under each direction.

Acknowledgments. The authors would like to thank the anonymous reviewers for their insightful comments and suggestions. In addition, the first and third authors' contribution to this work was supported by NSF under award No. CNS-1011984.

References

1. Guidelines for smart grid cyber security the smart grid interoper-ability panel cyber security working group. In: NISTIR 7628, August 2010
2. Atallah, M., Bykova, M., Li, J., Frikken, K., Topkara, M.: Private collaborative forecasting and benchmarking. In: Proceedings of the 2004 ACM Workshop on Privacy in the Electronic Society, pp. 103–114. ACM (2004)
3. Blake, I.F., Kolesnikov, V.: One-round secure comparison of integers. J. Math. Cryptolol. **3**(1), 37–68 (2009)
4. Bunn, P., Ostrovsky, R.: Secure two-party k-means clustering. In: Proceedings of the 14th ACM Conference on Computer and Communications Security, pp. 486–497. ACM (2007)
5. Cramer, R., Damgård, I.B., Nielsen, J.B.: Multiparty computation from threshold homomorphic encryption. In: Pfitzmann, B. (ed.) EUROCRYPT 2001. LNCS, vol. 2045, pp. 280–299. Springer, Heidelberg (2001)
6. Damgård, I.B., Geisler, M., Krøigaard, M.: Efficient and secure comparison for on-line auctions. In: Pieprzyk, J., Ghodosi, H., Dawson, E. (eds.) ACISP 2007. LNCS, vol. 4586, pp. 416–430. Springer, Heidelberg (2007)
7. Damgard, I., Geisler, M., Kroigard, M.: Homomorphic encryption and secure comparison. Int. J. Appl. Crypt. **1**(1), 22–31 (2008)
8. Drenker, S., Kader, A.: Nonintrusive monitoring of electric loads. IEEE Comput. Appl. Power **12**(4), 47–51 (1999)
9. Garay, J.A., Schoenmakers, B., Villegas, J.: Practical and secure solutions for integer comparison. In: Okamoto, T., Wang, X. (eds.) PKC 2007. LNCS, vol. 4450, pp. 330–342. Springer, Heidelberg (2007)
10. Goldreich, O.: Foundations of Cryptography: Volume 2, Basic Applications., vol. 2. Cambridge University Press, New York (2009)
11. Chun, H., Jiang, W., McMillin, B.: Privacy-preserving power usage control in the smart grid. In: Butts, J., Shenoi, S. (eds.) Critical Infrastructure Protection VI. IFIP Advances in Information and Communication Technology, vol. 390, pp. 127–137. Springer, Berlin Heidelberg (2012)
12. Huang, Y., Evans, D., Katz, J., Malka, L.: Faster secure two-party computation using garbled circuits. In: USENIX Security Symposium, vol. 201 (2011)
13. Jokar, N., Arianpoo, P., Leung, V.: A survey on security issues in smart grids. Secur. Comm. Netw. **7**(4), 414–424 (2012). doi:10.1002/sec.559.V.C.M
14. Kursawe, K., Danezis, G., Kohlweiss, M.: Privacy-friendly aggregation for the smart-grid. In: Fischer-Hübner, S., Hopper, N. (eds.) PETS 2011. LNCS, vol. 6794, pp. 175–191. Springer, Heidelberg (2011)
15. Lisovich, M.A., Mulligan, D.K., Wicker, S.B.: Inferring personal information from demand-response systems. IEEE Secur. Privacy **8**(1), 11–20 (2010)
16. Liu, J., Xiao, Y., Li, S., Liang, W., Chen, C.L.P.: Cyber security and privacy issues in smart grids. IEEE Commun. Surv. Tutorials **14**(4), 981–997 (2012)
17. Rongxing, L., Xiaohui Liang, X., Li, X.L., Shen, X.: Eppa: an efficient and privacy-preserving aggregation scheme for secure smart grid communications. IEEE Trans. Parallel Distrib. Syst. **23**(9), 1621–1631 (2012)
18. Melicher, W., Zahur, S., Evans, D.: An intermediate language for garbled circuits. In: IEEE Symposium on Security and Privacy Poster Abstract (2012)
19. Molina-Markham, A., Shenoy, P., Fu, K., Cecchet, E., Irwin, D.: Private memoirs of a smart meter. In: Proceedings of the 2nd ACM Workshop on Embedded Sensing Systems for Energy-Efficiency in Building, pp. 61–66. ACM (2010)

20. Nergiz, A.E., Nergiz, M.E., Pedersen, T., Clifton, C.: Practical and secure integer comparison and interval check. In: 2010 IEEE Second International Conference on Social Computing (SocialCom), pp. 791–799. IEEE (2010)
21. Quinn, E.L.: Privacy and the new energy infrastructure. SSRN E. J. (2009). http://dx.doi.org/10.2139/ssrn.1370731
22. Quinn, E.L.: Smart metering and privacy: existing laws and competing policies. SSRN eLibrary (2009). http://dx.doi.org/10.2139/ssrn.1462285
23. Rial, A., Danezis, G.: Privacy-preserving smart metering. In: Proceedings of the 10th annual ACM Workshop on Privacy in the Electronic Society, pp. 49–60. ACM (2011)
24. Rouf, I., Mustafa, H., Xu, M., Xu, W., Miller, R., Gruteser, M.: Neighborhood watch: security and privacy analysis of automatic meter reading systems. In: Proceedings of the 2012 ACM Conference on Computer and Communications Security, pp. 462–473. ACM (2012)
25. Salinas, S., Li, M., Li, P.: Privacy-preserving energy theft detection in smart grids. In: 2012 9th Annual IEEE Communications Society Conference on Sensor, Mesh and Ad Hoc Communications and Networks (SECON), pp. 605–613. IEEE (2012)
26. Samanthula, B.K., Chun, H., Jiang, W., McMillin, B.M.: Secure and threshold-based power usage control in smart grid environments. Int. J. Parallel, Emergent Distrib. Syst. 29(3), 264–289 (2014)
27. Saputro, N., Akkaya, K.: Performance evaluation of smart grid data aggregation via homomorphic encryption. In: 2012 IEEE Wireless Communications and Networking Conference (WCNC), pp. 2945–2950. IEEE (2012)
28. Shamir, A.: How to share a secret. Commun. ACM 22(11), 612–613 (1979)
29. Yao, A.C.-C.: How to generate and exchange secrets. In: 1986 27th Annual Symposium on Foundations of Computer Science, pp. 162–167. IEEE (1986)

Privacy-Preserving Public Transport Ticketing System

Milica Milutinovic[1]([✉]), Koen Decroix[2], Vincent Naessens[2],
and Bart De Decker[1]

[1] Department of Computer Science, iMinds/DistriNet,
KU Leuven, Leuven, Belgium
{milica.milutinovic,bart.dedecker}@cs.kuleuven.be
[2] TC Ghent, Department of Computer Science, MSec, iMinds/DistriNet,
KU Leuven, Ghent, Belgium
{koen.decroix,vincent.naessens}@cs.kuleuven.be

Abstract. The public transport ticketing systems are undergoing significant changes in recent years. The tickets can now be issued and presented in digital form, significantly improving the user experience. The digital data is also used to improve the services' efficiency. Travelling patterns and route occupancy can be analysed to adjust the frequency and coverage of the service. However, data recorded by the providers extends the information that is needed for simple analysis. The travel passes that are issued usually contain unique identifiers, allowing to trace the movement of users, which can even be linked to their identities. In order to tackle these privacy issues, we propose a novel, privacy-preserving ticketing system, based on a scheme for issuing and redemption of unlinkable certified tokens. The design also allows offering advanced services, such as reduction plans or monthly passes, without introducing privacy concerns. Even though the travellers' actions cannot be linked, the service providers are given assurances against possible misuse, and are able to control the usage of the issued products. Additionally, experimental evaluation shows that the system performance is adequate for practical applications.

1 Introduction

The public transport systems have a four centuries long history and have undergone a considerable evolution. However, the corresponding ticketing systems have only recently started to experience significant changes. The early systems were based on paper tickets, usually bought on site. With the technological advances, the travellers are now able to verify the seats availability, reserve or purchase a ticket online and present it in a digital form on their smartphone or tablet. Digital handling of travellers' data also allows the transportation providers to better inspect the travelling patterns and accordingly adjust the provided services. Examples are the organisation of transportation during rush hours or to less frequented areas. This improves the transportation network's efficiency and lowers the cost for the customers.

© IFIP International Federation for Information Processing 2015
P. Samarati (Ed.): DBSec 2015, LNCS 9149, pp. 135–150, 2015.
DOI: 10.1007/978-3-319-20810-7_9

However, the way these novel ticketing systems are deployed in practice is creating significant privacy concerns. Namely, the issued travelling passes usually contain unique identifiers, which are in most systems linked to the identities of their holders. This allows to make behaviour profiles, which is detrimental to the travellers' privacy. Even when the user identity is not given, powerful data mining techniques can be utilised to determine who is the holder of a pass. The users have little or no control over their data in such systems. Moreover, with some implementations, not only can the provider see the behaviour or identity of the traveller, but an external party can mount a successful attack and obtain this data as well. A notable example of a successful attack on a public transport ticketing system's technology is the attack on the MIFARE Classic card [8].

Contributions. In order to tackle the aforementioned privacy concerns, we have devised a privacy-preserving ticketing system (PPTS). It is based on a scheme for unlinkable certified tokens and utilises cryptographic primitives, such as commitment schemes [16], partially blind signatures [1] and anonymous credentials [6] and is designed for smartphone technology. The resulting system allows the travellers to manage their personal data and purchased travel products, issued in the form of digital tokens. The products are linked to the purchasing traveller and cannot be transferred to another entity without the approval of the provider. The provider is able to control the products' spending and verify the validity of the traveller's registration, but cannot obtain the identity of the traveller or link together different interactions performed with the same traveller. Finally, efficiency improvements of the offered services are still possible, as the service provider can see the routes' occupancy and usage of specific products.

This paper is organised as follows: Sect. 2 describes the existing systems, their architecture and the attacker model. Section 3 details the proposed scheme and the underlying protocols with Sect. 4 evaluating protocols' security, privacy and efficiency and presenting possible design extensions. Finally, Sect. 5 discusses the related work and concluding remarks are given in Sect. 6.

2   Public Transport Ticketing Systems

The novel commercial ticketing systems are usually based on a *Personal Transport Pass*. It represents a pass linked to a particular traveller, which cannot be utilised by other individuals. In order to achieve this property, the pass records personal identifiable information in addition to the transport products it stores. Some of the personal data is printed on the cover of the pass and some is stored in its embedded microchip. The chip can only be accessed by the ticketing system equipment. It can store the unique chip number, ePurse balance (which is reduced with every trip the traveller takes), travel transactions history (such as validations of entering or leaving a vehicle) and personal transport products (such as a monthly discount plan). The cover usually contains the traveller's name, passport picture, date of birth and gender. This personal identifiable information is visible to everyone with visual access to the card. It is also used by the inspectors who verify whether the pass belongs to the traveller.

When a pass is issued, the user provides the recorded personal details. With online pass ordering, some of the personal data is not verified. However, as the pass is delivered to the given address, the provider is assured about the validity of this attribute. When the traveller utilises the issued pass, a random inspection may request to check its validity. The picture and possibly other information can then be verified and the pass can be revoked in case of irregularities.

For privacy-aware users, *Anonymous Transport Passes* can be offered as well. In contrast to the personalised version, the anonymous pass can be shared with other travellers, as it contains no personal data. However, as a consequence, no personal transport products can be loaded on the pass and the range of provided services is limited. Even though such card is anonymous, it can still record the *travel transactions history*. This can lead to traveller profiling and raises serious privacy concerns as it allows to track movements and even link them to the identity of the traveller by using powerful data mining techniques.

2.1 System Architecture

The ticketing service is offered through collaboration of multiple stakeholders. They usually comprise the *ticketing system operator* (TSO), who issues travellers' passes and handles the related interactions, and the *public transport organisers* (PTO), who organize the actual public transport. One TSO usually collaborates with multiple PTO entities. It manages the personal information obtained in the registration procedures and the identifiers recorded in the passes. The PTO is able to record the trips taken and the disclosed data, such as the unique pass identifier [5,20]. The existing systems collect this travel data in order to optimize the provided services. However, recording unique identifiers, such as smart card serial numbers, is a major privacy concern. It allows for creating profiles and possibly linking them with registration information, including traveller's personal identifiable information. Some solutions for mitigating privacy concerns [17] rely on corporate level policies that separate travel transactions from user data and restrict access to only one of the databases. However, the privacy depends on the discipline inside the organization and may be prone to internal or external attacks which could link identifiable data to travel patterns.

2.2 Attacker Model

A public transport ticketing system needs to be resilient to the following attacks:

- Attacks on user privacy mounted by TSO and PTO entities. They can try to link the user activities, such as purchasing and utilising the travel products, and possibly even link them to the user identities.
- Attacks on user privacy by external entities. External parties may try reading the travel passes or intercepting the ongoing interaction with the provider.
- Inappropriate charging of users for the provided services.
- Unauthorised usage of the transport services. These attacks are carried out by travellers who try to make use of the service without obtaining the required

authorisations. This can refer to unregistered entities using the transport services or registered travellers who utilise spent or expired tickets, tickets of other travellers or simply have an insufficient ePurse balance or do not possess the right travel product.

2.3   Cryptographic Building Blocks

This section provides an overview of the cryptographic building blocks used in the proposed protocols.

Commitment schemes allow an entity to commit to a set of values while keeping them secret. They can be compared to sealed, non-transparent envelopes. When a commitment is disclosed, the user cannot change the values she committed to, without this being detectable by the verifier. The commitment hides the chosen values, while allowing to prove certain properties about them. For committing to a value, we assume usage of the Pedersen commitment scheme [16]. Thus, for a group G of prime order q and generators g_1 and $g_2 \in G$, the user commits to a message m, by choosing a random value r and computing the commitment:

$$C = g_1^m \times g_2^r.$$

Partially blind signature schemes allow to sign a data structure, parts of which are not disclosed to the signer. They are an extension of the blind signatures concept, where the contents of the signed message are hidden from the signer [7]. In the partially blind signature scheme (PBS), the signer (S) and the receiver (R) agree on some *public* information, that is also included in the signature [1]:

$$pbsig \leftarrow \{PBsign(SK_S; hidden_R; public)\}.$$

Zero-knowledge proofs of knowledge (ZKPK) allow one party to prove that she knows certain values or secrets [3]. Namely, a prover can convince a verifier that a certain statement is true, without revealing any additional information. In the proposed protocols, we utilise a non-interactive signature proof of knowledge, which additionally allows the prover to sign a message when creating the proof of knowledge [6]. For a public value y and a private value x, such that $y = g^x$, and for a message m, we denote the signed proof of knowledge of x with:

$$SPK\{(x) : y = g^x\}(m).$$

Anonymous credentials allow for authentication of users in a privacy-protecting manner [4,6]. This credential technology offers selective disclosure of attributes, i.e. disclosing only a part of the recorded attributes, while hiding the others. Additionally, it is possible to only prove properties of the embedded attributes, without disclosing the actual values. For instance, it is possible to prove that the holder of the credential is older than 18, without revealing the birthdate embedded in the credential. Possession of a valid credential and properties of the recorded attributes are proven with ZKPK. They additionally allow to prove equality of a value hidden in a commitment to a value contained in the credential. In the remainder of the text, we will assume the usage of Idemix credentials [6], as they allow unlinkable use of the same credential.

3   Privacy-Preserving Ticketing System

Similarly to existing systems, the proposed scheme consists of interactions between a traveller, a ticketing system operator (TSO) and a public transport organiser (PTO). Before participating in the PPTS system, every traveller needs to install a smartphone application, which interfaces with the ticketing system. All travellers are also issued with credentials which serve as personal passes. Before utilising the public transport services, a traveller makes a purchase of the desired products, such as single tickets or monthly passes. Even though the products are linked to the traveller's credential in order to prevent unauthorised sharing, no identifying data is disclosed at the time of purchase. In order to use the transport services, a traveller's application contacts the TSO to be issued with a single-use ticket for the desired ride. For this, the application spends or proves possession of a previously purchased product and demonstrates that it is linked to the credential the traveller owns. The acquired temporary ticket is validated by the PTO's validation machine on the vehicle. At the end of the journey, the traveller's phone interacts with the validation machine once more to be issued with change in case the spent product is not fully used. The obtained change proof can then be exchanged with TSO for a long-term token. Although there are multiple interactions with TSO/PTO, they are mostly transparent to the traveller, as she only initiates the ticket issuance and travel start/end, while all the other operations are automatically performed by the application.

3.1   Traveller Credential Issuance

After installing the PPTS application, a traveller interacts with the online ticketing application, to be issued with an anonymous credential which serves as a personalised pass and is denoted as the PPTS credential. Credential attributes include the traveller's personal information (such as the name and date of birth), the validity information and a secret number - the traveller's *ticketing system secret* (tss), which is different from the credential's master secret and is not disclosed to the TSO[1]. The personal information is provided by the traveller, as in the online registrations in the existing systems. In case additional assurances are needed, the traveller's eID card can be used for proving this data. In systems where the smart cards are delivered to the traveller's home address, there is additional confirmation of the provided address information. This can be offered with the PPTS, by sending a code via post, which is used upon reception to complete the registration and credential issuance. On the whole, this approach improves the efficiency, while providing the same guarantees as the currently issued passes in (Sect. 2). Idemix credential technology [6] allows for all subsequent interactions with the TSO to remain unlinkable to the credential issuance. Additionally, for a better privacy-protection we assume that the network layer meta data does not allow linking activities of the same user.

---

[1] The user sends a commitment to a random number to the TSO, which applies a random offset to it before including it in the credential, resulting in the *tss* attribute.

3.2   ePurse Balance Recharge

In order to recharge the ePurse balance, the traveller makes a request and pays the desired amount to the TSO. In return, the TSO issues a number of signed tokens to the traveller. The tokens represent a partially blind signature on a public part, i.e. the information on the token value, and a private part, which is not disclosed to the TSO. The public information in a token represents its denomination and possibly constraints that apply (such as a validity period). The hidden part of the signed data in a token is a commitment to the secret value in the traveller's PPTS credential (tss). It serves as a link to the traveller's credential and prevents transferring tokens to other travellers.

Protocol 1. ePurse recharge.

ePurseRecharge($amount$)

(1) $T_{app} \rightarrow TSO$: request($amount$)
(2) $T_{app} \leftarrow TSO$: $c \in_{\mathcal{R}} \mathbb{Z}_q$
(3) $T_{app} \rightarrow TSO$: $\pi \leftarrow SPK\{(MS) : Cred.validity\}(c)$
(4) TSO : if (!verify(π)) abort
(5) $T_{app} \leftrightarrow TSO$: pay$_{bank}$($invoice : \{reference, amount, account_{TSO}\}$)
(6) $T_{app} \leftarrow TSO$: $\{info : D_g\}_{i \in \{1...n\}} \leftarrow$ generate($amount$)
(7) T_{app} : $\{r\}_{i \in \{1...n\}} \leftarrow$ generate()
(8) T_{app} : $\{C\}_{i \in \{1...n\}} \leftarrow$ commit($\{r\}_{i \in \{1...n\}}, Cred.tss$)
(9) $T_{app} \leftrightarrow TSO$: $\{pbsig\}_{i \in \{1...n\}} \leftarrow$ PBSign($SK_{TSO}; \{C\}_{i \in \{1...n\}}; \{info\}_{i \in \{1...n\}}$)
(10) T_{app} : store($\{eToken : \{C, r, info, pbsig\}\}_{i \in \{1...n\}}$)

The detailed interaction for recharging the ePurse is illustrated with Protocol prot:topup. The traveller initially requests a recharge via the installed mobile application, T_{app} *(step 1)*. The request contains only the requested amount to be added to the ePurse. In order to be granted the recharge, T_{app} also proves that the traveller holds a valid PPTS credential, $Cred$, by creating a zero-knowledge proof of knowledge, π, to a fresh challenge c received from the TSO *(2)*. Proof creation requires knowledge of the credential master secret MS, which is known only to the credential holder. In case of successful proof verification, the TSO replies with an adequate invoice. The traveller then performs the online payment *(5)* through a third-party payment service provider. After a successful payment, the TSO is notified and generates the public details for the tokens to be issued *(6)*. These details contain the information on the denomination of every token (D_g), which add up to the requested recharge amount. The D_g value is the guaranteed amount for one journey, i.e. the amount that a traveller needs to hold in order to be allowed to start a journey. It usually corresponds to the maximal charge for a ride. This way, the service provider is assured that the full trip fee will be paid, because the traveller spends one token with the guaranteed amount when entering the vehicle and is reissued with the change if a cheaper ride was taken. The T_{app} then creates a fresh commitment to the tss secret from the traveller's credential for each of the n tokens to be issued *(7–8)*. This way, the tokens issued to the same *tss* will not be linkable in the spending phase (see Sect. 3.4). In an interaction with the T_{app}, the TSO signs the public details and the *hidden* commitment with the partially blind signature scheme *(9)*. For sharing prevention, the blinded commitments are signed only after verifying that they belong to the credential holder (more details on the properties of such unlinkable tokens can be found in [15]). In the final step, the traveller's application stores the signatures, the commitments and opening information with the tokens' details. These *eToken* structures represent the recharge of the ePurse.

3.3   Purchase of Travel Products

The proposed system also allows for the PTO providers to offer multiple-use products, such as monthly discounts, which is a service already present in current ticketing systems (e.g. the Dutch U-OV bus or NS railway services). The interaction is detailed in Protocol 2.

Protocol 2. Purchase of multiple-use products

---

purchaseTransportProduct(*monthlyDiscount*)

---

(1) $T_{app} \rightarrow PTO$: request(*monthlyDiscount*)
(2) $T_{app} \leftarrow PTO$: $c \in_R \mathbb{Z}_q$
(3) $T_{app} \rightarrow PTO$: $\pi \leftarrow SPK\{(MS, dob) : Cred.validity \wedge$
$\qquad\qquad\qquad\qquad 12 \leq$ age($Cred.dob$) $\leq 18\}(c)$
(4) $\qquad\qquad PTO$: if (!verify(π)) abort
(5) $T_{app} \leftrightarrow PTO$: pay$_{bank}$(*invoice* : {*reference, amount, account$_{TSO}$*})
(6) $T_{app} \leftarrow PTO$: $info_{tp}$: {*reduction, PTO, validity*} $\leftarrow$ generate()
(7) T_{app} $\qquad$: $\{r_{tp}\}_{i \in \{1...n\}} \leftarrow$ generate()
(8) T_{app} $\qquad$: $\{C_{tp}\}_{i \in \{1...n\}} \leftarrow$ commit($\{r_{tp}\}_{i \in \{1...n\}}$, $Cred.tss$)
(9) $T_{app} \leftrightarrow PTO$: $\{pbsig_{tp}\}_{i \in \{1...n\}} \leftarrow$ PBSign(SK_{PTO}; $\{C_{tp}\}_{i \in \{1...n\}}$; $info_{tp}$)
(10) T_{app} $\qquad$: store($\{eToken : \{C_{tp}, r_{tp}, info_{tp}, pbsig_{tp}\}\}_{i \in \{1...n\}}$)

The traveller initially requests a multiple-use product via his mobile application *(step 1)*. The request only records the kind of product that is requested. The traveller also proves ownership of a valid PPTS credential, *Cred*. It may additionally be required to prove certain properties, such as the age group, using the date of birth (*dob*) attribute of the credential *(step 3)*. The proof is provided in the form of a signed zero-knowledge proof (SPK) and it only convinces the provider that the attributes in the traveller's credential satisfy the given properties, and hide other information recorded in the credential. If the proof verifies, the PTO can generate an appropriate invoice for the traveller. The traveller makes the payment via a third-party payment service provider *(5)*. Similarly to the ePurse recharge, the requested product is issued in the form of partially blind signatures on the public *info* and fresh commitments to the *tss* secret *(6–9)*. The *info* is the same in all tokens and records the product specification, such as validity, type and issuing PTO[2]. These tokens are spent with the TSO

---

[2] The *info* is assumed to have a limited set of possible values, as unique values would allow to link different interactions with the same traveller.

before starting the journeys (Protocol 3). Until the limitation on these tokens (such as validity date) is met, the application interacts with the PTO before the last token is used; the last token can be spent with the TSO to obtain a new bundle of signature tokens on fresh commitments.

The system also allows for purchases of single-use products, such as discounted tickets for a specific journey, vouchers for carying a bike on the train, or tickets for a pet. Similarly to multi-use products, the single-use products are issued as *eToken* structures with *info* representing the product description.

3.4 Validation of the Trip Start

For using the PTO service and charging the ePurse, the T_{app} interacts with the TSO to spend an *eToken* and obtain a single-use ticket. This ticket is sent to the PTO's validation machine over an NFC channel upon entering the bus, where it is verified. The interaction is detailed in Protocol 3.

Protocol 3. Validation of the trip start using the ePurse.

---

validateStartTrip($ePurse$)

		Before boarding the vehicle:
(1) T_{app}	:	$\{C, r, info : D_g, pbsig\} \leftarrow$ load($eToken$)
(2) T_{app}	:	$\{C_{tp}, r_{tp}, info_{tp} : \{reduction, PTO, validity\}, pbsig_{tp}\}$
		$\leftarrow$ load($eToken_{tp}$)
(3) $T_{app} \rightarrow TSO$	:	request($startTrip$)
(4) $T_{app} \leftarrow TSO$	:	$c_{start} \in_{\mathcal{R}} \mathbb{Z}_q$
(5) T_{app}	:	$\pi \leftarrow SPK\{(MS, r, r_{tp}, tss) :$
		$Cred.validity \wedge C = g^{tss} \times h^r \wedge$
		$C.tss = Cred.tss \wedge C_{tp} = g^{tss} \times h^{r_{tp}} \wedge$
		$C_{tp}.tss = Cred.tss\}(c_{start})$
(6) $T_{app} \rightarrow TSO$	:	$loc_{start}, C, info, pbsig, C_{tp}, info_{tp}, pbsig_{tp}, \pi$
(7)	TSO	: if (seen($C, info$) $\vee$ seen($C_{tp}, info_{tp}$) $\vee$!verify($PK_{TSO}; pbsig, C, info$) $\vee$
		!verify($PK_{PTO}; pbsig_{tp}, C_{tp}, info_{tp}$) $\vee$!verify(π, c_{start})) abort
(8)	TSO	: $t_{val} \leftarrow$ generate()
(9)	TSO	: $sig_{val} \leftarrow$ sign($SK_{TSO}; \{c_{start}, t_{val}, loc_{start}, info_{tp}\}$)
(10)	TSO	: store($c_{start}, C, info, C_{tp}, info_{tp}, t_{val}$)
(11) $T_{app} \leftarrow TSO$	:	sig_{val}, t_{val}
(12) T_{app}	:	store($sig_{val}, c_{start}, t_{val}, loc_{start}, info_{tp}$), delete($eToken, eToken_{tp}$)
		On entering the vehicle:
(13) $T_{app} \rightarrow PTO_{VM}$	:	$sig_{val}, c_{start}, t_{val}, loc_{start}, info_{tp}$
(14)	PTO_{VM}	: if (!verify($PK_{TSO}; sig_{val}, c_{start}, t_{val}, loc_{start}, info_{tp}$)$\vee$
		!verify(loc_{start}) $\vee$!verify(t_{val}) $\vee$!verify($c_{start} \leftrightarrow t_{val}$)) abort
(15)	PTO_{VM}	: $\{t_{start}, id_{bus}\} \leftarrow$ generate()
(16)	PTO_{VM}	: $sig_{start} \leftarrow$ sign($SK_{PTO}; \{c_{start}, t_{start}, loc_{start}, id_{bus}, info_{tp}\}$)
(17) $T_{app} \leftarrow PTO_{VM}$	:	$val_{start} : \{sig_{start}, c_{start}, t_{start}, loc_{start}, id_{bus}, info_{tp}\}$
(18) T_{app}	:	store(val_{start})

Before taking the ride, the traveller performs certain precomputations and interacts with the TSO application server online. It spends an *eToken* representing the required guarantee amount and an applicable discount. This way, the efficiency of the protocol is improved and the time needed for the interaction between the traveller's application T_{app} and the validation machine PTO_{VM}, is reduced. The T_{app} initially loads the tokens and requests a temporary ticket from the TSO *(steps 1–3)*. Next, the *eToken* is spent with the TSO's application server *(steps 4–6)*, by showing the partially blind signatures, commitments, *info* descriptions, and providing a zero-knowledge proof π on a received challenge c_{start}. It proves ownership and validity of a PPTS credential and the fact that the commitments are created with the secret of the same credential. The application also sends the starting location of the trip, loc_{start}. The TSO checks if the same commitments were used before and verifies the signatures, validity information (recorded in the *info*) and the SPK *(7)*. It records the received commitment and *info*, to prevent the double spending of the token in future transactions *(10)*. The *info* field also contains the validity information, thus allowing the TSO to delete the expired commitments from the database of spent commitments. It also issues a temporary ticket, which is a signed timestamp t_{val}, starting bus stop loc_{start}, challenge c_{start} and reduction information, $info_{tp}$ *(9)*. When the temporary ticket is issued, the T_{app} stores it and can delete the *eTokens* *(12)*.

At the start of the ride, the traveller's application establishes a short-range anonymous channel[3] with the validation device PTO_{VM}, which corresponds to scanning a smart card in the existing systems. The application shows the signed ticket sig_{val} *(13)*. After verifying it, as well as the starting time and location *(14)*[4], the validation machine creates a signature on the current time and location, vehicle identifier, challenge c and reduction information *(16)*. The user stores the signed data as a ticket with a validated start *(18)*.

3.5   Validation of the Trip End Using the ePurse

In the existing systems, the travellers validate their cards when exiting the vehicle as well, in order to receive back the difference between the guaranteed amount and the price of their journey. Similarly, in PPTS the smartphone establishes an anonymous short-range communication with the validation machine to receive the change (Protocol 4). Initially, T_{app} sends the signature sig_{start} and corresponding information from the beginning of the journey *(2)*. The validation machine verifies the signature and the bus identifier *(3)* and calculates the applicable fare *(5)* before generating the trip-end ticket *(6)*. The trip details, including *fare* and a fresh nonce, c_{end}, are signed to create a single-use ticket. The ticket and corresponding details are sent to the traveller's application *(7)* and are used to have the change reissued from the TSO *(13–15)*. The change is received in the form of an *eToken*. The traveller is awarded with the change only if the trip was not refunded before, the signature of the PTO_{VM} verifies and the time duration of the trip is within the maximal boundaries, ensuring that the traveller is not trying to combine two different trips as one *(10)*. For a limited time the TSO stores the *trip* data to prevent double refunds *(11)*.

---

[3] We employ the establishment of communication based on device-generated identifiers, which change with every new ride the traveller takes [9].

[4] The PTO allows for a sufficient ticket validity, i.e. difference between t_{val} and t_{start}.

Protocol 4. Validation of the trip end using the ePurse.

validateEndTrip($ePurse$)	
(1) T_{app}	: $\{sig_{start}, c_{start}, t_{start}, loc_{start}, id_{bus}, info_{tp}\} \leftarrow$ load(val_{start})
(2) $T_{app} \rightarrow PTO_{VM}$	: $sig_{start}, c_{start}, t_{start}, loc_{start}, id_{bus}, info_{tp}$
(3) PTO_{VM}	: if (!verify($PK_{PTO}; sig_{start}, c_{start}, t_{start}, loc_{start}, id_{bus}, info_{tp}$) $\vee$
	!verify(id_{bus})) abort
(4) PTO_{VM}	: $\{t_{end}, loc_{end}, c_{end}\} \leftarrow$ generate()
(5) PTO_{VM}	: $fare = \Delta(loc_{end}, loc_{start}) \times tariff_{km} \times reduction$
(6) PTO_{VM}	: $sig_{trip} \leftarrow$ sign($SK_{PTO}; trip : \{c_{end}, fare, id_{bus}, t_{start}, t_{end}\}$)
(7) $T_{app} \leftarrow PTO_{VM}$	: $sig_{trip}, trip$
(8) T_{app}	: store($sig_{trip}, trip$), delete(val_{start})
	After exiting the vehicle:
(9) $T_{app} \rightarrow TSO$	: $sig_{trip}, trip$
(10) TSO	: if (seen(c_{end}) $\vee$!verify($PK_{PTO}; sig_{trip}, trip$)$\vee$
	!verify($\Delta(t_{end}, t_{start}) \subset boundary$)) abort
(11) TSO	: store($trip$)
(12) TSO	: $diff = \Delta(D_g, fare)$
(13) $T_{app} \leftarrow TSO$	: $info : D_{diff} \leftarrow$ generate($diff$)
(14) T_{app}	: $C \leftarrow$ commit($r, Cred.tss$)
(15) $T_{app} \leftrightarrow TSO$	: $pbsig \leftarrow$ PBSign($SK_{TSO}; C; info$)
(16) T_{app}	: store($eToken : \{C, r, info, pbsig\}$)

When the accumulated change tokens exceed the guaranteed amount, D_g, the T_{app} interacts with the TSO online to spend these smaller denominations and receive one token of value D_g. The spending is performed similarly as when a trip is started (Protocol 3, *steps 5–7*), without the reduction-related interactions, and a new *eToken* is issued with a fresh commitment to the secret *tss* (Protocol 4, *steps 13–15*). Using a new commitment makes the spending of this *eToken* unlinkable to its earning interaction, or the interactions when the change used for its creation was obtained.

3.6   Random Trip Inspection

With the PPTS system, it is also possible to perform random inspections of the travellers and their tickets. The protocol is performed between the inspection authority, i.e. the I_{MD} and the traveller's mobile application (Protocol 5). The channel that is established is anonymous and short-range communication is used to prevent interception [9]. The I_{MD} initially sends a challenge c_I and requests proof of the currently held ticket. Using the challenge, T_{app} creates a proof of possession of a valid PPTS credential and shows the picture attribute recorded in it. The provided proof is verified by the machine and the inspector can check the picture displayed on the machine's screen. In case the proof is not valid, the traveller is identified by showing the PPTS credential's name and address attributes and with a document, such as a driver's licence. In addition, if the PPTS credential picture belongs to another person, the credential is also revoked.

Protocol 5. Random Trip Inspection

tripInspection(*trip*)

(1) $T_{app} \leftarrow I_{MD}$: requestInspection(c_I)
(2) T_{app} : $\{sig_{start}, c_{start}, t_{start}, loc_{start}, id_{bus}, info_{tp}\} \leftarrow$ load(val_{start})
(3) T_{app} : $\pi \leftarrow SPK\{(MS) : Cred.validity \wedge$
                                    $Cred.picture\}(c_I)$
(4) $T_{app} \rightarrow I_{MD}$: $\pi, Cred.picture, c_{start}, t_{start}, loc_{start}, id_{bus}, sig_{start}$
(5) I_{MD} : if (!verify($PK_{PTO}; sig_{start}, c_{start}, t_{start}, loc_{start}, id_{bus}, info_{tp}$)$\vee$
                    !verify(π, c_I)) {
(6) $T_{app} \leftrightarrow I_{MD}$: $\{name, address\} \leftarrow$ showCred($Cred$)
                             }
(7) I_{MD} : if (!verify($Cred.picture$)) {
(8) $T_{app} \leftrightarrow I_{MD}$: $\{name, address\} \leftarrow$ showCred($Cred$)
(9) $TSO_{AS} \leftarrow I_{MD}$:   revoke($Cred$)
                             }

4   Evaluation

The proposed system allows for a privacy-preserving, yet full-fledged ticketing services. It aims to allow the travellers to manage their own data, without introducing security issues for the providers. Both the personal information and travelling history are held and managed by the traveller. All the travellers equipped with an NFC-enabled smartphone are able to benefit from this privacy-protecting scheme. The providers' equipment could at the same time support the interface with the contactless smart cards, thus allowing travellers to use the basic system flavour, however, without the privacy assurances of the PPTS scheme.

4.1   Security and Privacy of the System

This section evaluates the security and privacy of the system against the defined attacker model (Sect. 2.2). In the following analysis we assume that the traveller device is communicating with the provider's equipment over an encrypted channel with server-side authentication.

Traveller privacy refers to preventing disclosure of the travellers' identities and travel patterns. It is ensured by means of underlying cryptographic technologies. Traveller's personal information is only disclosed to the TSO at registration time. It is certified in an anonymous credential, which allows proving existence of a valid registration, while hiding all other data it records. The credential properties ensure that different uses of the same credential remain unlinkable [6]. The traveller also interact with the TSO to obtain the *eTokens*, which are partially blind signatures applied on the commitments to the secret *tss*. By signing a commitment to the credential secret, the token is linked to the traveller, while the commitment hides the actual value of the unique secret to prevent profiling. The link between the interactions for issuance of a token and its spending cannot be derived, due to properties of the partially blind signature scheme [15]. Similarly, the signed tickets issued by PTO_{VM} at the end of a journey have a fresh nonce included in them, preventing the TSO from linking the interactions for spending an *eToken* and obtaining the change. Even if the TSO and PTO entities collude by merging their databases, no new information would be learned. The individual rides of a traveller recorded by the PTO cannot be linked together or to any identifying information, as no unique identifiers are used. Finally, since the picture data disclosed during random inspections is a unique identifier, we assume these checks are infrequent and do not allow for profiling travellers.

The traveller data is also protected from *external attackers* trying to extract the data from the T_{app} or listen in on the communication with the server, with encrypted communication with authenticated entities. Moreover, no action, such as credential attributes disclosure, can be carried out without user knowledge.

The *unauthorised usage* of travel products refers to forging, double-spending, sharing or changing details of valid tokens. In order to create a new valid token, which is a partially blind signature, an attacker needs access to the secret signing key, which we assume is prevented. In the similar manner, the token details (*info*) cannot be altered, as they are part of the signed structure. For utilising a valid token, it is necessary to prove possession of a valid PPTS credential, linked to the token (*step 5*, Protocol 3). Only entities with the knowledge of the credential's master secret can create the required proofs. Even if registered users try to share *eTokens*, they are not able to provide proofs for products which are not linked to their credential (e.g. *steps 5–7* in Protocol 3). Although sharing credentials and their master secrets would allow to exchange travel products amongst users, we assume that existing mechanisms for credential sharing prevention are in place [6]. In order to prevent sharing the PTO-issued tickets, they include a nonce c_{start}. The validation machine at the end of a journey can verify that the ticket has been used only once, even without online contact with the backend. Finally, double-issuance of the change tokens is prevented with nonces added to the temporary tickets for trip end, c_{end}. The ticket verification carried out by TSO includes a check whether the nonce is already recorded in its database linked to a particular time period. As these tickets have temporary validity, the databases do not have unlimited growth. The scheme also prevents fare evasion, as travellers 'spend' the maximal ticket price when starting a journey and are not allowed to board the bus in case of insufficient balance (*step 14*, Protocol 3).

The users who interact for using their travel products are also protected from *seamless overcharging*, as the user is presented with the amount that is going to be spent and receive proofs of journey details.

4.2   System Efficiency

For improved efficiency, some of the operations are carried out offline. The mobile application can create commitments and store them to be used at the time of check-in or check-out. Additionally, when the ePurse recharge is performed, issued digital tokens have the value required to show when taking one standard ride. This means that when taking a ride, the user usually only spends one token.

When a user collects enough change tokens to create a new token with standard fee, the application interacts with the TSO to spend the tokens with smaller amount and have the standard-value token issued.

The performance evaluation was done by measuring the execution time for the cryptographic primitives utilised in the protocols[5]. The measurements for the client-side (T_{app}) and PTO's validation machine (PTO_{VM}) were performed on a Samsung Galaxy S3 (GT-I9300) with a quad-core 1.4 GHz Cortex-A9 processor, 1 GB of memory and Android 4.1.2. The TSO operations were done on a workstation with Intel® Core™ i7-3770 CPU, 16 GB of memory and Ubuntu 13.04.

The most time-critical operations of the scheme are interactions between the traveller's application and the validation machine at the start and end of a trip. The cryptographic operations they comprise, i.e. creation and verification of digital signatures, have proven to be very efficient. For 100 measurements using a 2048 bit RSA key pair, signing and signature verification took on average 40.93 ± 0.18 ms, with 95 % confidence intervals.

In addition to these operations, the traveller's application communicates with the TSO before boarding the vehicle to receive a temporary validation confirmation. This interaction incorporates creation of a signed zero-knowledge proof on the client side and verification of this proof and two partially blind signatures on the server side. The average time of client execution is 197.22 ± 33.4 ms for 100 measurements and 95 % confidence intervals. The server execution takes 60.15 ± 7.8 ms for verifying the SPK and 8.14 ± 2.9 ms for verifying a partially blind signature. When the traveller exits the vehicle, the interaction with the validation machine again incorporates digital signature creation and verification. In a subsequent interaction with the TSO, the traveller is issued with an *eToken*, which takes 104.62 ± 22.46 ms for client executions and 172.71 ± 43.74 ms on the server side. These values show adequate efficiency. In addition, they are performed after the user leaves the vehicle and are not time-critical. Overall, the results show that the protocol's efficiency with the mentioned efficiency improvements allows the approach to be deployed in a practical ticketing system.

4.3 Design Extensions

The described proposal focuses on local transport, such as bus services, but can easily be extended to other transport systems. Also, the issuance and utilisation of the transport products is designed in a way that allows for a flexible system. In some systems a maximal charge for a single day is set (e.g. 'capping' in London Oyster system). To achieve this property in PPTS, the users would be issued with a proof-of-spending *eToken* at the end of every ride. The issuance would be performed by the TSO, as in Protocol 4. After the maximal amount is reached, the application contacts the TSO to be issued with *eTokens* which correspond to single rides for

---

[5] For more information about the implementation utilised for the performance evaluation, please consult: https://mobcom.org/deliverables/inshopnito_code.

that day. There is no limit on the number of these additional rides, as the traveller can exchange one *eToken* for a new batch (see Sect. 3.3).

It is also possible to allow the providers to learn how buses should be synchronised, by linking together multiple jumps that comprise one journey. A traveller would create a domain pseudonym using the PPTS credential (which does not reveal any additional information), show it on all jumps of one journey and would change it for every new journey. The credential properties provide assurances that different credentials cannot produce same domain pseudonyms [6].

5   Related Work

As novel technologies advance the ticketing systems, research initiatives also increase their focus on this field. However, multiple studies identify that privacy is a serious issue in the novel designs, as they allow to collect information about the users, such as locations and movements [10,17]. The way some commercial systems are deployed also create grounds for concern [24]. For instance, the Washington D.C. Metro was functioning for years without a clearly defined privacy policy [11,22]. Many solutions rely on cards with unique identifiers and utilise other personal information, even credit card data [21]. To tackle these privacy concerns, there is a limited number of research proposals. One of the initial proposals by Heydt-Benjamin et al. [11] uses an e-cash payment scheme, anonymous credentials and proxy re-encryption for concealing personal data, while ensuring correct payment. However, the system describes the functioning on a higher level of abstraction and system flexibility is limited compared to currently offered services. On the other hand, work of Jorns et al. [12] focuses on the problem of location services. As the network operators gradually open their interfaces for mobile applications that use travellers' location and presence information, privacy issues arise. The paper proposes a pseudonymous system for protection of user identity. However, there are still possibilities for user profiling, as the users are pseudonymous and every ticket contains a unique identifier, linking its purchase and usage. For ensuring unlinkability, a proposal by Reza et al. [19] relies on trusted anonymisers and employing physically unclonable functions (PUFs) technology on all the used tokens. However, we focus on the software solutions and limit hardware requirements. Similarly, some proposals protect user privacy using anonymous credentials or e-cash schemes. A system based on anonymous credentials is designed by Verslype et al. [23]. However, the system is not flexible enough for public transport systems, as it does not consider the option of pricing per travelled distance or reduction plans. Rupp et al. [18] propose a lightweight payment scheme for transit based on Brands e-cash scheme and blind Boneh-Lynn-Shacham signatures. It is based on users purchasing bundles of credentials which represent single travel tickets. At the end of a ride, the traveller is refunded with change. While the scheme is protecting the privacy of the travellers, it does not allow for services such as discount plans or monthly passes, which we aim to support with our proposal. Finally, a practical proposal of Kerschbaum et al. [13] addresses the use case of the Singapore ticketing system where on every card top-up, the unique identifier is disclosed and the recorded travelling data is leaked from the card. They design a post-paid billing system based on partially homomorphic encryption that allows for data analysis, although requiring expensive computation on the server side. Unlike in this proposal, we only focus on the pre-paid schemes, while limiting server side computation. Additionally, similar systems for privacy-preserving travel billing exist in the domain of toll systems. The privacy-protecting solutions [2,14], however, are not applicable to the public transport ticketing systems, as they have different hardware assumptions, namely the existence of trusted on-board units.

6   Conclusion

In this work we have presented a privacy-preserving ticketing system, which ensures unlinkability of travellers' interactions and prevents creating identifiable or even pseudonymous profiles. The proposal is flexible and can offer the services delivered in the currently deployed ticketing solutions. Although the privacy of the user is protected and the products' issuance and utilisation cannot be linked together, the service providers are still receiving the needed security assurances and can impose restrictions on utilisation and sharing of the purchased products. Our system prevents traceability of user actions even if the traditional and linkable payment systems are used. The trust assumptions are also reduced, as the users do not need to rely on the service providers to handle their data in a way that corresponds to their privacy preferences and trust that the security of the stored information cannot be defeated. They can be assured that their personal data is not revealed and only need to trust the application developer, while the implementation itself can easily be audited to assure the users that the performed actions correspond to the expected behaviour. At the same time, the minimisation of information is done so that it is still possible to perform the statistical analyses for improving the efficiency of the provisioned services.

The deployment of the proposal in real systems is eased by limited requirements, as it relies on the NFC-enabled smarphone technology on the traveller's side. It also demonstrates a usable efficiency. Similarly to the existing solutions, the validation machines do not require real-time communication with the backend to verify the validity of presented products. Finally, the performance evaluation illustrates a usable and efficient system.

References

1. Abe, M., Okamoto, T.: Provably Secure Partially Blind Signatures. In: Bellare, M. (ed.) CRYPTO 2000. LNCS, vol. 1880, pp. 271–286. Springer, Heidelberg (2000)
2. Balasch, J., Rial, A., Troncoso, C., Preneel, B., Verbauwhede, I., Geuens, C.: PrETP: privacy-preserving electronic toll pricing. In USENIX Symposium (2010)
3. Bellare, M., Goldreich, O.: On defining proofs of knowledge. In: Brickell, E.F. (ed.) CRYPTO 1992. LNCS, vol. 740, pp. 390–420. Springer, Heidelberg (1993)
4. Brands, S.A.: Rethinking Public Key Infrastructures and Digital Certificates: Building in Privacy. MIT Press, Cambridge (2000)

5. Calypso. Calypso functional specification, card application. http://www.calypsostandard.net/index.php/documents/specifications/public-documents/78-010608-functional-card-application (2014)
6. Camenisch, J.L., Lysyanskaya, A.: An efficient system for non-transferable anonymous credentials with optional anonymity revocation. In: Pfitzmann, B. (ed.) EUROCRYPT 2001. LNCS, vol. 2045, pp. 93–118. Springer, Heidelberg (2001)
7. Chaum, D.: Blind signatures for untraceable payments. In: Chaum, D., Rivest, R.L., Sherman, A.T. (eds.) Advances in Cryptology, pp. 199–203. Springer, Boston (1982)
8. de Koning Gans, G., Hoepman, J.-H., Garcia, F.D.: A practical attack on the MIFARE classic. In: Grimaud, G., Standaert, F.-X. (eds.) CARDIS 2008. LNCS, vol. 5189, pp. 267–282. Springer, Heidelberg (2008)
9. Eun, H., Lee, H., Oh, H.: Conditional privacy preserving security protocol for NFC applications. IEEE Trans. Consum. Electron. 59(1), 153–160 (2013)
10. Foss, T.: Safe and secure intelligent transport systems (ITS). In: Transport Research Arena 5th Conference: Transport Solutions from Research to Deployment (2014)
11. Heydt-Benjamin, T.S., Chae, H.-J., Defend, B., Fu, K.: Privacy for public transportation. In: Danezis, G., Golle, P. (eds.) PET 2006. LNCS, vol. 4258, pp. 1–19. Springer, Heidelberg (2006)
12. Jorns, O., Jung, O., Quirchmayr, G.: A privacy enhancing service architecture for ticket-based mobile applications. In: The Second International Conference on Availability, Reliability and Security, ARES 2007, pp. 139–146. IEEE (2007)
13. Kerschbaum, F., Lim, H.W., Gudymenko, I.: Privacy-preserving billing for e-ticketing systems in public transportation. In: Proceedings of the 12th ACM Workshop on Workshop on Privacy in the Electronic Society, WPES 2013 (2013)
14. Meiklejohn, S., Mowery, K., Checkoway, S., Shacham, H.: The phantom tollbooth: privacy-preserving electronic toll collection in the presence of driver collusion. In: USENIX Symposium (2011)
15. Milutinovic, M., Dacosta, I., Put, A., De Decker, B.: An efficient and unlinkable incentives scheme. CW Reports CW659, Department of Computer Science, KU Leuven (2014)
16. Pedersen, T.P.: Non-interactive and information-theoretic secure verifiable secret sharing. In: Feigenbaum, J. (ed.) CRYPTO 1991. LNCS, vol. 576, pp. 129–140. Springer, Heidelberg (1992)
17. Pelletier, M.-P., Trpanier, M., Morency, C.: Smart card data use in public transit: a literature review. Transp. Res. Part C Emerg. Technol. 19(4), 557–568 (2011)
18. Rupp, A., Hinterwälder, G., Baldimtsi, F., Paar, C.: P4R: privacy-preserving prepayments with refunds for transportation systems. In: Sadeghi, A.-R. (ed.) FC 2013. LNCS, vol. 7859, pp. 205–212. Springer, Heidelberg (2013)
19. Sadeghi, A., Visconti, I., Wachsmann, C.: User privacy in transport systems based on RFID e-tickets. In: Proceedings of the 1st International Workshop on Privacy in Location-Based Applications, Malaga, Spain, 9 Oct 2008 (2008)
20. N. Semiconductors. Mifare standard 4kbyte card IC functional specification (2012)
21. The Smart Card Alliance. Hong Kong Octopus Card (2006). (January issue)
22. The Smart Card Alliance. Smart Card Talk Standards (2006). (January issue)
23. Verslype, K., De Decker, B., Naessens, V., Nigusse, G., Lapon, J., Verhaeghe, P.: A privacy-preserving ticketing system. In: Atluri, V. (ed.) DAS 2008. LNCS, vol. 5094, pp. 97–112. Springer, Heidelberg (2008)
24. Winters, N.: Personal privacy and popular ubiquitous technology. In: Proceedings of Ubiconf (2004)

Authentication and Information Integration

Expiration and Revocation
of Keys for Attribute-Based Signatures

Stephen R. Tate[1] and Roopa Vishwanathan[2]($\boxtimes$)

[1] Department of Computer Science, UNC Greensboro,
Greensboro, NC 27402, USA
srtate@uncg.edu
[2] Department of Computer Science, SUNY Poly,
Utica, NY 13502, USA
vishwar@sunyit.edu

Abstract. Attribute-based signatures, introduced by Maji *et al.*, are signatures that prove that an authority has issued the signer "attributes" that satisfy some specified predicate. In existing attribute-based signature schemes, keys are valid indefinitely once issued. In this paper, we initiate the study of incorporating time into attribute-based signatures, where a time instance is embedded in every signature, and attributes are restricted to producing signatures with times that fall in designated validity intervals. We provide three implementations that vary in granularity of assigning validity intervals to attributes, including a scheme in which each attribute has its own independent validity interval, a scheme in which all attributes share a common validity interval, and a scheme in which sets of attributes share validity intervals. All of our schemes provide anonymity to a signer, hide the attributes used to create the signature, and provide collusion-resistance between users.

Keywords: Attribute-based signatures · Key revocation · Key expiration

1 Introduction

In some situations, users authenticate themselves based on credentials they own, rather than their identity. Knowing the identity of the signer is often less important than knowing that a user possesses certain credentials or attributes, e.g., "over 21 years old," or "computer science major." This form of authentication is ideal for loosely-knit situations where anonymity and unforgeability are desired, and one needs to be sure that users cannot collude to combine attributes from each other to satisfy authentication challenges. To this end, Maji *et al.* [8] introduced *attribute-based signatures* as a primitive that allows users to sign messages anonymously using a combination of their attributes. The parties involved in attribute-based signatures are a signature trustee (ST), an attribute-issuing authority (AIA), and potentially many signers and verifiers.

This material is based upon work supported by the National Science Foundation under Grant No. 0915735.

© IFIP International Federation for Information Processing 2015
P. Samarati (Ed.): DBSec 2015, LNCS 9149, pp. 153–169, 2015.
DOI: 10.1007/978-3-319-20810-7_10

The signature trustee acts as a globally trusted source that sets the global system parameters correctly (e.g., honestly generates a common reference string), and the attribute-issuing authority, which is trusted in more limited ways, issues signing keys for attributes to users. Although the AIA knows the signing keys and attributes of all users, it cannot tell which attributes have been used in a given valid signature, and hence cannot identify the signatures made by any user and/or link signatures made by a single user.

In the original work of Maji et al. [8], the basic scheme uses attributes that do not have any time restrictions on validity – once an attribute is issued, it good forever (or at least as long as the global public verification key is valid). Maji et al. [8] informally describe some ideas for attribute expiration and revocation, but these issues are simply mentioned in passing. In this paper, we initiate a careful study of restricting attribute validity in attribute-based signature schemes, providing a formal framework as well as implementations that are significantly more efficient than those that were suggested in earlier work.

A user who receives a key for a set of attributes from an AIA can sign a message with a predicate that is satisfied by their attributes. Predicates, or claim predicates, are Boolean expressions over a set of attributes, and satisfying a predicate involves supplying a valid combination of attributes such that the Boolean expression evaluates to true. Signature verification tests if the signature was performed by a user with a satisfying set of attributes, without needing to know the signer's attributes or identity. The main interesting properties of attribute-based signatures are *anonymity* of both the signer's identity and specific attributes used in generating the signatures, even if one has full information about which users were issued which attributes, and *collusion-resistance*, where two or more users cannot pool their attributes together to satisfy a predicate that they cannot individually satisfy. Note that since traditional digital signatures are verified using a user-specific public key, such a signature cannot provide the anonymity property required of an attribute-based signature.

In real-world situations, a user may be issued a time-limited attribute that has a well-defined validity period consisting of an issue date and expiry date. Since explicit revocation is not possible in the anonymous setting of attribute-based signatures, attributes can be used until they expire, forcing frequent expiration. As a simple example that motivates revocation, an organization could issue Employee attributes to its employees, which they use for authentication. Once an employee leaves the organization, they should no longer be able to authenticate using their Employee attribute. In addition to the expiry date, it is also important to check the issue date of an attribute, or the start of validity. Consider an organization where employees can anonymously certify or sign internal company documents, as long as they have valid credentials. Alice is an employee that joined the organization in March 2012, and was issued an Employee attribute. She should not be able to use this attribute to produce valid signatures over documents for February 2012, or any time before her start date. This property is referred to as *forward security*, in the signature literature.

In this paper we take an abstract view of time, with concrete instantiations for traditional notions of time (which we call "clock-based time") and a trusted server instantiation (which we call "counter-based time") which allows for instant revocation by incrementing a counter on a trusted time server.

Related Work. Attribute-based signature revocation was briefly mentioned by Maji *et al.* [8], but they don't give any specifics on how attribute sets can incorporate signing key revocation or attribute set revocation. Escala *et al.* [3] introduce schemes for revocable attribute-based signatures, but in their paper, "revocability" refers to revoking the anonymity of a user who created a signature (revealing their identity), and not revoking signing keys or attribute sets. Their revoke function is run by a party whose role is similar to that of a group manager in group signatures, and takes in an attribute-based signature, some public parameters and state information, and outputs the identity of the user who created the signature. Li *et al.* [7], Shahandashti and Safavi-Naini [12], and Herranz *et al.* [5] present attribute-based signature schemes, but do not deal with attribute and key revocation and expiry. Okamoto and Takashima [9,10] propose efficient attribute-based signature schemes which support a rich range of predicates, and do not require any trusted setup, respectively, but do not consider revocation.

In this paper we focus exclusively on authentication and attribute-based *signatures*. A significant amount of work has been done recently in the area of attribute-based *encryption* [2,4,6,11,14], but those techniques do not carry over into the signature realm and can be viewed as orthogonal to our work.

Our Contributions. The contributions of this paper are briefly summarized as follows:

- Extension of attribute-based signature definitions to support attribute expiration;
- A generic notion of time that includes instantiations for not only traditional ("clock-based") time, but also a trusted counter based notion that allows instant revocation;
- Key-update mechanisms that allow efficient extension of issued attribute sets; and
- Three implementations that vary in granularity of associating intervals with attributes and have various efficiency trade-offs.

2 Definitions

In this section we develop definitions for a time-aware attribute-based signature (ABS) scheme, and since the motivation is to support attribute expiration for revocation, we call this a Revocable Attribute-Based Signature scheme, or "RABS." The starting point for our definition is the ABS definition from Maji *et al.* [8]. At the core of any attribute-based scheme are the attributes, defined by a universe of attributes $\mathbb{A}$. An attribute $a \in \mathbb{A}$ is a generic name (e.g., `Employee`), and when we say that an attribute is "issued" to a user we are really talking about a private signing key associated with that attribute being generated by the AIA and provided to the user. Keys are associated with sets of attributes, and each instance of a attribute set signing key has a public identifier *pid* (users do not have individual public keys).

Attribute-based signatures are made with respect to a predicate Υ over attributes. For RABS we use monotone span programs to specify Υ, the same as Maji *et al.* [8]. A span program $\Upsilon = (\mathbf{M}, a)$ consists of an $\ell \times k$ matrix $\mathbf{M}$ over a field $\mathbf{F}$, with a labeling function $a : [\ell] \rightarrow \mathbb{A}$ that associates each of the ℓ rows of $\mathbf{M}$ with an attribute. The monotone span program is satisfied by a set of attributes $\mathcal{A} \subseteq \mathbb{A}$, written $\Upsilon(\mathcal{A}) = 1$, if and only if

$$\exists \boldsymbol{v} \in \mathbf{F}^{1 \times \ell} \; : \; \boldsymbol{v}\mathbf{M} = [1, 0, 0, \cdots, 0] \text{ and } (\forall i : v_i \neq 0 \Longrightarrow a(i) \in \mathcal{A}) \qquad (1)$$

Another way to view this is that the monotone span program is satisfied if and only if $[1, 0, 0, \cdots, 0]$ is in the span of the row vectors corresponding to the attributes held by the user.

2.1 Time and Validity Intervals

In this paper, times can be drawn from any partially ordered set $(T, \leq)$. There is a trusted time source that can report an authenticated "current time" to any party in the system, and it is required that the sequence of reported times be a totally ordered subset of T. Time intervals are specified as closed intervals such as $[t_s, t_e]$, where $t_s \leq t_e$, and a time value t is said to be in the interval (written $t \in [t_s, t_e]$) if $t_s \leq t \leq t_e$. In RABS, attributes have associated *validity intervals*, so if $a \in \mathbb{A}$ is a non-time-specific attribute, in RABS we would typically refer to $(a, [t_s, t_e])$ meaning that this attribute is valid at all times $t \in [t_s, t_e]$. As a more compact notation, we will sometimes use ι to denote an interval, so a time-specific attribute might be denoted (a, ι).

RABS signatures include a specific time $t \in T$ in the signature, so we typically write a RABS signature as $\sigma = (t, \phi)$, and we call this a "time-t signature." A valid time-t signature can only be made by a user who has been issued attributes $(a_i, [t_{s_i}, t_{e_i}])$ for $i = 1, \ldots, n$, such that $\Upsilon(\{a_i \,|\, i = 1, \ldots, n\}) = 1$ and $t \in [t_{s_i}, t_{e_i}]$ for all $i = 1, \ldots, n$. While it is tempting to refer to a "signature made at time t," it is clearly impossible to restrict when a signature is actually created — a time t signature could in fact be created at any time, as long as the signer holds (possibly old) keys that were valid at time t. Note that in one prominent application, a real-time authentication scenario in which a challenger provides the current time t and a nonce to the prover, who is then required to produce a time-t signature over the nonce, it *does* make sense to think of this as a signature being made at time t.

The everyday notion of time (which we will refer to as "clock-based time") easily meets these requirements, where each element of T is actually an interval defined with respect to some level of granularity of time, such as seconds, days, weeks, or months. For example, if T were the set of all months, then there might be a time value such as $t = 2014\text{-March}$. These times form a totally ordered set, and larger intervals can be specified such as $[2014\text{-March}, 2014\text{-June}]$. In clock-based time, we assume that there are a limited set of *standard validity intervals* that are used for attributes. For example, if T contains individuals days, then we could have standard validity intervals that represent monthly, weekly, or daily intervals, so a single-day time $t = $ 2014-Jan-09 could be in standard validity intervals [2014-Jan-01, 2014-Jan-31] (monthly), [2014-Jan-06, 2014-Jan-12] (weekly), or [2014-Jan-09, 2014-Jan-09] (daily).

As an alternative to clock-based time, we can let T be a set of vectors over integer counter variables, where two times $t_1 = \langle t_{1,1}, t_{1,2}, \cdots, t_{1,k} \rangle$ and $t_2 = \langle t_{2,1}, t_{2,2}, \cdots, t_{2,k} \rangle$ are compared by

$$t_1 \leq t_2 \quad \Longleftrightarrow \quad \forall i \in 1, \cdots, k, \quad t_{1,i} \leq t_{2,i}.$$

In this case the trusted time source could maintain a set of monotonic counters for each vector entry so that counters could be independently incremented on demand. While the set T is only partially ordered, since the individual counters are monotonic, the trusted time source would never output two times that are incomparable, such as $\langle 1, 2 \rangle$ and $\langle 2, 1 \rangle$.

While using vectors of counters for time requires more space to specify a time, it is a significantly more powerful notion. In particular, a counter can correspond to a set of attributes, and then when an attribute in that set needs to be revoked the counter can be incremented on demand. This allows for immediate expiration of issued attributes, rather than having to wait until the end of the current time period (e.g., the end of the month) as you would have to do with clock-based time.

2.2   Basic Techniques

A fundamental part of making or verifying a time-t signature in RABS implementations is the conversion of a span program $\Upsilon = (\mathbf{M}, a)$ that does not take time into consideration into a span program $\Upsilon' = (\mathbf{M}', a')$ that includes requirements that t is in the validity interval of all attributes used to satisfy Υ. The precise form of our transformation depends on the specific implementation, so we will introduce these transformations in later sections. Recall that "issuing an attribute set" means providing a user with a signing key that corresponds to a set of attributes. We write a generic secret key as SK, and we can also add designations to this secret key to indicate that it has certain properties. For example, $SK_\mathcal{A}$ refers to a signing key for the specified set of attributes, $SK_\mathcal{A}^t$ refers to a signing key in which all attributes in $\mathcal{A}$ are valid at time t.

Another novel idea that we introduce in this paper is the idea of a "key change." Some RABS operations can be accomplished with a small change to an already-issued signing key, so rather than communicate a full and nearly-identical key we communicate a Δ which describes how to change the existing key into a new key. Consider the following situation: a user has been issued a large attribute set $\mathcal{A}$, with hundreds of attributes — this is a very large signing key. At some point, these attributes expire and we wish to renew or reissue them for a new time period. Our goal then is to produce a small, compact Δ that describes changes to an existing signing key, say $SK_\mathcal{A}^t$, so that we can apply this Δ to update the key. While the precise format of Δ depends on a specific implementation, our implementations treat Δ as a sequence of commands such as $\langle \text{NEW}, id, SK \rangle$ for replacing a component of a key, identified as id, with a new key SK. All of these notions are combined to yield the definition of a RABS scheme, given in Definition 1.

Definition 1. *A Revocable ABS (RABS) scheme has the following functions:*

- RABS.TSetup(1^λ) $\rightarrow$ (TPK, TSK): *Run by the signature trustee to generate a common public key or reference string, TPK, and a secret key TSK.*
- RABS.Register(TSK, uid) $\rightarrow$ τ: *Run by the signature trustee to register a user. τ can bind user-specific parameters chosen by the trustee to a user id (uid). For example, in one of Maji et al.'s implementations, τ consists of some trustee and user-specific public parameters, signed by the trustee.*
- RABS.ASetup($TPK, 1^\lambda$) $\rightarrow$ (APK, ASK): *Run by the attribute-issuing authority (AIA) to generate a keypair (APK, ASK).*
- RABS.AttrGen($\tau, TPK, ASK, \mathcal{A} = \{(a_1, \iota_1), \ldots, (a_u, \iota_u)\}$) $\rightarrow$ $(SK_{\mathcal{A}}, pid, \psi)$: *Run by the AIA to issue a signing key for time-specified attribute set $\mathcal{A}$ for a user identified in τ. We assume that AIA has verified τ before using this function. Outputs include the private signing key $SK_{\mathcal{A}}$ to be given to the user, the public identifier pid for this key, and ψ which is the user-specific state that is maintained by the AIA as required to work with this set efficiently on future requests, such as Reissue and Extend.*
- RABS.Sign($TPK, APK, SK_{\mathcal{A}}, m, \Upsilon, t$) $\rightarrow$ σ: *Run by a user that possesses signing key $SK_{\mathcal{A}}$ for attributes $\mathcal{A}$ which are all valid at time t, to produce a time-t signature on message m. Note that the time t is embedded in the signature, so we will sometimes write $\sigma = (t, \phi)$ to make the time explicit.*
- RABS.Ver($TPK, APK, m, \Upsilon, \sigma$) $\rightarrow$ $v \in \{$ "accept", "reject"$\}$: *Run by a verifier to validate signature $\sigma = (t, \phi)$. Verifies that the signature was made by some user that was issued attributes $\mathcal{A}$ that were valid at time t such that $\Upsilon(\mathcal{A}) = 1$.*
- RABS.Reissue($\tau, \psi, pid, TPK, ASK, \mathcal{A} = \{(a_1, \iota_1), \ldots, (a_u, \iota_u)\}$) $\rightarrow$ (Δ, ψ'): *Run by the AIA to extend the valid time intervals for all of the associated attributes. For this function, pid should reference an existing issued attributed set for an $\mathcal{A}' = \{(a_1, \iota_1'), \ldots, (a_u, \iota_u')\}$ with the same attributes at different (typically earlier) time intervals, and the output includes a signing key update description Δ and updated AIA state information ψ'. Δ compactly describes how to update the current signing key, and is sent to the user.*
- RABS.Extend($\tau, \psi, pid, TPK, ASK, \mathcal{A}' = \{(a_1, \iota_1), \ldots, (a_u, \iota_u)\}$) $\rightarrow$ (Δ, ψ'): *Run by the attribute-issuing authority, to add new attributes to the already-issued set pid, which currently covers attribute set $\mathcal{A}$. The outputs are the same as RABS.Reissue, where Δ contains information that allows the user to update their signing key so that it covers extended attribute set $\mathcal{A} \cup \mathcal{A}'$.*
- RABS.Update(TPK, APK, Δ, SK) $\rightarrow$ (SK'): *This is a deterministic algorithm that is run by the user, where the user takes in an old signing key, an update description Δ generated by the attribute authority, and outputs a new signing key SK'.*

3 Threat Model and Security Properties

In the attribute-based signature (ABS) model, the adversary could either be a user who was issued attributes and keys valid for a fixed time period, or could be an external party that compromised the user's attributes and keys. Additionally, the attribute issuing authority could itself be considered an adversary colluding with a malicious user and/or external parties. We note that in our model, as well as in previous work in attribute-based signatures, the attribute-issuing authorities are considered malicious only in the sense that they will try to violate the anonymity of a user signing a message, and they are still trusted to correctly distribute attributes and signing keys among users. In particular, in the ABS model, one generally does not consider issues such as the attribute authorities unilaterally issuing (or re-issuing) signing keys, and using them to sign on behalf of a user. Furthermore, the signature trustee is considered to be a trusted party.

We now give a formal definition of security for any RABS scheme. Consider two adversaries, $\mathfrak{S}_1$ and $\mathfrak{S}_2$. Both adversaries know general system parameters, such as the set T, and are given public keys of the signature trustee and attribute authority when they are generated. The goal of $\mathfrak{S}_1$ is to guess which attributes were used to satisfy Υ, and the goal of $\mathfrak{S}_2$ is to forge a signature that passes verification, despite not having been issued satisfying attributes that are good at the time t embedded in the signature. The definition follows, and is derived from the ABS definitions of Maji *et al.* [8] — more discussion is in that paper.

Definition 2. *A secure RABS scheme possesses the following properties:*

1. **Correctness:** *A RABS scheme is said to be correct if for all $(TPK, TSK) \leftarrow$ RABS.TSetup(1^λ), all $(APK, ASK) \leftarrow$ RABS.ASetup($TPK, 1^\lambda$), all messages m, all attribute sets $\mathcal{A}$, all claim-predicates Υ such that $\Upsilon(\mathcal{A}) = 1$, all keys $(SK_{\mathcal{A}}, pid, \psi) \leftarrow$ RABS.AttrGen($\tau, TPK, ASK, \mathcal{A}$), and all signatures $\sigma \leftarrow$ RABS.Sign($TPK, APK, SK_{\mathcal{A}}, m, \Upsilon, t$), we have RABS.Ver($TPK, APK, m, \Upsilon, \sigma$) = "accept".*

2. **Perfect Privacy:** *A RABS scheme has perfect privacy if, for TPK that are all honestly generated with RABS.TSetup, all APK, all attribute sets $\mathcal{A}_1$ and $\mathcal{A}_2$, all $SK_1 \leftarrow$ RABS.AttrGen($.., \mathcal{A}_1$) and $SK_2 \leftarrow$ RABS.AttrGen($.., \mathcal{A}_2$), and all Υ such that $\Upsilon(\mathcal{A}_1) = \Upsilon(\mathcal{A}_2) = 1$, the distributions RABS.Sign($TPK, APK, SK_1, m, \Upsilon, t$) and RABS.Sign($TPK, APK, SK_2, m, \Upsilon, t$) are identical.*

3. **Existential Unforgeability:** *A RABS scheme is existentially unforgeable if adversary $\mathfrak{S}_2$, given black-box access to a RABS oracle $\mathcal{O}$, has negligible probability of winning the following game:*
   - *Run $(TPK, TSK) \leftarrow$ RABS.TSetup(1^λ), and $(APK, ASK) \leftarrow$ RABS.ASetup($TPK, 1^\lambda$). TPK, APK are given to $\mathfrak{S}_2$.*
   - *$\mathfrak{S}_2$ runs a probabilistic polynomial time algorithm in which it can make queries to registration oracle $\mathcal{O}^{\text{RABS.Register}(TSK, \cdot)}$, key generation and modification oracles $\mathcal{O}^{\text{RABS.AttrGen}(\cdot, \cdot, ASK, \cdot)}$, $\mathcal{O}^{\text{RABS.ReIssue}(\cdot, \cdot, \cdot, \cdot, ASK, \cdot)}$, and $\mathcal{O}^{\text{RABS.Extend}(\cdot, \cdot, \cdot, \cdot, ASK, \cdot)}$.*
   - *$\mathfrak{S}_2$ outputs (m', Υ', σ').*

$\mathfrak{S}_2$ *succeeds if* RABS.Ver$(TPK, APK, m', \Upsilon', \sigma') = $ *"accept"*, $\mathcal{O}^{\text{RABS.Sign}}$ *was never queried with* (m', Υ'), *and* $\Upsilon'(\mathcal{A}) = 0$ *for all* $\mathcal{A}$ *queried to* $\mathcal{O}^{\text{RABS.AttrGen}}$.

4   Implementations

In this section, we present several implementations for RABS. The implementations differ in how attributes use validity intervals: each attribute can be assigned a validity interval that is independent of the others; all attributes can share the same validity interval; or attributes can be grouped into sets that share the same validity interval. All of our implementations are built on top of a secure non-time-specific ABS scheme — for Implementations 1 and 2, any ABS scheme that satisfies the security properties in Maji *et al.* [8] will work, but Implemention 3 has more strict requirements, as described in Sect. 4.4.

4.1   Implementation 1: Independent Validity Intervals

For this implementation, each attribute is assigned a validity interval that is independent of any other validity interval used by any other attribute. To accomplish this, we incorporate the validity interval into the attribute name. For example, a time-specific attribute (Employee, $[2014\text{-}\text{Jan-}06, 2014\text{-}\text{Jan-}12]$) would be named Employee-2014-Jan-06-2014-Jan-12.

Using the notion of standard validity intervals from Sect. 2.1, consider a time t that is contained in k standard validity intervals: $\iota_1, \ldots, \iota_k$. Viewing the condition Υ as a Boolean formula, when calling the RABS.Sign function to make a time-t signature we would first change every occurrence of an attribute a in the Boolean formula to a disjunction of all attributes that incorporate a standard time interval that includes time t. In other words, an occurrence of attribute a in the Boolean formula would be replaced with $(a\text{-}\iota_1 \vee \cdots \vee a\text{-}\iota_k)$. Viewing the condition $\Upsilon = (\mathbf{M}, a)$ as a monotone span program, since each row $i = 1, \ldots, \ell$ of the original $\mathbf{M}$ corresponds to attribute $a(i)$, we simply duplicate this row k times, and map the time-specific attributes to these rows. In the example of standard validity intervals from Sect. 2.1, if $a(i) = $ Employee then we duplicate that row 3 times and map the monthly, weekly, and daily validity intervals to these 3 rows. We will refer to the expanded matrix as $\Upsilon' = (\mathbf{M}', a)$.

This implementation is an obvious way of adding support for validity intervals to attribute-based signatures, and the overhead for signatures is not large: If $\mathbf{M}$ is $\ell \times k$ and there are c time intervals that are valid for each attribute (e.g., $c = 3$ in our example above), then the resulting Υ' used in making signatures includes a $c\ell \times k$ matrix $\mathbf{M}'$. However, this implementation has a major disadvantage, which was the motivation for this work: the AIA has a motivation to expire attributes frequently so that attributes can be effectively revoked without a long delay, but most of the time a user's set of attributes will simply be reissued for the following time interval. This implementation requires the AIA to frequently reissue all attributes for every user in this situation, and if users hold lots of fine-grained attributes this is very expensive.

Theorem 1. *Given a secure non-time based ABS scheme, Implementation 1 is a secure RABS scheme.*

Proof. First, note that, given a time t, Υ' is satsfied by set of time-specific attributes $\mathcal{A}' = \{(a_1, \iota_1), \ldots, (a_s, \iota_s)\}$ if and only if $t \in \iota_i$ for all $i = 1, \ldots, s$ and $\Upsilon(\{a_1, \ldots, a_s\}) = 1$. The Correctness and Perfect Privacy properties of Implementation 1 follow directly from this fact and the corresponding properties of the underlying ABS scheme. For Existential Unforgeability, note that an adversary playing against a RABS oracle can be easily converted into an adversary playing against an ABS oracle since none of the RABS-to-ABS conversion uses oracle-only secrets such as TSK, ASK, or signing keys for Sign oracle calls. As a result, any RABS adversary that wins with non-negligible probability can become a ABS adversary that wins with non-negligible probability — but since the ABS scheme is existentially unforgeable, this is impossible. □

4.2 Validity Attributes

The next two implementations rely on a special type of attribute called a *validity attribute*. When a validity attribute is issued as part of an attribute set it indicates that all attributes in the set are valid during the validity attribute's interval. A single set may contain validity attributes with different validity intervals, making the set valid for multiple time intervals (which is essential for our efficient RABS.ReIssue operation), but attribute sets that are separately issued cannot be combined due to the non-collusion property of the underlying ABS scheme. In other words, a user could not take a current validity attribute and combine it with an expired, previously-issued set of attributes, even if all of these attributes had been properly issued to the same user.

There can be multiple, distinct validity attribute names, and we denote the full set of validity attribute names as $\mathbb{V}$. Different regular attributes may use different validity attributes from $\mathbb{V}$, but each regular attribute has a single validity attribute that it can use. We define a map $v : \mathbb{A} \to \mathbb{V}$ that gives the validity attribute $v(a)$ that can be used for attribute $a \in \mathbb{A}$. We define the following set to restrict attention to validity attributes that can be used for a specific attribute at a specific time $t \in T$:

$$\mathbb{V}_{a,t} = \{(v(a), \iota) \mid \iota = [t_s, t_e] \text{ is a standard validity interval with } t \in [t_s, t_e]\}$$

If the set of standard validity intervals for any time t is small, as we expect it would be in practical applications, then $|\mathbb{V}_{a,t}|$ will be bounded by a small constant.

Incorporating Validity Attributes into the Monotone Span Program. When creating or verifying a time-t signature using validity attributes, we modify a non-time-specific monotone access program $\Upsilon = (\mathbf{M}, a)$, where $\mathbf{M}$ is an $\ell \times k$ matrix, to create a time-specific monotone access program $\Upsilon' = (\mathbf{M}', a')$ for time t as follows. For each row $i = 1, \cdots, \ell$ we add a single new column, which we refer to as column $nc(i)$, and add a new row for each $v \in \mathbb{V}_{a(i),t}$ which we refer to as row $nr(i, v)$. Each new row $nr(i, v)$ contains a 1 in column $nc(i)$ and zeroes in all other columns. In addition to those 1's, new column $nc(i)$ also has a 1 in row i, and zeroes in all other entries. To expand the labeling function a to a', we map each new row $nr(i, v)$ to validity attribute v. We call this transformation of span programs T, and since it depends on both the original monotone span program Υ and the time t, we can denote this as $\Upsilon' = T(\Upsilon, t)$.

The following Lemma shows that a user can satisfy Υ' if and only if she has been issued attributes that satisfy the non-time-specific Υ as well as validity attributes that validate each attribute she uses at time t.

Lemma 1. *Given a non-time-specific monotone access program Υ, the constructed time-specific monotone access program $\Upsilon' = T(\Upsilon, t)$, and two sets of attributes $\mathcal{A} \subseteq \mathbb{A}$ and $\mathcal{V} \subseteq \mathbb{V}$, $\Upsilon'(\mathcal{A} \cup \mathcal{V}) = 1$ if and only if $\Upsilon(\mathcal{A}) = 1$ and for every $a \in \mathcal{A}$ there exists a $v \in \mathcal{V}$ such that $v \in \mathbb{V}_{a,t}$.*

Proof. Let $\Upsilon = (\mathbf{M}, a)$ and $\Upsilon' = (\mathbf{M}', a')$, where $\mathbf{M}$ is $\ell \times s$ and $\mathbf{M}'$ is $\ell' \times k$. For the first direction of the proof, let $\mathcal{A}$ and $\mathcal{V}$ be as described in the final clause of the lemma, so that $\Upsilon(\mathcal{A}) = 1$, and for every $a \in \mathcal{A}$ there is a $v \in \mathcal{V}$ such that $v \in \mathbb{V}_{a,t}$. We will show that $\Upsilon'(\mathcal{A} \cup \mathcal{V}) = 1$. Since $\Upsilon(\mathcal{A}) = 1$, there must be some vector $\boldsymbol{w} \in \mathbf{F}^{1 \times \ell}$ such that $\boldsymbol{w}\mathbf{M} = [1, 0, \cdots, 0]$, where every non-zero coordinate w_i corresponds to an attribute $a(i) \in \mathcal{A}$. Constructing a $\boldsymbol{w}' \in \mathbf{F}^{1 \times \ell'}$ so that $\boldsymbol{w}'\mathbf{M}' = [1, 0, \cdots, 0]$ is then fairly straightforward: The first ℓ coordinates of $\boldsymbol{w}$ are copied to $\boldsymbol{w}'$, and for each original row $i \in \{1, \ldots, \ell\}$ we pick one $v \in \mathbb{V}_{a(i),t}$ and set coordinate $w'_{nr(i,v)} = -w_i$. All other $\boldsymbol{w}'$ coordinates are zero. It is easy to verify that the first k columns in $\boldsymbol{w}'\mathbf{M}'$ keep the same value as in $\boldsymbol{w}\mathbf{M}$ and each new column has two coordinates that exactly cancel each other out, so the result is that $\boldsymbol{w}'\mathbf{M}' = [1, 0, \cdots, 0]$. Therefore, $\Upsilon(\mathcal{A}') = 1$.

For the other direction of the "if and only if," let $\mathcal{A}'$ be a set of attributes such that $\Upsilon'(\mathcal{A}') = 1$, and partition $\mathcal{A}'$ into sets $\mathcal{A}$ and $\mathcal{V}$ for the original attributes and validity attributes, respectively. Then there must be a $\boldsymbol{w}' \in \mathbf{F}^{1 \times \ell'}$ such that $\boldsymbol{w}'\mathbf{M}' = [1, 0, \cdots, 0]$ and each $w_i \neq 0$ corresponds to an attribute $a(i) \in \mathcal{A}'$. Taking the first ℓ coordinates of $\boldsymbol{w}'$ to form $\boldsymbol{w}$, and noting that the first ℓ columns of $\mathbf{M}'$ have zeroes in rows $\ell + 1$ and higher, it follows that $\boldsymbol{w}\mathbf{M} = [1, 0, \cdots, 0]$ and so $\Upsilon(\mathcal{A}) = 1$. Next, consider column $nc(i)$ that was added when $\mathbf{M}'$ was created, which we will denote as $\mathbf{M}'_{\cdot, nc(i)}$. Since $\boldsymbol{w}'\mathbf{M}' = [1, 0, \cdots, 0]$, we know that $\boldsymbol{w}' \cdot \mathbf{M}'_{\cdot, nc(i)} = 0$. Furthermore, since $\mathbf{M}'_{\cdot, nc(i)}$ is zero everywhere except row i and rows $nr(i, v)$, which are 1's, if $w'_i \neq 0$, meaning $a(i) \in \mathcal{A}$, and the dot product is non-zero, then at least one of the $\boldsymbol{w}'$ coordinates corresponding to rows $nr(i, v)$ must also be nonzero. Let v be such that $w'_{nr(i,v)} \neq 0$, and so $v \in \mathcal{V}$ and $v \in \mathbb{V}_{a(i),t}$, which completes the proof. $\qquad \square$

Transformation T results in an expanded matrix $\mathbf{M}'$ that has $\ell + \sum_{i=1}^{\ell} |\mathbb{V}_{a(i),t}|$ rows and $s + \ell$ columns. We expect that in practice the set of possible validity intervals at time t will be a fixed set that does not depend on the attribute, so we can write this simply as $(|\mathbb{V}_t| + 1)\ell$ rows by $s + \ell$ columns.

4.3   Implementation 2: Common Validity Interval

In this implementation, there is only a single validity interval that applies to all issued attributes, and so all attributes will share that validity interval. The big advantage that we gain is that an entire set of attributes can be reissued for a new validity interval by just issuing a single new validity attribute to the user, making the "common case" much more efficient than Implementation 1. Furthermore, implementation is still straightforward using any standard non-time based attribute-based signature scheme, and the basic setup and key management functions (TSetup, Register, ASetup, Update) carry over without modification. AttrGen and Reissue require a check to make sure that all specified validity attributes are the same, and Sign, and Ver require modifications based on transforming $\Upsilon' = T(\Upsilon, t)$ and incorporating the time t into the signature. For space reasons, definitions for the basic functions is left to the full version of this paper [13]. The one tricky function is Extend, which is defined and explained below:

– RABS.Extend$(\tau, \psi, pid, TPK, ASK, \mathcal{A}' = \{(a'_1, \iota'_1), \ldots, (a'_u, \iota'_u)\}) \rightarrow (\Delta, \psi')$:
  Recover the current attribute set $\mathcal{A}$ for set pid from ψ, and let U be the union of validity intervals for all validity attributes that have been issued with this set (note that U may not be a contiguous interval). Next, check that all ι'_i designate the same standard validity interval $[t'_s, t'_e]$ and that $[t'_s, t'_e] \subseteq U$, returning an error if this is not true. Finally, if $[t'_s, t'_e] = U$ we call ABS.Extend$(\tau, \psi, pid, TPK, ASK, \mathcal{A}')$, returning the resulting (Δ, ψ'); otherwise, $[t'_s, t'_e]$ is a proper subset of U, and this operation generate an entirely new signing key by pairing each attribute of $\mathcal{A}$ with $[t'_s, t'_e]$ and calling RABS.AttrGen$(\tau, TPK, ASK, \mathcal{A} \cup \mathcal{A}')$ to get (SK, ψ), giving $(\langle \text{NEW}, SK \rangle, \psi)$ as the result of the Extend operation.

The extra check in Extend is subtle, but important: Since we can reissue an attribute set for a new time interval by just issuing a new validity attribute, there may be older validity attributes that are carried along with the attribute set. If we did not make this test, then a new attribute added by using Extend would be in the same attribute set as an older validity attribute, allowing a dishonest user to create a signature with a time that pre-dates when they were authorized to use the new attributes. Note that in all cases the underlying attribute set is extended, even if the validity interval for the set is being restricted in this special case. A proof for the following theorem is in the full version of this paper [13].

Theorem 2. *Given a non-interactive witness indistinguishable proof of knowledge, and a secure credential bundle scheme, Implementation 2 is a secure revocable attribute-based signature scheme.*

4.4   Implementation 3: Grouped Validity Intervals

In Implementation 1, each attribute was given a validity interval that was independent of all other attributes, while in Implementation 2, all attributes shared a common validity interval. In Implementation 3 we take the middle ground: we partition the attribute set $\mathbb{A}$ into b buckets of size $p = |\mathbb{A}|/b$ so that all attributes in the same bucket share a common validity interval. While Implementation 2 supported efficient reissue of all attributes, excluding (revoking) a single attribute on reissue would require reissuing the entire set. While Implementation 3 is considerably more complex, it supports efficient full-set reissue involving a single validity attribute, and partial with with $O(\log b)$ overhead.

To refer to an attribute $a \in \mathbb{A}$ that was issued as part a specific attribute set, say set pid, we will use a subscript like a_{pid}. For example, an Employee attribute issued in set 512 could be written as $Employee_{512}$. When we explicitly specify the pid for an issued attribute, like a_{pid}, we call this as an "identified attribute."

We define a special type of attribute, called a *link attribute*, which will serve as a bridge between two issued attribute sets. Like any other attribute, a link attribute is issued as part of a particular issued attribute set, say set pid, but it also specifies the issued attribute set to which it is linking, which we will denote $opid$ (for "other pid"). The name of such an attribute is written as $link\sharp opid$, and once issued we can identify a specific identified link attribute as $link\sharp opid_{pid}$. A link attribute indicates that issued attributes from sets pid and $opid$ can be used together in making a signature, as if they had been issued in the same set.

Attribute Trees. As described above, we partition the set $\mathbb{A}$ into b buckets of $p = |\mathbb{A}|/b$ attributes each. While we can generalize to any sizes, in this section we assume that b is powers of two. Consider a complete binary tree with b leaves, where each node in the tree can have an independently issued attribute set. The leaves correspond to the b attribute buckets, and each internal node of the tree corresponds to an attribute set that can contain only link attributes. We use the standard 1-based numbering of nodes in a complete binary tree (as used in heaps) to identify positions in the tree, so "Node 1" is the root of the tree.

The AIA maintains such a tree for each user, with that user's current issued attributes. An example is shown in Fig. 1, where leaf nodes 10, 11, and 12 have issued attribute sets (with $pids$ as shown in the figure), but other leaf nodes do not (indicated with $pid = null$). The AIA maintains a mapping between tree nodes and $pids$, and we can write $pid[u, node]$ to refer to the current pid for user u and node $node$, or just $pid[node]$ when the user is known. For example, in Fig. 1 the AIA's mapping contains $pid[1] = 92$, $pid[5] = 75$, $pid[9] = null$, etc.

As in the previous implementations, issued attribute sets contain validity attributes, and a validity attribute stored in any node of the tree overrides validity intervals specified in its children and by transitivity all of its descendants. This enables the reissue of the entire attribute set by simply adding a new validity attribute to the root node. We define two functions that are useful in describing how attribute issue and reissue work.

Given a set of attributes $\mathcal{A}$, define the *bucket set* $bs(\mathcal{A})$ to be the set of leaf nodes containing attributes from $\mathcal{A}$, and define the *ancestor set* $as(\mathcal{A})$ to be set of all proper ancestors of the bucket set. In the example in Fig. 2,

$$bs(\{a_{2p+1}, a_{3p+1}, a_{4p+1}\}) = \{\text{Node } 10, \text{Node } 11, \text{Node } 12\}, \text{ and}$$

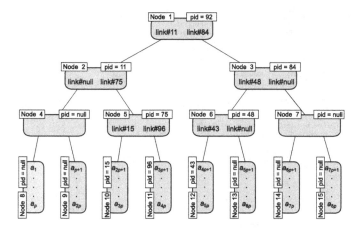

Fig. 1. Example Attribute Tree

$$as(\{a_{2p+1}, a_{3p+1}, a_{4p+1}\}) = \{\text{Node 1}, \text{Node 2}, \text{Node 3}, \text{Node 5}, \text{Node 6}\}.$$

Whenever the AIA issues an attribute set $\mathcal{A}$, it issues sets for nodes in $bs(\mathcal{A})$ as well as the internal nodes $as(\mathcal{A})$. The ancestor set always forms a connected subset of the attribute tree, and therefore if link attributes are interpreted as meaning "attribute sets *pid* and *opid* can be used together," then proving possession of the link attributes for the nodes in the ancestor set proves that all associated attribute sets can be used together to satisfy the predicate. After a set is issued (as represented by a connected subset of an attribute set), whenever a leaf node needs to be reissued by, for example, removing an attribute from a bucket, then we issue a new set for that leaf and link the new set in by issuing issue new sets for the internal nodes on the path from that leaf to the root.

The key management operations, AttrGen, ReIssue, and Extend can all be handled uniformly using the UpdateTree function shown in Fig. 2. These functions are given access to the state ψ that the AIA saves regarding the keys in this attribute tree. For simplicity of notation, we define the following functions which extract parts of the information represented by ψ: Set($node, \psi$) denotes the set of attributes associated with any node in the tree, State($node, \psi$) denotes the *node*-specific state, and Params(ψ) denote the τ parameters for the attribute tree's user. We also use IntervalIntersection($\mathcal{A}$) to denote the intersection of all intervals represented in a time-specific attribute set $\mathcal{A}$. AttrGen calls UpdateTree with a null state ψ since this does not modify or build on an existing tree, whereas the two update functions (ReIssue and Extend) provide the saved state associated with the root of the tree.

Sign and Verify Operations. The previous description of attribute trees could be applied to any attribute-based signature scheme, but to handle link attributes in the RABS.Sign and RABS.Ver operations we use the specific credential-bundle implementation of attribute-based signatures given by Maji *et al.* [8], where the credential bundles are implemented using Boneh-Boyen signatures [1]. In particular,

ProcessLeaf($node, pid, \psi, ASK, \mathcal{A}$)
    if IntervalIntersection($\mathcal{A}$) $= \emptyset$ **then return** $\langle$ERROR$, \perp, \perp, \perp\rangle$
    $\mathcal{A}' \leftarrow$ Set($node, \psi$) // The pre-update attribute set
    if $\mathcal{A}'$ is empty **or** $|\mathcal{A}' - \mathcal{A}| > 0$ **then**
        $(SK, pid', \psi') \leftarrow$ RABS1.AttrGen(Params(ψ), $TPK, ASK, \mathcal{A}$)
        return $\langle$ISSUE, link$\sharp pid', \{(node, \langle$NEW$, SK\rangle)\}, \{(node, \psi')\}\rangle$
    else
        $v \leftarrow$ (validity, IntervalIntersection($\mathcal{A}$)) // new validity attribute
        $(\Delta, \psi') \leftarrow$ RABS1.Extend(Params(ψ), State($node, \psi$), $pid, TPK, ASK,$
                          $(\mathcal{A} - \mathcal{A}') \cup \{v\})$
        return $\langle$EXTEND$, v, \{(node, \Delta)\}, \{(node, \psi')\}\rangle$

UpdateTree($node, \psi, pid, ASK, \mathcal{A}$)
    if $node$ is a leaf node **then return** ProcessLeaf($node, \psi, pid, ASK, \mathcal{A}$)
    $\mathcal{A}' \leftarrow$ Set($node, \psi$) // The pre-update attribute set
    if $\mathcal{A} = \mathcal{A}'$ **and** IntervalIntersection($\mathcal{A}$) $\neq \emptyset$ **then**
        $v \leftarrow$ (validity, IntervalIntersection($\mathcal{A}$)) // new validity attribute
        $(\Delta, \psi') \leftarrow$ RABS1.Extend(Params(ψ), State($node, \psi$), $pid, TPK, ASK, \{v\})$
        return $\langle$EXTEND$, v, \{(node, \Delta)\}, \{(node, \psi')\}\rangle$
    else
        $action \leftarrow$ EXTEND
        $V \leftarrow \{\}$
        for $c \in$ children($node, \psi$) **do**
            $\langle label, attr, SK', \psi'\rangle \leftarrow$ UpdateTree($c, \psi, pid[c], ASK,$ PartitionAttr($c, \mathcal{A}$))
            if $label =$ERROR **then return** $\langle$ERROR$, \perp, \perp, \perp\rangle$
            if $label =$ISSUE **then**
                $action \leftarrow$ ISSUE
                Replace link attr in $\mathcal{A}'$ with $attr$
            $V \leftarrow V \cup \{attr\}$
            $SK_{new} \leftarrow SK_{new} \cup SK'$
            $\psi_{new} \leftarrow \psi_{new} \cup \psi'$

        $v \leftarrow$ (validity, IntervalIntersection(V)) // new validity attribute
        if $action =$ ISSUE **then**
            $(SK, pid', \psi') \leftarrow$ RABS1.AttrGen(Params(ψ), $TPK, ASK, \mathcal{A}' \cup \{v\})$
            return $\langle$ISSUE, link$\sharp pid', SK_{new} \cup \{(node, \langle$NEW$, SK\rangle)\}, \psi_{new} \cup \{(node, \psi')\}\rangle$
        else
            $(\Delta', \psi') \leftarrow$ RABS1.Extend(Params(ψ), State($node, \psi$), $pid, TPK, ASK, \{v\})$
            return $\langle$EXTEND$, v, SK_{new} \cup \{(node, \Delta')\}, \psi_{new} \cup \{(node, \psi')\}\rangle$

Fig. 2. Key-management functions. RABS1 is a single-set RABS scheme.

the AIA's keypair (APK, ASK) is a Boneh-Boyen signature keypair, and the "secret key" for attribute a in issued attribute set pid is the digital signature DS.Sign($ASK, pid\|a$). Since only the AIA could have created such a signature, proving possession of this signature is the same as proving that this attribute was issued by the AIA. To issue a link attribute link$\sharp opid_{pid}$ the AIA computes DS.Sign($ASK, pid\|$link$\sharp opid$). In the example in Fig. 2, the right child link attribute pictured for Node 5 would be the signature DS.Sign($ASK, 75\|$link$\sharp 96$).

A signature in this attribute-based signature then is a non-interactive witness indistinguishable (NIWI) proof showing that the signer knows signatures corresponding to a set of attributes that satisfy the predicate Υ. For a predicate Υ that depends on ℓ attributes, $a_1, \ldots, a_\ell$, a signer may not have been issued all attributes, so we use notation $\perp$ to denote a "null signature" — a value that is in the form of a proper signature, but does not verify. The signer then creates a list of signatures $\sigma_1, \ldots, \sigma_\ell$ which may be either actual secret keys (Boneh-Boyen signatures) or the value $\perp$. Any non-$\perp$ signature provided should be a verifiable signature, and these should correspond to a set of attributes that satisfy Υ. Therefore, in Maji *et al.*'s signature scheme (without attribute trees), the signature is a NIWI proof of (modified slightly from Maji *et al.*):

$$\exists pid, \sigma_1, \cdots, \sigma_\ell : \left(\bigwedge_{i=1,\ldots,\ell} (\sigma_i = \perp) \vee \mathsf{DS.Ver}\left(APK, pid\|a_i, \sigma_i\right) = 1 \right)$$
$$\wedge \Upsilon\left(\{a_i \mid \sigma_i \neq \perp\}\right) = 1. \tag{2}$$

Modifying this technique to use attribute trees, first note that a predicate Υ that refers to attribute set $\mathbb{A}_\Upsilon$ will reference a subset of the attribute tree with a total of $nn = |bs(\mathbb{A}_\Upsilon)| + |as(\mathbb{A}_\Upsilon)|$ nodes. Therefore, Υ references nn separately issued attribute sets and hence there are nn distinct $pids$ to account for in the NIWI statement. In this subset of the attribute tree there are $nn - 1$ link attributes, and since each link attribute and each base attribute is issued as a signature from the AIA, there are a total of $ns = |\mathbb{A}_\Upsilon| + nn - 1$ signatures.

To construct the NIWI statement, we order the ns signatures into a sequence so that $\sigma_1, \ldots, \sigma_{|\mathbb{A}_\Upsilon|}$ are signatures for base attributes and $\sigma_{|\mathbb{A}_\Upsilon|+1}, \ldots, \sigma_{ns}$ are signatures for link attributes. We order the nn nodes of the attribute subtree arbitrarily so that $pid_1, \ldots, pid_{nn}$ are the $pids$ of the sets issued at all relevant nodes. We define a map $n : [1, \ldots, ns] \to [1, \ldots, nn]$ so that $n(i)$ gives the node containing signature/attribute σ_i, so issued set for signature σ_i is $pid[n(i)]$. Since every node except the root node is linked from its parent by a link attribute, given as a signature, we define $p : [1, \ldots, ns] \to [0, \ldots, ns]$ so that $p(i)$ is the parent link to the node containing σ_i; for the root node r we define $p(r) = 0$. Finally, we let $lnk : [|\mathbb{A}_\Upsilon| + 1, \ldots, ns] \to [1, \ldots, nn]$ be such that if σ_i represents a link attribute then $lnk(i)$ is the child node that this link attribute connects to. To simplify notation, we will use $\ell(i)$ to denote node i's label, which is either $pid[n(i)]\|a_i$ (for a leaf node) or $pid[n(i)]\|\mathsf{link}\sharp pid[lnk(i)]$ (for an internal node). The RABS.Sign and RABS.Verify operations then create and verify a NIWI proof of the following predicate:

$$\exists pid_1, \cdots, pid_{nn}, \sigma_1, \cdots, \sigma_{ns} :$$
$$\bigwedge_{i=1,\ldots,ns} \left((\sigma_i = \bot) \vee \left[(\mathsf{DS.Ver}(APK, \ell(i), \sigma_i) = 1) \wedge \left(p(i) = 0 \vee \sigma_{p(i)} \neq \bot \right) \right] \right)$$
$$\wedge \ \Upsilon(\{a_i \mid 1 \leq i \leq n \ \wedge \ \sigma_i \neq \bot\}) = 1$$

Just like in (2), a user does not have to have signatures for all attributes in $\mathbb{A}_\Upsilon$ to satisfy this statement, but if the user *does* supply a signature for a non-root attribute then it must also provide a signature for the link from its parent. This ensures that the attributes used by the signer (which must satisfy Υ by the last clause) are all connected by link attributes indicating that they can all be used together even though issued in different attribute sets. A proof of the following theorem can be found in the full version of this paper [13].

Theorem 3. *Given a NIWI proof of knowledge and a secure credential bundle scheme, Implementation 3 is a secure RABS scheme.*

Efficiency: Since the tree is a complete binary tree with b leaves (i.e., buckets), there are $\log_2 b$ link nodes on the path from any attribute to the root. Therefore, $|as(\mathbb{A}_\Upsilon)| \leq |\mathbb{A}_\Upsilon| \log_2 b$ (with equality when $|\mathbb{A}_\Upsilon| = 1$), and since $|bs(\mathbb{A}_\Upsilon)| \leq |\mathbb{A}_\Upsilon|$ we have $nn \leq |\mathbb{A}_\Upsilon|(1 + \log_2 b)$ and $ns \leq |\mathbb{A}_\Upsilon|(2 + \log_2 b)$. Therefore, compared to the single-set NIWI proof, this implementation adds an overhead factor of $O(\log b)$. Smaller numbers of buckets require less overhead, but this savings must be balanced against the increased cost of issuing new attribute sets for leaves (which can be substantial if there are large numbers of attributes in each bucket).

5   Conclusion

In this paper we have initiated a careful study of incorporating time intervals into attribute-signatures, so that attributes can be given a finite lifespan when they are issued. This allows for attribute revocation either at pre-defined time instances (in our clock-based techniques) or on demand (in our counter-based technique). This is preliminary work in this direction, and there are many open questions related to supporting different models of time as well as improving efficiency. One possible direction of future work is to explore revoking attributes while using non-monotone span programs [15], as this would help represent a richer range of predicates. From an efficiency standpoint, it would be useful to explore revocability in the setting of attribute-based signature construction techniques that avoid the use of non-interactive witness indistinguishable proofs.

References

1. Boneh, D., Boyen, X.: Short signatures without random oracles. In: Cachin, C., Camenisch, J.L. (eds.) EUROCRYPT 2004. LNCS, vol. 3027, pp. 56–73. Springer, Heidelberg (2004)
2. Boneh, D., Sahai, A., Waters, B.: Functional encryption: a new vision for public-key cryptography. Commun. ACM **55**(11), 56–64 (2012)
3. Escala, A., Herranz, J., Morillo, P.: Revocable attribute-based signatures with adaptive security in the standard model. In: Nitaj, A., Pointcheval, D. (eds.) AFRICACRYPT 2011. LNCS, vol. 6737, pp. 224–241. Springer, Heidelberg (2011)
4. Garg, S., Gentry, C., Halevi, S., Sahai, A., Waters, B.: Attribute-based encryption for circuits from multilinear maps. In: Canetti, R., Garay, J.A. (eds.) CRYPTO 2013, Part II. LNCS, vol. 8043, pp. 479–499. Springer, Heidelberg (2013)
5. Herranz, J., Laguillaumie, F., Libert, B., Ràfols, C.: Short attribute-based signatures for threshold predicates. In: Dunkelman, O. (ed.) CT-RSA 2012. LNCS, vol. 7178, pp. 51–67. Springer, Heidelberg (2012)
6. Hohenberger, S., Waters, B.: Online/offline attribute-based encryption. In: Krawczyk, H. (ed.) PKC 2014. LNCS, vol. 8383, pp. 293–310. Springer, Heidelberg (2014)
7. Li, J., Au, M.H., Susilo, W., Xie, D., Ren, K.: Attribute-based signature and its applications. In: ASIACCS, pp. 60–69 (2010)
8. Maji, H.K., Prabhakaran, M., Rosulek, M.: Attribute-based signatures. In: Kiayias, A. (ed.) CT-RSA 2011. LNCS, vol. 6558, pp. 376–392. Springer, Heidelberg (2011)
9. Okamoto, T., Takashima, K.: Efficient attribute-based signatures for non-monotone predicates in the standard model. In: Catalano, D., Fazio, N., Gennaro, R., Nicolosi, A. (eds.) PKC 2011. LNCS, vol. 6571, pp. 35–52. Springer, Heidelberg (2011)
10. Okamoto, T., Takashima, K.: Decentralized attribute-based signatures. In: Kurosawa, K., Hanaoka, G. (eds.) PKC 2013. LNCS, vol. 7778, pp. 125–142. Springer, Heidelberg (2013)
11. Rouselakis, Y., Waters, B.: Practical constructions and new proof methods for large universe attribute-based encryption. In: ACM CCS, pp. 463–474 (2013)
12. Shahandashti, S.F., Safavi-Naini, R.: Threshold attribute-based signatures and their application to anonymous credential systems. In: Preneel, B. (ed.) AFRICACRYPT 2009. LNCS, vol. 5580, pp. 198–216. Springer, Heidelberg (2009)

13. Tate, S.R., Vishwanathan, R.: Expiration and revocation of keys for attribute-based signatures. Cryptology ePrint Archive, report 2015/xxx (2015). http://eprint.iacr.org/2015/xxx

14. Waters, B.: Functional encryption: origins and recent developments. In: Kurosawa, K., Hanaoka, G. (eds.) PKC 2013. LNCS, vol. 7778, pp. 51–54. Springer, Heidelberg (2013)

15. Yamada, S., Attrapadung, N., Hanaoka, G., Kunihiro, N.: A framework and compact constructions for non-monotonic attribute-based encryption. In: Krawczyk, H. (ed.) PKC 2014. LNCS, vol. 8383, pp. 275–292. Springer, Heidelberg (2014)

Detecting Opinion Spammer Groups Through Community Discovery and Sentiment Analysis

Euijin Choo[1]([✉]), Ting Yu[1,2], and Min Chi[1]

[1] North Carolina State University, Raleigh, USA
{echoo,mchi,tyu}@ncsu.edu
[2] Qatar Computing Research Institute, Doha, Qatar
tyu@qf.org.qa

Abstract. In this paper we investigate on detection of opinion spammer groups in review systems. Most existing approaches typically build pure *content-based* classifiers, using various features extracted from review contents; however, spammers can superficially alter their review contents to avoid detections. In our approach, we focus on user relationships built through interactions to identify spammers. Previously, we revealed the existence of implicit communities among users based upon their interaction patterns [3]. In this work we further explore the community structures to distinguish spam communities from non-spam ones with sentiment analysis on user interactions. Through extensive experiments over a dataset collected from Amazon, we found that the discovered strong positive communities are more likely to be opinion spammer groups. In fact, our results show that our approach is comparable to the existing state-of-art content-based classifier, meaning that our approach can identify spammer groups reliably even if spammers alter their contents.

Keywords: Opinion spammer groups · Sentiment analysis · Community discovery

1 Introduction

There has been a rapid and growing interest in recent years in opinion spamming [8–10,13,15,17,19]. Opinion spamming refers to malicious activities that aim to influence normal users' decisionmaking for profit.

While a number of methods have been proposed to detect opinion spam, most of them focus primarily on developing pure *content-based* classifiers [4,10,13,17, 19]. The basic idea behind these approaches is to detect opinion spam through the analysis of review content. Such pure content-based classifiers, however, are limited for several reasons. First, spammers can easily manipulate review content to avoid detection [10,17]. For example, if duplicated text reviews are considered to be spam, spammers may simply paraphrase the content. Second, they are often designed for specific application domains such as travel reviews, and cannot be applied easily to different domains such as movie reviews [13]. Third, while most

© IFIP International Federation for Information Processing 2015
P. Samarati (Ed.): DBSec 2015, LNCS 9149, pp. 170–187, 2015.
DOI: 10.1007/978-3-319-20810-7_11

content-based classifiers generally require ground truth labels, it is often hard to obtain for real datasets. Some previous researchers have hired human experts to manually label data. The high cost of this approach, however, makes it impossible to do so reliably for large-scale datasets [9].

In this paper we explore an alternative approach by examining what we call *promotional opinion spammers* through the analysis of user relationships rather than review content. Promotional opinion spammers refer to attackers who try to improve the influence of their opinions by malicious artificial boosting. For example, many review systems employ some sort of reviewer/review ranking systems e.g., a top reviewer list on Amazon, most helpful reviews on Amazon, or most recommended reviews on Yelp. Spammers may thus artificially boost the rank of their reviews to attract more attention.

To obtain high ranking, spammers need to collect significantly more positive responses than negative ones. For example, review and reviewer ranks on Amazon are based primarily on the number of *helpful* votes received. Since multiple votes from the same user on one review are often counted as one vote, spammers need to boost their ranks by gathering positive votes from different users (i.e., collusion). One possible way to do this is for spammers to collaborate to vote high. We thus hypothesize that such malicious artificial boosting activities would eventually lead to construct spammer communities in which spammers are strongly positively connected with each other through review-response interactions (e.g., votes and text replies on the review). Our goal is thus to find these strongly or even abnormally positively connected communities among users and we argue that it is more likely to detect collusive spamming behavior among these users than those who are not part of these communities.

Our work is grounded in the context of a review ecosystem on Amazon. In our prior work we identified the existence of implicit communities built through review/response activities on Amazon [3]. In this paper we further explore positively and negatively connected communities through review and response activities via sentiment analysis. The intuition behind this approach is that: if a user has an unusual positive or negative relationship with another, they may be posting fraudulent positive and negative responses to each other's items and/or reviews to boost or demote the reputation of specific reviews or reviewers. In this paper we focus on spammers' boosting behavior.

In our approach, we first build general user relationship graphs representing how users *interact* with one-another. Then, we derive the sentiment of each relationship by aggregating sentiments of all responses between any two users. We then extract *positive* relationship graphs from the general user relationship graphs to capture boosting behavior. More specifically, motivated by link-based web spam detection, we focus on strongly connected communities in positive relationship graphs. Finally, we analyze extracted strongly positively connected communities to find opinion spammer groups.

Note that non-spammers may also form natural communities based upon their genuine similar interests [3]. However, we argue that spammer communities have distinguishing characteristics in terms of structures and the strength of their relationships. Concretely, we show that the stronger a community the user appears in, the more likely the user is involved in spamming-like activities.

Our main contributions are summarized as follows.

(1) We propose a general unsupervised hybrid approach that is based on user interactions coupled with sentiment analysis. To the best of our knowledge, this is the first attempt to identify opinion spammer groups through analyzing users' interactions rather than their review content. A key advantage of our approach is that it can detect opinion spammers even when traditional review content-based approaches fail.

(2) We introduce a new angle of collusive spamming behavior that spammers deliberately build strong positive communities to make their own opinions influential. We thus propose to explore community structures and a strength of relationships (i.e., how much the relationships are likely to be built intentionally) as spam indicators.

(3) We run extensive experiments over a dataset collected from Amazon to evaluate the effectiveness of the proposed approach. Our experiments show that even though our community-based approach differs markedly from pure content-based approaches, it reaches the same level of accuracy as the state-of-art content-based approaches.

The remaining parts of this paper are organized as follows. In Sect. 2, we review related work. Section 3 presents an abstract model of review systems, and introduces basic concepts and notations used through this paper. Section 4 offers the proposed approach to analyze and detect spammer groups. In Sect. 5, we discuss experimental results. Finally, Sect. 6 concludes the paper.

2   Related Work

Unlike traditional spam analysis in the context of Web and email, it is often hard to get ground truth for opinion spam. Previous research employed different mechanisms to obtain ground truth data. Early work manually inspected reviews and extracted simple features such as duplicated reviews or unexpected rating patterns [4–7]. These approaches were limited as they depend largely on heuristics [9,10].

A few researchers have created ground truth data by hiring Turkers to write spams [12,13]. They then developed content-based classifiers that compare the linguistic features of genuine and spam reviews. While these classifiers have been shown to be successful, it is questionable whether they can be applied in other domains as they are content specific. For example, linguistic features of hotel and book reviews may be different. More importantly, there have been unresolved debates on whether datasets generated by Turkers can be representative of actual spams in practice [9].

Mukherjee et al. generated ground truth by hiring domain experts who manually detected spams given a few intuitive features [9,10]. The authors observed some abnormal behavior regarding spam, and they classified the typical behavioral features of opinion spam and spammers into nine indicators.

While existing efforts discussed above present promising results, it is often easy for spammers to avoid content-based spamming detection by making superficial alterations to their reviews [10,17]. Also, such pure content-based detection methods often need to develop different classifiers for each purpose and domain [12,13]. By contrast, our approach detects spammers by analyzing user relationships and communities built through unusual interactions; which is much harder to fake than to reword their review content, as we shall describe later in this paper.

3   Review System

We focus on two types of user actions in a review system: reviewing items as *a reviewer* and commenting on reviews as *a commenter*. A *review* refers to one's opinion towards an item and a *comment* refers to one's response to a review or other comments. Both reviews and comments may take a variety of forms including assigning scores, voting, and writing text. For instance, Amazon users can assign a star rating along with text reviews, post text comments, and vote on the helpfulness of a review; while Urbanspoon users can only vote on the helpfulness of a review but cannot post text comments.

Interactions are defined between two different users. More specifically, an interaction from a user u to a user v is formed if u made a comment on v's review or v's comment. Note that users may build threads of comments. In this paper, however, we will only consider the interactions made by commenting on a review for simplicity reasons. Also, we count multiple comments from the same user on the same review as a single interaction for the sake of fairness.

4   Discovering Opinion Spammer Groups

Our proposed approach aims to detect opinion spammer groups who artificially form communities through the coordinated positive interactions.

Generally speaking, our approach can be divided into four stages and Fig. 1 depicts the general four stages through four sub-graphs, one sub-graph per stage. The four stages are: (1) building a general user relationship graph, Fig. 1(a);(2) annotating the general graph through sentiment analysis, Fig. 1(b); (3) pruning the general graph to a positive relationship graph, Fig. 1(c); and finally (4) identifying strongly positively connected communities within the positive relationship graph, Fig. 1(d). In the following, we will describe each stage in more details.

4.1   Stage 1: Building a General User Relationship Graph

We extend the definitions of a *user relationship* and a *community* proposed in our previous work [3], which we describe in this section.

We represent users and their interactions on a review system as a directed multigraph $G = (U, E)$ in which U represents users (vertices) and E represents

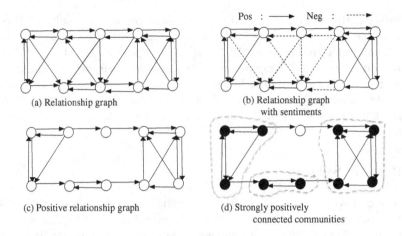

(a) Relationship graph

(b) Relationship graph
with sentiments

(c) Positive relationship graph

(d) Strongly positively
connected communities

Fig. 1. The general idea of the proposed approach

interactions (edges). Each edge $\overrightarrow{e_{uv}}$ is a 2-tuple (u, v) having direction from a commenter u to a reviewer v. A commenter has outgoing edges, and a reviewer has incoming edges in a graph. An *out-degree* of commenter u is the total number of edges from u to other users, which essentially reflects u's tendency as a commenter (i.e., how much u is willing to comment); an *in-degree* of reviewer v is the total number of edges from other users to v, which essentially reflects v's tendency as a reviewer (i.e., how popular v is to get comments). We further model those tendencies using incoming and outgoing probabilities defined as a reviewer's probability to get incoming edges and a commenter's probability to generate outgoing edges respectively.

Generally speaking, if we assume that there is no external relationship between commenter u and reviewer v, the typical interaction between u and v can be modeled as a random process. u simply stumbles upon v's review by chance when browsing the system. He does not know v and seek out v's review deliberately. In other words, without prior relationship from u to v, interactions from u to v should happen randomly depending on u's tendency as a commenter and v's tendency as a reviewer. Accordingly, we can represent all users interactions as a random graph in which edges (i.e., interactions) are randomly created following the incoming/outgoing probability of each user [3,11]. Specifically, if the outgoing probability of u is p and the incoming probability of v is q in an original interaction graph G, $\overrightarrow{e_{uv}}$ is built with the probability $p * q$ in a random graph. Hence, we get a random graph $G_r = (U, E')$ in which the total number of all edges, and each user's degree distribution are the same as G. The random graph thereby preserves the same nature of each individual as a commenter or a reviewer, which is independent of any prior relationships between users. The only main difference between the two graphs is that: all edges are randomly generated in G_r and so the number of edges between each pair of users will be different from G.

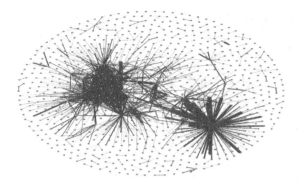

Fig. 2. An example of 99.5 % strength of user relationship graphs found in Amazon

Given the random graph model, we examine the real interaction patterns and see how much they are deviated from the random graph. We define users' relationship and its strength based upon the distance between users' original interaction graph and its corresponding random graph. Intuitively, the larger the difference between the real interaction pattern and the random model is, the more likely the relationships are to have been artificially orchestrated. We measure the distance by building confidence intervals based on the random graph. We denote that u has a relationship with v with τ strength, when the probability for edge $\overrightarrow{e_{uv}}$ to form in the real graph is outside of the given confidence interval τ. Then, the larger τ a relationship has, the farther the real interaction pattern is from the random graph and thus the higher strength the relationship has.

The concept of strength can be naturally extended to communities. Concretely, edge $\overrightarrow{e_{uv}}$ (in turn, user u and v) belongs to τ % community, if the strength of a relationship from u to v is τ. The larger τ is, the higher strength relationships in a community have and thus the higher strength the community has. Details of definitions can be found in our previous work [3].

For this work it is important to note that relationships belonging to higher strength of communities are excluded from lower ones. For instance, if a relationship is in 99.5 % community, it is excluded from all lower strength of communities such as 98 %.

Given the definitions above, we extract separate *user relationship graphs* for each τ community in which vertices are users and edges are their relationships defined by interactions, as illustrated in Fig. 1(a). Figure 2 presents an example of 99.5 % strength of user relationship graph found in Amazon.

4.2   Stage 2: Sentiment Analysis on User Relationships

Given τ strength of user relationships graphs, we further analyze the sentiment of relationships. To do so, we aggregate the sentiments of all comments between any pair of users from which we derive the sentiment of each relationship.

If comments are in the form of explicit votes, it is straightforward to obtain sentiment values. However, in many systems including Amazon and Yelp, it is often unknown who made the vote, while only aggregated information is publicly available. For example, we may know a certain review got 50 positive votes total, but we cannot know who made those votes. We thus focus specifically on the commenting text in order to define the sentiment of a relationship. We chose to employ a publicly available tool, AlchemyAPI [1], for this purpose. AlchemyAPI is known to present high accuracy on identification of sentiments in various applications including reviews and tweets [14,16], which gives us good confidence in using the API.

AlchemyAPI takes text contents as input, identifies a sentiment of the text contents, and output sentiment score. The score ranges from -1 to 1, where positive/negative scores represent the strength of positivity/negativity, and 0 means neutral.

There are many possible ways to derive the sentiment of a relationship from the sentiment of each comment. In this paper we employ a straightforward approach where the sentiment of a relationship from commenter u to reviewer v is the average of the sentiments of all u's comments on v's reviews. Specifically, to decide whether a relationship between users u and v is positive or negative, we first analyze the sentiments of all comments between u and v, and aggregate them. We then build relationship graphs in which sentiments of all relationships are analyzed, as illustrated in Fig. 1(b). We consider the relationship is positive if the average sentiment score is bigger than 0.

4.3   Stage 3: Positive Relationship Graphs

Once sentiments are analyzed, we prune the user relationship graphs to build τ strength of positive relationship graphs by extracting only positive relationships (Fig. 1(c)).

4.4   Stage 4: Identify Spammer Candidates by Decomposing Positive Relationship Graphs

We identify spammer candidates by analyzing community structures in τ strength of positive relationships graphs. Note that we are interested in spammer groups who work together, not individual spammers. As mentioned before, to boost their opinions, each spammer needs to collect a significant amount of positive interactions from others, usually her colluders; as it is expected that non-spammers rarely post positive comments to spam in general, whereas groups of spammers post positive comments to each other so that most of them can obtain a dominant position (i.e., reviewers whose opinions are believed to be trustworthy) in a system. In other words, interaction from a non-spammer to a spammer are not likely to appear in positive relationship graphs; and spammers will have strong interconnections through positive interactions. This motivates us to extract strongly connected components from positive relationship graphs. In other words, we believe that deliberate positive interactions among spammers will lead to the formation of strongly connected communities in a positive relationship graph, as illustrated in Fig. 1(d). Accordingly, we cast the problem of detecting opinion spammers as the problem of finding strongly positively connected communities.

A *strongly connected component* $G' = (V, E')$ is a subgraph of given graph $G = (U, E)$ such that there is a directed path in each direction between every pair of vertices $u,v \in V \subset U$. In our context, we define a *strongly positively connected community* $G' = (V, E')$ as follows.

Definition 1. G' is a *strongly positively connected community*, if G' is a subgraph of positive relationship graph G such that

(i) $\exists$ at least two vertices in G'
(ii) G' is a strongly connected component of G
(iii) G' is maximal, i.e., $\nexists$ strongly connected component $H \subset G$ containing G'.

We find all strongly positively connected communities in each τ strength of positive relationship graph and consider them as possible spammer candidates.

As noted before, non-spammers may form natural communities due to their similar interest on items. For example, in a random fashion, u has a few positive interactions with v through multiple items. This is likely to happen because v may have reviewed similar items, and u may look at those items to buy so that multiple interactions from u to v occur. And natural communities can arise from such random relationships. On the other hand, spammers construct artificial non-random communities. We thus argue that we can differentiate natural and spammer communities by measuring the level of randomness within the relationships. By our definition in Sect. 4.1, the strength of the relationships captures such a level of randomness, which we have in fact shown in [3]. We show that how the strength and spammicity are correlated in Sect. 5.

Table 1. Dataset.

Category	#items	#reviews	#comments	#reviewers	#commenters
Books	116,044	620,131	533,816	70,784	164,209
Movie	48,212	646,675	201,814	273,088	72,548
Electronics	35,992	542,085	128,876	424,519	72,636
Tools	22,019	229,794	32,489	151,642	21,977
Across	222,267	2,038,685	896,995	901,812	295,118

5 Experimental Results and Analysis

In this section we will present the characteristics of the *discovered reviewers* who appear in the strongly positively connected communities identified by our approach. Table 1 summarizes the dataset collected from four popular categories of Amazon reviews: Books, Movies, Electronics, and Tools. In our experiment, we investigated the characteristics of the discovered reviewers in each category individually and across the four categories. This is because spammers may launch attacks not only in specific categories but also across categories. We will refer to the cross-category dataset as *Across*. Due to space limits, in the following we primarily report results for the Across dataset. We note that the same observations were found for the category-specific datasets.

We will compare three groups of reviewers: the *discovered* reviewers identified by our approach, the *top* reviewers recognized by Amazon, and the *total* reviewers which includes all reviewers appearing in our dataset. The top reviewers set contained 10,000 top ranked reviewers recognized by Amazon and to be on the list, a reviewer needs to demonstrate credible resources of high-quality reviews. Since Amazon is a well-known system, we assume that most top reviewers are trustworthy. Based on this assumption, we focus primarily on comparing our discovered reviewers with Amazon's top reviewers to show that although the discovered reviewers can appear to be as "helpful" as top reviewers, they are strong spammer candidates.

We begin by presenting statistical characteristics of discovered reviewers in Sect. 5.1. Then, we compare the behavior of three groups of reviewers in terms of verified purchase ratio (Sect. 5.2) and spam indicators introduced in [9, 10] (Sect. 5.3). Finally, in Sect. 5.4 we illustrate the effectiveness of our community-based detection by comparing it to the state-of-the art content-based approach.

In following sections we will describe each of the measures used for our study and will present the results in a series of plots where: the x-axis demonstrates the strengths of the recovered communities; the y-axis presents the strength of the appropriate measure; and we have one line per reviewer group.

5.1   User Statistics

Figure 3 shows the number of reviewers in each discovered community. In the Across dataset, no communities were found with strengths $10\,\% \sim 40\,\%$ and $70\,\%$. So they are not presented in the following graphics.

First and most importantly, we measured the average number of reviews of three groups of reviewers as shown in Fig. 4. Figure 4 shows that both

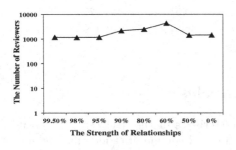

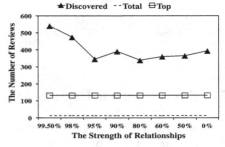

Fig. 3. The number of discovered reviewers

Fig. 4. The average number of reviews

discovered and top reviewers have reviews more than 100 on average while the total reviewers have relatively less reviews on average, < 10. This result agrees with the observations of prior researchers who found that the majority of reviewers writes only a few reviews [18]. One important observation from Fig. 4 is that both the discovered and the top reviewers are *active reviewers* (i.e., who actively participate in discussion on items) and more importantly, our discovered reviewers are much more active on average than the top reviewers regardless of the strength of community they are in: > 300 reviews on average for discovered reviewers vs. 150 for the top reviewers. Additionally, the higher strength of communities (e.g., 99.5 % and 98 %) had more reviews on average, > 450, than those in the lower strength of communities (e.g., 0 %) 300–400 range on average.

To determine whether the behavior differences reported in the following were due to the number of reviews a user submitted, we grouped the reviewers by the number of reviews they each submitted. We found that each group demonstrated similar patterns and behaviors as those for total population. Due to the space limit, we will not present the results here. However, this analysis showed the results presented in the following were not simply due to the reason that the discovered reviewers reviewed more.

As our goal is to find opinion spammesr who artificially boost their reviews, we first need to know whether their reviews are actually boosted in the system (i.e., whether their reviews are marked as helpful). In a common sense, reviews marked as helpful will have more influence on others. We thus calculated the positive vote ratio (PVR), ranging from 0 to 1, of the three groups of reviewers. We calculated PVR for each reviewer as the percentage of positive votes over the total number of votes each reviewer got. The higher PVR is, the more helpful their reviews appeared to be in general.

As shown in Fig. 5, the PVRs of the discovered reviewers are relatively high and in fact, close to that of the top reviewers, nearly 80 %. Both groups have much higher PVR than the total reviewers whose value is closer to 55 %. This indicates that the opinions of discovered reviewers do indeed appear to be quite helpful in general, as much as that of the top reviewers. Additionally, PVRs of discovered reviewers vary across different strengths and 60 % community has the lowest PVR ratio: close to 70 %. In the following we show that although the PVR analysis indicates that reviews of discovered reviewers may have a similar level of influence on others as that of top reviewers, they are more likely to be spammers.

5.2 Verified Purchase Analysis

Amazon tags each review with Verified Purchase to indicate whether the reviewer made a purchase through Amazon. Although it is not the case that every non-spammer made a purchase through Amazon, reviewers who purchased the item are less likely to be spammers than those who submitted a review without doing so. We therefore defined the verified purchase ratio (VPR) as the percentage of verified reviews over the number of total reviews of each user and believe that VPR is good indicator for spammicity.

180   E. Choo et al.

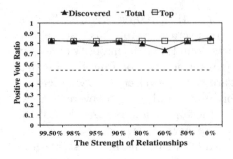

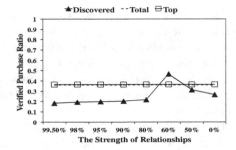

Fig. 5. Positive vote ratio (PVR)   **Fig. 6.** Verified purchase ratio (VPR)

Figure 6 shows the average VPRs of the three groups of reviewers. Interestingly, it also shows that there was no difference between the top and the total reviewers in terms of their VPRs. In other words, the top reviewers were no more likely to purchase the reviewed item than normal users. As we expected, our discovered reviewers have lower VPRs than the other two groups in general except for the 60 % communities. In fact, the VPRs for the 80 % ∼ 99.5 % communities are substantially lower than those for the top and the total reviewers. For the reviewers in the 0 % ∼ 60 % communities we see that the stronger the community the higher the VPRs observed. However, as shown in Fig. 6, the trend is different for reviewers in the 80 % ∼ 99.5 % communities. In that case the strength of the community is negatively correlated with VPR. We believe that this occurs because the members of those communities are more likely to be spammers as we will show in the following sections.

5.3 Spammicity Analysis

In this subsection we will measure the spammicity (i.e., how likely users are to be spammers) of the discovered reviewers across the various community strengths. We used nine content-based spam indicators suggested by existing research to measure the level of spammicity of reviewers [9,10]. Each value for the spam indicators ranges from 0 (non-spammers) to 1 (spammers).

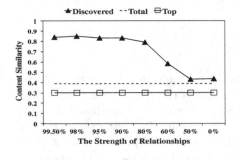

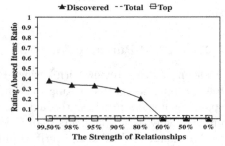

Fig. 7. Contents similarity(CS)   **Fig. 8.** Rating abused item ratio (RA)

Content Similarity (CS): Measures how similar the user's reviews are, as spammers often copy their own reviews across items. Following [9,10], we measured the maximum of pairwise similarity of two reviews by each reviewer to capture the worst case. Figure 7 presents the average CSs of three groups of reviewers. Mukherjee *et al.* stated that the expected value of CS of spammers was 0.7 [9]. As shown in Fig. 7, we observe that the CSs of reviewers in 80 % ~ 99.5 % communities are over 0.7. Note that there is a big drop between the 80 % and 60 % communities, and the CSs of 0 % community is very close to the CSs of total reviewers. This result suggests that 80 % ~ 99.5 % communities are more likely to be spammers with much higher CSs than others.

Rating Abused Item Ratio (RA): Checks whether a user posted multiple reviews with similar ratings on the same item, as non-spammers post multiple reviews usually when her opinion changes. Following [9,10], we measured the similarity by computing the difference between the maximum and minimum ratings of each reviewer for an item; and we assumed a reviewer abused ratings, if she posted the similar ratings more than twice on the same item. We then measured how many items were involved in rating abuse for each user. Figure 8 shows the average RAs of three groups of reviewers. In general, non-spammers are not likely to involve in rating abuse. Indeed, RAs of reviewers in 0 % ~ 60 % communities and top reviewers are close to 0, whereas RAs of reviewers in 80 % ~ 99.5 % communities range from 0.2 to 0.4[1].

Maximum One Day Review Ratio (MOR): Measures how many reviews a user posted in one day compared with the maximum across all reviewers, as a massive amount of reviews in one day often looks suspicious. In the Across dataset, the maximum per day was 96, which we can undoubtedly say is a suspicious amount of reviews for a day. Figure 9 shows the average MORs of three groups of reviewers. Mukherjee *et al.* stated the maximum number of reviews per day was 21 in their dataset, and the expected MOR of spammers was 0.28 and that of non-spammers was 0.11 (i.e., the expected number of reviews per day of spammers was $0.28 \times 21 \approx 5$ and that of non-spammers was $0.11 \times 21 \approx 2$) [9]. The maximum number of reviews per day was higher in our dataset than that used in [9] and this produced a correspondingly different MOR. However, we found that the maximum number of reviews per day ranged from 7 ($\approx 0.07 \times 96$) to 17 ($\approx 0.18 \times 96$) for reviewers in the 80 % ~ 99.5 % communities, which is more than the expected number for spammers; whereas it was 3 ($\approx 0.03 \times 96$) for those in 0 % ~ 60 % communities, which is similar to the expected number for non-spammers. It is interesting to see that the MOR of the top reviewers was also relatively high, compared to that of the total reviewers. One possible

---

[1] In [9,10], a measure called **DUP(Duplicated Reviews)** was also suggested, which focuses on multiple review content, not ratings. Our observations of the DUP were similar to our observations of RA. We therefore elected not to report the DUP due to space limitations.

182   E. Choo et al.

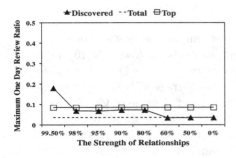

Fig. 9. Maximum one day review ratio (MOR)

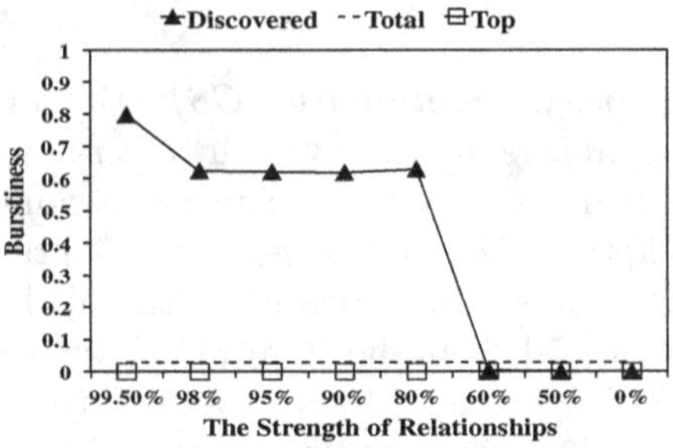

Fig. 10. Review Burstiness (BST)

reason might be that Amazon invites some top reviewers to get advance access to not-yet-released items and to write reviews [2].

Review Burstiness (BST): Measures the interval between a user's first and last reviews, as spammers often post reviews in a short period of time. Mukherjee *et al.* compared each reviewer's history with an estimated threshold of 28 days [9,10]. The shorter the interval, the larger the BST. The BST was 0 if a reviewer has a history equal to or longer than 28 days. Figure 10 shows the average BSTs of the three groups of reviewers. Note that top reviewers are expected to be valued customers who have a relatively long history with high-quality reviews. Indeed, top reviewers have the lowest BSTs (close to 0) as shown in Fig. 10. By contrast, we observe that reviewers in the 80 % and 99.5 % communities have rather high BST scores. Recall that both the top reviewers and the reviewers in the 80 % and 99.5 % communities have high PVRs, but the BST score analysis suggests that the latter are likely to be spammers since do not have a long history but collect many positive comments in a short period of time to appear to be very "helpful".

First Review Ratio (FRR): Measures how many of user's reviews are the first review for the target item, as spammers often post reviews early in order to maximize the impact of their reviews. Figure 11 presents the average FRRs of three groups of reviewers. As shown in Fig. 11, the top and the total reviewers have very close FRRs overall but for our discovered reviewers, we observe that FRR increases, as the strength of a community increases. Note that this result may simply reflect the fact that reviewers in the higher strength of communities are more active and thus are more likely to author the first review. However, the high FRRs for reviewers in 80 % ~ 99.5 % communities still reflect their spammicity, when combined with other spam indicators[2].

---

[2] In [9,10], a measure called *ETF (Early Time Frame)* has also been suggested. The intuition behind this is the same as for the FRR, because if not for the first review, earlier reviews may have a bigger impact. Our observations of the ETF were similar to our observations of FRR.

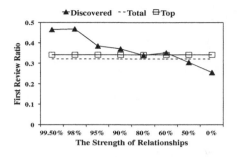

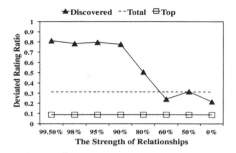

Fig. 11. First review ratio (FRR)   **Fig. 12.** Deviated rating ratio (DEV)

Deviated Rating Ratio (DEV): Checks the difference between a user's rating and the average rating of others for the same item, as spammers often try to inflict incorrect projections which deviate from the common consensus. We employed a threshold (of 0.63) estimated in [9, 10] to decide whether a rating is deviated, and measured the percentage of a user's reviews deviated. Figure 12 shows the average DEVs of the three groups of reviewers. Note that DEV of the top reviewers is the lowest. This suggests that their reviews are actually reliable or consistent with others' perceptions, whereas most reviews by reviewers in the 80 % ∼ 99.5 % communities deviate greatly from the common consensus. This deviance reaches as high as 0.8 deviation for the 99.5 % community[3].

Summary. In short, our findings from spammicity analysis can be summarized as follows. First, we find a clear distinction in terms of spammicity values between reviewers in the 80 99.5 Concretely, the behavior of the former groups tends to exhibit strong spamming behavior (high spammicity) although their positive vote ratio is high. The latter groups by contrast tend to be similar to the total and top reviewers (low spammicity). This result suggests that there exist reviewers whose reviews are maliciously endorsed to make more them influential. Indeed, prior researchers have argued that votes from users are not reliable and easy to abuse [7, 9].

Second, we see that the spammicity increases, as the strength increases for reviewers in the 80 other words, reviewers in the higher strength communities (e.g., 99.5 %) have a higher probability of being spammers; whereas reviewers in 0 % ∼ 60 % communities tend to have low spammicity in general, although the spammicity scores vary.

5.4   Analysis on Spammer Classification

In this section we show the correlation between the strength of each community and the probability of being spammers. Our goal is to suggest a way to

---

[3] In [9, 10], a measure called *EXT (Extreme rating ratio)* was also suggested to determine whether a user's rating is extreme, as spammers' ratings tend to be extreme while that of non-spammers tend to be more moderate and item specific.

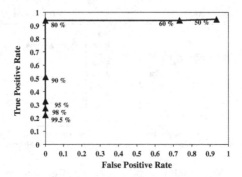

Fig. 13. ROC curve with different strengths as thresholds for classification

incorporate distinctive characteristics of different strengths of communities for spammer detection with the analysis of false positive rate and true positive rate.

The most direct way to evaluate our approach is to compare our detection process to the state-of-the-art content-based scheme with ground-truth data. However, after several attempts, we were unable to obtain access to datasets with ground-truth labels used in previous research such as [9,17]. Therefore we opted to compare our approach to the existing state of the art content-based classifier [9] on our dataset. Specifically, Mukherjee *et al.* suggested that when reviewers are ranked in descending order based on the sum of nine spammicity values, top and bottom 5 % ranked reviewers can be classified as spammers and non-spammers respectively [9,10]. We thus generated a "pseudo ground truth set" by applying Mukherjee *et al.*'s approach to our dataset, as it is the state-of-art classifier shown to have high accuracy over Amazon dataset with ground truth. We thereby show that although the proposed community-based approach does not look into details on review contents, it successfully identifies spammers without loss of accuracy.

Figure 13 shows the ROC curve by varying different strengths as thresholds to define spammers. The x-axis represents the false positive rate and the y-axis represents true positive rate. Each point represents true positive rate against false positive rate given τ strength as a threshold. We assume that reviewers in communities with strengths greater than or equal to τ are spammers; those in communities with strengths less than τ are non-spammers. For example, a point labelled as 90 % represents that we assume reviewers in 90 % $\sim$ 99.5 % communities are spammers and those in 0 % $\sim$ 80 % communities are non-spammers. Note that in Fig. 13, we present results regarding whether or not discovered reviewers in different strengths of communities are spammers. We thus do not plot when 0 % is used as a threshold, as we could not get false or true negative results.

When 80 % $\sim$ 99.5 % are used as thresholds, there was no false positive as shown in Fig. 13. This means that all reviewers in 80 % $\sim$ 99.5 % communities appeared in the top 5 % ranked reviewers (i.e., spammers); which is expected, as their spammicity values were high as discussed in Sect. 5.3. Note that the larger threshold τ, the lower true positive rate. For example, when 99.5 % is used as threshold, true positive rate is 0.2 due to many false negative results including reviewers in 80 % ∼ 98 % communities. On the other hand, when 50 % or 60 % was used as thresholds, the false positive rate dramatically increased (over 0.7), meaning that 0 % ∼ 60 % communities are likely to be non-spammers. As more non-spammers (i.e., reviewers in 0 % ∼ 60 % communities) are classified as spammers with 50 % or 60 % as thresholds, the number of false positive results increased. In such a case, the number of false negative results would be small, resulting in higher true positive rate.

Note that we get the best result (i.e., 0 % false positive rate and high (close to 1) true positive rate), when 80 % is used as a threshold; and the classifying results get worse with thresholds lower than 80 %. This implies a clear distinction between reviewers in 80 % ∼ 99.5 % communities and those in 0 % ∼ 60 % communities. This lends support to our claim that strengths of communities can be used to distinguish spam communities from non-spam ones.

Summary. In short, our findings from ROC analysis indicate that while strongly positively connected communities may be naturally constructed with different strengths, communities with a strength higher than 80 % are strong spammer candidates. We note that it is hard to evade our community-based scheme as spammers essentially need to build such high strength of communities to make their opinions influential; whereas spammers can easily fake their content features (e.g., reword their contents to lower content similarity value) to evade detection by content-based classifiers. It is also important to note that discovered communities not only include reviewers but also commenters who may not write any spam reviews. Existing pure content-based approaches will not be able to discover such *supporting commenters*, though they are also suspicious and indirectly contribute to opinion spams. In other words, our approach can discover both spam reviewers and suspicious commenters, which is a great advantage over pure content-based approaches.

6   Conclusion

In this paper we proposed a novel approach to find opinion spammer groups by analyzing community structures built through abnormally non-random positive interactions based on the intuition that spammers need to form artificial communities to make their opinions influential. We thereby exposed two types of spammers: spam reviewers who post spam reviews and supporting commenters who extensively endorse those reviews. Through extensive experimental analysis, we demonstrated the effectiveness of our community-based approach in terms of accuracy and reliability. We showed that our approach can successfully identify without relying on review contents, while achieving the same level of accuracy as the state-of-art pure content-based classifier.

Some challenges still must be surmounted. First, the proposed approach has focused mainly on spammer groups so it cannot find individual non-group spammers. We may combine our approach with content-based classifiers (e.g., [9,18]) to detect such non-group spammers. Second, while we have discussed the effectiveness of our approach in terms of detection accuracy, it would also be useful to develop a model to measure the effect of various spamming strategies (e.g., manipulate contents and build artificial communities). We thereby plan to investigate the robustness of our approach (i.e., to what degree attackers can manipulate their behavior to avoid detection).

Acknowledgement. This work is supported in part by the National Science Foundation under the awards CNS-0747247, CCF-0914946 and CNS-1314229, and by an NSA Science of Security Lablet grant at North Carolina State University. We would also like to thank the anonymous reviewers for their valuable feedback.

References

1. AlchemyAPI. http://www.alchemyapi.com/
2. AmazonVine. http://www.amazon.com/gp/vine/help
3. Choo, E., Yu, T., Chi, M., Sun, Y.: Revealing and incorporating implicit communities to improve recommender systems. In: Proceedings of the 15th ACM Conference on Economics and computation, pp. 489–506. ACM (2014)
4. Feng, S., Xing, L., Gogar, A., Choi, Y.: Distributional footprints of deceptive product reviews. In: ICWSM (2012)
5. Jindal, N., Liu, B.: Opinion spam and analysis. In: Proceedings of the WSDM, pp. 219–230. ACM (2008)
6. Jindal, N., Liu, B., Lim, E.P.: Finding unusual review patterns using unexpected rules. In: Proceedings of the 19th CIKM, pp. 1549–1552. ACM (2010)
7. Lim, E.P., Nguyen, V.A., Jindal, N., Liu, B., Lauw, H.W.: Detecting product review spammers using rating behaviors. In: Proceedings of the 19th CIKM, pp. 939–948. ACM (2010)
8. Lu, Y., Zhang, L., Xiao, Y., Li, Y.: Simultaneously detecting fake reviews and review spammers using factor graph model. In: Proceedings of the 5th WebSci, pp. 225–233. ACM (2013)
9. Mukherjee, A., Kumar, A., Liu, B., Wang, J., Hsu, M., Castellanos, M., Ghosh, R.: Spotting opinion spammers using behavioral footprints. In: Proceedings of the 19th ACM KDD, pp. 632–640. ACM (2013)
10. Mukherjee, A., Liu, B., Glance, N.: Spotting fake reviewer groups in consumer reviews. In: Proceedings of the 21st WWW, pp. 191–200. ACM (2012)
11. Newman, M.E.J., Strogatz, S.H., Watts, D.J.: Random graphs with arbitrary degree distributions and their applications. Phys. Rev. E **64**, 026118 (2001)
12. Ott, M., Cardie, C., Hancock, J.T.: Negative deceptive opinion spam. In: HLT-NAACL, pp. 497–501 (2013)
13. Ott, M., Choi, Y., Cardie, C., Hancock, J.T.: Finding deceptive opinion spam by any stretch of the imagination. arXiv preprint arXiv:1107.4557 (2011)
14. Quercia, D., Askham, H., Crowcroft, J.: Tweetlda: supervised topic classification and link prediction in twitter. In: Proceedings of the 3rd WebSci, pp. 247–250. ACM
15. Sheibani, A.A.: Opinion mining and opinion spam: A literature review focusing on product reviews. In: 6th IST. pp. 1109–1113. IEEE (2012)

16. Singh, V., Piryani, R., Uddin, A., Waila, P.: Sentiment analysis of movie reviews: a new feature-based heuristic for aspect-level sentiment classification. In: Proceedings of iMac4s, pp. 712–717. IEEE (2013)
17. Wang, G., Xie, S., Liu, B., Yu, P.S.: Review graph based online store review spammer detection. In: 11th ICDM, pp. 1242–1247. IEEE (2011)
18. Xie, S., Wang, G., Lin, S., Yu, P.S.: Review spam detection via temporal pattern discovery. In: Proceedings of the 18th SIGKDD, pp. 823–831. ACM (2012)
19. Yoo, K.H., Gretzel, U.: Comparison of deceptive and truthful travel reviews. Inf. Commun. Technol. Tourism **2009**, 37–47 (2009)

Constructing Inference-Proof Belief Mediators

Joachim Biskup and Cornelia Tadros$^{(\boxtimes)}$

Fakultät für Informatik, Technische Universität Dortmund, Dortmund, Germany
{joachim.biskup,cornelia.tadros}@cs.tu-dortmund.de

Abstract. An information owner might interact with cooperation partners regarding its belief, which is derived from a collection of heterogeneous data sources and can be changed according to perceptions of the partners' actions. While interacting, the information owner willingly shares some information with a cooperation partner but also might want to keep selected pieces of information confidential. This requirement should even be satisfied if the partner as an intelligent and only semi-honest attacker attempts to infer hidden information from accessible data, also employing background knowledge. For this problem of inference control, we outline and discuss a solution by means of a sophisticated mediator agent. Based on forming an integrated belief from the underlying data sources, the design adapts and combines known approaches to language-based information flow control and controlled interaction execution for logic-based information systems.

Keywords: Attacker simulation · Security policy · Controlled interaction execution · Declassification · Inference control · Information flow control · Integrated belief · Mediation · Multiagent system · Reasoning

1 Introduction

Today's IT-security technologies provide a broad variety of effective and efficient mechanisms to prohibit unauthorized reading of any kind of raw *data*, e.g., authenticated access control and private-key or certified public-key encryption. And these technologies also offer somehow limited approaches to confine the *information* content of data made accessible to cooperation partners, e.g., language-based information flow control, information systems with controlled interaction execution, confidentiality-preserving data publishing and cryptographic multiparty computations. However, independently of its carrier and its representation, information is the fundamental *asset* of an individual pursuing self-determination or an enterprise doing business. Moreover, information arises not only from accessible data but essentially also from social *contexts* as well as from a priori *knowledge* and *intelligence* of a reasoning observer and, additionally, is *accumulated* over the time, and *revised* by new events. So, being

This work has been supported by the Deutsche Forschungsgemeinschaft (German Research Council) under grant SFB 876/A5 within the framework of the Collaborative Research Center "Providing Information by Resource-Constrained Data Analysis".

© IFIP International Federation for Information Processing 2015
P. Samarati (Ed.): DBSec 2015, LNCS 9149, pp. 188–203, 2015.
DOI: 10.1007/978-3-319-20810-7_12

widely unsolved so far, the challenge is to enable an individual or an enterprise, respectively, an *owner* agent for short, to exercise a *holistic control* over the information conveyed to communication partners by means of transferred data.

Notably, the direct *objects of control* are not the partners, which are seen as independent and autonomous entities, but the information owner's messages made observable to others. Thus the topic is disciplined *self-restriction* regarding a specific aspect of the owner itself. This aspect is its *belief*, as virtually derived from actual data sources by reasoning, about matters of joint interest. An unrestricted partner can watch "reality" and access other sources by himself and thus gain information about those matters (including "external" properties of the owner) in potentially many ways; but, basically, the owner's "internal" belief has to be learnt solely from the owner's behavior.

While we see the partners learning belief as an agreed primary goal of cooperation, and thus *permissions* to share data as the default, we argue that nevertheless the owner might want to hide specific pieces of belief to selected partners as an exception, declared as dedicated *prohibitions* in some security policy. Thus, regarding that policy, the owner perceives a partner as a semi-honest *attacker* agent, potentially aiming to gain more information than wanted. Having no control on the attacker, the owner has no other chance than proceeding as follows: before releasing any data, it has to explore the attacker's options to exploit the data to infer information to be kept hidden, and to block all such options by *filtering* and *modifying* the data appropriately. Clearly, any such simulation has to be based on convincing but in principle unverifiable *assumptions* about the attacker. In other words, the owner has to perform *adversarial reasoning*.

Finally, interactions between the owner and a partner might occur during a longer *period of time* and include any kind of *program execution*. These properties demand for keeping track of all information previously released and considering not only direct data flows but also implicit information flows caused by the control flow during a program execution. Thus, all reasonings about an attacker's gain of pieces of belief have to be *state-dependent*, both in long and short terms.

The discussion above points to the inherent difficulties of the challenge:

– the *targets* of protection are pieces of the holder's virtual integrated belief;
– the *requirements* of protection imply the need of an attacker assumption;
– the *application field* of protection is history-aware and procedure-oriented;
– any *mechanism* of protection has to be based on three kinds of reasoning, for the holder's integrated belief, for the attacker's inference options, and for tracing the overall history and tracking a single control flow.

Though admitting the impossibility of a general approach, in this report we will present a framework to construct solutions for instantiations of a narrower scenario. We describe their flavor and requirements in Sects. 2 and 3, respectively, leading to a mediator-based design. In Sect. 4 we outline the suggested kind of an inference control mechanism, which applies language-based information flow control with declassification based on controlled interaction execution, under some restrictions on the expressiveness of the programming constructs involved. The achievements are discussed in the concluding Sect. 5.

2   Scenario and Overall Problem

While processing *interactions* with cooperation *partners*, the information *owner* wants to employ inference control to confine the *information* content of *data* delivered by *external actions*, which might be responses to *perceptions* including explicit requests. More specifically, such an *inference control* aims at disabling a cooperating receiver to gain a piece of information that the owner wants to keep *secret*, as declared in the owner's security *policy*. The required hiding effect should be achieved solely by *filtering* and *modifying* the interaction data according to meaningful *assumptions* about the receiver which is then seen as an intelligent and only semi-honest "attacker" *reasoning* about both data perceived over the time and further *background knowledge*.

The owner's assumptions might refer to a large variety of the attacker's capabilities, ranging from the kind and the extent of the attacker's background knowledge over the attacker's *means* and *preferences* for reasoning to the attackers's *awareness* of the owner's configuration of both the underlying *information processing system* and the employed *security mechanism* for inference control. In defending, the owner exploits these assumptions for *simulating* possible behavior of the attacker, and for then blocking a harmful one by appropriately distorting external actions.

The scenario sketched above can have diverse instantiations which might vary in several dimensions, e.g.: an information "owner" might be an individual, a group of them, or even an enterprise; "information" might refer to facts of an objective world or to somebody's belief about such facts; an owner's information "basis" might be a single relational database, a collection of diverse data sources or a dedicated virtual view derived from a federation of heterogeneous data sources; interaction "processing" might be simple generation of answer relations to database queries, more involved treatment of update and revision requests, or even execution of programs written in a general programming language; the owner's overall "system" including the control mechanism might be monolithic or based on loosely coupled components; the "interactions" with the devices of the cooperation partners might be based on shared storage or message exchanges.

Obviously, each dimension will have an impact on the general design and various more specific aspects of the anticipated inference control. Elaborating seminal proposals for inference control in information systems, and being in the spirit of many similar approaches to secrecy as concisely exposed in [14], previous work on Controlled Interaction Execution, CIE, originally only dealt with a single owner of a logic-oriented database system like a relational one solely employed for querying, and later also included updates and non-monotonic belief management, see the summaries [4,5], and the abstraction [6]. Based on that, and grossly summarized, in our vision [7] we proposed an architecture of an inference control front-end for uniformly shielding a possibly heterogeneous collection of data sources.

Further expanding on and extending that vision, in the present article we will consider an instantiation of the scenario of the following kind:

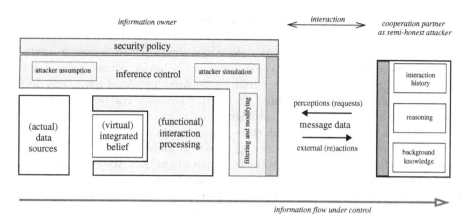

Fig. 1. Inference control for the focused scenario showing only one cooperation partner

- the owner might be *any subject* being willing and able to formulate a *coherent security policy* regarding a cooperation partner;
- data is representing information in the form of (subjective) *belief*, possibly including (objective) *knowledge* as a special case;
- the belief is derived as a dedicated *virtual integrated view* from a *federation* of existing heterogeneous data sources;
- interaction processing in terms of the virtual integrated belief might be governed by a *Java-like program* that complies with some syntactic restrictions, actually operating on the underlying heterogeneous data sources;
- the owner's system is understood as a subpart of a *multiagent system*;
- the cooperation partners' systems are also seen as *intelligent agents*;
- interactions between agents are solely based on *messages* representing *perceptions* and *actions*, including *requests* from and *reactions* to a partner's agent, respectively.

For such an instantiation we will focus on controlling the information flow

- from the owner's actual data sources
- over the owner's virtual integrated belief derived from the sources
- via the (re)action data transmitted by messages
- to a partner's system
- as caused by the owner's interaction processing.

More specifically, we consider the following problem of inference control: How to analyze and to block the partner's opportunities for successful inferences of pieces of belief the owner wants to keep confidential, as roughly visualized in Fig. 1? This problem in particular includes the following subproblems: How to form the virtual integrated belief whose pieces are the main targets of protection? And how to treat not only explicit direct information flows conveyed by message data and indirect ones due to evaluating expressions but also implicit information flows caused by guarded commands in the protocols?

3   Requirements within the Agent Paradigm

Both *advanced interaction processing* alone and sophisticated *inference control* alone require autonomously performed intelligent behavior: formal reasoning in some appropriate logic, pro-active pursue of declared high-level goals, and decision making guided by an accepted norm [1]. Moreover, computational *belief management* alone demands for intelligent engineering. Consequently, for the combined task under consideration these requirements are mandatory, too.

Local autonomy and intelligence together with global cooperation based on messages are fundamental issues of the agent paradigm [17]. Accordingly, we will present our *requirements* mostly in terms of this paradigm, subsequently aiming to design the *architecture* and *selected components* of a *mediator agent* meeting our requirements. The requirements will be explained in three layers, from the underlying belief management over the functional interaction processing to the comprehensive inference control. The explanations will be informal in style.

3.1   Basic Belief Requests for the Virtual Integrated Belief

Assuming a collection of possibly *heterogeneous data sources*, we require that all interactions with a specific cooperation partner are based on a dedicated *unified view* on the data sources, forming an *integrated belief*, continuously maintained by the owner [10,12]. This strict requirement reflects the need to protect information independently from its data representation and its physical storage. Furthermore, information to be hidden should refer to the owner's presumably consistent belief on the matters of an interaction, rather than on the storage state of the underlying data sources or some "facts of the real world". To handle different views dedicated for specific partners, such a belief should not be fully materialized but only be *virtually derived*, as far as possible and convenient.

Leaving open the status of the underlying data sources and the channels to access them, we prefer to derive a virtual integrated belief following a *mediation* approach, as visualized in Fig. 2. Each actually materialized data source is *wrapped* to be seen as a *local knowledge base*, comprising both its own *background knowledge* and *evidential knowledge* as well as *meta knowledge* regarding the mediation framework, and exporting a *local belief*. The *virtual integrated belief* is then formed by means of a *knowledge base as a mediated schema*, being equipped with background knowledge (about the intended application) and meta knowledge (regarding the mediation framework), and further components to handle a *basic belief request*, in particular a query, an update or a revision. At suitable commit points in time, this approach has to satisfy a *fundamental invariant*, namely that the virtual integrated belief "correctly reflects" the materialized sources.

A request is handled by *translating* it into subrequests directed to the underlying sources over a *communication network* via their *wrappers* and then *combining* the subreactions to an overall *basic belief reaction*. The further components for *request handling* are briefly explained by outlining the expected conceptual control flow and data flow for a basic belief request, which we suppose to be

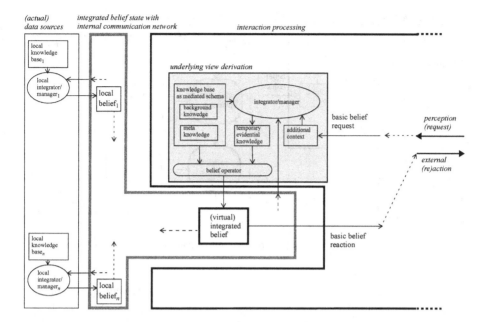

Fig. 2. Forming a virtual integrated belief and executing basic belief requests

submitted by the remaining parts of the interaction processing possibly based on perceptions. Depending on the kind of request, first some so-called *additional context* is generated that is then forwarded to the *integrator/manager* to inform it about the details of the request. The integrator/manager also has access to the integrated belief state assumed to satisfy the fundamental invariant, and to the knowledge base as mediated schema. From these three inputs, the integrator/manager generates appropriate *temporary evidential knowledge* that in turn, together with the knowledge base, is employed by the *belief operator* to form a relevant part of the virtual integrated belief, more precisely to return a pertinent *basic belief reaction* and, if applicable in case of changes, to sent appropriate *materialization requests* to the sources, in particular in order to re-establish the fundamental invariant.

3.2   Advanced Interaction Processing

Interaction processing actually performs the information owner's part of the intended cooperation with another partner and, thus, is dependent on the concrete application. Accordingly, we imagine that a *Java-like program* for some kind of a cooperation protocol is executed. Following the agent paradigm [17], we exemplify our requirements by considering the typical *looping behavior* of a rational reasoner that is *querying and maintaining belief, pro-actively planning* while pursuing *goals*, and *making decisions* while *respecting norms* [1], as visualized in Fig. 3. Such a behavior shows the following characteristic properties:

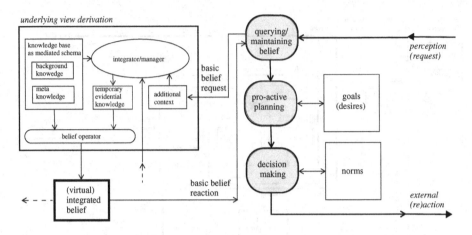

Fig. 3. Exemplified interaction processing (without inference control)

a sequence of uniformly repeated history-aware activities, branchings dependent on a possibly changing belief, submission of basic belief requests, and branchings within the execution of a basic belief request. So we require inference control of interaction processing summarized as follows:

- started with the (hidden) **input** of an *initial belief* and
- supplied with a further (open) **input** of a *sequence of perceptions*, received via a dedicated interface,
- *performing a loop*, for each of the perceptions the interaction processing **system** uniformly *executes a body* that
  - might contain *branchings* and involves calls of *basic belief requests* whose *reactions* are communicated via a *belief–program interface*, and
  - finally generates an action, sent via a dedicated interface,
- resulting in an overall (open) **output** of a *sequence of actions*.

3.3 Inference Control

For each of the information owner's cooperation partners, interaction processing (as outlined in Subsect. 3.2) based on a (virtual) integrated belief (as sketched in Subsect. 3.1) should be *generally permitted*, possibly somehow restricted according to granted *access rights*. However, each actual execution should also be continuously monitored in order to block the respective partner's options to infer pieces of belief the owner wants to keep secret to that partner. Accordingly, a partner-specific *security policy* expressed in terms of belief sentences should declare *prohibitions* as exceptions from the general permission.

The policy only specifies *what* should be kept confidential and leaves open *how* confidentiality will be enforced. For an enforcement we aim at a two-layered approach of employing existing concepts:

- language-based *information flow control* with declassification for the Java-like implemented interaction protocol
- based on *inference-usability confinement* with filtering and modification by CIE for the logic-oriented belief management.

Moreover, we want to apply a suitable variant of CIE-like *semantics* of a security policy for the overall system, see [5]. Informally expressed, the wanted semantics basically requires the following for each belief sentence (traditionally called a *potential secret*) in the security policy for a specific cooperation partner:

the *actual validity* (held to be true in the owner's integrated belief) should be *kept secret* to the attacker (though being a cooperation partner), whereas an actual negated validity (held to be false in the owner's integrated belief or having an undecided status) may be learnt.

The sketched semantics can equivalently be expressed in terms of either "absence of knowledge" – the attacker should *not know* the potential secret's *validity* – or "ensurance of possibility" – the attacker should be *sure about* the *possibility of the potential secret being not valid*. We also could distinguish whether a confidentiality requirement should refer to either the *initial* status of a potential secret or its *current* status or its full status *history* or, in some extension, even to any selection of *points in time* of its history.

The meaning of phrases like "kept secret to", "not knowing", or "being sure" applied to an intelligent attacker strongly depends on its background, in particular its *a priori knowledge* about the integrated belief, its *awareness* about details of the controlled interaction system, and its *reasoning* methods [7]. However, in general the (defending) owner can only form reasonable *assumptions* about the (attacking) partner's background. So we require that the mediator for the owner should be able to *simulate* the partner agent's behavior in attempting to infer belief to be kept secret according to *partner-specific parameter* values, which are provided via an *administration interface*. This simulation should be based on a *conservative* approach to security, considering a kind of *worst case* regarding the *general part* of the attacker's background: the mediated schema and, thus, the expressive means of declaring potential secrets; the security policy actually employed in the interaction; the owner's kind of forming and changing the integrated belief, i.e., the syntax and semantics of basic belief requests; the owner's Java-like program for the overall looping of interaction processing; and, additionally, the owner's confidentiality enforcement mechanism to be designed for the required inference control.

Taken all together, the wanted protection should be achieved against an attacker that knows the overall programming code of controlled interaction processing based on CIE including its parameter values, and thus the *complete system definition* in terms of *traces* associated with the respective *inputs* and *outputs*. Under this perspective, the semantics of a security policy can be rephrased in terms of the system definition by traces like a *non-interference property* [16].

4   A Mediator Framework for Unified Inference Control

In this section we outline a mediator framework to comply with the requirements developed in Sect. 3. The framework applies language-based information
flow control with declassification supported by controlled interaction execution.
Rather than establishing a single inference control mechanism for a specific interaction protocol programmed in Java, as done in previous work, e.g., [8], we more
ambitiously aim at providing a *general framework* to implement any inference-
proof interaction protocol of the kind described in Subsect. 3.2. The main goal
of the framework is to *uniformly* and *securely relate* CIE-like inference control
regarding logically expressed pieces of belief on the one hand to information flow
control regarding data objects stored in containers and manipulated by means
of Java commands like evaluation of expressions, assignment and procedure call,
or conditionals (guarded commands) on the other hand.

For lack of space, we will present the framework by summarizing the nine
main steps of the line of reasoning for its justification and by discussing an
informative example. A detailed exposition of a full abstract model and a formal
verification of the achievements are left to a forthcoming report, complemented
by an implementation employing Paragon [11].

Paragon is a Java-based programming language supporting *static checking*
of a specification of permitted information flows and offering *dynamic declassification* [16] by means of current states of *flow locks*. Roughly summarized, a programmer should associate a *flow policy* of form {*receivers : list_of_flowlocks*}
to an *object* declaration, and in the program code he might employ operations
to *open* or *close* declared flow locks.

The Paragon *compiler* then checks whether (the semantics of) all commands
appearing in the program code comply with the (semantics of the) declared
policies in the following sense: in any program execution, the information content
of an object can only flow to the intended receivers under the condition that the
associated flow locks have been opened. Accordingly, the *runtime* system of
Paragon only maintains and checks the lock states.

This implies that a Paragon *programmer* has to take care that all declassification relevant procedures are appropriately *encapsulated* such that the wanted
effects cannot unintendedly or maliciously be modified. In particular, the programmer has to safely protect any code that leads to open flow locks after checking some conditions. In our suggested framework, this code would be concentrated
in a *belief–program interface* that contains a *flow tracker* as its main component.
Accordingly, this interface has to be generically provided as part of the general
framework such that an application-oriented programmer of an interaction protocol cannot modify or circumvent the security enforcing procedures.

4.1   Overall Design of the Framework

To provide the general framework, we have to define appropriate *structures*,
to be implemented as *Java/Paragon classes*, and to describe a corresponding
programming discipline. In the following we will introduce these items by a brief

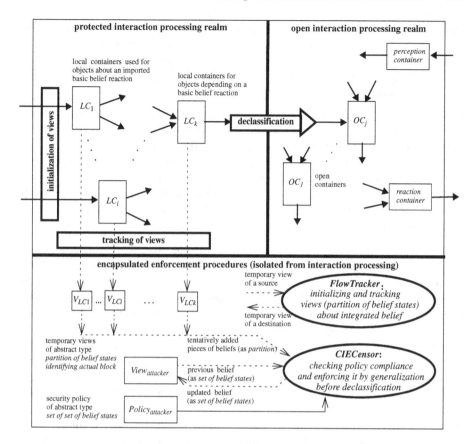

Fig. 4. Concepts of the belief–program interface underlying the mediator framework

summary of the line of reasoning that justifies our approach, complemented by
a partial visualization shown in Fig. 4.

1. *Isolation by typing.* The working space of an interaction protocol has to be
strictly divided into a *protected realm* where potentially confidential information
stemming from basic belief reactions is processed and an *open realm* where the
final external reaction is prepared. We will employ *typing* with *flow lock policies*
to achieve a complete (but preliminary) isolation of these realms.

2. *Sharing by declassification.* To nevertheless enable *discretionary sharing* of
information about the integrated belief, i.e., a controlled information flow from
a container in the protected realm to a container in the open realm, we will
use *declassification* by means of temporarily *opening* the flow lock on the source
container.

3. *History-aware policy compliance by FlowTracker and CIECensor.* Before temporarily opening a flow lock to permit a requested data transfer, we have to
ensure that the transfer would be harmless, i.e., complying with the *security*

policy under the simulated history-dependent *previous view* of the attacker on
the owner's integrated belief. For this complex task, we will provide a dedicated encapsulated component called *FlowTracker* which can delegate subtasks,
namely (1) evaluations of harmlessness and (2) actions of filtering and modifying,
to a further component called *CIECensor*.

4. *Need of local flow tracking.* For an *evaluation of harmlessness* of a requested
data transfer, the *CIECensor* needs to know both the explicit and the implicit
information about the integrated belief contained in the source container as the
result of the preceding processing in the protected realm. I.e., the *CIECensor*
needs an additional input, namely the view on the owner's integrated belief,
solely resulting from preceding processing and to be tentatively combined with
the attacker's previous view. This *tentative addition* will be dynamically generated by the *FlowTracker*.

5. *Identifying implicit flows by symbolic executions.* Implicit information – as
caused by guarded commands – not only depends on the actually performed execution path but also on the possibly followed (alternative) paths – which could
be selected for different values of the pertinent guards. Accordingly, the *Flow-
Tracker* will base the dynamic generation of the tentative addition on *code annotations* that stem from *symbolic program executions* performed at compile time,
as inspired by [2].

More specifically, as part of the *programming discipline*, a data transfer from
the protected realm to the open realm may only be requested by an explicit
assignment command, or any equivalent like a procedure call, that is *outside the
scope* of any guard. For such a command, *code analysis* will perform symbolic
executions of *all* paths leading to the pertinent command, and combine their
results to an annotation which contains a symbolic expression referring to the
usage of a container in a path by a (still uninterpreted) symbol and denoting
the information content of the source container regarding the integrated belief.

6. *Determining local flows by FlowTracker.* To prepare for manipulating the
flow lock, the *FlowTracker* will evaluate the symbolic code annotation using the
actual information contents of the local containers involved. These information
contents are dynamically determined as *temporary views* associated with the
local containers. More specifically, these temporary views are *initialized* when
storing a basic belief reaction as an object in a local container and for an evaluation further *tracked* according to the operators in the code annotation. In
abstract terms, such an information content is represented as a mapping of possible values to sets of belief states such that all these sets together form a *partition* of the possible belief states, similarly as in [6]. Moreover, the mapping is
complemented with an identification of the *actual value and block*, respectively.

7. *Evaluation of harmlessness by CIECensor.* Called by the *FlowTracker* with
the tentative addition, the *CIECensor* checks whether the *combined information content* of the tentative addition resulting from preceding processing and
the previous view resulting from the history could possibly violate the *security
policy*. In abstract terms, this combination is obtained by taking all nonempty

intersections of a block in (the partition of) the tentative addition with the previous view, and a *possible violation* occurs if there is a block in the combination that is *completely contained* in an element of the security policy, assuming that a policy element is abstractly represented as a set of belief states, as described in [6]. If the check confirms harmlessness, the previous view is updated to its intersection with the actual block and the *FlowTracker* is informed accordingly, and the *FlowTracker* then temporarily opens the flow lock in turn.

8. *Filtering and modifying by generalization.* If the check indicates a possible violation, the *CIECensor* considers whether there would be an *actual violation*. Clearly, this is the case if the block in the combination that corresponds to the actual value is contained in a policy element, and thus this value may not be revealed. However, to avoid meta-inferences such a hiding has to be made *indistinguishable* from the treatment of at least one different value. Accordingly, the *CIECensor* has to apply a precomputed *distortion table*, as exemplified in [9], that (i) clusters possible values such that the union of their blocks is not contained in any policy element and (ii) determines for each cluster a suitably *generalized value*, similarly as for k-anonymity. Applying the distortion table then means that the *CIECensor* updates the previous view with the partition derived from the clustering and returns the generalized value determined by the cluster containing the actual value to the *FlowTracker*, which then replaces the actual value of the source container by the generalized one and finally temporarily opens the flow lock.

As part of the *programming discipline*, the set of possible return values of a basic belief reaction and the set of (crucial) values of external reactions (depending on the integrated belief state) has to be kept suitably small to manage the precomputation of the distortion table.

9. *Processing generalized values by overloading operators.* To enable further processing of generalized values within the *open realm*, all operators used in the pertinent program code have to be suitably *redefined* by overloading.

So far, to enable manageable procedures, we rely on two restrictions. First, only *closed queries* are accepted as basic belief requests (but no open queries, updates and revisions), since they have only two or a few more return values (e.g., corresponding to *valid, invalid, unknown, . . .*) and can be handled without a sophisticated transaction management including commits and aborts. Second, only two-sided conditionals are allowed in a program for interaction processing (but no repetitions with dynamically determined number of rounds), to enable the symbolic program executions according to Item 5. Moreover, as already indicated before, the effectiveness of the proposed procedures crucially depends on the suitable protection of the *FlowTracker* and the related components, which might restrict the usage of some further programming features.

Based on an assignment of pertinent flow policies to basic belief reactions and the reaction container, type-checking the interaction program by Paragon will ensure isolation of the two realms and, by exception, sharing via declassification as permitted by the lock state. Additionally, write-access to the necessary locks can be limited to the *FlowTracker* class by using Java access level modifiers.

Regarding the CIE-like semantics of the security policy (Subsect. 3.3), we will prove that the attacker's information gain is limited, locally, to explicit assignments across the realms and, in extent, to the information content of the possibly generalized value so assigned. The proof will be based on the gradual release property, to be established by Paragon, and an extension to conditioned gradual release [3], to be established by symbolic execution for local flow tracking.

4.2   An Informative Example

We will discuss the following abstract, imperative interaction program:

$$\underline{c_1} := val_2; c_2 := val_2;$$
$$\underline{c_3} := breq_1(ibs, c_{per}); \underline{c_4} := breq_2(ibs, c_{per}); \underline{c_5} := breq_3(ibs, c_{per});$$
$$\text{if } q_1(c_{per}) \text{ then}$$
$$\quad \text{if } q_2(\underline{c_4}) \text{ then } \underline{c_1} := \oplus_1(\underline{c_3}, \underline{c_5}) \text{ else } \underline{c_1} := \underline{c_3} \text{ endif}$$
$$\text{endif}$$
$$ic(\underline{c_1}, c_6); ic(\underline{c_3}, c_7);$$
$$c_{rea} := \oplus_2(c_6, c_2, c_7)$$

Data from the integrated belief state ibs is imported into containers c_3, c_4 and c_5 via basic belief requests depending on the perception container c_{per}. Consequently, according to Item 1 (Isolation), these containers belong to the protected realm as indicated by their underlining and determined by the not represented flow policies of the respective basic belief reactions and so does the container c_1 due to its dependence on basic belief reactions. The remaining containers c_2, c_6 and c_7 belong to the open realm, contributing to the preparation of the reaction container c_{rea}, as determined by its not represented flow policy. To transfer data from containers c_1 and c_3 in the protected realm to the open realm into containers c_6 and c_7, respectively, the programmer employs the assignment ic controlled by the *FlowTracker* for declassification according to Item 2 (Sharing).

According to Item 5 (Implicit Flows), dependencies of c_1 on basic belief reactions in execution paths, which lead through the two guarded commands to the declassification command for c_1, are represented in a precomputed symbolic expression for c_1. In the precomputation, uninterpreted symbols are introduced for each basic belief reaction. Following all paths, symbolic expressions for c_1 are generated for each assignment to c_1 in the scope of the guarded commands which are $\oplus_1(\alpha, \gamma)$ (for the operation $\oplus_1$ dependent on the basic belief reactions $breq_1(ibs, c_{per})$ and $breq_3(ibs, c_{per})$, respectively) and α (for the basic belief reaction $breq_1(ibs, c_{per})$). The visit of a branch conveys information about the validity of the guard as denoted by the symbolic expressions q_1 and $q_2(\beta)$, respectively (the latter dependent on the basic belief reaction $breq_2(ibs, c_{per})$). At the join of two complementary branches, the symbolic expressions assigned to c_1 in each branch are refined with the respective expression for the validity or falsity of the enclosing guard and then combined for the join. Here, leaving the branches of the inner guard, the symbolic expressions for c_1 of each branch are $q_2(\beta) * \oplus_1(\alpha, \gamma)$

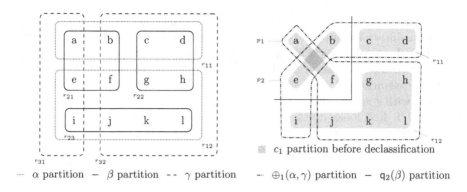

$\cdots$ α partition $-$ β partition $--$ γ partition $\cdots$ $\oplus_1(\alpha,\gamma)$ partition $-$ $q_2(\beta)$ partition

Fig. 5. Indexed partitions of the set of belief states for local flow tracking

and $\overline{q_2(\beta)} * \alpha$, respectively, joined to the expression $(q_2(\beta) * \oplus_1(\alpha,\gamma)) + (\overline{q_2(\beta)} * \alpha)$. Leaving the scope of the outer guard, the symbolic expression for c_1 becomes $(q_1 * ((q_2(\beta) * \oplus_1(\alpha,\gamma)) + (\overline{q_2(\beta)} * \alpha))) + \overline{q_1}$ as used for the declassification.

Assume that the integrated belief state *ibs* is an element from the abstract set $\mathcal{IBS} = \{a, b, \ldots, l\}$ and that the input to the perception container c_{per} is fixed. Then, dependent on the actual choice of *ibs*, the basic belief reactions may vary within small ranges R_1, R_2 and R_3 of values and partition the set $\mathcal{IBS}$ according to the value (Fig. 5 on the left). According to Item 6 (Tentative Addition), the *FlowTracker* initializes the symbols for the respective belief reactions and the temporary views of the containers into which these are imported to the respective partition. A view $(w, (B_r)_{r \in R})$ for container c means the following: knowing the value of c is r enables the partner to infer to which block the actual integrated belief state belongs, namely B_r. Note that the partner is always able to determine the partition from his background and the fixed open input.

Term-wise, being synchronized with interaction processing by (not represented) code annotations, the *FlowTracker* evaluates pertinent subterms of the symbolic expression for container c_1 yielding an evaluation of the whole expression to be used as the tentative addition during declassification (Item 6), as shown in Fig. 5 on the right. Being informed about the return value of the boolean function q_1, the *FlowTracker* extracts the subterm of the symbolic expression according to the validity of q_1 and discards the rest. For the subterm built with symbol $\oplus_1$, it first computes the lower bound of the two input partitions, α and γ, maps the index of each block to the result of operator $\oplus_1$, and unions all blocks with the same index. Lastly, for the boolean function q_2 dependent on the partition β, the *FlowTracker* unions all blocks B_r from β with the same value $q_2(r)$, leading to two blocks, and intersects the partitions for the subterms $\oplus_1(\alpha,\gamma)$ and α with the pertinent block. This way, the *FlowTracker* obtains the tentative addition for the declassification of c_1.

Consider now the security policy $\{\{a\}, \{g, h\}\}$, the actual integrated belief state $e \in \mathcal{IBS}$ and the history-dependent previous view containing $\mathcal{IBS} \setminus$

$\{c, d, f\}$. Regarding Item 3 (Compliance), before the transfer from c_1 to c_6 via the declassification command ic, the *CIECensor* checks whether a set in the security policy comprises a block from the tentative addition for c_1 intersected with the previous view according to Item 7 (Harmlessness). The check is positive for policy element $\{a\}$ so that policy violation is possible and the *CIECensor* proceeds with generalization according to Item 8 (Generalization). In the distortion table, it first looks up the highlighted row as determined by the view of c_1 intersected with the previous view and the security policy and then it looks up the column for the actual value p_2 of c_1:

sets of indices per harmful union of blocks	actual container value			
	p_1	p_2	r_{11}	r_{12}
$\{p_1\}$	p	p	r_{11}	r_{12}
$\{p_2\}$	p	p	r_{11}	r_{12}
$\{p_1, p_2\}$	#	#	#	#
...				

The so looked up cell contains the value to be transferred to container c_6. Accordingly, the *CIECensor* updates the view for the partner to the set $\{a, b, e\}$ and then forwards the value p to the *FlowTracker*.

5   Conclusions

As already mentioned in the introductory Sect. 1, we started a highly ambitious project to construct solutions for the inherently difficult challenges of a uniform information confinement of protocols for interaction processing based on an integrated belief. Briefly summarized, we have had to combine adapted technologies from various fields of expertise, including logic-based belief forming [10], adversarial reasoning [15], information system integration and mediation [12], data–program interfacing [13], logic-based inference control [4], and language-based information flow control with declassification [16], for each of which alone the state of science already provides impressive achievements.

So, the conjecture underlying our project is that time is come to construct a novel kind of systems to manage and share information while discretionarily protecting dedicated pieces of it. Our main contribution, a framework for designing and implementing such a system by employing available technologies from the various fields, supports our conjecture by a technical argument. The technicalities employed consist of interfacing data sources and programming code not only at the syntactic layer of the data's bytes but on the semantic layer of the data's information content in terms of the owner's integrated belief, actually even more striving in terms of (a simulation of) the attackers's view on that belief.

Obviously, we have only exhibited one possible approach for the indicated scenario; in other scenarios and under other circumstances alternative approaches might be possible as well. However, we believe that bridging the gap between the underlying raw data and the effectively released information will be at the core of any attempt. Moreover, we still have to experimentally evaluate the practicality of several mediators constructed by employing a future prototype implementation of the framework. As usual, acceptable computational complexity and scalability will demand appropriate approximations and some simplification.

References

1. Andrighetto, G., Governatori, G., Noriega, P., van der Torre, L.W.N. (eds.): Normative Multi-Agent Systems. Dagstuhl Follow-Ups, vol. 4. Schloss Dagstuhl - Leibniz-Zentrum fuer Informatik (2013)
2. Balliu, M., Dam, M., Guernic, G.L.: Encover: symbolic exploration for information flow security. In: Chong, S. (ed.) IEEE Computer Security Foundations Symposium - CSF 2012, pp. 30–44. IEEE Computer Society, Los Alamitos (2012)
3. Banerjee, A., Naumann, D.A., Rosenberg, S.: Expressive declassification policies and modular static enforcement. In: IEEE Symposium on Security and Privacy - S & P 2008, pp. 339–353. IEEE Computer Society, Los Alamitos (2008)
4. Biskup, J.: Inference-usability confinement by maintaining inference-proof views of an information system. Int. J. Comput. Sci. Eng. $7(1)$, 17–37 (2012)
5. Biskup, J.: Logic-oriented confidentiality policies for controlled interaction execution. In: Madaan, A., Kikuchi, S., Bhalla, S. (eds.) DNIS 2013. LNCS, vol. 7813, pp. 1–22. Springer, Heidelberg (2013)
6. Biskup, J., Bonatti, P.A., Galdi, C., Sauro, L.: Optimality and complexity of inference-proof data filtering and CQE. In: Kutyłowski, M., Vaidya, J. (eds.) ICAIS 2014, Part II. LNCS, vol. 8713, pp. 165–181. Springer, Heidelberg (2014)
7. Biskup, J., Tadros, C.: Idea: towards a vision of engineering controlled interaction execution for information services. In: Jürjens, J., Piessens, F., Bielova, N. (eds.) ESSoS. LNCS, vol. 8364, pp. 35–44. Springer, Heidelberg (2014)
8. Biskup, J., Tadros, C.: Preserving confidentiality while reacting on iterated queries and belief revisions. Ann. Math. Artif. Intell. $73(1-2)$, 75–123 (2015)
9. Biskup, J., Weibert, T.: Keeping secrets in incomplete databases. Int. J. Inf. Sec. $7(3)$, 199–217 (2008)
10. Brewka, G.: Multi-context systems: specifying the interaction of knowledge bases declaratively. In: Krötzsch, M., Straccia, U. (eds.) RR 2012. LNCS, vol. 7497, pp. 1–4. Springer, Heidelberg (2012)
11. Broberg, N., van Delft, B., Sands, D.: Paragon for practical programming with information-flow control. In: Shan, C. (ed.) APLAS 2013. LNCS, vol. 8301, pp. 217–232. Springer, Heidelberg (2013)
12. Doan, A., Halevy, A.Y., Ives, Z.G.: Principles of Data Integration. Morgan Kaufmann, San Francisco (2012)
13. Fowler, M.: Patterns of Enterprise Application Architecture. Pearson, Boston (2003)
14. Halpern, J.Y., O'Neill, K.R.: Secrecy in multiagent systems. ACM Trans. Inf. Syst. Secur. $12(1)$, 5.1–5.47 (2008)
15. Kott, A., McEneaney, W.M. (eds.): Adversarial Reasoning: Computational Approaches to Reading the Opponent's Mind. Chapman & Hall/CRC, London (2007)
16. Sabelfeld, A., Sands, D.: Declassification: dimensions and principles. J. Comput. Secur. $17(5)$, 517–548 (2009)
17. Wooldridge, M.J.: An Introduction to MultiAgent Systems, 2nd edn. Wiley, Chichester (2009)

Privacy and Trust

Personalized Composition of Trustful Reputation Systems

Johannes Sänger$^{(\boxtimes)}$, Christian Richthammer, André Kremser,
and Günther Pernul

Department of Information Systems, University of Regensburg, Regensburg, Germany
{Johannes.sanger,Christian.richthammer,Andre.kremser,
Gunther.pernul}@wiwi.uni-regensburg.de

Abstract. The vast amount of computation techniques for reputation systems proposed in the past has resulted in a need for a global online trust repository with reusable components. In order to increase the practical usability of such a repository, we propose a software framework that supports the user in selecting appropriate components and automatically combines them to a fully functional computation engine. On the one hand, this lets developers experiment with different concepts and move away from one single static computation engine. On the other hand, our software framework also enables an explorative trust evaluation through user interaction. In this way, we notably increase the transparency of reputation systems. To demonstrate the practical applicability of our proposal, we present realistic use cases and describe how it would be employed in these scenarios.

Keywords: Trust management · Reputation systems · Reusability · Component repository

1 Introduction

New environments such as eCommerce platforms and content communities offer manifold opportunities but also pose many challenges. Unlike in traditional settings, electronic interaction partners are usually strangers whose trustworthiness is unknown. To cope with this, trust and reputation models have emerged in recent decades. They allow to rate a set of objects (e.g. actors, products) and calculate a reputation value based on the feedback given. Since Resnick et al.'s paper [1] on the use of reputation systems to facilitate trust in Internet transactions, a vast number of reputation systems has been proposed. One major problem in this context is that most of them are completely designed from scratch and that established ideas are rarely considered [2]. To address this, Sänger and Pernul [3] decompose common reputation systems into single functional building blocks and describe and implement them in a publicly available repository.

One important factor that can be observed in connection with the repository is the subjective nature of trust, meaning that the trust value regarding one

© IFIP International Federation for Information Processing 2015
P. Samarati (Ed.): DBSec 2015, LNCS 9149, pp. 207–214, 2015.
DOI: 10.1007/978-3-319-20810-7_13

entity might be different from the view of various end users. Many trust models try to cover this by involving individualized information on the current end user in the computation process. However, while the output value is based on distinct input data, the computation methods applied are alike for every user in such systems. In this work, we choose a different path. We take existing concepts and let the user make up his "new" personalized trust model. Thereto, we develop a software framework that allows to combine the reusable components provided in the aforementioned repository [3]. The benefits of such an approach are manifold. From the end user's point of view, we allow the dynamic adaption of a reputation system to a specific situation, enable an explorative trust evaluation through user interaction, and notably increase the transparency of reputation systems as the user himself composes the computation methods. Considering the increasing number and sophistication of attacks on reputation systems [4], these benefits constitute important aspects to raise situational awareness and thus to foster trust in reputation systems. We argue that being able to actively add and remove particularly designed computation components greatly facilitates the discovery of manipulations such as multiple referrals between colluding entities.

The remainder of the paper is based on the design science research paradigm including the guidelines for conducting design science research by Hevner et al. [5]. In particular, we follow the design science research methodology introduced by Peffers et al. [6]. In Sect. 2, we delineate the scientific background and related work important with respect to this work. Thereby, we outline our research goals. After that, we introduce our concept for flexible and dynamic trust model composition. We expose the conceptual design in Sect. 3 and describe how it is implemented in Sect. 4. Subsequently, we demonstrate the proper functioning of our software framework and discuss the benefits of our approach in Sect. 5. Finally, we sum up our contribution and conclude in Sect. 6.

2   Background and Related Work

In this section, we discuss previous work that forms the basis for this paper. The information presented directly leads us to our research goals.

2.1   Reusability for Trust and Reputation Systems

The ongoing interest in trust and reputation systems has resulted in a large number of different proposals. The computation methods applied to come up with an ultimate trust value making a statement about the trustworthiness of a particular entity range from simple arithmetic via statistical approaches through to graph-based models. Moreover, they involve multiple factors such as context information, propagation, and personal preferences.

Since most of the reputation systems proposed in literature use computation methods that are entirely built from scratch [2], well-established approaches are rarely considered and promising concepts get lost in the shuffle. In order to foster reusability of the particular components of reputation systems, Sänger and Pernul [3] propose a hierarchical component taxonomy of computation engines.

The taxonomy forms the basis for setting up a repository containing design knowledge both on a conceptual and an implementation level[1]. On the conceptual level, the components are described in design pattern-like artifacts. On implementation level, all components are provided in form of reusable web services. This repository, in turn, is supposed to serve as a natural framework for the design of new reputation systems.

2.2 Research Gap

Compared to [3], we want to go one step further. The selection and interpretation of adequate components for new reputation systems in a specific application area requires time, effort, and to some extent knowledge of the area. Therefore, we argue that there is a need for an application that supports this development process by enabling the software-supported selection and composition of components. On the one hand, this further supports the objectives of fostering the reuse of existing ideas, encouraging researchers and platform operators to focus on the design of single components, and allowing them to experiment with different concepts. On the other hand, the software-supported selection and composition of components also gives platform operators the ability to dynamically combine particular functional blocks and move away from one single static computation engine. Furthermore, we now take the end users of reputation systems as another group of stakeholders into consideration. With the help of an application for the dynamic composition of reputation-based trust models, we want to enable an explorative trust evaluation through user interaction. Since end users themselves can compose the computation methods, such an application notably increases the transparency of reputation systems. Moreover, end users are able to dynamically adapt a computation engine to the specific situation and to their own needs.

3 Conceptual Design

In this section, we describe the conceptual design for a software framework, where single components of a reputation system (implemented as web services) can be initially selected by the user, are gradually composed to a fully functional reputation system and where the selection can finally be flexibly and dynamically refined. At each step, our system supports the user by filtering further possibilities based on composition rules, input data and previous user decisions.

Figure 1 depicts the overall process of our component-based reputation system with user interaction. The phases "selection" and "composition" are iteratively run through so that a user can successively adapt and refine the selection of components. In this way, he can experiment with different compositions, exploratively evaluate reputation and approach to the most suitable reputation system. To develop the conceptual design of our framework, we carry out the four major steps described in the following.

---

[1] Available online: http://trust.bayforsec.de/.

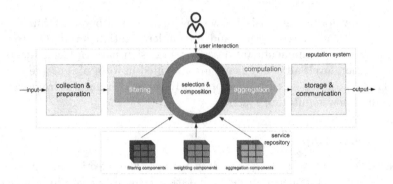

Fig. 1. Component-based reputation system with user interaction

3.1 Standard Input Format

As the provision of suitable input data is crucial for the proper functioning of a component (web service) and as the single components can be dynamically exchanged, a standard input format needs to be defined. Based on this standardized structure, we adapt each component to implement their interface accordingly. Consequently, the framework can only be used if input data is provided according to this standard.

3.2 Matching Input Data and Components

Despite the input being provided in a standardized format, it is not ensured that it contains all data necessary for the proper functioning of each component. Time-based filtering, for instance, is only applicable if referrals contain a timestamp. Therefore, the next step that needs to be considered is the analysis of necessary input data for each component. Thus, based on the requirements of each service in the service repository, we firstly set up a global list of data necessary for the proper functioning of all components. Secondly, we match every computation component to the standard input data on the list to reveal the type of input data required by each service. Applying these information, our software framework can ensure that the user can only select services compatible to the input data provided.

3.3 Interactive Component Selection

The interactive component selection enables the user to choose between the different components via a graphical user interface (GUI). Based on the selections made, a workflow description is generated. Using this workflow description, it is no longer necessary to call each component (web service) individually. Instead, the input data and the workflow description serve as input for the automated component composition service that delivers the final reputation value as output.

3.4 Automated Component Composition Service

After the selection has been made, the framework needs to automatically compose the selected components to a fully functional reputation system. Thereto, composition rules need to be defined. Filtering services, for instance, can only be executed in sequence whereas weighting services can be processed in parallel. To guarantee the correct execution of these rules, a workflow handler and a workflow engine need to be implemented. The workflow handler validates the syntax and semantics of the submitted workflow description. It then creates an execution list that is handed over to the workflow engines. The workflow engine gradually processes the execution list. It calls each computation component with its settings that are specified in the task. Having processed the complete execution list, the reputation value result is transmitted back to the workflow handler which returns the result to the user.

4 Implementation

To demonstrate the feasibility of our conceptual design, we implemented the dynamic composition framework in a software prototype. In order to allow the dynamic addition of computation components without altering the web service, we set up a plug-in orientated framework. In this way, the computation components can be developed independently and are made available to the framework by configuration. Thereby, they can be used either with an internal API or via REST-API. The interactive component selection is implemented in a web-based application using the current web standards HTML5, JavaScript and CSS3. These enable the user to select computation components in order to generate a workflow description in JSON format via the browser. The automated component composition service is implemented in PHP. Here, it is only necessary to provide the workflow description along with the referrals as input data. The automated component composition service processes the input and delivers a reputation value as output.

5 Evaluation

To rigorously demonstrate the proper functioning and goodness of our solution, we carry out a descriptive scenario-based evaluation in which we demonstrate how the framework could be used to build a reputation engine in practice. Here, we present a realistic scenario from the viewpoint of two potential user groups – system developers and end users. According to Hevner et al. [5], the evaluation procedure employed by us is a standard approach for innovative artifacts like ours.

5.1 Scenario Analysis, Part 1: System Developer

The fictitious web developer Arthur Dent runs an eBay-like electronic marketplace platform. Similar to eBay's reputation system, his current system calculates the seller reputation value based on the sum of positive ($+1$) and negative (-1)

ratings. Furthermore, it provides the share of positive ratings during the last 12 months.

As his current reputation system is quite vulnerable against a variety of attacks, he decides to integrate a new computation engine in order to enhance the security of his platform. Analyzing his environment, he comes up with the following list of requirements:

1. The reputation value should directly reflect changes in seller behavior.
2. Ratings pushing one's reputation by means of fake transactions between two friends should not be considered.
3. The reputation value should reflect the seller's behavior for a specific product group to deter dishonest sellers from building high reputation in one product group while cheating on other products.

As Arthur does not really know how to implement such an engine, he makes use of our dynamic composition framework. To decide which components best fit his requirements, he firstly reads the functionality description of each component in the knowledge repository[2]. Based on this, he experiments with different compositions and finally chooses a combination of the four components "weighting:TimeDiscountingAbsolute" (requirement 1), "filter:MultipleReferrals" (requirement 2), "weighting:ContextDiscountingAbsolutCongruence" (requirement 3) and "aggregation:SharePositive". Having selected the components on the user interface, a workflow description is generated by the framework as shown on Listing 1.

Listing 1. Workflow generated for the four selected components

```
''MultipleReferrals''->
(
''TimeDiscountingAbsolute'':[{''time_limit'':365}] |
''CongruenceAbsolute'':[{''context-text'':
    [''product_category_1'',''product_category_2'']
    }]) ->
''SharePositive''
```

Using this workflow description along with the referrals, Arthur only needs to call the automated component composition service, and will receive a reputation value that is calculated using the specified components.

This first part of the scenario demonstrates that a system developer can easily arrange a new computation engine that perfectly fits his requirements without any need to implement the logic. In this way, he is encouraged to reuse existing ideas and build on findings made by others. Besides the systems developers, the second user group that can profit from our framework are the end users.

5.2 Scenario Analysis, Part 2: End User

Having started to integrate the new static reputation engine in the platform, Arthur has an idea. Why not let the user compose his "own" reputation engine?

---
[2] http://trust.bayforsec.de/ngot/index.php.

To accomplish this, he pre-defines the available input data and integrates the resulting component selection form in his platform.

To evaluate if the dynamic reputation engine actually fulfills his requirements and to see how seller reputation can be exploratively analyzed from a user's point of view, he creates a fictional profile of a malicious seller on his platform who carried out 20 transactions (one per day, starting on 2015-01-01). For the first 10 transactions, he behaved honestly to build a high reputation. He thereby sold trading cards. Subsequently, he started to cheat on transactions involving mobile phones for 5 times resulting in negative ratings. To recover his reputation, he finally asked a friend to rate him positively after 5 fake transactions attributed to mobile phones as well.

Having set up the seller profile, Arthur gradually composes the reputation engine designed in the previous part. Figure 2 depicts the resulting reputation values. The four lines on the chart reflect the different composition phases.

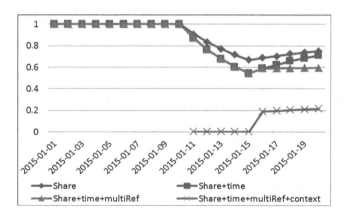

Fig. 2. Reputation values calculated over time

The first engine, which only consists of the aggregation component, provides a value of 1 (100 Nevertheless, the multiple positive ratings provided by the same buyer are still equally considered. Adding the MultipleReferrals filter this problem is sufficiently addressed. Note that the user can only become aware of the fact that the seller has been rated unfairly high by one buyer, if he actively filters these multiple referrals. Whereas initially presenting the lower reputation value may indeed reflect the real seller reputation, but still hide information about the multiple unfair ratings. Finally, Arthur extends the engine by the context-based weighting component. The corresponding values on the chart depict the reputation values calculated for the context-description "phone" and "mobile". As there is no evidence for this context at the beginning, the first value is provided for the 2015-01-11. The reputation values involving context stay considerably low, since the seller did not perform well in this context for all referrals considered.

214 J. Sänger et al.

6 Discussion and Conclusion

Overall, this scenario elucidates that our dynamic composition framework has an obvious utility from a practical point of view for system developers and end users. Developers, on the one hand, can experiment with different combinations, easily build reputation computation engines and even let the end user decide which combination to apply without having to implement various systems. End users, on the other hand, can add and remove single components, exploratively analyze seller reputation, create a personalized computation engine and in this way strengthen their situational awareness. All in all, we reduce efforts, allow to increase the robustness of reputation systems by extending their capabilities, and enhance the transparency of reputation systems as well as the situational awareness through involving the user in the decision process.

Acknowledgement. The research leading to these results was supported by the "Bavarian State Ministry of Education, Science and the Arts" as part of the FORSEC research association.

References

1. Resnick, P., Kuwabara, K., Zeckhauser, R., Friedman, E.: Reputation systems. Commun. ACM **43**(12), 45–48 (2000)
2. Tavakolifard, M., Almeroth, K.C.: A taxonomy to express open challenges in trust and reputation systems. J. Commun. **7**(7), 538–551 (2012)
3. Sänger, J., Pernul, G.: Reusability for trust and reputation systems. In: Zhou, J., Gal-Oz, N., Zhang, J., Gudes, E. (eds.) Trust Management VIII. IFIP AICT, vol. 430, pp. 28–43. Springer, Heidelberg (2014)
4. Hoffman, K., Zage, D., Nita-Rotaru, C.: A survey of attack and defense techniques for reputation systems. ACM Comput. Surv. **42**(1), 1–31 (2009)
5. Hevner, A.R., March, S.T., Park, J., Ram, S.: Design science in information systems research. MIS Q. **28**(1), 75–105 (2004)
6. Peffers, K., Tuunanen, T., Rothenberger, M.A., Chatterjee, S.: A design science research methodology for information systems research. J. Manage. Inf. Syst. **24**(3), 45–77 (2007)

FamilyID: A Hybrid Approach to Identify Family Information from Microblogs

Jamuna Gopal[1], Shu Huang[2]($\boxtimes$), and Bo Luo[3]($\boxtimes$)

[1] IBM, San Jose, CA, USA
[2] Microsoft, Seattle, WA, USA
shuang@microsoft.com
[3] Department of EECS, University of Kansas, Lawrence, KS, USA
bluo@ku.edu

Abstract. With the growing popularity of social networks, extremely large amount of users routinely post messages about their daily life to online social networking services. In particular, we have observed that family related information, including some very sensitive information, are freely available and easily extracted from Twitter. In this paper, we present a hybrid information retrieval mechanism, namely FamilyID, to identify and extract family related information of a user from his/her microblogs (tweets). The proposed model takes into account part-of-speech tagging, pattern matching, lexical similarity, and semantic similarity of the tweets. Experiment results show that FamilyID provides both high precision and recall. We expect the project to serve as a warning to users that they may have accidentally revealed too much personal/family information to the public. It could also help microblog users to evaluate the amount of information that they have already revealed.

1 Introduction

With the growing popularity of online social networks, the data that is publicly available has increased by numerous folds. This data includes personal, employment, education, relationship, and family-related information. Figure 1 shows a microblog example – a tweet message that was broadcasted to the public, and effectively reveals his mother's Twitter ID, birthdate and last name.

Numerous commercial products or research projects have been developed to discover user information from online social networking data. Such information is used to improve the accuracy of advertisement delivery, to make sensible suggestions to users, and to predict events or trends. Moreover, the media industry (radio, movie, television) now highly depends on feedback from public OSN data for market study, user preference analysis, hot topic identification, etc. Although such products/projects may benefit both OSN providers and end users, they pose significant privacy threats to all users, while many of them are unaware of

S. Huang and B. Luo—This work was partially supported by NSF CNS-1422206, NSF IIS-1513324, NSF OIA-1308762, and University of Kansas GRF-2301876.

P. Samarati (Ed.): DBSec 2015, LNCS 9149, pp. 215–222, 2015.
DOI: 10.1007/978-3-319-20810-7_14

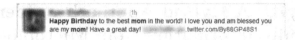

Fig. 1. A Tweet message that reveals sensitive family-related information.

such threats. An online stalker with limited hacking capability but ample time can effectively figure out lots of details about a targeted user with this publicly available data. For instance, message with birthday or anniversary wishes exposes users' age, date of birth and family information.

Extracting family-related information from Twitter is challenging: (1) it is cumbersome to manually identify such posts, as we have discovered that less than 1 % of the tweets are family-related; and (2) although it is possible to develop an automated mechanism to identify family-related tweets, the task is nontrivial, due to the size of data, the use of short text and informal language, and large amount of synonyms. In this paper, we present FamilyID, a multi-phase approach that automatically identifies family-related information from publicly available Twitter data. Our algorithm considers multiple features of tweets, including part-of-speech tagging, term distribution similarity, and semantic similarity. Experimental results show that FamilyID produces good accuracy.

The key contributions of this paper are: (1) We make the first attempt to automatically identify family-related microblogs – they usually disclose sensitive personal information, and they are the primary targets for both adversaries and defenders. (2) The proposed mechanisms exploit multiple lexical and semantic features, with a good balance of efficiency and precision. Our approach could handle large amount of data and provide relatively high accuracy.

2   Related Work

Private Information Disclosure. People may publicize private information for social advantages [7]. Users' privacy settings violate their sharing intentions, and they are unable or unwilling to fix the errors [11,13] explores three types of private information disclosed in the textual content of tweets. Impersonation attacks are proposed in [2] to steal private (friends-only) attributes.

Information Aggregation Attacks. Information aggregation attacks were introduced in [8,10,17]: significant amount of privacy is recovered when small pieces of information submitted by users are associated. [1] confirms that a significant amount of user profiles from multiple SNSs could be linked by email addresses.

Inference Attacks. Hidden attributes are inferred from friends' attributes with a Bayesian network [4,5] developed a model to predict user's birth year (i.e., age). Unknown user attributes could be accurately inferred when as few as 20 % of the users are known [14]. Friendship links and group membership information can be used to identify users [16] or infer sensitive hidden attributes [18].

Microblog Mining. Knowledge discovery in social networks is a hot research area. For instance, methods have been proposed to identify user attributes, such as gender, age, location [12], location type [9], activities [6], personalities [15], etc. There are also proposals to make predictions based on information and activities in social networks, e.g., to predict stock rates based on user tweets [3].

3   The FamilyID Approach

3.1   Problem Definition and Solution Overview

The goal of this research is to identify family-related posts from microblogs. Due to the volume of the data, manually reading each tweet and classifying it is an almost impossible task. Formally, the objective of the research is: *For each tweet, efficiently and accurately identify whether it is related to one or more family members of the message owner (the user who posted the message).*

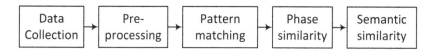

Fig. 2. Overview of the FamilyID approach

As illustrated in Fig. 2, we first use a customized crawler to collect user information and messages from Twitter. Each message is pre-processed to remove all the special characters and other unwanted contents, such as multimedia data (images, audio and video files). Each message from a user (denoted as the *owner* of the account/tweet) is processed through three steps: pattern matching, lexical (phrase) similarity measurement, and semantic similarity measurement. These steps are used to predict the likelihood of each tweet being family-related.

3.2   Data Collection

Using the *twitter4j* API, we have collected 150 twitter users' information, including username, screen name, friends (follower and following) list, tweets and tweets time-stamp. Twitter does not have the concept of *friends*. Hence, we considered the intersection of the followers list and the following list as the friends list. We have randomly selected users with the following criteria: (1) Users with more than 1500 followers are omitted as they have higher chances of being celebrities. Tweets of celebrities are not used in this research, since they demonstrate significantly different styles and contents from tweets of regular users. (2) Users with fewer than 2000 tweets are not crawled. (3) Users with majority of tweets in foreign languages (anything other than English) are discarded.

3.3   Pre-Processing

Messages from Twitter are extremely noisy. We develop several heuristics to pre-process raw tweets: *(1) Term Expansion.* Twitter users like to use abbreviations and very informal terms that do not exist in the dictionary. Certain steps in

Fig. 2 cannot process irregular words. Hence, we construct a table for Twitter term expansion for family-related terms (some examples are shown in Table 1). *(2) URL Truncation.* Tweets sometimes have URLs embedded in them. Since these URLs are not utilized in pattern matching, lexical similarity or semantic similarity assessments, we truncate all URLs. *(3). Stop Words.* FamilyID does not remove stop words, since words like "my", "our" are important in predicting family relationships. *(4) Special Characters.* All special characters other than the English words and numbers are truncated. Although we do not process numbers, we keep them for future use, e.g., to identify patterns related to year.

Table 1. Term expansion examples

Base word	Expanded word	Base word	Expanded word
mum	mother	sissy	sister
gf	girlfriend	bro	brother

3.4   Pattern Extraction and Matching

In Sects. 3.4–3.6, we present a series of operations to identify family-related tweets. The design philosophy is to first employ computationally inexpensive methods to eliminate the majority of irrelevant tweets, and then refine the results with methods that are more effective but expensive.

Iterative Pattern Discovery. The first step in family-related tweet identification is to discover natural language patterns that are highly likely to mention family member(s). We first employ the Stanford NLP tagger for part-of-speech tagging on all crawled tweets. Next, we extract N-Gram histograms ($N = 2, 3, 4$) across the dataset to collect the common patterns containing family terms. Pattern discovery is performed in an iterative manner: for each discovered pattern, we attempt to relax it, and validate the relaxed pattern on the dataset.

Example 1: In our dataset, POS-tagged text snippet
    my_PRP$ little_JJ sister_NN
has repeated 48 times, while text snippet
    my_PRP$ little_JJ sister_NN @UserName_NN
has appeared 32 times. Therefore, we have extracted the following pattern:
    _PRP$ _JJ _NN

Pattern Matching. Every POS-tagged tweet is matched against the seed patterns. With a matched pattern, the tweet has the potential to contain family-related information. Note that pattern matching is the first filter in the whole process, it leads to lot of noise outputs since many phrases could match one of our seed patterns. For instance, phrases such as "my dear dog", "my sweet neighbor" are matched to the _PRP$ _JJ _NN pattern, although they have nothing to do with family members.

3.5 Lexical Similarity Assessment

This phase finds if a pattern-matched tweet contains family-related words. We first create a seed tweet set covering all possible relationships and frequent non-relationship components from the patterns. We then employ the *UMBC ebiquity* text similarity system to calculate the lexical similarities for pairs of tweets. *Stanford WebBase Corpus* is used to find possible synonyms of the given words. Table 2 shows some examples of similarities computed in FamilyID.

Lexical similarity assessment effectively eliminates most of the noise from pattern matching. In particular, messages such as "my dog", "my neighbors", are effectively eliminated. However, tweets such as "my dear dog is my best companion" pass the pattern matching phase ("my dear dog" matches _PRP\$ _JJ _NN), and the lexical similarity assessment phase, due to the existence of terms "dear", "best", "companion". Since such tweets are clearly not family-related, we need another layer of semantic analysis to handle them.

Table 2. Lexical similarity examples

Text compared	Score
Happy birthday mother *vs.* happy birthday father	0.902
Happy anniversary sister *vs.* birthday wishes sister	0.749
Grandma is the best *vs.* my life is boring	0.033
I love you the most father *vs.* Jesus is great	0.122

3.6 Semantic Similarity Assessment

Semantic similarity assessment, which is relatively slower, is the last step to remove irrelevant tweets that have passed through the first two filters.

To generate a seed set for this model, we first take a seed such as "my little sister", and ran the sliding window algorithm on it. This is a recurring model that matches patterns in windows' length of up to 5. It replaces each word in the seed, and finds substitutions for the word, as shown below:

```
my little sister
*** little sister       my *** sister       my little ***
my *** little sister     my little *** sister
```

To calculate semantic similarity, we employ the *UMBC GetStsSim API*. This API takes 2 text snippets and returns a value between 0 and 1 as a similarity measure. Every candidate tweet is compared with the seed tweets, to measure the pairwise semantic similarity. As shown in Table 3, similarity score of 0.75 or above indicates an almost perfect match, while similarity score of 0.6 or above indicates relatively similar texts. Tweets with the highest similarity scores higher than the threshold are finally labeled as family-related. As shown in the previous example, tweet "my dear dog is my best companion" passes first two phases. When we evaluate its semantic similarity with the seed tweets in this phase, the highest similarity score is 0.33, which indicates that it is not similar with any of the seeds. In this way, this message is labeled as non-family-related.

Table 3. Semantic similarity examples

Compared tweets	Scores
Happy birthday mother *vs.* birthday wishes mother. You are the best	0.611
My sweet little sister *vs.* my handsome young brother	0.624
My sweet sister *vs.* my awesome dog	0.21
Long day. I miss you my dear mother. Come back soon *vs.* feeling extremely tired. Its a long day	0.38

4 Experimental Results

Tweet Identification. First, we have performed *tweet identification* on the collected dataset (150 Twitter users, more than 450,000 tweets). On average, FamilyID has identified approximately 30 tweets from each user as family-related, as shown in Fig. 3 (users are sorted by total number of tweets crawled). Less than 1 % of the tweets are identified to be related to family members. These include a small amount of false positives (to be

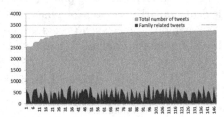

Fig. 3. Total number of tweets and family-related tweets for each user.

discussed later). With the numbers and by looking into the identified tweets, we have found that the results reflect our previous observations: (1) for most of the Twitter users, family-related tweets are very sparse. It is extremely time-consuming, if not impossible, to manually identify such tweets. (2) The identified family-related tweets almost always bring additional information about the family members, including the relationship, Twitter username, date of birth, age, interests, etc.

Comparing with Keyword-based Retrieval. To evaluate the effectiveness of FamilyID in reducing false-positives, we compare it with a keyword-based approach – identifying family-related tweets with keyword spotting. That is, when a pre-selected relationship keyword (e.g., "sister", "mother", the same as we used in Sect. 3.4) is found in the tweet, it is labeled as "family-related".

In order to manually examine the results, we perform keyword-based retrieval on 75 randomly selected users. We have evaluated 225,886 tweets. Keyword-based retrieval has found 6,121 tweets to be family-related, while FamilyID has identified 2301 of them as family-related. Note that due to the selection of the keywords, each tweet identified by keyword spotting is a candidate tweet in FamilyID. Therefore, more than 62 % of the tweets containing family-related keywords are identified as *irrelevant* to family relationships through content-based analysis in FamilyID. We further manually look into such irrelevant tweets, and find that more than 90 % of them are true negatives (not relevant to family members). This also indicates that the precision of the keyword spotting approach is low, since it has included large amount of non-family tweets.

Table 4. Examples of true positives and false positives.

True positives (Family-related tweets)
I'm gon be an uncle *smiles* "@Bintah_Adam: I can't imagine my mum having another baby now"
Oh my god my sister is annoying
False positives
When one of my boys tells me he's in love
If your not my girl don't be jealous of my other girls

Precision. We invite human evaluators to examine the tweets identified as family-related from 50 random users, to determine whether each tweet is truly related to family members. As the most important performance metric of FamilyID, the *precision* is defined as: $Precision = \frac{TP}{P}$, where TP indicates the number of true positives (tweets labeled as family-related that are determined to be family-related by human evaluators), and P indicates the number of positives (tweets labeled as family-related by FamilyID).

The evaluators have examined 1346 tweets that are identified as family-related by FamilyID. They have found 1110 tweets to be true positives. Therefore, the *precision of FamilyID is 83%*. Table 4 shows examples of true/false positives. The precision is high, especially consider the difficulty of the task. For some tweets, the human evaluator could hardly determine if they are family-related. For instance, for the message "When one of my boys tells me he's in love", the evaluator has referred to many other posts from the user, to find that she is a teacher and she is very likely talking about a student, instead of a child. However, the evaluator is less confident about the verdict.

Finally, we would like to point out that we have not evaluated the overall recall of FamilyID, for two reasons: (1) the size of the data set (450K tweets in total) makes it infeasible to manually examine all tweets; and (2) due to the heavy use of urban slang, abbreviations and short texts, it is even difficult for human evaluators to determine whether some of the tweets are family-related.

5   Conclusion

With the growing popularity of online social networks, large amounts of private information have been voluntarily posted to the Internet. From attackers' perspective, they could stalk a targeted user and attempt to extract such private information. However, manually identifying family-related tweets that are scattered in millions of microblog posts is very labor intensive. The FamilyID project demonstrates the capabilities of an automated mechanism to identify family-related microblogs and extract family member information from the microblogs. By utilizing lexical and semantic features in a multi-phase approach, we are able to achieve high accuracy. Moreover, most of the identified tweets carry additional (very sensitive) information about the family, such as birthdates, hobbies, family events, etc. FamilyID could be used by social network users to self-assess the amount of family-related information that they have posted to the public. We also expect the project to serve as a warning to Twitter users who carelessly disclose too much information in online socialization.

References

1. Balduzzi, M., Platzer, C., Holz, T., Kirda, E., Balzarotti, D., Kruegel, C.: Abusing social networks for automated user profiling. In: Jha, S., Sommer, R., Kreibich, C. (eds.) RAID 2010. LNCS, vol. 6307, pp. 422–441. Springer, Heidelberg (2010)
2. Bilge, L., Strufe, T., Balzarotti, D., Kirda, E.: All your contacts are belong to us: automated identity theft attacks on social networks. In: WWW (2009)
3. Bollen, J., Mao, H., Zeng, X.-J.: Twitter mood predicts the stock market. In: CoRR, abs/1010.3003 (2010)
4. Dey, R., Tang, C., Ross, K., Saxena, N.: Estimating age privacy leakage in online social networks (2012)
5. He, J., Chu, W.W., Liu, Z.V.: Inferring privacy information from social networks. In: Mehrotra, S., Zeng, D.D., Chen, H., Thuraisingham, B., Wang, F.-Y. (eds.) ISI 2006. LNCS, vol. 3975, pp. 154–165. Springer, Heidelberg (2006)
6. Huang, S., Chen, M., Luo, B., Lee, D.: Predicting aggregate social activities using continuous-time stochastic process. In: Proceedings ACM International Conference on Information and knowledge management (2012)
7. Huberman, B.A., Adar, E., Fine, L.R.: Valuating privacy. IEEE Secur. Priv. **3**(5), 22–25 (2005)
8. Li, F., Chen, J.Y., Zou, X., Liu, P.: New privacy threats in healthcare informatics: when medical records join the web. In: BIOKDD (2010)
9. Liu, H., Luo, B., Lee, D.: Location type classification using tweet content. In: ICMLA, vol. 1, pp. 232–237. IEEE (2012)
10. Luo, B., Lee, D.: On protecting private information in social networks: a proposal. In: M3SN Workshop (2009)
11. Madejski, M., Johnson, M., Bellovin, S.M.: The failure of online social network privacy settings. Technical report CUCS-010-11, Columbia University (2011)
12. Mahmud, J., Nichols, J., Drews, C.: Home location identification of twitter users. ACM Trans. Intell. Syst. Technol. **5**(3), 1–47 (2014)
13. Mao, H., Shuai, X., Kapadia, A.: Loose tweets: an analysis of privacy leaks on twitter. In: WPES (2011)
14. Mislove, A., Viswanath, B., Gummadi, K.P., Druschel, P.: You are who you know: inferring user profiles in online social networks. In: WSDM (2010)
15. Quercia, D., Kosinski, M., Stillwell, D., Crowcroft, J.: Our twitter profiles, our selves: predicting personality with twitter. In: IEEE PASSAT (2011)
16. Wondracek, G., Holz, T., Kirda, E., Kruegel, C.: A practical attack to de-anonymize social network users. In: IEEE Security and Privacy (2010)
17. Yang, Y., Lutes, J., Li, F., Luo, B., Liu, P.: Stalking online: on user privacy in social networks. In: ACM CODASPY (2012)
18. Zheleva, E., Getoor, L.: To join or not to join: the illusion of privacy in social networks with mixed public and private user profiles. In: WWW (2009)

Sanitization of Call Detail Records via Differentially-Private Bloom Filters

Mohammad Alaggan[1], Sébastien Gambs[2], Stan Matwin[3]([✉]),
and Mohammed Tuhin[3]

[1] Helwan University, Cairo, Egypt
[2] Université de Rennes 1 - Inria, Rennes, France
[3] Dalhousie University, Halifax, Canada
stan@cs.dal.ca

Abstract. Publishing directly human mobility data raises serious privacy issues due to its inference potential, such as the (re-)identification of individuals. To address these issues and to foster the development of such applications in a privacy-preserving manner, we propose in this paper a novel approach in which Call Detail Records (CDRs) are summarized under the form of a differentially-private Bloom filter for the purpose of privately estimating the number of mobile service users moving from one area (region) to another in a given time frame. Our sanitization method is both time and space efficient, and ensures differential privacy while solving the shortcomings of a solution recently proposed. We also report on experiments conducted using a real life CDRs dataset, which show that our method maintains a high utility while providing strong privacy.

1 Introduction

One of the key ingredients of the digital economy of the future is the opportunity to exploit large amounts of data. In particular, Call Detail Records (CDRs) that are generated by users of mobile devices and collected by telecom operators could potentially be used for the socio-economic development and well-being of populations. For instance, such data can be used for scientific research (*e.g.*, the study of the human mobility), and also for practical objectives that can benefit the society (*e.g.*, to find the best place to build an infrastructure such as a bridge or to create a new bus line). However, learning the location of an individual is one of the greatest threats against his privacy, because it can be used to derive other personal information. For example, from the movements of an individual it is possible to infer his points of interests (such as his home and place of work) [10], to predict his past, current and future locations [9], or to conduct a de-anonymization attack [8]. Thus, it is of paramount importance to develop new methods that can mine CDRs while preserving the privacy of the individuals contained in this data. To counter these threats, we propose a novel data sanitization method based on Bloom filters [4] that produces a privacy-preserving data structure out of CDRs.

© IFIP International Federation for Information Processing 2015
P. Samarati (Ed.): DBSec 2015, LNCS 9149, pp. 223–230, 2015.
DOI: 10.1007/978-3-319-20810-7_15

2 Preliminaries

Bloom filter. A *Bloom filter* [4] is widely used as a summary data structure originally designed for membership testing (*i.e.*, testing whether a particular element is contained in the set considered). A Bloom filter can summarize a large dataset using linear space, is very simple to construct and inserting an element or testing its membership can be done in constant time. A Bloom filter is composed of an array of m bits and equipped with a set of k independent hash functions. An element can be inserted into a Bloom filter by passing it as input to each of the hash functions. The k outputs of the hash functions correspond to k positions of the Bloom filter, which are all set to one independently of their previous values. Testing the membership is done in a similar manner by considering that an item is contained in the filter only if the k corresponding bits are all set to 1. Due to the collisions generated by the hash functions, false positives can arise by having an element erroneously considered as being a member of the filter. The accuracy of a query to a Bloom filter depends on the number k of hash functions used, the size m of the filter as well as the number of items inserted. Disclosing directly a plain Bloom filter easily jeopardize privacy. For instance is possible for an adversary observing this Bloom filter to query exhaustively for all items to reconstruct the set encoded in this Bloom filter. Thus, it is necessary to ensure that the summary released also ensure strong privacy guarantees such as differential privacy, which we present hereafter.

Differential privacy [6] aims at providing strong privacy guarantees with respect to the input of some computation by randomizing the output of this computation. In our setting, the input of the computation is a summary of the CDRs observed by a cellular antenna and the randomized output is a perturbed version of this summary (*i.e.*, a Bloom filter). Two databases $\mathbf{x}$ and $\mathbf{x}'$ are said to *differ in at most one element*, or equivalently to be *neighbors*, if they are equal except for possibly one entry.

Definition 1 (Differential privacy [7]). *A randomized function* $\mathcal{F} : \mathcal{D}^n \to \mathcal{D}^n$ *is ϵ-differentially private, if for all neighbor databases* $\mathbf{x}, \mathbf{x}' \in \mathcal{D}^n$ *and for all* $\mathbf{t} \in \mathcal{D}^n$:

$$\Pr[\mathcal{F}(\mathbf{x}) = \mathbf{t}] \leqslant e^{\epsilon} \cdot \Pr[\mathcal{F}(\mathbf{x}') = \mathbf{t}] \ .$$

This probability is taken over all the coin tosses of $\mathcal{F}$ and e is the base of the natural logarithm.

The privacy parameter ϵ is public and may take different values depending on the application (for instance it could be 0.1, 0.25, 1.5, 5 or even more) [11]. The smaller the value of ϵ, the higher the privacy but also as a consequence the higher the impact on the utility of the resulting output. Differential privacy is known to compose well. In particular, if two functions F_1 and F_2, that are respectively ϵ_1 and ϵ_2 differentially private, then the function G combining their outputs $G(\mathbf{x}) = (F_1(\mathbf{x}), F_2(\mathbf{x}))$ is $(\epsilon_1 + \epsilon_2)$ differentially private. For a computation applying several differentially private algorithms on the same dataset, the sum of their differential privacy parameters is called the *privacy budget*.

Originally, differential privacy was developed within the context of private data analysis. The main guarantee is that if a differentially private mechanism is applied on a dataset composed of the personal data of individuals, no output would become significantly more (or less) probable whether or not a *single* participant contributes to the data set. This means that an adversary observing the output of the mechanism only gains negligible information about the presence (or absence) of a particular individual in the database. This statement is a statistical property about the behavior of the mechanism (*i.e.*, function) and holds independently of the auxiliary knowledge that the adversary might have gathered. In our setting, the database that we want to protect is a CDRs dataset and the objective of a differentially private mechanism is to hide the presence or absence of a particular user in these CDRs.

To compute privately the similarity between profiles in a social platform, Alaggan, Gambs and Kermarrec [1] have introduced a privacy-preserving summary technique called BLIP (for *BLoom-then-fLIP*). In this context, the profile of each user is represented compactly using a Bloom filter and the main objective of BLIP is to prevent an adversary with unlimited computational power from learning the presence or absence of an item in the profile of a user by observing the Bloom filter representation of this profile. BLIP ensures ϵ-differential privacy [6] by flipping each bit of Bloom filter with some probability before publishing it. BLIP has the advantage of having the same communication cost as a plain Bloom filter, while guaranteeing privacy at the expense of a slight decrease of utility. We use BLIP as a fundamental building block in our approach.

3   Mining CDRs via Differentially-Private Summaries

System model. Our main objective is to perform data mining operations on differentially-private summaries learnt directly from CDRs. For instance, we would like to be able to count the number of distinct users represented in a particular summary or to compute the size of the intersection between two summaries. To realize this, we will leverage the BLIP mechanism described in the previous section. Our system model is illustrated in Fig. 1. More precisely, we consider as our model a network composed of a large number of cellular antennas that are responsible for recording the CDRs related to their neighborhood (basically the events generated by calls or text messages sent or received in their corresponding region). Each of these cellular antennas publishes at a regular interval (*e.g.*, every 6 hours or each day) a summary of the users it has seen during this period. This summary takes the form of a Bloom filter in which each element inserted is actually the identifier of a user associated with a CDR. One of the advantages of using a Bloom filter is that even if a user is inserted several times (*e.g.*, if he has received or made several calls during the same period), his impact on the Bloom filter is the same. In addition, Bloom filter can be updated incrementally and in an online manner. Once the end of the period is reached, all cellular antennas BLIPed their summaries before publishing them and then erase their memories.

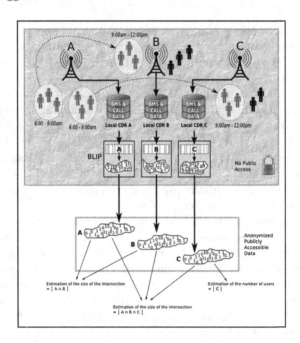

Fig. 1. Illustration of the system model.

Estimating the size of the intersection between two summaries. Broder, Mitzenmacher and Mitzenmacher [5] described a method to approximate the intersection of two sets, S_1 and S_2, given their Bloom filter representation, B_1 and B_2. Basically, they provided a relationship between the inner product of two Bloom filters and the cardinality of the set intersection of the two sets encoded in those Bloom filters. This expected value for the inner product $\sum_i B_1[i] \times B_2[i]$ corresponds to the probability that a particular bucket is simultaneously set to one in both Bloom filters, multiplied by the total number of buckets: $m \times \Pr\left[B_1[i] = 1 \wedge B_2[i] = 1\right]$. We extended their method to the case in which the bits of both Bloom filters are flipped with some probability (such as in BLIP) prior to computing the inner product, which enables to estimate the cardinality of set intersection in a privacy-preserving way.

Our main result is summarized by the following theorem.

Theorem 1 (Size of the intersection of two sets). *Given two sets S_1 and S_2 with respective cardinalities n_1 and n_2, and their flipped Bloom filters B_1 and B_2 whose bits were flipped independently with probability p, let Q be the inner product of B_1 and B_2. Let also*

$$g(x) = -\ln(x/m - C_1)/C_2 + C_3, \tag{1}$$

in which $q = 1 - p$, k is the number of hash functions employed by the Bloom filter, m is its number of bits, $\phi = 1 - 1/m$, $C_1 = (pq - q^2)(\phi^{kn_1} + \phi^{kn_2}) - q^2$,

$C_2 = k \ln \phi$ and $C_3 = \ln((p - q)^2)/k \ln \phi + n_1 + n_2$. Then, $W = g(Q)$ is an estimator for $|S_1 \cap S_2|$ with expected value:

$$\mathbb{E}[W] \approx |S_1 \cap S_2| + \mathrm{var}(Q)/(2C_2(\mathbb{E}[Q] - C_1m)^2). \tag{2}$$

Proof. Consider $\mathbb{E}[W] = \mathbb{E}[g(Q)]$. The expectation of the second degree Taylor expansion (*i.e.*, truncated after the third term[1]) around $\mathbb{E}[Q]$ of $g(Q)$ is

$$g(\mathbb{E}[Q]) + \mathrm{var}(Q)/(2C_2(\mathbb{E}[Q] - C_1m)^2). \tag{3}$$

We further detail the bias $\mathrm{var}(Q)/(2C_2(\mathbb{E}[Q] - C_1m)^2)$ later.

We now compute $\mathbb{E}[Q]$ and prove that $g(\mathbb{E}[Q]) = |S_1 \cap S_2|$. Consider two standard unflipped Bloom filter representations of two sets S_1 and S_2. The j-th bit of both Bloom filters will be set to 1 simultaneously if it was set by an element in $S_1 \cap S_2$ or by some element in $S_1 - S_2$ and a different element in $S_2 - S_1$. Consider the probability space of the choice of the hash functions used and let A_j be the event that the j-th bit is set in the first Bloom filter by an element of $S_1 - S_2$, B_j be the event that the j-th bit is set in the second Bloom filter by an element of $S_2 - S_1$, and C_j as the event that the j-th bit in both Bloom filters was set by an element in $S_1 \cap S_2$. The event that the j-th bit is set in both Bloom filters is $(A_j \cap B_j) \cup C_j$ and its probability is [5]:

$$\Pr[C_j] + (1 - \Pr[C_j]) \times \Pr[A_j] \times \Pr[B_j] = \quad 1 - \phi^{kn_1} - \phi^{kn_2} + \phi^{k(n_1+n_2-|S_1 \cap S_2|)}.$$

For the case of flipped Bloom filters let $A = 1 - \Pr[A_j], B = 1 - \Pr[B_j]$, and $C = 1 - \Pr[C_j]$, and we obtain

$$\Pr[C_j] + (1 - \Pr[C_j]) \times \Pr[A_j] \times Pr[B_j] = \quad (1 - C) + C(1 - A)(1 - B).$$

For a bit to be set to 1 in the flipped Bloom filter it either had to be 1 in the unflipped Bloom filter and remained unchanged despite the probabilistic flipping or the converse. Therefore, it is easy to verify that the probability that the j-th bit is set to 1 is both *flipped* Bloom filters is

$$q^2(1 - C) + C[q^2(1 - A)(1 - B) + pqA(1 - B) + \quad pqB(1 - A) + p^2AB],$$

which is equal to

$$(pq - q^2)(\phi^{kn_1} + \phi^{kn_2}) + q^2 + (p - q)^2\phi^{k(n_1+n_2-|S_1 \cap S_2|)}. \tag{4}$$

Now, considering that the inner product Q between two flipped Bloom filters is the sum of m binary random variables, each of which has the probability of being 1 given by Eq. (4). One can easily verify by simple algebraic manipulation that $g(\mathbb{E}[Q]) = |S_1 \cap S_2|$. By independence, we also have that $\mathbb{E}[Q]$ itself is the same as (4) multiplied by m. Hence, the result follows. $\square$

In the proof of Theorem 1, we truncated the Taylor expansion after the third term, which naturally introduces an error. However, we demonstrate that for

---

[1] We discuss later the error introduced by this truncation.

standard values of the parameters, the error is negligible. For instance consider the following standard values for the parameters: $\epsilon = 3$, $m = 187500$, $k = 2$ and $n_1 = n_2 = 50000$. With probability at least 99.9 %, when Q is in the range $\mathbb{E}[Q] \pm 3\sqrt{m}$ [1], the absolute error introduced by the truncating beyond the third term is at most 0.003 for all values of $|S_1 \cap S_2|$. This error is clearly negligible compared to $|S_1 \cap S_2|$. Moreover, for the same settings, the ratio of the fourth term to the third term is 0.002, which justifies its truncation.

The bias of the estimator as described in Eq. (2) can be bounded using the Bhatia-Davis inequality [3]: $\mathrm{var}(Q) \leq (m - \mathbb{E}[Q])\mathbb{E}[Q]$. Using this bound, the absolute ratio of the bias

$$\mathrm{var}(Q)/(2C_2(\mathbb{E}[Q] - C_1 m)^2) \tag{5}$$

to the set intersection $|S_1 \cap S_2|$ is at most 30 % for $|S_1 \cap S_2| \leq 12000$, using the same set of values considered in the previous paragraph. We will see in the next section that this value represents a Mean Relative Error (MRE) of 0.3, which is very small.

Counting the number of users in a summary. The computation of the intersection requires knowledge of n_1 and n_2, the true cardinalities of the two sets under consideration. One possibility is to release directly the set sizes by applying the ϵ-differentially private Laplacian mechanism [7] with error $O(1)$. In that case, the total privacy budget will be 2ϵ instead of ϵ. Alternatively, these cardinalities can be estimated directly from the flipped Bloom filters with no cost to the privacy budget using the method introduced recently by Balu, Furon and Gambs in [2]. This method defines a probabilistic relation between the number of items in a set and the number of bits in its Bloom filter, before extending this relation to the flipped Bloom filter. In a nutshell, given an unflipped Bloom filter with m bits, k hash functions and a set of c items, the probability[2] that a particular bit is set to 1 is $\pi_c = 1 - \phi^{ck}$, which corresponds to the probability that at least one hash function of at least one item chooses this bit. Note that this probability is not known in advance since c is precisely the quantity that we want to estimate. This relationship extends to a Bloom filter flipped with probability p, obtaining $\tilde{\pi}_c = (1 - p)\pi_c + p(1 - \pi_c)$, the probability that a bit is set to 1 in the flipped Bloom filter. The parameter p is known since ϵ is public and $p = 1/(1 + \exp(\epsilon/k))$, thus the only unknown value is c, the size of the set encoded in the Bloom filter. Their method is based on the observation that the ratio of bits set to 1 in the flipped Bloom filter (*i.e.*, its Hamming weight) to the total number of bits m is an unbiased estimator for $\tilde{\pi}_c$. Since this ratio can be computed directly from the released flipped Bloom filter, the equation for $\tilde{\pi}_c$ can be used to derive a value for π_c, from which an estimate for c can be obtained.

4   Experimental Results and Conclusion

Experimental setting. In this section, we report on the results obtained by applying our method on a real dataset from a telecom operator. This large dataset includes

---

[2] Assuming that the hash functions are independent and uniform.

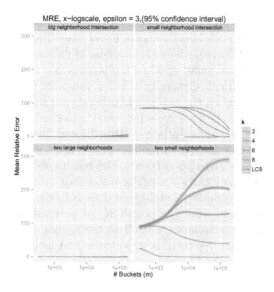

Fig. 2. Mean relative error for different number m of buckets with a differential privacy $\epsilon = 3$. The non-private linear counting sketch (LCS) baseline is also plotted.

coarse-grained phone call data for users in a city divided into a number of neighborhoods. More precisely for each call made by the user, his location as well as the time of the call are recorded. In our experiments, we have first extracted the set of users for each neighborhood and for each month and encode them within a Bloom filter. Afterwards, the Bloom filter was flipped according to the recipe of BLIP before release. Then, we use the algorithm from the previous section to estimate the intersection between each pair of neighborhoods given their flipped Bloom filters. To observe the behavior of our algorithm under different conditions, we specifically selected four sets of neighborhood couples. The choice of these four sets was based on the different number of users in the neighborhoods. For instance, the first set contains two neighborhoods with 57 000 and 42 000 users, and we call it "two large" in the figures while the next set contains two neighborhoods with 600 and 1 000 users, and we call it "two small". For the two other sets, there is a small neighborhood and a large one, but one set has a small intersection between the two neighborhoods while the other one has a (relatively) big intersection. In particular, the first set has 15 000 and 1 200 users and an intersection of 180 users, thus we call it "small intersection". The second set has 3 400 and 39 000 users with an intersection of 3 339 users and we call it "big intersection". All the experiments reported involving BLIP are averaged over 100 independent trials.

Evaluation. To assess the utility of our method, we compute the Mean Relative Error (MRE), which is defined as the absolute difference between the estimated intersection and the true intersection, divided by the true intersection. We also plot the standard deviation of the MRE for selected parameters. Figure 2 show the MRE obtained for a privacy level $\epsilon = 3$ and for different values of Bloom filter parameters: k, the number of hash functions, as well as m the number of buckets. The value $\epsilon = 3$ is rather strict and provides high privacy guarantees.

The MRE changes based on the properties of the neighborhoods considered. In particular, when the two neighborhoods are big or when the intersection is large, the MRE is less than 12 %, regardless of the choice of parameters. However, when the two neighborhoods are small or when the intersection is small, the choice of parameters becomes critical. Generally, a lower value for k and a higher value for m is better, except when the two neighborhoods are small.

Conclusion. In this paper, we have proposed a method by which CDRs are sanitized in the form of a differentially-private Bloom filter for the purpose of privately counting of the number of mobile service users moving from one area (region) to another in a given time frame. The results obtained show that our method achieves - in most cases - a performance in terms of utility similar to another method (linear counting sketch) that does not provide any privacy guarantees. We leave as future work the possibility of performing other operations on differentially-private summaries as well as the design of privacy variants of more complex data structures such as trajectories and mobility models.

Acknowledgments. This work was partially supported by the MSR-INRIA joint lab as well as the INRIA project lab CAPPRIS, and by NSERC Canada.

References

1. Alaggan, M., Gambs, S., Kermarrec, A.-M.: BLIP: Non-interactive differentially-private similarity computation on bloom filters. In: Richa, A.W., Scheideler, C. (eds.) SSS 2012. LNCS, vol. 7596, pp. 202–216. Springer, Heidelberg (2012)
2. Balu, R., Furon, T., Gambs, S.: Challenging differential privacy:the case of non-interactive mechanisms. In: Kutyłowski, M., Vaidya, J. (eds.) ICAIS 2014, Part II. LNCS, vol. 8713, pp. 146–164. Springer, Heidelberg (2014)
3. Bhatia, R., Davis, C.: A better bound on the variance. Am. Math. Mon. **107**(4), 353–357 (2000)
4. Bloom, B.H.: Space/time trade-offs in hash coding with allowable errors. Commun. ACM **13**(7), 422–426 (1970)
5. Broder, A., Mitzenmacher, M., Mitzenmacher, A.B.I.M.: Network applications of bloom filters: a survey. In: Internet Mathematics, pp. 636–646 (2002)
6. Dwork, C.: Differential privacy. In: Bugliesi, M., Preneel, B., Sassone, V., Wegener, I. (eds.) ICALP 2006. LNCS, vol. 4052, pp. 1–12. Springer, Heidelberg (2006)
7. Dwork, C., McSherry, F., Nissim, K., Smith, A.: Calibrating noise to sensitivity in private data analysis. In: Halevi, S., Rabin, T. (eds.) TCC 2006. LNCS, vol. 3876, pp. 265–284. Springer, Heidelberg (2006)
8. Gambs, S., Killijian, M., del Prado Cortez, M.N.: De-anonymization attack on geolocated data. In: TrustCom, pp. 789–797 (2013)
9. González, M.C., C.A.H.R., Barabási, A.: Understanding individual human mobility patterns. CoRR, abs/0806.1256 (2008)
10. Krumm, J.: Inference attacks on location tracks. In: LaMarca, A., Langheinrich, M., Truong, K.N. (eds.) Pervasive 2007. LNCS, vol. 4480, pp. 127–143. Springer, Heidelberg (2007)
11. Lee, J., Clifton, C.: How much is enough? choosing ϵ for differential privacy. In: Lai, X., Zhou, J., Li, H. (eds.) ISC 2011. LNCS, vol. 7001, pp. 325–340. Springer, Heidelberg (2011)

Access Control and Usage Policies

Protecting Personal Data: Access Control for Privacy Preserving Perimeter Protection System

Annanda Thavymony Rath[(✉)] and Jean-Noël Colin

Faculty of Computer Science, University of Namur, Namur, Belgium
{rath.thavymony,jean-noel.colin}@unamur.be

Abstract. In this paper, we address the issues of personal data protection for privacy preserving perimeter protection system, particularly, the access control for real-time data streamed from surveillance tools and also for data stored in facility's storage. Furthermore, we also provide an access control model proposed specifically for such system and access control system implemented in Java.

Keywords: Access control · Purpose enforcement · Perimeter protection system · Privacy-aware policies · Access control system architecture

1 Introduction

Critical buildings and infrastructures (e.g. nuclear power plants) require strong and unlikely breakable physical security protection from physical or forceful attacks. To protect such infrastructures beyond the use of conventional methods such as fences, we normally use different surveillance tools (e.g. visual cameras) to observe and detect activities around the protected infrastructures. In most cases, the surveillance covers only the private zones, but sometimes it goes beyond by covering a larger area (e.g. public area) in order to have an early warning, which provides enough time to react in case of attack. However, including the public area into the surveillance perimeter poses challenges for personal data protection since surveilling the public areas, without the approval from concern government authority, are not permitted in some countries like in EU or USA [4]. Thus, when designing perimeter protection system covering public area, one needs to take into account the personal data protection aspect [3,8]. We introduce, in this paper, an access control model and system designed particularly for P5 (Privacy Preserving Perimeter Protection Project) system [2]. The proposed access control system aims at ensuring that personal data are properly protected and only authorized

The work presented in this paper is supported by the European Commission's FP7 programme P5 Project (Grant agreement No: 312784). The content of this paper is the sole responsibility of the authors and it does not represent the opinion of the European Commission and the Commission is not responsible for any use that might be made of information contained herein.

P. Samarati (Ed.): DBSec 2015, LNCS 9149, pp. 233–241, 2015.
DOI: 10.1007/978-3-319-20810-7_16

people can use those data for purpose they intend for. The rest of the paper is organized as follows. Section 2 is about P5 project and system architecture. Section 3
introduces the privacy-aware access control model. Section 4 presents the access
control scenarios and policies definition for P5 system. Section 5 talks about access
control architecture and implementation. Section 6 is related work and contributions while Sect. 7 is conclusion.

2   P5 Project and P5 System Architecture

P5 is the European and FP7 FUNDED (http://www.foi.se/p5) project for the
protection of critical infrastructures to benefit the sustainability of society and
future well-being of the European Citizens. The goal of the P5 project is an intelligent perimeter proactive surveillance system that works robustly under a wide
range of weather and lighting conditions and that has strong privacy preserving
features. In P5's system architecture (see Fig. 1), there are many modules forming the entire P5 system, from the the lowest layer hosting sensors that provide
different data types to the upper layer modules, such as "attributes analysis",
"detection/localization", "multi-source heterogeneous data fusion", "object classification, tracking and behavior and intents recognition", "early warning" and
"man machine interface". Each one of the modules is a problem by itself, however, in this paper we address only the issue of access control for real-time data
streamed from surveillance tools and data stored in facility's storage. There are

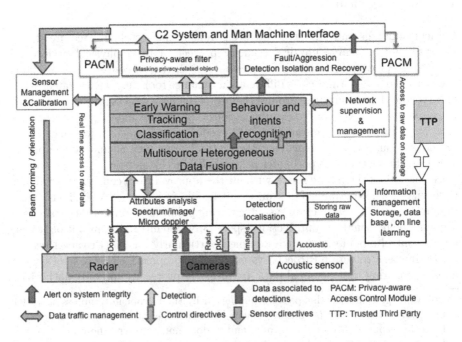

Fig. 1. Privacy preserving perimeter protection system architecture.

three modules, in the proposed architecture, which ensure privacy preservation and personal data protection: (1) Privacy-aware access control module (PACM) is responsible for controlling access to raw data. This module is responsible also for enforcing access control policies. (2) Privacy-aware filter is responsible for filtering the privacy-related information. (3) Trusted Third Party (TTP) module provides a way to manage access control policies, to protect the raw data and to audit the access to raw data. *TTP administrator* can be a trusted private or government entity, which is authorized for the job. It is important to note that since our main addressing issue in this paper is the design of privacy-aware access control system, we address only PACM.

3   Privacy-Aware Access Control Model

Access Control Requirements. To identify the access control requirements for privacy preserving perimeter protection system, we conducted two different studies. Firstly, we worked with legal group to study the EU Directive 95/46/EC [4]. Secondly, we did a formal survey and also conducted a broad range of data collection and analysis. For the field works, we visited existing perimeter protection systems installed in the protected facilities in United Kingdom (UK) and Sweden, such as National Air Traffic control in UK and OKG Nuclear Power Plant in Sweden. Based on the result of our survey and legal studies, we can classify the access control and data protection requirements into four main points.

1. **Legal Requirements:** based on the article 2, 10 and 11 of Directive 95/46/EC, we can define the following legal requirements. (1) Data controller needs to notify data subject every time of access. (2) Processing of private data is limited to the purpose for which data are intended for. (3) Consent from data subject is required when processing personal data.
2. **User Management Requirements:** security personnel manages access to control room as well as sensors. An assigned group of users, while they are on duty, is allowed to be in control room to view real time data streamed from sensors. In case of emergency where there are intruders attacking the facility, users in control room are allowed to access raw data. Other assigned group of users can access raw data in storage, but special access permission is needed. The main purpose of storing data from sensors is for forensic purpose.
3. **System Performance Requirements:** since we deal also with real-time data, access control to such data stream must be reasonably fast to avoid the delay to data stream.
4. **Security and Data Protection Requirements:** processing of private data must be secured. We need to make sure that only authorized people can get access to data. Data controller should be a trusted entity that overlooks the management of access control policies as well as data in storage.

Based on the above requirements, we define the following access control model.

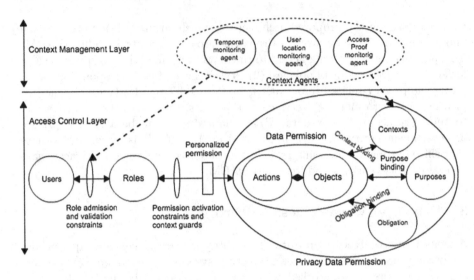

Fig. 2. Context- and Privacy-aware Role-Based Access Control Model (CP-RBAC).

Access Control Model. We introduce Context- and Privacy-aware RBAC [3] (CP-RBAC), an access control model designed for controlling access to private data in privacy-preserving perimeter protection system. In CP-RBAC, access authorization is based not only on the user's role, but also on contextual information, such as temporal-, spatial- and environment-context. Furthermore, the concept of privacy is also introduced into the model. In the proposed model, contextual information is used as constraint for both the role admission and data permission assignment (see Fig. 2). The purpose of access and obligation are also the binding constraints on data permission to preserve and protect the privacy.

CP-RBAC (see Fig. 2) consists of the following entities.

- U is a set of users (u) where $u \in U$. R is a set of roles (r) where $r \in R$.
- A is a set of actions (a) where $a \in A$. D is a set of data where $d \in D$.
- P is a set of purposes (p) where $p \in P$. O is a set of obligations (o) where $o \in O$. C is a set of contextual variables (c) where $c \in C$.

Then, we formulate the privacy-sensitive policy (RP): $RP \subseteq R \times ((A \times D) \times (P \times C \times O))$. The detailed formulation of privacy-sensitive policy is as follows.

- The set of Data Permission $DP = \{(a,d) \mid a \in A, d \in D\}$
- The set of Privacy-sensitive Data Permission $PDP = \{(dp,p,c,o) \mid dp \in DP, p \in P, c \in C, o \in O\}$
- Privacy-sensitive Data Permission to role Assignment PDPA $\subseteq R \times PDP$, a many-to-many mapping privacy-sensitive data permission to role.

Contextual Data are the information surrounding user, data and reason that user needs to execute the action. Contextual information can be anything, such as user's personal data, location or time.

Definition 1. Contextual variables expression

Let C be a set of contextual variables (c), where $c \in C$. "c has the finite domain of possible values, denoted as DC where $dc \in DC$. "c" is equipped with the relational operators (Oprs) " $=, \neq, \geq, and \leq$". The condition of c has the form $(c \ opr \ dc)$. Let c_1 and c_2 are two contextual variables in the form of the atomic condition. Then, $(c_1 \land c_2)$ or $(c_1 \lor c_2)$ is also condition.

Obligation is defined as the action that user or system needs to fulfill before or after accessing data. For example, notifying data controller every access.

Definition 2. Obligation expression

Let O be a set of obligation variables (o), where $o \in O$. "o" has the finite domain of possible values, denoted as B where $b \in B$. "o" is equipped with the relational operators (Oprs) " $=, \neq, \geq, and \leq$". The condition of "o" has the form $(o \ opr \ b)$. For example, a payment obligation has the form: $payment \geq 50\$$.

---

4   Access Scenarios and Policy Definition for P5

We present the access scenarios and access control policies for P5. Then, we express those policies with the access control model we presented in Sect. 3.

1) Access Raw Data in Real Time (P1): we define the role "guardian"and users in this role are able to view real-time raw data streamed from sensors. However, they can do so only in case of emergency. Users can trigger emergency if and only if there is a positive acknowledgement from early warning module, which is responsible for providing a warning message when it detects an abnormal behavior of the objects. Moreover, to be able to keep track user's activities, users are required to notify system every time access to raw data. With above policy description, we are able to mine the following information.

- Role of user: "Guardian". Action: "View". Data: "streaming video".
- Context: "acknowledgement-from-early-warning".
- Purpose: "Observing-suspicious-object". Obligation: "notify".

With the above information and policy expression in Sect. 3, we can formulate the following access policy.

PDPA to role "Guardian"(P1)= (Guardian, (View, streaming video), Observing-suspicious-object, (acknowledgement-from-early-warning= positive), Notify=yes))

2) Replay Recent Past Raw Data (P2): this happens when guard in the control room wants to replay recent past video stream. We define "recent past video stream" as the video stream that has been recorded within the last 30 min Users in role "guardian" are allowed to review recent past video stream. The same rule in P1 is applied in P2. However, one more context is required that is the life of video stream, which is set to be 30 min. The life of video stream context limits the access to the past videos, which are older than 30 min. Any access to older past video streams needs to be controlled by policy P3. With the above policy description, we are able to define the policy (P2) as follows.

PDPA to role "Guardian" (P2)= (Guardian, (View, streaming video), Observing-suspicious-object, (acknowledgement-from-early-warning= positive ∧ life-of-video ≤ 30 min), Notify=yes))

3) Access Raw Data in Storage (P3): authority may need to access past raw data for an investigation (e.g. a crime scene in the coverage area). However, in order to get access to raw data facility manager needs to send the request to TTP with proof. Proof is an official document justifying the mission. We define the role "Facility-security-manager" and users in this role are able to request TTP for accessing raw data in storage. In addition to that, users need to mention their purpose of request. We define three types of purpose: (1) Internal auditing, (2) Investigation and (3) Observing-suspicious-object. Moreover, to be able to keep track users' activities, users are required to notify system every access. With above policy description, we are able to mine the following information.
- Role of user: "Facility-security-manager". Action: "View". Context: "proof".
- Data: "raw-video-in-storage". Purpose: "Investigation". Obligation: "notify". With the above information, we can formulate P3 as follows.

PDPA to role "Facility-security-manager" (P3)= (Facility-security-manager, (View, raw-video-in-storage), Investigation, (proof= yes), Notify=yes))

5   Access Control: Architecture and Implementation

The access control system (see Fig. 3) consists of the following components. Policy Enforcement Point (PEP) handles request from user and forwards it to PDP; PEP also enforces the policy by using different policy enforcement mechanisms: role to purpose alignment and notification. Policy Decision Point (PDP) is responsible for validating access control policies with the support of information provided by Policy Information Point (PIP). PIP is responsible for providing all needed information to PDP during policy validation phase. We define four contextual variables. (1) Proof is an official mission document that user needs to provide when requesting access to raw data in storage. (2) Early warning, this module is a part of P5's architecture (see Fig. 1). (3) User to role alignment provides information concerning the assignment of users to roles. (4) Working hours is the timetable of each user. We have implemented a context- and privacy-aware access control (CP-RBAC) system based on our proposed architecture (see Fig. 3) using Java. We have used XACML version 2 as the format for access control requests, responses and policies [1]. We have also made use of Java Enterprise XACML library[1] as the policy decision point engine. We developed our program in Eclipse Standard/SDK (version Kepler) installed on Macbook air OS version 10.8.4, processor 1.3 Ghz Intel Core i5 with memory 8 GB DDR3. We created 48 policies and expressed them with XACML policy language. The policies P1, P2 and P3 (see Sect. 4) are used as the models for the 48 policies. We performed six different tests with the same request structure, but different number of policies in the policy storages. There are two criteria we want to assess. The first criterion is the accuracy of the access control system we developed. This means it should provide 100 % correct policy evaluation. The second criterion is the time required to evaluate a request. To evaluate second criteria, we created different access control policies with different level of complexity; then we find out the validation time for each request with different number of policies in storage. After several performance tests with the 6 different scenarios, we find that as the number of policies in storage increases, the time required to evaluate a request also increase; this is as expected. The first test scenario where there is only one policy in the policy storage, the time required to validate the policy is 344 milliseconds. With 48 policies, it takes 954 ms.

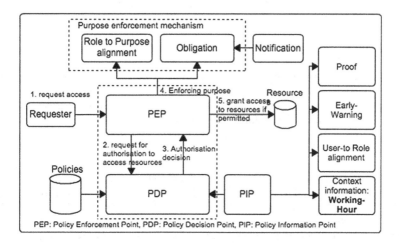

Fig. 3. Privacy-aware Access Control Architecture for P5 System.

---

[1] https://code.google.com/p/enterprise-java-xacml/.

6   Related Work and Contributions

After our thorough study of different access control models, we arrive to the conclusion of using RBAC [3] in P5 project, but with extension. We have also studied different models, such as DAC, MAC [3,5,6], ABAC [10] and OrBAC [9]. In context of P5 environment setting, most of access control models (like DAC and MAC) fail to respond to the requirements since such systems generally have very complex access control policies as we have illustrated in Sect. 3. P-RBAC [3] is another family of RBAC where the concept of privacy is introduced, but it does not address the contextual information. Moreover, it does not have the concepts of context-aware role admission and personalised role permission. With above reasons, we propose an access control model that takes into account the aspects like privacy [2,7]. To provide privacy preservation feature, the concept of purpose and obligation are introduced.

Contributions. Firstly, we propose the privacy preserving perimeter protection system architecture. Secondly, access control model that can be used to express privacy-aware access control policies in P5 system. The third contribution is the implementation of such access control system.

7   Conclusion

In this paper, we present a detailed architecture of privacy preserving perimeter protection system. We also present the context- and privacy-aware access control model that is designed specifically for such system. The access control system implemented in Java is also presented. Our future work is to focus on the development of TTP and the privacy-aware filter module.

References

1. Anderson, A.: XACML profile for Role Based Access Control, 13 February 2004. http://www.oasis-open.org/committees/xacml
2. European Community Research And Development Information Service, 7 Framework Program. http://www.foi.se/p5. Accessed April 2014
3. Qun, N., Elisa, B., Jorge, L., Carolyn, B., Karat, C.-M., Alberto, T.: Privacy-aware role-based access control. ACM Trans. Inf. Syst. Secur. **13**, 24:1–24:31 (2010)
4. Directive 95/46/EC of the European Parliament and of the Council of 24 October 1995. http://www.dataprotection.ie/. Accessed December 2014
5. Ferraiolo, D.F., Sandhu, R., Gavrila, S., Kuhn, D.R., Chandramouli, R.: Proposed NIST standard for role-based access control. ACM Trans. Inf. Syst. Secur. **4**(3), 222–274 (2001)
6. Hu, V.C., Ferraiolo, D.F., Kuhn, D.R.: Assessment of Access Control System. National Institute of Standards and Technology, Gaithersbur (2006)
7. Ardagna, C.A., Cremonini, M., De Capitani di Vimercati, S., Samarati, P.: A privacy-aware access control system. J. Comput. Secur. (JCS) **16**(4), 369–392 (2008)

8. Rath, A.T., Colin, J.-N.: Towards enforcement of purpose for privacy policy in distributed healthcare. In: The 3rd IEEE International Conference on Consumer eHealth Platforms, Services and Applications (CeHPSA), IEEE CCNC 2013
9. Cuppens, F., Cuppens, N.: Modeling contextual security policies in OrBAC. Int. J. Inf. Secur. (IJIS) **7**(4), 285–305 (2008)
10. Yuan, E., Tong, J.: Attribute based access control a new access control approach for service oriented architectures (soa). In: Workshop on New Challenges for Access Control, Ottawa, ON, Canada, April 2005

Integrating Attributes into Role-Based Access Control

Qasim Mahmood Rajpoot[1][(✉)], Christian Damsgaard Jensen[1],
and Ram Krishnan[2]

[1] Department of Applied Mathematics and Computer Science,
Technical University of Denmark, DK-2800, Kgs. Lyngby, Denmark
{qara,cdje}@dtu.dk
[2] Department of Electrical and Computer Engineering,
University of Texas at San Antonio, San Antonio, USA
ram.krishnan@utsa.edu

Abstract. Role-based access control (RBAC) and attribute-based access control (ABAC) are currently the most prominent access control models. However, they both suffer from limitations and have features complimentary to each other. Due to this fact, integration of RBAC and ABAC has become a hot area of research recently. We propose an access control model that combines the two models in a novel way in order to unify their benefits. Our approach provides a fine-grained access control mechanism that takes into account the current contextual information while making the access control decisions.

Keywords: Context-aware access control · RBAC · Attributes · Role-permission explosion

1 Introduction

RBAC [6] is the most popular access control model and has been a focus of research since last two decades. The RBAC paradigm encapsulates privileges into roles, and users are assigned to roles to acquire privileges, which makes it simple and facilitates reviewing permissions assigned to a user. It also makes the task of policy administration less cumbersome, as every change in a role is immediately reflected on the permissions available to users assigned to that role.

With the advent of pervasive systems, authorization control has become complex as access decisions may depend on the context in which access requests are made. The contextual information represents a measurable contextual primitive and may entail such information being associated with a user, object and environment. It has been recognized that RBAC is not adequate for situations where contextual attributes are required parameters in granting access to a user [12]. Another limitation of RBAC is that the permissions are specified in terms of object identifiers, referring to individual objects. This is not adequate in situations where a large number of objects in hundreds of thousands exist and leads to role-permission explosion problem.

P. Samarati (Ed.): DBSec 2015, LNCS 9149, pp. 242–249, 2015.
DOI: 10.1007/978-3-319-20810-7_17

Attribute-Based Access Control (ABAC) [17] has been identified to overcome these limitations of RBAC [5]. ABAC is considered more flexible as compared to RBAC, since it can easily accommodate contextual attributes as access control parameters [12]. However, ABAC is typically much more complex than RBAC in terms of policy review, hence analyzing the policy and reviewing or changing user permissions are quite cumbersome tasks. As discussed above, both RBAC and ABAC have their particular advantages and disadvantages. Both have features complimentary to each other, and thus integrating RBAC and ABAC has become an important research topic [5,9,10]. Recently, NIST announced an initiative to integrate RBAC and its various extensions with ABAC in order to combine the advantages offered by both RBAC and ABAC. We take a step in this direction and present the idea of an integrated RBAC and ABAC access control model, called the Attributes Enhanced Role-Based Access Control model. The proposed model retains the flexibility offered by ABAC, yet it maintains RBAC's advantages of easier administration, policy analysis and review of user permissions.

The rest of the paper is organized as follows: Sect. 2 summarizes related work and compares our approach to prior work. In Sect. 3, we present the components of the proposed access control model and how access control decisions may be calculated. Section 4 discusses potential benefits offered by the proposed approach and identifies future directions.

2   Related Work

The limitations of RBAC led to announcement of the NIST initiative to incorporate attributes into roles [12]. The initiative identified three possible ways in which roles and attributes may be combined. The first option is *dynamic roles*, where attributes determine the roles to be activated for a user. Al-Kahtani et al. [1] and Kern et al. [14] explored this option for automated user-role assignment, in large organizations, using attribute-based rules. These solutions consider only user attributes and do not address the issues of role explosion and role-permission explosion. In the second approach, roles and attributes may be combined in an *attribute-centric* manner. The roles are not associated to permissions; rather they are treated as just one of many attributes. This approach is essentially the same as ABAC and does not inherit any benefit from RBAC. In the third approach, called *role-centric*, roles determine the maximum permissions available to a user, and attributes are used to constrain these permissions. Kuhn et al. [12] identify this approach as a direction for future research, since it may retain the advantages of RBAC while adding the much needed flexibility.

In response to the above initiative, Jin et al. [10] present first formal access control model called RABAC using the role-centric approach. They extend RBAC with user and object attributes and add a component called permission filtering policy (PFP). The PFP requires specification of filtering functions in the form of Boolean expression consisting of user and object attributes. Their solution is useful to address the role-explosion problem and as a result facilitates user role assignment. However, the approach does not incorporate environment attributes and is not suitable for systems involving frequently changing attributes, e.g., location and time. Also, we make a fundamental modification in RBAC by using attributes of the objects in the permissions, addressing the issue of role-permission explosion. Huang et al. [9] present a framework to integrate RBAC with attributes. The approach consists of two levels: underground and aboveground. The underground level makes use of attribute-based policies to automate the processes of user-role and role-permission assignment. The above-ground level is the RBAC model, with addition of environment attributes, constructed using attribute-based policies. Their work is different than ours in that it focuses on automated construction of RBAC.

Several efforts have been reported which extend RBAC to include the context of access. Examples include: environment roles [2], spatio-temporal RBAC [16], context-aware RBAC [13] and others. They add context into RBAC, however these extensions typically require creation of a large number of closely related roles, causing the role-explosion problem. Ge et al. [8], and Giuri et al. [7] focus on resolving the issue of role explosion by providing the mechanism of parametrized privileges and parametrized roles. However, the permissions in these solutions refer to objects using their identifiers. Few approaches propose a variant of RBAC categorizing the objects into groups or types in an attempt to resolve the role-permission explosion issue [3,11,15]. Grouping the objects allows us to associate a single attribute with each object. The permissions are then specified using the group attribute, where each permission refers to a set of objects in that group. Moreover, as the number of object attributes grow, the number of groups (referred to as views in [11] and object classes in [3]) increase exponentially. This makes task of policy administration complex since for every new object to be added in the system it has to be associated with all those groups to which it belongs.

3   Components of the Proposed Model

This section presents the components of the proposed Attributes Enhanced Role-Based Access Control (AERBAC) model. We also discuss briefly how an access request may be evaluated. Figure 1 depicts our access control model and its components. The entities users, roles, objects and operations have the same semantics as in RBAC. Users and objects in our model are associated with attributes too. We also incorporate the environment attribute to fully capture the situation in which access needs to be authorized. Below, we first describe these attributes and then discuss semantics of the components in our access control model, including permissions, conditions, sessions and request evaluation.

Attributes: Attributes capture the properties of specific entities (e.g. user). We define an attribute function for each attribute that returns the value of that attribute. Each attribute is represented by a range of finite sets of atomic values. For example, the range of branch attribute is a set of names of branches semantically relevant for the application domain.

User attributes capture the properties of the user who initiates an access request. Examples of user attributes are title, specialization, location, security clearance etc. *Object attributes* are used to define the properties of the resources

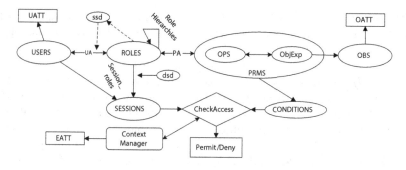

Fig. 1. Attributes extended role-based access control model

protected by the access control policy. Examples of object attributes include type, status, location, time of object creation etc. *Environment attributes* capture external factors of the situation in which the access takes place. Temperature, occurrence of an incident, system mode or other information which not only pertains to a specific object or user, but may hold for multiple entities, are typically modelled as environment attributes.

An attribute may be either static or dynamic. The values of *static attributes* rarely change e.g. designation, department, type etc. On the other hand, *dynamic attribute* values may change frequently and unpredictably, so they may well change during the lifetime of a session. This means that they may need to be checked more frequently, depending on the application requirements. Examples of such attributes include officer in command, location, occurrence of an incident etc. They are also referred to as contextual attributes in the literature [4].

Permissions and conditions: Our aim is to provide a dynamic, yet easy to manage and efficient solution to enforce the access control model. In our model, we achieve this by incorporating attributes associated with user, objects and environment in the permission. In contrast to the traditional approaches in RBAC, the permissions in AERBAC refer to objects indirectly, using their attributes, so a permission grants access to a set of objects having those attributes rather than a single object. A permission refers to a set of objects sharing common attributes, e.g. type or branch, using a single permission, in contrast to separate permissions for each unique object. This is particularly relevant in those domains where several objects share common attribute values. This helps in significantly reducing the number of permissions associated with a role, while increasing the expressiveness and granularity of access control in a role-centric fashion.

A permission consists of an object expression and an authorized operation on the object set denoted by the expression. Object expressions are formed using the attributes of objects. Each permission is associated with one or more conditions, which must be evaluated to be true in order for the user to exercise that permission. A condition associated with a permission may contain attributes of the users, objects and environment. When a user requests a specific permission, it is granted to the user if the permission exists in the user's session and the associated condition is satisfied, i.e. the current values of attributes match the constraints given by the condition.

An example of a permission is: $p= ((oType(o) = secret ? oStatus(o) = active), read)$ which states that a role having this permission can perform read operation on the objects denoted by the given object expression. Here $oType$ and $oStatus$ are object attribute functions that return the values of respective attributes for a given object. Suppose that the permission p is constrained by a condition $c= (uMember(u) = premium \land time\_of\_day() \le uDuty\text{-}Expire(u))$ where $uMember$ and $uDutyExpire$ are user attribute functions that return the attribute values of a given user, whereas $time\_of\_day()$ is an environment attribute function. This condition implies that, in order to be granted the permission p, the user must be a premium user and time of access must be before the end of user's duty timing.

Session: A session contains a list of permissions associated with the roles activated by the user. As described earlier, the permissions are different from standard RBAC permissions in terms of referring to the objects using their attributes and being tied with the conditions that are evaluated every time a permission is to be exercised. Hence, the CheckAccess function needs to be re-defined.

The Context Manager is responsible for propagating the updated values of dynamic attributes of the users, objects and environment. Depending on the application, some of these attribute values may also be provided by the user while placing an access request, however the application must ensure the authenticity of such information before using it.

3.1   Access Decisions

The main role of the access control mechanism is to verify whether a user u, requesting access to object o, using an operation op, is authorized to do so. An important consideration, in environments motivating the proposed approach, is that the user's request may also be based on the attributes of the objects. For instance, in a medical imaging application, a user might want to view all images containing specified characteristics e.g., objects with $type = tumor$ and $domain = hospital\text{-}nw$. The permissions in AERBAC are constrained by conditions. For a user request to be granted, there must exist an object expression in the user's session that denotes the requested objects, and the condition tied to that object expression must be evaluated to be true, as illustrated in Fig. 2.

Request Evaluation: As mentioned above, a user request can either explicitly specify an object, by listing its identifier, or can implicitly denote a set of objects using the attributes of the objects. If the user request is not for a specific object but rather a set of objects, the system must consider the given criteria to return the requested objects. Once a user submits an access request, the request must be evaluated against the policy. The function checkAccess in RBAC needs to be modified such that it takes the user request as input, processes the request as

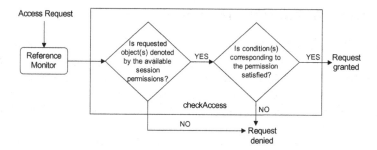

Fig. 2. Access request evaluation

per the format of a given request, and returns the result. In the following, we elaborate on evaluation of both identifier-based and attribute-based requests.

(a)Identifier-based request: In identifier-based request, the user specifies the identifier of the object to be accessed. The evaluation of such type of request is straight-forward. In this case, the input of the function checkAccess consists of a session *se*, an operation *m*, and an object *obj*. Recall that a permission consists of an object expression and an operation and is constrained by a condition. The checkAccess function returns true if and only if (i) there exists a permission *p*, in the available session permissions in session *se*, that contains an object expression which evaluates to true for *obj*, (ii) *m* matches *op*, and (iii) the corresponding condition *c* evaluates to true.

(b)Attribute-based request: Using the second form of request, the user may specify the attributes of the object in his/her request, rather than a unique identifier of the object. Specifying the object attributes in the request implies that the user wishes to access all those objects which have the specified attribute values. In this approach, an example user request could be: $Req = < se, (otype = secret \land odept = admin \land ostatus = inactive), write>$ which states that the owner of the session *se* wishes to exercise the *write* operation on the objects denoted by the given object expression. The checkAccess function receives as input the access request *Req* and returns the authorized objects to the user, if request is granted, otherwise the request is denied. The given expression is converted to a query and the resulting objects are retrieved from the resource database. The object expressions existing in the user's session are evaluated against each retrieved object and if an object expression and its corresponding condition evaluate to true for an object, the object is added into the list of authorized objects to be granted to the user. Finally, the user is granted access to all those objects for which an object expression and its corresponding condition return true. Since the object expressions are to be evaluated for each returned object, this approach may prove to be expensive in cases where several objects are returned by the query formed based on user's request. We plan to work further on it and propose a more efficient algorithm to process such a request.

4   Discussion And Future Work

Our motivation to integrate RBAC with attributes is to obtain advantages associated with both RBAC and ABAC, while addressing the limitations of RBAC and ABAC. In a pure ABAC approach, when a user request needs to be evaluated, the relevant rules are identified using the attributes associated with requesting user, requested object and current environment. These shortlisted rules are then evaluated one-by-one unless we find a rule which allows the request. In contrast, our approach requires evaluation of only those object expressions which are associated with the roles activated by a user in his/her session. Note that this would significantly reduce the number of rules to be evaluated. Compared to ABAC, our approach provides a systematic mechanism to evaluate a subset of policy rules which are determined based on the user's roles, yet retaining the advantages offered by RBAC including quick assignment and revocation of roles to users, reviewing of permissions assigned to a user or role, and reduced complexity of administration in large organizations. Our approach also provides significant advantages when compared to RBAC. First, RBAC requires that the permissions must refer to the objects based on their identity, which may lead to role-permission explosion issue in applications involving large number of objects. Our model allows to use object attributes in the permissions. Second, RBAC cannot easily handle dynamically changing attributes [5]. It typically does not support making contextual decisions unless many similar roles are created causing role-explosion problem. We provide a mechanism to incorporate these dynamically changing attributes in a role-centric manner, yet without requiring creation of a large number of roles.

The model we proposed integrates RBAC and ABAC bringing together the features offered by both models. In our model, the attributes may be associated with users, objects and environment allowing the request context to be considered in making access control decisions. In the future, we plan to work on formally defining the proposed model and provide a deeper analysis of merits offered by the proposed model as compared to existing access control model including ABAC and RBAC. Moreover, we aim to extend the model with continuous enforcement to deactivate a role or revoke a permission when context conditions fail to hold, and to develop an XACML profile of the proposed model.

Acknowledgments. The work of first two authors is supported by a grant from the Danish National Advanced Technology Foundation. The work of the third author is supported by a US National Science Foundation grant CNS-1423481.

References

1. Al-Kahtani, M.A., Sandhu, R.: A model for attribute-based user-role assignment. In: Annual Computer Security Applications Conference, pp. 353–362. IEEE (2002)
2. Covington, M.J., Long, W., Srinivasan, S., Dev, A.K., Ahamad, M., Abowd, G.D.: Securing context-aware applications using environment roles. In: Symposium on Access Control Models and Technologies, pp. 10–20. ACM (2001)

3. Chae, J.H., Shiri, N.: Formalization of RBAC policy with object class hierarchy. In: Dawson, E., Wong, D.S. (eds.) ISPEC 2007. LNCS, vol. 4464, pp. 162–176. Springer, Heidelberg (2007)
4. Covington, M.J., Sastry, M.R.: A contextual attribute-based access control model. In: Meersman, R., Tari, Z., Herrero, P. (eds.) OTM 2006 Workshops. LNCS, vol. 4278, pp. 1996–2006. Springer, Heidelberg (2006)
5. Coyne, E., Weil, T.R.: ABAC and RBAC: scalable, flexible, and auditable access management. IT Prof. **15**(3), 14–16 (2013)
6. Ferraiolo, D.F., Sandhu, R., Gavrila, S., Kuhn, D.R., Chandramouli, R.: Proposed NIST standard for role-based access control. ACM Trans. Inf. Syst. Secur. (TISSEC) **4**(3), 224–274 (2001)
7. Giuri, L., Iglio, P.: Role templates for content-based access control. In: Workshop on Role-Based Access Control, pp. 153–159. ACM (1997)
8. Ge, M., Osborn, S.L.: A design for parameterized roles. In: Farkas, C., Samarati, P. (eds.) Research Directions in Data and Applications Security XVIII. IFIP, vol. 144, pp. 251–264. Springer, Boston (2004)
9. Huang, J., Nicol, D.M., Bobba, R., Huh, J.H.: A framework integrating attribute-based policies into RBAC. In: Symposium on Access Control Models and Technologies, pp. 187–196. ACM (2012)
10. Jin, X., Sandhu, R., Krishnan, R.: RABAC: role-centric attribute-based access control. In: Kotenko, I., Skormin, V. (eds.) MMM-ACNS 2012. LNCS, vol. 7531, pp. 84–96. Springer, Heidelberg (2012)
11. Kalam, A.A.E., Baida, R.E., Balbiani, P., Benferhat, S., Cuppens, F., Deswarte, Y., Miege, A., Saurel, C., Trouessin, G.: Organization based access control. In: IEEE 4th International Workshop on Policies for Distributed Systems and Networks (2003)
12. Kuhn, D.R., Coyne, E.J., Weil, T.R.: Adding attributes to role-based access control. IEEE Comput. **43**, 79–81 (2010)
13. Kulkarni, D., Tripathi, A.: Context-Aware role-based access control in pervasive computing systems. In: Symposium on Access Control Models and Technologies, pp. 113–122. ACM (2008)
14. Kern, A., Walhorn, C.: Rule support for role-based access control. In: Symposium on Access Control Models and Technologies, pp. 130–138. ACM (2005)
15. Moyer, M.J., Abamad, M.: Gener alized role-based access control. In: International Conference on Distributed Computing Systems, pp. 391–398. IEEE (2001)
16. Ray, I., Toahchoodee, M.: A spatio-temporal role-based access control model. In: Barker, S., Ahn, G.-J. (eds.) Data and Applications Security XXI 2007. LNCS, vol. 4602, pp. 211–226. Springer, Heidelberg (2007)
17. Yuan, E., Tong, J.: Attributed based access control (ABAC) for web services. In: IEEE International Conference on Web Services (2005)

Automated Translation of End User Policies for Usage Control Enforcement

Prachi Kumari[✉] and Alexander Pretschner

Technische Universität München, München, Germany
{kumari,pretschn}@cs.tum.edu

Abstract. In existing implementations of usage control, policies have been specified at the implementation level by intelligent users who understand the technical details of the systems in place. However, end users who want to protect their data are not always technical experts. So they would like to specify policies in abstract terms which could somehow be translated in a format that technical systems understand. This paper describes a generic and automated policy derivation where end users can specify their usage control requirements in structured natural language sentences, from which system-understandable technical policies are derived and deployed without further human intervention.

1 Introduction

The problem of enforcing policies about what can and what must not happen to specific data items is ubiquitous. Different enforcement infrastructures, both generic [1] and specific [2], have been proposed. The configuration of these infrastructures requires technical *implementation-level policies* (ILPs). End users, however, often cannot directly specify ILPs but require a higher level of abstraction, that of *specification-level policies* (SLPs). The problem we tackle in this paper is the automatic derivation of ILPs from SLPs. We show how to translate SLPs written in OSL [3] to ILPs that come as ECA rules [4].

The object of data usage control enforcement is abstract *data* (photo, song etc.), that we need to distinguish from concrete technical representations called *containers* (specific files, dom elements etc.). Policies on data usually need to be interpreted as policies on *all representations* of that data. We therefore rely on a data flow model [5] that defines system states as mappings between data and containers at a moment in time. The transition relation on states is the change in these mappings. Policy enforcement on data is done on the basis of data flow tracking which is monitored on grounds of the transition relation [5].

Because data and actions on data are specific to an application domain, a three-layered domain meta-model for refining data and actions has been proposed in [6]. This meta-model (Fig. 1) describes a domain to be composed of classes of data and actions at the end user's level (platform-independent model: PIM), both of which are refined in terms of classes of technical concepts (platform-specific model: PSM) and classes of various implementations of them

© IFIP International Federation for Information Processing 2015
P. Samarati (Ed.): DBSec 2015, LNCS 9149, pp. 250–258, 2015.
DOI: 10.1007/978-3-319-20810-7_18

(implementation-specific model: ISM) at the lower levels in the meta-model. The refinement of user action and data is given by the vertical mappings between the model elements (data classes mapped to container classes and action classes mapped to transformer classes which are further mapped to other classes of containers and transformers at the PSM and the ISM levels). Figure 2 (taken from [7]) shows an example instance of the meta-model in Fig. 1 that refines "copy photo" in different ways in an Online Social Network (OSN).

The formal semantics of the refinements are given by combining the domain meta-model with the aforementioned data flow model. Policies are derived using this formal action refinement. The detailed formalism is described in [7].

Running Example. In an OSN implementation, user Alice wants to specify and enforce a policy "friends must never copy this data" for her photos, without any technical knowledge. We will refer to this SLP and the action refinement in Fig. 2 throughout this paper. In Sect. 3, we describe the technicalities of one implementation that helps Alice prevent her friends from copying her photos.

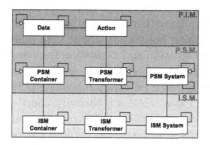

Fig. 1. The Domain Meta-model

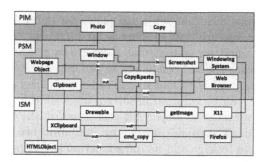

Fig. 2. An OSN instance of Fig. 1

Contribution. This paper presents a generic methodology for automating policy derivation for usage control enforcement. A proof of concept is realized for a specific context (i.e. OSN). However, the approach is generic and can be applied to any other domain model.

2 The Generic Approach to Policy Derivation

Connecting Instances to Classes. The domain model specifies general *classes* of data. A specific policy is concerned with specific data items, which we need to connect to the classes in the domain model. Conceptually, we use a generic function *getClass* for this. The definition of the *getClass* function varies according to the application domain. We illustrate this with a simple example: In the OSN context, a specific image (data d) can be a profile photo, logo, banner or a cover photo (data classes). Different data classes might mean different storage and different technical refinements of the instances. E.g. (small) logos stored as blobs vs. (large) photos stored as links in a table. Relevant data classes and assignment of data elements to one or many of them is intuitive and is driven by the domain design and its implementation. This is because data classes describe how users understand different types of data in a particular context and there is no universal rule for classifying them. However, for a given context, it is easy to define *getClass*. In Sect. 3 we show how this can be done for a particular case.

The Policy Derivation Methodology. Although end users would like to specify security requirements, in particular usage control policies [8], they are in general not capable of reasoning holistically about such policies [9]. This motivates the need for a policy specification and derivation framework that requires simple and limited user input for the specification of usage control policies. Our policy derivation approach is based on *policy templates* that are *classes of policies*. Human intervention is in two roles: a technical expert called the **power user** specifies the domain model and other configurations, using which, an **end user** specifies and automatically translates and deploys the policies. The power user only configures the policy derivation at the start, no further human intervention is needed. Policies are automatically derived in the following *five* steps:

Step 1: Setting up the Policy Derivation. The power user specifies the domain model used for action refinement. The power user also specifies two types of policy templates: a *first* set of templates for the SLPs, to be instantiated by an end user for each data element to be protected. We studied several application domains and recognized that most relevant usage control policies could be specified using limited combinations of OSL operators. Based on this, we came up with *classes of SLPs that specify constraints upon classes of data and actions*. As one SLP can be enforced in several ways [4], the *second* set of templates specifies enforcement *strategies* for each class of SLPs. E.g. a company enforces a policy "don't copy document" by inhibition because the company wants to prevent data leakage and its infrastructure supports it; or, a film producer enforces "don't play unpaid videos" by allowing corresponding events with a lower quality video because either it's technically not feasible to inhibit the events or he wants to give a limited preview to its prospective customers. As the reasons for deciding upon an enforcement strategy don't change very often, it is reasonable to specify the enforcement strategy for ECA rules generation in a template in order to automate the process.

Step 2: Policy Specification. End users instantiate the policy classes using templates to specify data elements, actions and other constraints like time, cardinality etc. (e.g. max. copies allowed, min. payable amount, currency etc.).

Step 3: Policy Derivation. First, we get the class of data addressed in the policy using *getClass*. Then, data and actions are refined according to the formal policy derivation described in [7] and the resulting OSL formulas are converted into ECA rules using predefined templates.

Step 4: Connecting Data and Container. As such, data does not exist in real world, except in the mind of the humans who want to protect or abuse it. In real systems, only corresponding containers exist. Therefore, an end user writes policies on containers and specifies if he means to address the data in that container (i.e. all copies of the container) or the container itself. This is done by specifying the *policy type* in the SLP. Conceptually, data enters a system in an *initial container* and gets a data ID assigned. This process of initially mapping containers to data is called the *initial binding of data and container*. After the initial binding, policies that are finally deployed for enforcement are of two types: *dataOnly* policies apply to all representations of data at and across layers of abstraction in a machine while *containerOnly* policies apply to the specific container mentioned in the policy.

Step 5: Adding Context-Specific Details. According to the domain and its implementation, there are many context details that might be added to the ECA rules before deployment. E.g. policies in an OSN might address specific users and their relationships to the profile owner, and this information is known only at runtime by identifying the browsing session. Together, step 4 and 5 are called *policy instantiation* and they might be switched in order, depending upon the context detail to be added and the corresponding system implementation.

Generic Architecture: We build upon an existing generic usage control infrastructure with three main components: a *Policy Enforcement Point* (PEP), able to observe, intercept, possibly modify and generate events in the system; a *Policy Decision Point* (PDP), representing the core of the usage control monitoring logic; and a *Policy Information Point* (PIP), which provides the data-container mapping to the PDP [5]. This infrastructure was extended with a *Policy Management Point* (PMP) with a dedicated sub-component, the *Policy Translation Point* (PTP) for policy derivation using action refinement. Policy specification, instantiation and deployment is handled by the PMP.

During policy enforcement, when an event is intercepted and notified by the PEP to the PDP, the object parameter is always a container as only concrete containers exist in running systems. For a *dataOnly* policy, the PDP queries the PIP for the data-container mapping before deciding upon the enforcement mechanism. In case of *containerOnly* policies, the PDP needs no communication with the PIP as the policy and the event notification address containers.

3   Implementation and Evaluation

We instantiated the generic architecture to derive policies for the online social network SCUTA, which already had basic usage control capabilities [2]. We extended SCUTA with two types of policy specification for two classes of end users. As shown in Fig. 3, *basic users* only specify how sensitive they consider a particular data. Based on the sensitivity rating and a predefined trust model, SLPs are generated by the system on behalf of the user (for details, see [2]). *Advanced Users* specify their policies by instantiating admin-defined SLP templates that are loaded every time the page is requested. In Fig. 3, we also see an SLP template in edit mode.

In our attacker model, all the policies *protect end users' data from misuse by other social network users*. The SCUTA provider is trusted. SLPs are specified by Alice. They are translated at the data receiver Bob's end, to be enforced at two layers of abstraction in the system: Mozilla Firefox web browser [2] and Windows 7 operating system (for protecting cache files) [10].[1]

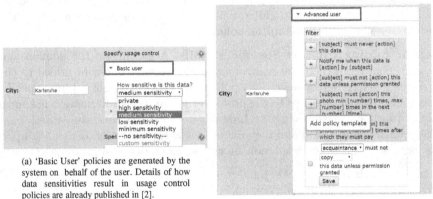

(a) 'Basic User' policies are generated by the system on behalf of the user. Details of how data sensitivities result in usage control policies are already published in [2].

(b) 'Advanced Users' can specify their policies using admin-defined SLP templates

Fig. 3. Screenshot of SCUTA showing basic and advanced policy specification

Connecting instances to classes. In order to connect data elements to their classes, we used the database schema of SCUTA: the class of a data element is represented by the name of the table where that element is stored. E.g. an image stored in table "profile_photo" is a profile photo. As mentioned in Sect. 1, a data flow model is used to keep track of data in multiple containers. The data flow model of a particular system describes all sets of containers in that system. E.g., C_{File} is the set of all files in the data flow model of Windows 7. We reused this

---

[1] A video demonstrating policy specification and translation for this use case is available at https://www.youtube.com/watch?v=6i9Mfmbj2Xw.

information in our implementation to connect containers to their classes, e.g., all members of C_{File} are of the type File.

Example Policy Derivation. Now we describe the derivation of our example policy introduced in Sect. 1: "friends must never copy this data". Action refinement is based on the domain model shown in Fig. 2. The SLP templates (specified by the power user) and their instances (specified by end users) are stored in the SCUTA database. Figure 4 shows an example SLP template.

Template ID	102
Template Text	#{[subject]}# must never _[[action]]_ this data
Data Class	city;email;photo
Policy Class	\<policy subject=\"#{subject}#\"\>\<obligation\>\<always\>\<not\> \<action name=\"_[action]_\" type=\"desiredEv\"\>\<params\>\<param class=\"@{class}@\" name=\"object\" policyType=\"dataUsage\" value=\"@{object}@\"/\>\</params\>\</action\>\</not\>\</always\> \</obligation\>\</policy\>

Fig. 4. An example SLP template, specified by the power user

Each template is identified by an *ID*. The *template text* appears in the front end without the special character delimiters; the delimiters are used by the web application logic to create the GUI. *Data class* refers to the type of data for which the policy could be instantiated. *Policy class* is the XML representation of the template text with placeholders delimited by special symbols. In the GUI, the end user sees the template text with editable parts. When a template is instantiated, data and other parameter values substitute the placeholders. Generated policies are shown to the user as structured sentences in natural language.

Policy derivation and deployment is a one-click process. ECA templates are specified per SLP template. Listing 1.1 shows the ECA template (as a JSON object) for the SLP template shown in Fig. 4. Note how the template ID from Fig. 4 is used to connect the two templates. This ECA template states that in the generated ECA rule, the trigger *event* is a *-event which matches all events in the system; the *condition* comes from the action refinement whose input is the past form of the specified OSL policy; the *action* is to inhibit the event.

```
{"id":"102",
"templates":[
  {"event":"<*/>",
    "condition":"<actionRef(pastForm)
      />",
    "action":["<inhibit/>"],
    "type":"preventive"
} ]    },
```

Listing 1.1. ECA generation template for "inhibit" enforcement strategy

```
{"id":"102",
"templates":[
  {"event":"<*/>",
    "condition":"<actionRef(pastForm)
      />",
    "action":["<modify/>","object", "
      icon/error.jpg"],
    "type":"preventive"
} ] },
```

Listing 1.2. ECA generation template for "modify" enforcement strategy

Using this ECA template, ECA rules are generated automatically. An ECA rule for the Firefox web browser is shown in Listing 1.3. The scope in line 3 of

Listing 1.3 is added to the policy as part of the context information that identifies each logged-in SCUTA user (and his browsing session) uniquely. "cmd_copy" in line 6 comes from the refinement of copy action (Fig. 2). In line 7, "dataUsage" means that the container "9c73d9b7ff.jpg" is to be interpreted as data and substituted by a data ID.

```
1   <preventiveMechanism name="Mechanism_102_1_preventive">
2       <trigger action="*"tryEvent="true">
3           <paramMatch name="scope"value="536a624a87644"/>
4       </trigger>
5       <condition>
6           <eventMatch action="cmd_copy"tryEvent="true">
7               <paramMatch name="object"value="9c73d9b7ff.jpg"type="dataUsage"
                    />
8           </eventMatch>
9       </condition>
10      <authorizationAction name="Authorization␣1">
11          <inhibit/>
12      </authorizationAction>
13  </preventiveMechanism>
```

Listing 1.3. ECA rule for "inhibit copy" in Firefox web browser

Listing 1.2 shows another ECA template that generates ECA rules with "modify" enforcement strategy for the SLP template of Fig. 4: the *action* part says that the enforcement mechanism must replace the object in question by "icon/error.jpg". One of the generated ECA rules is shown in Listing 1.4.

```
<preventiveMechanism name="Mechanism_102_1_preventive">
    <trigger action="*"tryEvent="true">
        <paramMatch name="scope"value="536a62466a42e"/>
    </trigger>
    <condition>
        <eventMatch action="cmd_copy"tryEvent="true">
            <paramMatch name="object"value="9c73d9b7ff.jpg"type="dataUsage"/>
        </eventMatch>
    </condition>
    <authorizationAction name="Authorization␣1">
        <allow>
            <modify>
                <parameter name="object"value="icon/error.jpg"/>
            </modify>
        </allow>
    </authorizationAction>
</preventiveMechanism>
```

Listing 1.4. ECA rule for "modify copy" in Firefox web browser

As we use templates for ECA rules generation, changing enforcement strategies is easy. The power user modifies the ECA templates and notifies the PMP for retranslating, revoking and deploying policies. In the current implementation, all deployed policies are overwritten. Modifying the PMP to selectively revoke and redeploy only those policies whose enforcement strategy has changed is trivial.

4   Related Work and Relevance

Policy derivation for access control has been investigated based on resource hierarchies [11], goal decomposition [12], action decomposition [13], data classification

[14], ontology [15], etc. In **usage control**, several enforcements exist at and across different layers of abstraction in various types of systems [2,3,5,16–18]. In all these implementations, the focus has been on the implementation of event monitors; policy derivation has not been addressed. While [19] describes an approach where high-level usage control policies are automatically refined to implementation-level policies using policy refinement rules, the refinement rules are specific to the domain in consideration. In contrast, the very idea of our work is a more generic approach that relies on instantiated domain meta models; this is the gap in usage control policy refinement that is filled by this work. A model-based semi-automated approach to usage control policy derivation is described in [6,7]. We build on this work and achieve automated policy derivation.

5   Conclusions and Future Work

This paper provides a methodology for automating usage control policy derivation. We have also proposed the usage of policy templates in order to enable end users to specify usage control policies without having to know the underlying policy language. We do not propose any concrete syntax or design for the templates. We have *deliberately* kept our implementation of the templates simple with user inputs limited to multiple-choice format. In principle, policy templates could be written in XML, in plain structured text, in simple graphical format with dropdowns and checkboxes or, in advanced graphical format by dragging and connecting different blocks to write policies (along the lines of MIT Open Blocks). Policies could also be specified using free text in any natural language or standardized solutions like ODRLC (a translation from OSL to ODRLC and vice versa is shown in [3]). Also, technically-proficient users can write policies directly at the implementation level. This work does not exclude such possibility.

One limitation of this work is the static domain structure. This is a deliberately introduced limitation which does not affect the automation of policy derivation, which was the goal of this work. This limitation is being addressed in ongoing work and is therefore out of the scope of this paper.

References

1. Kelbert, F., Pretschner, A.: Towards a policy enforcement infrastructure for distributed usagecontrol. In: Proceedings of SACMAT 2012, pp. 119–122 (2012)
2. Kumari, P., Pretschner, P., Peschla, P., Kuhn, J.: Distributed data usage control for web applications: a social network implementation. In: Proceedings of the First ACM Conference on Data and Application Security and Privacy, CODASPY 2011, pp. 85–96 (2011)
3. Hilty, M., Pretschner, A., Basin, D., Schaefer, C., Walter, T.: A policy language for distributed usage control. In: Biskup, J., López, J. (eds.) ESORICS 2007. LNCS, vol. 4734, pp. 531–546. Springer, Heidelberg (2007)
4. Pretschner, A., Hilty, M., Basin, D., Schaefer, C., Walter, T.: Mechanisms for Usage Control. In: Proceedings of ASIACCS, pp. 240–245 (2008)

5. Pretschner, A., Lovat, E., Buechler, M.: Representation-independent data usage control. In Proceedings of 6th International Workshop on Data Privacy Management (2011)
6. Kumari, P., Pretschner, A.: Deriving implementation-level policies for usage control enforcement. In: Proceedings of CODASPY 2012, pp. 83–94. ACM (2012)
7. Kumari, P., Pretschner, A.: Model-based usage control policy derivation. In: Proceedings of ESSOS 2013, pp. 58–74 (2013)
8. Rudolph, M., Schwarz, R., Jung, C., Mauthe, A., Shirazi, N.: Deliverable 3.2 - policy specification methodology. Technical report, SECCRIT, June 2014
9. Fang, L., LeFevre, K.: Privacy wizards for social networking sites. In: Proceedings of WWW 2010, pp. 351–360. ACM, New York (2010)
10. Wüchner, T., Pretschner, A.: Data loss prevention based on data-driven usage control. In: Proceedings of ISSRE 2012, pp. 151–160 (2012)
11. Su, L., Chadwick, D., Basden, A., Cunningham, J.: Automated decomposition of access control policies. In: Proceedings of POLICY 2005, pp. 6–8 (2005)
12. Bandara, A.K., Lupu, E.C., Moffett, J., Russo, A.: A goal-based approach to policy refinement. In: Proceedings of POLICY 2004, pp. 229–239 (2004)
13. Craven, R., Lobo, J., Lupu, E., Russo, A., Sloman, M.: Decomposition techniques for policy refinement. In: Proceedings of CNSM 2010, pp. 72–79 (2010)
14. Udupi, Y.B., Sahai, A., Singhal, S.: A classification-based approach to policy refinement. In: Proceedings of 10th IFIP/IEEE IM, pp. 785–788 (2007)
15. Guerrero, A., Villagrá, V.A., de Vergara, J.E.L., Sánchez-Macián, A., Berrocal, J.: Ontology-based policy refinement using swrl rules for management information definitions in OWL. In: State, R., van der Meer, S., O'Sullivan, D., Pfeifer, T. (eds.) DSOM 2006. LNCS, vol. 4269, pp. 227–232. Springer, Heidelberg (2006)
16. Harvan, M., Pretschner, A.: State-based usage control enforcement with data flow tracking using system call interposition. In: Proceedings of NSS, pp. 373–380 (2009)
17. Pretschner, A., Buechler, M., Harvan, M., Schaefer, C., and T. Walter. Usage control enforcement with data flow tracking for x11. In: Proceedings of STM 2009, pp. 124–137 (2009)
18. Kumari, P., Kelbert, F., Pretschner, A.: Data protection in heterogeneous distributed systems: a smart meter example. In: DSCI (2011)
19. Neisse, R., Doerr, J.: Model-based specification and refinement of usage control policies. In: Proceedings of PST'2013, pp. 169–176 (2013)

Network and Internet Security

Defensive Resource Allocations with Security Chokepoints in IPv6 Networks

Assane Gueye[1]([✉]), Peter Mell[2], Richard Harang[3], and Richard J. La[1]

[1] University of Maryland, College Park, MD, USA
{agueye,hyongla}@umd.edu
[2] National Institute of Standards and Technology, Gaithersburg, USA
peter.mell@nist.gov
[3] U.S. Army Research Laboratory, Adelphi, MD, USA
richard.e.harang.civ@mail.mil

Abstract. Securely configured Internet Protocol version 6 networks can be made resistant to network scanning, forcing attackers to propagate following existing benign communication paths. We exploit this attacker limitation in a defensive approach in which heightened security measures are deployed onto a select group of chokepoint hosts to enhance detection or deter penetration. Chokepoints are chosen such that, together, they connect small isolated clusters of the communication graph. Hence, attackers attempting to propagate are limited to a small set of targets or have to penetrate one or more chokepoints. Optimal placement of chokepoints requires solving an NP-hard problem and, hence, we approximate optimal solutions via a suite of heuristics. We test our algorithms on data from a large operational network and discover that heightened security measures are only needed on 0.65 % of the nodes to restrict unimpeded attacker propagation to no more than 15 % of the network.

Keywords: Chokepoints · IPv6 · Moving target · Vertex partitioning · Security

1 Introduction

Consider an attacker stealthily compromising an internal host on an Internet Protocol version 6 (IPv6) network. Leveraging this vantage point, the attacker then attacks other internal hosts, using some of them as launching points for additional attacks. The attacker's goal is to either find a particular resource or to simply gain control of as many internal hosts as possible. We further assume that the attacker will execute attacks at the transport layer and above because the vast majority of network-based attacks operate at these layers [10].

A securely configured IPv6 network can be made resistant to network scanning [7] and other forms of target acquisition [4], limiting the attacker's ability to discover new hosts and subnets. As a consequence, attacker propagation is mostly limited to existing benign communication pathways. We exploit this limited attacker movement in a new defensive model by augmenting a set of

© IFIP International Federation for Information Processing 2015
P. Samarati (Ed.): DBSec 2015, LNCS 9149, pp. 261–276, 2015.
DOI: 10.1007/978-3-319-20810-7_19

hosts with heightened security measures such that they form internal choke-points for attacker propagation. The attacker will then be required to penetrate these chokepoints or else be limited to a small set of targets. We thus enable a novel defense-in-depth layer that complements traditional security approaches.

The heightened security measures at the chokepoints may take many forms, be detective or preventative, and include a combination of different approaches. The nodes may be hardened to a similar degree as network perimeter devices, may have increased monitoring (human or automated), or may have an enhanced deployment of security software. They may be special purpose servers with lim-ited functionality (thus reducing the overall attack surface). These chokepoints then represent a more difficult target than standard network nodes and/or ones with increased detection capabilities.

We assume that there is budget to place heightened security measures on up k nodes. The question of interest to us then becomes: how do we assign these k nodes in order for them to be effective chokepoints? In this paper, we consider two objective functions: *minimizing the number of hosts an attacker could penetrate without compromising a chokepoint node* and *maximizing the number of chokepoints between the attacker and any random goal host*.

Optimal assignment of chokepoints requires solving the NP-complete [5] vertex separator problem; for this reason, we developed a suite of four greedy heuristic solutions. Aiding our identification of chokepoints is that our empirical evaluation indicates that transport layer communication graphs have two prop-erties: (i) there are many nodes of low degree and few nodes of high degree, while (ii) low degree nodes tend to be connected to high degree nodes and vice versa (i.e., the graph of the network is *disassortative* [18]). The result is that there are many communication paths that tend to overlap onto a subset of hosts, which helps in our design of heuristics for choosing the set of k chokepoints.

To evaluate the effectiveness of our approach and proposed algorithms, we collected transport layer communication data throughout a large operational network consisting of 15509 nodes. We used the empirical degree sequence of this data to generate a suite of uniformly distributed random graphs conformant with the degree distribution within the network. We were thus able to create a variety of test graphs to broaden our test cases beyond the single monitored network. Finally, we ran our algorithms on each random graph and evaluated the performance according to two metrics: (a) the size of the largest cluster and (b) the average number of chokepoints between a pair of nodes.

Once the chokepoints are chosen, periodic monitoring of the communication patterns is necessary to detect ongoing changes and their impact on current chokepoint placement. While the link connectivity remains stable over time (from empirical observation), operational networks change slowly but continually as new users and hosts are added. This dynamic aspect to the communication graph can be accommodated by a mobile defensive technologies (those that can be repositioned rapidly and with little cost). Without mobile defensive measures being available, cluster sizes can always be minimized by adding new chokepoint at an increased cost. With mobile defensive measures, the chokepoints can be repositioned to near-optimally account for changing communication conditions. Even if the communication graph remains stable, a moving defense regimen may be implemented where the chokepoints migrate over time (e.g., between locally optimal configurations) to prevent attackers from mapping out the defensive topology or learning of chokepoint placement using out-of-band methods.

The remainder of this paper is structured as follows. Section 2 discusses our threat model while Sect. 3 describes network configuration requirements. Section 4 provides our chokepoint approach. Section 5 shows how to minimize the maximal cluster size. Section 6 illustrates how to maximize the mean of the minimum number of chokepoints that must be traversed between pairs of nodes. Section 7 describes our experimental data and Sect. 8 provides empirical results. Section 9 details related work and Sect. 10 concludes.

2   Threat Model

We assume that an attacker has broken through a network's, often porous [14], perimeter security and penetrated an internal host. We also assume that this penetrated host is equally likely to be any node of the network. From this vantage point, the attacker attempts to reach the rest of the network. This includes attacking nodes in order to perform malicious actions directly on those nodes as well as penetrating the nodes to use them as launching points for other malicious activities. Because of the security network configuration discussed in the next section, we model attackers as being limited to propagating through existing or previous transport layer communication channels (using only network knowledge available from the set of compromised hosts). With respect to attacks, we assume that all attacks take place at the ISO transport layer or above. This is where the vast majority of attacks take place [10] since network devices are usually not directly penetrable through the Internet Protocol layer. The presumed goal of the attacker is to either propagate through the network to reach a particular goal host or simply to gain control of as many hosts as possible.

3   Network Configuration Requirements

We model the defended network as IPv6 only. The actual network may contain IPv4 hosts and dual stack IPv4/IPv6 hosts, but our defensive approach applies solely to the IPv6-only subset. This means that as a network slowly migrates to IPv6, our approach will provide monotonically increasing benefits and may thus provide further motivation for a full transition.

We further assume that an attacker is only able to discover new hosts to attack by using the knowledge resident on previously compromised hosts (i.e., the neighbor discovery table). We can do this because we will discuss how it is possible to configure an IPv6 network to mitigate other target acquisition methodologies.

A primary method for target acquisition in IPv4 is network scanning (sending out probes to subnet addresses looking for active hosts). However, in IPv6 the size of a standard subnet is the square of the number of addresses in the entire IPv4 address space. In a securely configured IPv6 subnet, this makes network scanning infeasible since the number of addresses to be probed is insurmountable [7]. Other methods for target acquisition exist [4] but can be mitigated through a combination of perimeter security and secure configurations.

A method not easily addressed is that of an attacker monitoring layer 2 multicast traffic to "sniff" the addresses of active hosts on a subnet. The primary hurdle is the native IPv6 Neighbor Discovery (ND) protocol that serves as a replacement for the IPv4 Address Resolution Protocol (ARP) (and that has many of the same security weaknesses). However, other layer 2 multicasting protocols exist such as Apple's Bonjour [3] that present similar challenges.

The address disclosures inherent in layer 2 multicasting protocols can be accounted for in our chokepoint approach by incorporating the layer 2 intra-subnet communication along with the set of monitored transport layer flows. This has the effect of making each IPv6 subnet a complete sub-graph in our communication graph because ND will cause all hosts to multicast to all other hosts in a subnet. This is not a desirable situation with respect to our defensive solution.

Thus to limit this effect, we propose making the subnets as small as possible in order to limit the size of these complete sub-graphs. This results in a security versus functionality tradeoff. If the subnets are too small, then automated service discovery protocols (e.g., ND and Apple's Bonjour) will be unable to automatically find services, thus requiring a manual setup. If they are too big, then attackers will gain additional knowledge of network targets.

In evaluating our approach, we assume a high security implementation for the network where administrators are willing to sacrifice automated service discovery to achieve enhanced security. Hence, we model the enterprise taking the security/functionality tradeoff to its limit, using an IPv6/126 subnet for each host. This approach eliminates all layer 2 information leakage by restricting subnets to covering a single host and its related switch port. We then randomly assign these mini-subnets within the larger network address space to preserve network scanning resistance. By doing this, we essentially force layer 2 routing up to layer 3 and gain security advantages by doing so (while giving up some functionality in the form of automatic neighbor discovery and service configuration).

Given this security configuration, an attacker is limited to propagating using only the target address knowledge resident on the previously compromised hosts (i.e., existing benign communication paths). Our work then is to counter an attacker using this knowledge to expand their influence within a network.

4   Chokepoint Approach and Metrics

Our approach is to leverage limited attacker propagation in securely configured IPv6 enterprise networks to inhibit attacker movement or enhance detection by setting up security 'chokepoints'. A chokepoint is a preexisting host that is given heightened security measures where the security measures can be protective, detective, or a combination of both. The nodes not chosen to be chokepoints are referred to as 'ordinary'. The primary thrust of our work is then in determining how to best choose the chokepoints.

Our goal is to place the chokepoints so that attackers are maximally restricted in their ability to propagate through the network. We do this by modeling the layer 4 network communication as a graph with the nodes being hosts. We then choose the chokepoints in such a way that the graph is broken into isolated clusters when the chokepoints are removed. Each cluster represents an island of available targets to an attacker. To reach nodes in other clusters, however, the attacker needs to penetrate one or more chokepoint nodes. The heightened security at a checkpoint may impede attacker propagation, increase the chance of detecting an attacker, or both (depending upon the type of heightened security deployed).

We consider two metrics to optimize with our choice of chokepoints: (i) minimizing the maximal cluster size and (ii) maximizing the mean of the minimum number of chokepoints that lie between pairs of nodes. The former metric aims to constrain the attacker to as small a cluster as possible, and the second seeks to maximize the number of chokepoints that an attacker must penetrate on average while seeking a particular network target. The next two sections describe algorithms designed to achieve these goals.

Notations: We assume that the network is represented as an un-weighted undirected graph $G = (V, E)$, where V is the set of nodes and E is the set of edges, with $|V| = n$ and $|E| = m$. E is the set of observed benign communication links in the network (not the permissible links). We further assume that there is a budget to deploy enhanced security at up to k nodes. We use S to denote the set of (at most) k designated chokepoint nodes. With a little abuse of notation, we let $G \backslash S$ represent G with the nodes in S removed along with edges incident to them. This graph may be disconnected into a set of isolated clusters or components.

5   Minimizing the Maximum Cluster Size

Our primary goal is to choose the chokepoints in such a way that they maximally bound attacker propagation (either providing impedance points or enhanced detection points). To do this, the communication graph should break into clusters upon removal of the chokepoints. Note that the removal of chokepoint nodes and creation of isolated clusters is solely to model the optimization problem. It does not reflect actual removal of hosts or imply that the chokepoints themselves are invulnerable.

Within the same cluster, any node can attack any other node without encountering a chokepoint. The size of the maximum cluster is hence the largest set of nodes that could potentially be accessed by an attacker without being impeded or detected by a chokepoint. The first goal of chokepoint placement is to minimize the size of this maximal cluster. Unfortunately, this problem is an instance of the vertex separator problem which is known to be NP-hard [5] and has only received little attention in the literature. In this paper, we consider four heuristic algorithms to find approximate solutions to the problem. The algorithms are iterative in nature and exploit well-known features of the network.

1. Iterative removal of maximal degree node (DEG): This approach is motivated by the observation that engineered networks, such as the Internet, are very sensitive to attacks that target nodes with largest degrees [9]. In our DEG algorithm, we iteratively remove (i.e., choose as chokepoint) the node with the maximum degree in the remaining graph as well as all edges that are incident to it. After each iteration, we re-compute the degree of all nodes and recall the routine until k nodes are removed.

2. Iterative removal of maximal betweenness node (BET): This approach is inspired by the observation that in communication networks there are many low degree nodes that tend to talk to a few high degree 'hub' nodes while the few hub nodes talk to the many low degree nodes. As a consequence, most paths go through the hubs nodes. The fraction of shortest paths from all vertices to all others that pass through a given node is defined as its "betweenness centrality". Our BET algorithm is similar to DEG, but here we remove nodes with largest betweenness centrality.

3. Iterative greedy removal (GRD): In this approach, as in previous heuristics, nodes are removed one-by-one. However, instead of removing the node with the largest degree/betweenness, at each step we remove the node that minimizes the size of the current largest cluster. After each iteration, we update the graph and iterate until k nodes are removed.

4. Iterative Vertex Bisection (IVB): In this approach, we attempt to iteratively bisect the largest remaining cluster until all k nodes are removed. For each bisection attempt, we randomly choose pairs of nodes and iteratively grow two non-overlapping trees until we can no longer do so. We take the pair of trees that best optimizes the objective and then compare them against the output of the DEG algorithm (limited to the number of nodes removed in the tree bisection), with the best result being chosen.

In general, we have observed that IVB and GRD provided slightly better results, but not uniformly. While not immediately apparent, DEG can be implemented in $O(n + m)$ linear time and is reasonably effective overall. BET is the slowest among all algorithms but can occasionally produce the best answer. For our analysis, we run all four algorithms for each data points and simply choose the best one (i.e., has the minimum size of maximum cluster) as approximation to the problem.

6   Maximizing Chokepoint Traversal

Our secondary goal is to maximize the mean of the minimum number of chokepoints that an attacker must traverse to reach any given target node. The motivation for this is the observation that each traversed chokepoint increases the chance of impeding or detecting the attacker.

For the analysis, we assume that the attack propagates from some initial node s to some target node t $(s, t \in V)$ by following the path containing the smallest number of chokepoints (which corresponds to the best case from the attacker's point of view). In practice, the attack propagation path is determined by the attacker's mode of operation, which we often do not know. However, the aforementioned path with the minimum number of chokepoints offers a *universal lower bound* to the actual number of traversed chokepoints.

We say that an $s - t$ path is "*minimal*" if it contains a minimum number of chokepoints amongst all $s - t$ paths. For a given chokepoint assignment S, we ask the following question: what is the empirical distribution of the number of chokepoints in the minimal $s - t$ paths (i.e., the fraction of minimal $s - t$ paths containing $0, 1, 2, 3, \ldots$ chokepoints)? With this distribution, we can compute the average length of a minimal $s - t$ path. Our goal is to choose the chokepoint so as to maximize this average length of $s - t$ path.

To calculate any minimal $s - t$ path, we would like to use standard shortest path algorithms. However, they do not directly apply because there are both ordinary and chokepoint nodes in the graph whereas our distance metric is only concerned with the number of chokepoints along the paths. To enable the use of standard shortest path algorithms, we need a graph transformation such that, in the transformed graph, all nodes (except s and t) are chokepoint nodes and it retains the connectivity relations of the original communication graph. To this end, we propose the following three-step transformation:

Transformation 1 - (Collapsed Clusters): For each cluster in $G \backslash S$ (clusters may be single nodes), we create a single node in a new graph $G2$. For each node in S, we create a node in $G2$. For each edge $e \in G$, we create a corresponding edge in $G2$ if e is incident to at least one node in S. If one of the incident nodes is not in S, then we use the node in $G2$ that corresponds to the appropriate cluster in G. Finally, we replace any multi-edges in $G2$ with single edges. From its construction, in $G2$ no two ordinary nodes will have an edge between them. The chokepoints may have edges to both other chokepoints and ordinary nodes.

Transformation 2 - (Collapsed Leaves): Collapse all leaves surrounding each chokepoint into a single leaf node to form a second graph CG from $G2$.

Transformation 3 - (Ordinary Node Substitution): The previous two transformations can be done once on the entire graph regardless of the location of s and t. To compute the number of chokepoint in a minimal $s - t$ path, we now construct a final graph, HG, as follow: Make a copy of CG and, for each ordinary node x (except for s and t), add edges connecting x's neighbors (forming complete subgraphs) and remove x. Duplicate edges are removed.

This construction provides us with a graph containing s and t in which all other nodes are chokepoints. The edges in the graph represent the connectivity of the original graph G and thus we can use shortest path algorithms on the final graph HG to determine the minimal number of chokepoints between s and t in G. We now compute all minimal paths from each pair of points in the graph. Our work can be substantially reduced by realizing the all nodes in a single cluster in G can be computed as a single node in CG and HG (since they will all have the same path length to any target node). By computing these values for each (s,t) pair in the collapsed graph CG and making the appropriate updates after each run, we derive the empirical distribution of minimal $s-t$ paths containing l ($l = 0, 1, \ldots, n-1$) chokepoints. Note that using this procedure, we have considerably reduced the number of (s,t) pairs to consider. Also, the shortest path algorithm is now run on a much small graph (HG) which has only $k+2$ nodes.

7 Experimental Data

For our experiments, we generate random graphs that conform to the degree sequence we obtained by observing the transport layer communication between nodes in a large operational network of 15509 nodes. Unlike typical flow monitoring done on the network perimeter, we monitored flows internal to the network in order to obtain a complete view of the transport layer connectivity.

Note that the monitored network was an IPv4 network while our study pertains to IPv6 networks. However, the flow data represents communications above the IP layer and thus would be similar (if not the same) on an IPv6 substrate.

We monitor the network for 11 days and use all observed links and nodes to construct its connectivity graph. Figure 1a shows the number of nodes observed over time and Fig. 1b shows the number of observed links. By hour 116, almost all of the nodes and links have been observed. This indicates that most of the nodes can be seen communicating with other nodes within 4.83 days. The latter 6 days add only 0.72 % of the total observed nodes and 5.83 % of the total observed links. This indicates that the cumulative data obtained at hour 264 is an accurate description of the real network.

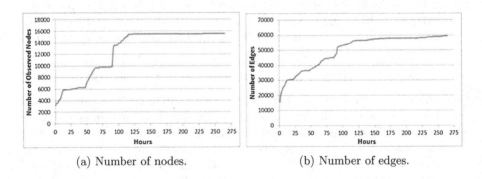

(a) Number of nodes. (b) Number of edges.

Fig. 1. Evolution over time.

We use the cumulative degree distribution of the built connectivity graph to generate random graphs that are "uniformly" sampled from the set of possible graphs with the given distribution. We do so by using to the following two-step algorithm:

- First, we build an initial random realization of a network according to the given degree sequence using the known Havel-Hakimi algorithm [12,13].
- Second, we use this initial realization to create a random graph by performing a series of random double edge swaps as follows: randomly choose two edges (u, v) and (x, y), where (u, x) and (v, y) are not already in the graph, remove the chosen edges from the graph, and add new edges (ux) and (v, y).

These edge swaps preserve the degree distribution of the graph, and generates a Markov chain that is ergodic over the space of all random graphs with the same degree distribution. Individual samples from this chain at steady state–assuming that the samples are separated by sufficiently large intervals–can then be treated as graphs sampled uniformly at random from the set of all graphs having the same degree distribution. Although the best known upper bound to the convergence rate is very large ($\approx n^{24}$) [11], it has been observed that in practice, the algorithm converges very quickly. In fact, the bound is conjectured to be $O(mlog(m))$, but it still remains an open question [11].

8 Empirical Results

We first examine the degree distribution of the operational network, and compare it to a power law distribution fit to the same data. We use the above algorithm to generate 10000 random graphs with the same degree sequence as the real operational network, and examine the effect of the sampling on the assortativity of the graph. We evaluate the effectiveness of our chokepoint placement procedure by varying the number of chokepoints k. We use the heuristic algorithms described earlier to select the chokepoint nodes and examine the two aforementioned metrics for chokepoint placement. First, we analyze the size of the single largest connected component in the graph formed by removing all nodes designated as chokepoints. Next, we consider the average minimum (again, worst-case for the defender) number of chokepoint nodes that an attacker would have to pass through to target a specific node given a random entry node. For this, we use the graph transformations and algorithm that we describe above in Sect. 6. Our analysis shows that the heuristic node selection method we describe above produces good results for both metrics simultaneously.

8.1 Degree Distribution

We first analyze the degree distribution of the operational network to test whether the network is scale-free [8] or not. We test both the size–rank relationship, as well as the frequency–size relationship proposed respectively in [15] and [8] to check for scale-freeness. Figure 2a shows a log-log plot of the values of the node degrees as a function of their ranks (in reversed order, i.e., highest degree value has lowest rank). Figure 2b shows a log-log plot of the (non-normalized) empirical complementary cumulative distribution function (CCDF) (i.e., for a given degree d, $y(d)$ is the number of nodes with degree strictly larger than d). Notice that these two plots are related–the former produced by ranking the degrees and the latter produced by looking at the proportion of each degree [1].

Both plots show a linear trend in the log-log plot indicating that the degree distribution of the network follows an approximate power law. In both cases, the exponent of the fitted power law is close to 2. This conforms to the widely observed phenomenon that many engineered networks have a power law distribution (which many authors refer to as scale-free networks).

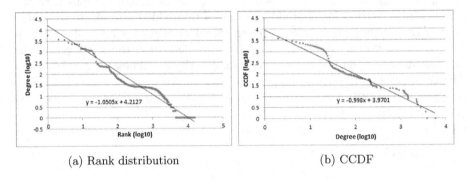

(a) Rank distribution   (b) CCDF

Fig. 2. Log-log plots of (a) the degrees as function of the rank in reverse order. (Slope) $s = -1.05 \implies$ (Exponent) $\alpha = 1.951(1+1/|s|)$. (b) the CCDF of the degree sequence as function of the degree. $s = -0.992 \implies \alpha = 1.992(1+|s|)$.

8.2 Assortativity

Figure 3 shows the empirical cumulative distribution function of the assortativity coefficient of the sampled networks. All sampled graphs had an assortativity coefficient less than zero. This is consistent with previous studies that show that engineered networks such as the Internet, the World Wide Web, the power grid, and many other communication networks are disassortative [18]. Indeed, in this network, on average 51 % of the links are between a low-degree node and a hub. Only 7 % of the edges join low-degree nodes and connections between large hubs are 1 % of the links. A degree is said to be low if it is in the bottom 15 % (i.e., less or equal to 23) and it is said to be high if it is in the top 15 % (i.e., greater or equal to 753). Notice that the assortativity of the operation network falls close to the center of the CDF indicating that our sampling procedure approximates a uniform sampling.

8.3 Size of Maximum Cluster

In this section, we analyze the size of the largest set of nodes that an attacker could potentially have access to–upon compromising some arbitrary (non-chokepoint) host–without encountering a chokepoint. This corresponds to the size of the maximum cluster after the chokepoints are removed from the graph.

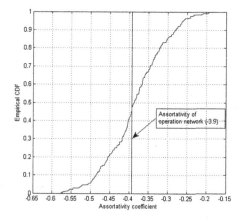

Fig. 3. Empirical distribution of the assortativity coefficient.

We place the chokepoints using the heuristics described earlier. We consider different values of the parameter k. Figure 4a shows the empirical distribution of the fraction of nodes in the largest cluster for different values of k.

As we can see from the figure, the fraction of nodes in the largest component is less than 40 % of the total number of nodes for all values of k considered in this study. As expected, this fraction of nodes in the maximum cluster decreases as k increases, from around 40 % $k = 20$ to less than 15 % for the maximum value of $k = 200$. It can be observed visually that there is a point of diminishing returns for values of k greater than or equal to roughly 100, beyond which the empirical distribution does not change drastically. This indicates that, for the network under consideration, deploying enhanced security measures to only 100 nodes (0.65 %) of the network is sufficient to reduce the size of the maximum cluster to about 15 % of the total number of nodes, while the use of additional resources produces a relatively minor benefit.

Another way to see this is to plot the size of the largest component as a function of the number of chokepoints, as shown in Fig. 4b. We can see that there is a sharp decrease in the size of the maximum cluster when the number of chokepoints increases from 20 to 80. However, once again diminishing returns can be observed after more than 100 chokepoints.

8.4 Number of Traversed Chokepoints

With the chokepoint defense architecture, an attack may be contained to a small set of nodes (those nodes that share the same cluster) with high probability before being detected. In order to infect other nodes in the network, the attacker needs to traverse one or more chokepoints. In this section, we study the empirical distribution of the minimum number of chokepoints an attacker needs to go through to infect other nodes. In Sect. 6, we have discussed how the minimum number of chokepoints between a pair of nodes is computed. Figure 5a shows

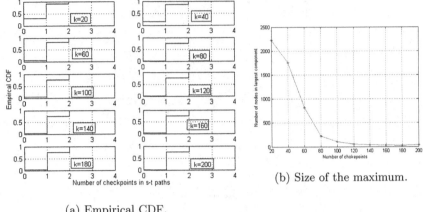

(a) Empirical CDF.

Fig. 4. Characteristics of the size of the maximum cluster. (a) Empirical cumulative distribution of the fraction of nodes in the largest cluster for a varying k. (b) Size of maximum cluster as a function of k.

the cumulative distribution function for different values of the parameter k. Figure 5b is an alternative representation where we plot the fraction of minimal paths with a varying number of chokepoints as a function of the number of deployed chokepoints.

First, notice that, an attacker only needs to traverse two chokepoints to reach any node. Recall that this is a lower bound to the actual number of traversed chokepoints. Also, this number is not the shortest path in the network. In fact, an attacker might need to traverse some clusters between the chokepoints and, within each cluster; the attacker might traverse many nodes before reaching a chokepoint (both of these cases are ignored when we compute the minimum number of traversed chokepoints.

Second, observe (Fig. 5a) that the distribution of the number of chokepoints in minimal paths does not change significantly for $k > 100$. This can also be seen in Fig. 5b where the plots become "flat" for the values of k greater than 100. This implies that, similarly to the maximum cluster size metric, approximately 100 hubs (0.65 %) are sufficient to achieve a significant improvement in security.

The fraction of pairs with zero chokepoints between them represents the fraction of attacks that are undetectable or unpreventable by the chokepoint approach. Figure 5a and b both demonstrate that this fraction decreases as the number of placed chokepoints increases, indicating that placement of chokepoints according to our approach can significantly reduce the mobility of attackers.

The figures also show that most of the minimal paths (around 72 % for $k > 100$) traverse only one chokepoint, suggesting that most nodes in the network are separated by only one chokepoint. This is consistent with (and could be explained by) the observation that about 71 % of the nodes are leaves. Indeed, two leaves are only separated by their common hub.

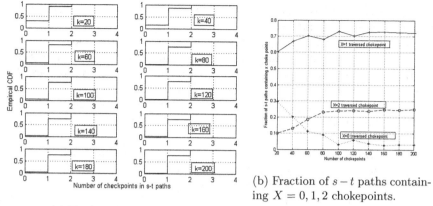

(a) Empirical distribution.

(b) Fraction of $s-t$ paths containing $X = 0, 1, 2$ chokepoints.

Fig. 5. Characteristics of the minimum number of chokepoints that a node needs to traverse to infect another node.

Finally, we see that the number of minimal paths with one or two chokepoints increases as the number of deployed chokepoints increases (while the fraction of minimal paths with zero chokepoint decreases). At the same time, we never observe the appearance of minimal paths with three or more chokepoints. This suggests that, for this data and this range of values for k, the partially collapsed graph ($G2$) has a diameter of at most 4.

9 Related Work

The problem of placement of monitors for network intrusion detection has been evaluated in a number of other contexts. The recent work by Talele et al. [25,26] addresses a similar problem: that of finding a minimal set of IDS placements that will obtain a given graph property. Their work, however, requires knowledge of information flows which we do not consider.

Noel and Jajodia [20] describe the combination of attack graphs with network maps and other security information such as firewalls and known vulnerabilities to construct a topological vulnerability analysis for a network. Sawilla and Ou [22] use attack graphs with a ranking method as a tool for monitor placement, explicitly invoking minimal graph cuts as a method for selecting remediation or focused monitoring. While exploring a closely related problem space to the one we consider, both works makes use of significant side information in the form of attack graphs and the result of vulnerability scans and analysis that we do not consider.

Anjum et al. [2] investigates the placement of costly "tamper resistant sensor" nodes within a sensor network that may be under attack by an adversary attempting to compromise the 'sink' node responsible for collecting the sensor data. This work is specialized to the sensor network case, in which all data flows to a single sink node. We consider a different problem where any node can be the source/target of an attack.

The work by Shaikh et al. [24] is the only work to explicitly model cost, modeling a value function for the deployment of intrusion detection sensors within a network. Each sensor location is characterized by its value, and sensors are then deployed in order of descending location value up to the available budget. Unlike our work, they do not incorporate any topological data regarding the network (although some related cost metrics are likely to be influenced by topological considerations).

Mell and Harang [17] examine the use of flow-based analysis (such as we consider here) to perform a triage operation on a network following a compromise. In contrast to the pre-emptive analysis of static graphs that we consider here, [17] focuses on identification of critical nodes ("hubs") for examination following the discovery of an intruder, in such a way that these hubs separate some minimal set of nodes containing the intruder's entry point from the rest of the network.

A very related problem is that of immunization where the goal is to find a set of 'agents' to immunize in order to suppress the spreading of a disease under various propagation models. Those nodes can be viewed as chokepoints as they impede the propagation of a disease. Tong et al. [27] has proposed a greedy algorithm that iteratively selects the current node with highest eigen-drop as the one to be immunized next. However, this algorithm was designed for a different metric and a quick test has shown that it performs poorly in our framework. In [19] Nian and Wang propose a high-risk immunization approach that targets susceptible nodes whose neighbors have been infected. This requires knowing all infected nodes in advance making it inapplicable to our problem. A greedy approach based on immunizing the most connected nodes has been proposed by several authors [16, 21]. In this paper, we have implemented a version of such an approach (Iterative removal of nodes with largest degree-DEG) that runs in linear time. Our BET algorithm is also very similar to the immunization approach in [23].

Finally, the work by Chen and Hero [6] considers the same problem of removing a set of nodes to minimize the size the maximum cluster in the remaining graph (although for a different purpose). They relate the optimization problem to the spectrum of the graph and propose a heuristic approximation algorithm. Their algorithm has similar performance as DEG in a small test algorithm of 300 nodes. Unfortunately, it involves solving a eigenvalue problem which makes it computationally very expensive for large graphs. For this reason we did not include Chen-Hero's heuristic algorithm in our suite of heuristic approximations.

10 Conclusion and Discussion

Properly configured IPv6 networks are resistant to scanning and other forms of target acquisitions. Attackers attempting to propagate through the network are hence limited to existing benign communication paths. We leverage this limitation of attacker movement to propose a chokepoint-based defensive approach that maximally bounds attacker propagation. With this approach, attackers are forced to limit their propagation to a small set of nodes or have to penetrate one or more chokepoints. We have considered two optimization criteria to choose the chokepoints: (1) minimizing the maximum number of nodes an attacker can compromise without encountering a chokepoint and (2) maximizing the average number of chokepoints an attacker has to traverse to attack a random target. Optimal placement of these chokepoints is a NP-hard problem and, as a consequence, we have used a set of heuristics to approximate the solution. We have tested our approach and algorithms using data from a large operation network of over 15500 nodes. Our experiments have shown that enhanced security solutions have to be deployed to only 0.65 % of the nodes to limit the propagation of a random attack to less 15 % if the nodes of the network. Our approach thus enables a novel defense-in-depth approach that complements traditional security approaches.

Acknowledgements. This research was sponsored by the U.S. Army Research Labs (ARL) and the National Institute of Standards and Technology (NIST). It was partially accomplished under NIST and University of Maryland, College Park Cooperative Agreement No.70NANB13H012.

References

1. Adamic, L.A.: Zipf, Power-laws and Pareto - a ranking tutorial (2002)
2. Anjum, F., Subhadrabandhu, D., Sarkar, S., Shetty, R.: On optimal placement of intrusion detection modules in sensor networks. In: Proceedings of the 1st International Conference on Broadband Networks, 2004. pp. 690–699, October 2004
3. Apple-Inc: Bonjour for developers. https://developer.apple.com/bonjour/index.html. Accessed on 12 November 2014
4. Bellovin, S.M., Keromytis, A., Cheswick, B.: Worm propagation strategies in an IPv6 internet. Login **31**, 70–76 (2006). Please check the edit made in Ref. [4]
5. Bui, T.N., Jones, C.: Finding good approximate vertex and edge partitions is NP-hard. Inf. Process. Lett. **42**(3), 153–159 (1992)
6. Chen, P., III, A.O.H.: Node removal vulnerability of the largest component of a network. CoRR abs/1403.2024 (2014)
7. Chown, T.: RFC 5157: IPv6 implications for network scanning. Internet Eng. Task Force (IETF) RFC (March 2008). https://tools.ietf.org/html/rfc5157
8. Clauset, A., Shalizi, C.R., Newman, M.E.J.: Power-law distributions in empirical data. SIAM Rev. **51**(4), 661–703 (2009)
9. Cohen, R., Erez, K., ben Avraham, D., Havlin, S.: Breakdown of the internet under intentional attack. Phys. Rev. Lett. **86**, 3682–3685 (2001)
10. Convery, S., Miller., D.: IPv6 and IPv4 threat comparison and best-practice evaluation. http://www.cisco.com/web/about/security/security_services/ciag/documents/v6-v4-threats.pdf. Accessed on 11 June 2014
11. Gkantsidis, C., Mihail, M., Zegura, E.: The markov chain simulation method for generating connected power law random graphs. In: In Proceedings of 5th Workshop on Algorithm Engineering and Experiments (ALENEX), SIAM (2003)
12. Hakimi, S.L.: On realizability of a set of integers as degrees of the vertices of a linear graph. I. J. SIAM **10**(3), 496–506 (1962)

13. Havel, V.: A remark on the existence of finite graphs. Casopis Pest. Mat. **80**, 477–480 (1955)
14. Landry, B.J.L., Koger, M.S., Blanke, S., Nielsen, C.: Using the private-internet-enterprise (PIE) model to examine it risks and threats due to porous perimeters. Inf. Secur. J.: Glob. Perspect. **18**(4), 163–169 (2009)
15. Li, L., Alderson, D., Doyle, J.C., Willinger, W.: Towards a theory of scale-free graphs: definition, properties, and implications. Internet Math. **2**(4), 431–523 (2005)
16. Madar, N., Kalisky, T., Cohen, R., ben Avraham, D., Havlin, S.: Immunization and epidemic dynamics in complex networks. Eur. Phys. J. B Condens. Matter Complex Syst. **38**(2), 269–276 (2004)
17. Mell, P., Harang, R.E.: Using network tainting to bound the scope of network ingress attacks. In: SERE 2014, pp. 206–215 (2014)
18. Newman, M.E.J.: Mixing patterns in networks. Phys. Rev. E **67**(2), 026126 (2003)
19. Nian, F., Wang, X.: Efficient immunization strategies on complex networks. J. Theor. Biol. **264**(1), 77–83 (2010)
20. Noel, S., Jajodia, S.: Optimal ids sensor placement and alert prioritization using attack graphs. J. Netw. Syst. Manag. **16**(3), 259–275 (2008)
21. Pastor-Satorras, R., Vespignani, A.: Immunization of complex networks. Phys. Rev. E **65**, 036104 (2002)
22. Sawilla, R.E., Ou, X.: Identifying critical attack assets in dependency attack graphs. In: Jajodia, S., Lopez, J. (eds.) ESORICS 2008. LNCS, vol. 5283, pp. 18–34. Springer, Heidelberg (2008)
23. Schneider, C.M., Mihaljev, T., Havlin, S., Herrmann, H.J.: Suppressing epidemics with a limited amount of immunization units. Phys. Rev. E **84**, 061911 (2011)
24. Shaikh, S.A., Chivers, H., Nobles, P., Clark, J.A., Chen, H.: A deployment value model for intrusion detection sensors. In: Park, J.H., Chen, H.-H., Atiquzzaman, M., Lee, C., Kim, T., Yeo, S.-S. (eds.) ISA 2009. LNCS, vol. 5576, pp. 250–259. Springer, Heidelberg (2009)
25. Talele, N., Teutsch, J., Erbacher, R.F., Jaeger, T.: Monitor placement for large-scale systems. In: Proceedings of the 19th ACM Symposium on Access Control Models and Technologies. pp. 29–40 (2014)
26. Talele, N., Teutsch, J., Jaeger, T., Erbacher, R.F.: Using security policies to automate placement of network intrusion prevention. In: Jürjens, J., Livshits, B., Scandariato, R. (eds.) ESSoS 2013. LNCS, vol. 7781, pp. 17–32. Springer, Heidelberg (2013)
27. Tong, H., Prakash, B., Tsourakakis, C., Eliassi-Rad, T., Faloutsos, C., Chau, D.: On the vulnerability of large graphs. In: 2010 IEEE 10th International Conference on Data Mining (ICDM), pp. 1091–1096, December 2010

A Topology Based Flow Model for Computing Domain Reputation

Igor Mishsky[1], Nurit Gal-Oz[2], and Ehud Gudes[1($\boxtimes$)]

[1] Ben-Gurion University, 84105 Beer-sheva, Israel
igormishsky@gmail.com,ehud@cs.bgu.ac.il
[2] Sapir Academic College, D.N. Hof Ashkelon, 79165 Ashkelon, Israel
galoz@sapir.ac.il

Abstract. The Domain Name System (DNS) is an essential component of the internet infrastructure that translates domain names into IP addresses. Recent incidents verify the enormous damage of malicious activities utilizing DNS such as bots that use DNS to locate their command&control servers. Detecting malicious domains using the DNS network is therefore a key challenge.

We project the famous expression *Tell me who your friends are and I will tell you who you are*, motivating many social trust models, on the internet domains world. A domain that is related to malicious domains is more likely to be malicious as well.

In this paper, our goal is to assign *reputation* values to domains and IPs indicating the extent to which we consider them malicious. We start with a list of domains known to be malicious or benign and assign them reputation scores accordingly. We then construct a DNS based graph in which nodes represent domains and IPs.

Our new approach for computing domain reputation applies a flow algorithm on the DNS graph to obtain the reputation of domains and identify potentially malicious ones. The experimental evaluation of the flow algorithm demonstrates its success in predicting malicious domains.

1 Introduction

Malicious botnets and Advanced Persistent Threats (APT) have plagued the Internet in recent years. Advanced Persistent Threat, often implemented as a botnet, is advanced since it uses sophisticated techniques to exploit vulnerabilities in systems, and is persistent since it uses an external command and control (C&C) site which is continuously monitoring and extracting data of a specific target. APTs are generated by hackers but are operated from specific domains or IPs. The detection of these misbehaving domains (including zero day attacks) is difficult since there is no time to collect and analyze traffic data in real-time, thus their identification ahead of time is very important. We use the term *domain reputation* to express a measure of our belief that a domain is benign or malicious. The term reputation is adopted from the field of social networks and virtual communities, in which the reputation of a peer is derived from evidences regarding its past behavior but also from its relations to other peers [12].

© IFIP International Federation for Information Processing 2015
P. Samarati (Ed.): DBSec 2015, LNCS 9149, pp. 277–292, 2015.
DOI: 10.1007/978-3-319-20810-7_20

A domain reputation system can support the decision to block traffic or warn organizations about suspicious domains. Currently lists of domains which are considered legitimate are published by web information companies (e.g., Alexa [1]) while black-lists of malware domains are published by web threat analysis services (e.g., VirusTotal [14]). Unfortunately the number of domains appearing in both types of lists is relatively small, and a huge number of domains is left unlabeled. Therefore, the problem of assigning reputation to unlabeled domains is highly important.

The Domain Name Service (DNS) maps domain names to IP addresses and provides an essential service to applications on the internet. Many botnets use a DNS service to locate their next C&C site. For example, botnets tend to use short-lived domains to evasively move their C&C sites. Therefore, DNS logs have been used by several researchers to detect suspicious domains and filter their traffic if necessary. Choi and Lee [4], analyzed DNS traffic to detect APTs. Such analysis requires large quantities of illegitimate DNS traffic data.

An alternative approach was proposed in the Notos system [2] which uses historical DNS information collected passively from multiple recursive DNS resolvers to build a model of how network resources are allocated and operated for legitimate Internet services. This model is mainly based on statistical features of domains and IPs that are used for building a classifier which assigns a reputation score to unlabeled domains. The main difference between the DNS data used for computing reputation and the data used for malware detection is that the first consists of mainly static properties of the domain and DNS topology data, while the latter requires behavioral and time-dependent data. While DNS behavior data may involve private information (e.g., the domains that an IP is trying to access), which ISPs may be reluctant to analyze or share, DNS topology data is much easier to collect. Our research also focuses on computing domain reputation using DNS topology data.

Various definitions of the terms trust and reputation have been proposed in the literature as the motivation for a computational metric. Trust is commonly defined following [11] as *a subjective expectation an agent has about another's future behavior based on the history of their encounters*. The history is usually learned from ratings that peers provide for each other. If such direct history is not available, one derives trust based on reputation. Reputation is defined [11] as *the aggregated perception that an agent creates through past actions about its intentions and norms.*, where this perception is based on information gathered from trusted peers. These definitions are widely used in state of the art research on trust and reputation as the logic behind trust based reputation computational models in web communities and social networks. However, computing reputation for domains raises several new difficulties:

- Rating information if exists, is sparse and usually binary, a domain is labeled either "white" or "black".
- Static sources like blacklists and whitelists are often not up-to-date.
- There is no explicit concept of trust between domains which make it difficult to apply a flow or a transitive trust algorithm.
- Reputation of domains is dynamic and changes very fast.

These difficulties make the selection of an adequate computational model for computing domain reputation a challenging task. The focus of our paper and its main contribution is therefore a flow model and a flow algorithm for computing domain reputation which uses a topology-based network that maps connections of domains to IPs and other domains. Our model uses DNS IP-Domain mappings and statistical information but does not use DNS traffic data.

Our approach is based on a flow algorithm, commonly used for computing trust in social networks and virtual communities. We are mainly inspired by two models: the Eigentrust model [8] that computes trust and reputation by transitive iteration through chains of trusting users; and the model by Guha et al. [9] which combines the flow of trust and distrust. The motivation for using a flow algorithm is the hypothesis that IPs and domains which are neighbors of malware generating IPs and domains, are more likely to become malware generating as well. We construct a graph which reflects the topology of domains and IPs and their relationships and use a flow model to propagate the knowledge received in the form of black list, to label domains in the graph as suspected domains. Our preliminary experimental results support our proposed hypothesis that domains (or IPs) connected to malicious domains have a higher probability to become malicious as well.

The main contribution of this paper lies in the novelty of the algorithm and the strength of the supporting experimental study.

The experimental study supporting our results, uses a sizable DNS database (more than a one million IPs and domains) which proves the feasibility of our approach. The rest of this paper is organized as follows. Section 2 provides a more detailed background on DNS and IP characteristics and on the classical flow models, and then surveys the related work. Section 3 discusses the graph construction, the weight assignment problem and the flow algorithm. Section 4 presents the results of our experimental evaluation and Sect. 5 concludes the paper and outlines future research.

2   Background and Related Work

The domain name system (DNS) translates Internet domains and host names into IP addresses. It is implemented as an hierarchical and distributed database containing various types of data, including host names and domain names, and provides application level protocol between clients and servers. An often-used analogy to explain the Domain Name System is that it serves as the phone book for the Internet by translating human-friendly computer host names into IP addresses. Unlike a phone book, the DNS can be quickly updated, allowing a service's location on the network to change without affecting the end users, who continue to use the same host name. Users take advantage of this when they use meaningful Uniform Resource Locators (URLs). In order to get the IP of a domain, the host usually consults a local recursive DNS server (RDNS). The RDNS iteratively discovers which authoritative name server is responsible for each zone. The result of this process is the mapping from the requested domain to the IP requested.

Two categories of models are related to our work. The first category deals with ways to compute domain reputation. The second deals with flow algorithms for the computation of trust and reputation in general. Domain reputation is a relatively new research area. The Notos model for assigning reputation to domains [2] was the first to use statistical features in the DNS topology data and to apply machine learning methods to construct a reputation prediction classifier. Notos uses historical DNS information collected passively from multiple DNS resolvers to build a model of how network resources are allocated and operated for professionally run Internet services. Specifically it constructs a set of clusters representing various types of popular domains statistics and computes features which represent the distance of a specific domain from these clusters. Notos also uses information about malicious domains obtained from sources such as spam-traps, honeynets, and malware analysis services to build a set of features representing how network resources are typically allocated by Internet miscreants. With the combination of these features, Notos constructs a classifier and assigns reputation scores to new, previously unseen domain names.(Note that Notos uses heavily, information about highly popular sites such as Acamai which is not publicly available and therefore make it difficult to compare to). The Exposure system [10] collects data from the DNS answers returned from authoritative DNS servers and uses a set of 15 features that are divided into four feature types: time-based features, DNS answer-based features, TTL value-based features, and domain name-based features. The above features are used to construct a classifier based on the J48 decision tree algorithm [16] in order to determine whether a domain name is malicious or not. Kopis [3] is a system for monitoring the high levels of the DNS hierarchy in order to discover the anomaly in malicious DNS activities. Unlike other detection systems such as Notos [2] or Exposure [10], Kopis takes advantage of the global visibility of DNS traffic at the upper levels of the DNS hierarchy to detect malicious domains. After the features are collected it uses the random forest technique as the machine learning algorithm to build the reputation prediction classifier.

In the category of flow algorithms for computation of trust in general, two models are of specific interest to our work. The first is Eigentrust [8], a reputation management algorithm for peer-to-peer network. The algorithm provides each peer in the network a unique global trust value based on the peer's history of uploads and thus aims to reduce the number of inauthentic files in a P2P network. The algorithm computes trust and reputation by transitive iteration through chains of trusting users. The page-rank algorithm [12] uses a similar approach, however it contains special features related to URL referencing. Guha et al. [9] introduce algorithms for implementing a web-of-trust that allows people to express either trust or distrust in other people. Two matrices representing the trust and distrust between people are built using four types of trust relationships. They present several schemes for explicitly modeling and propagating trust and distrust and propose methods for combining the two, using weighted linear combination. The propagation of trust was also used by Coskun et al. [6] for detecting potential members of botnets in P2P networks. Their proposed technique is based on the observation that peers of a P2P botnet with an unstructured topology, communicate with other peers in order to receive commands and updates. Since there is a significant probability that a pair of bots within a network have a mutual contact, they construct a mutual contact graph. This graph is different than the DNS topology graph we rely on, the attributes and semantics underlying our approach are different and accordingly the algorithm we propose. Wu et al. [17] use the distrust algorithm presented by Guha et al. [9] for detecting spam domains but use URL references rather than DNS data to derive the edges between domain nodes. They also discuss trust attenuation and the division of trust between a parent and its "children". Yadav et al. [18] describe an approach to detect malicious domains based mainly on their names distribution and similarity. They claim that many botnets use the technique of DGA (domain generating algorithm) and they show that domains generated in this form have certain characteristics which help in their detection. The domain names usually have a part in common, e.g. the top level domain (TLD), or a similar distribution of alpha-numeric characters in their names. The success of using the above characteristics in [18] motivates the construction of domain-domain edges in our graph as well.

There are quite a few papers which use DNS data logs to detect Botnets and malicious domains. However these papers use the DNS traffic behavior and not the mapping information used by Notos and in our work. Villarmin et al. [13] provide C&C detection technique motivated by the fact that bots typically initiate contact with C&C servers to poll for instructions. As an example, for each domain, they aggregate the number of non-existent domains (NXDOMAIN) responses per hour and use it as one of the classification features. Another work of this category, presented by Choi and Lee [4] monitor DNS traffic to detect botnets, which form a group activity in similar DNS queries simultaneously. They assume that infected hosts perform DNS queries at several occasions and using this data they construct a feature vector and apply a clustering technique to identify malicious domains. As discussed above, although DNS traffic data has significant features, it is difficult to obtain comparing to DNS topological data.

To summarize, although there are some previous works on domain reputation using DNS statistical features (e.g., Notos), and there exist flow algorithms in other trust and reputation domains, the combination of the two as used in this paper is new.

3   The Flow Model

The goal of the flow algorithm is to assign domains with reputation scores given an initial list of domains with known reputation (good or bad). The first step is the construction of the Domain-IP graph based on information obtained from a large set of successful DNS transactions represented as *A-records*. The A-records are used to construct the DNS topology graph, where vertices represent IPs and domains, and the weighted edges represent the strength of their connections. This is described next. In Sect. 3.2 we present in detail the flow algorithm, and describe the method for combining good and bad reputation scores. Finally we discuss an optimization of the algorithm needed for large graphs.

3.1   Constructing the Graph and Assigning Edge Weights

The DNS topology graph consists of two types of vertices: domains and IPs, deriving four types of edges between them. To construct the graph we use A-records, and also data available from public sources to estimate the strength of connections between any two vertices, IP or domain, by the amount of common data between them. The **IP data** for each IP consists of the following five characteristics available from sources such as e.g., WHOIS databae [15]:

- Autonomous System Number (ASN): a collection of connected Internet Protocol (IP) routing prefixes under the control of one or more network operators that present a common, clearly defined routing policy to the Internet. The ASN number is the indexation of the collection.
- Border Gateway Protocol (BGP) Prefix: a standardized exterior gateway protocol designed to exchange routing and reachability information between autonomous systems (AS) on the Internet. The protocol defines the routing of each ASN.BGP prefix as a range of IPs to which it routes.
- Registrar: the name of the organization that registered the IP.
- Country: the country to which the IP belongs.
- Registration date: the date and time at which the IP was registered.

For **Domain Data** the key concept is the parent of a domain. A k-Top Level Domain (kTLD) is the k suffix of the domain name [2]. For example: for domain finance.msn.com, the 3TLD is the same as the domain name: finance.msn.com, the 2TLD is .msn.com and the 1TLD is .com.

We use the following notation:

Set_{IP} is the set containing all the IPs.
Set_{domain} is the set containing all the domains.
$Set_{parent} \subseteq Set_{domain}$ is the set containing all the parents.
$Set_{commonAtt}$ is the set of attributes vectors derived from IP data. Attribute appear in the following order: country, ASN, BGP prefix, registrar, registration date. Missing information is replaced with 'none'. For example
$(DE, none, none, STRATO.DE, none) \in Set_{CommonAtt}$ is the vector element in which the only information available is the country and the registrar.

We define a weight function that assigns a weight to each edge in the graph. Let w be a weight function $w : (u, v) \rightarrow [0, 1]$ used to assign weight to the edge (u, v) where $u, v \in Set_{IP} \cup Set_{domain}$, for each edge type we consider three alternative weight functions as follows:

1. IP to Domain: For $ip \in Set_{IP}$ and the list of A-records, let D_{ip} be all the domains mapped to ip. For each $d \in D_{ip}$ we define: $w(ip, d) = \frac{1}{|D_{ip}|}; \frac{1}{\log|D_{ip}|}; 1$.
2. Domain to IP: For $d \in Set_{domain}$ and a list of A-records, let I_d be all the IPs that were mapped to d. For each $ip \in I_d$ we define: $w(d, ip) = \frac{1}{|I_d|}; \frac{1}{\log|I_d|}; 1$.

3. IP to IP: Let *commonAtt* be a combination of the five attributes of IP data. Let $Set_{commonAtt}$ be the set of all IPs with the attribute combination $Common_Att$. For each $ip_1, ip_2 \in Set_{commonAtt}$ s.t. $ip_1 \neq ip_2$ we define:
   $w(ip_1, ip_2) = \frac{1}{|Set_{commonAtt}|}; \frac{1}{\log|Set_{commonAtt}|}; 1.$
4. Domain to Domain: Let P_d be the set of all domains with the same parent domain d. For each $d1, d2 \in P_d$ s.t. $d1 \neq d2$ we define: $w(d_1, d_2) = \frac{1}{|P_d|}; \frac{1}{\log|P_d|}; 1.$

The intuition behind the above definition of weights is that, the effect of a domain reputation on the IPs it is mapped to, increases, as the amount of mapped IPs decreases. We use three approaches for computing weight, which produce 81 different combinations from which a subset was tested. We represent our graph as an adjacency matrix M, in which the value of an entry (i, j) is the weight between vertex i and j computed according to the selected combination.

3.2 The Flow Algorithm

The flow algorithm models the idea that IPs and domains affect the reputation of IPs and domains connected to them. This is done by propagating a node's reputation iteratively, so that the reputation in each iteration is added to the total reputation accumulated within a domain or IP node, using some attenuation factor. The attenuation factor is a means to reduce the amount of reputation accumulated by transitivity. The flow algorithm is executed separately to propagate good reputation and bad reputation. The algorithm is presented in two parts, the first is the *Basic Flow*, which describes the flow algorithm in general, and the second is the *Combined Algorithm*, which focuses on the way bad reputation and good reputation are combined.

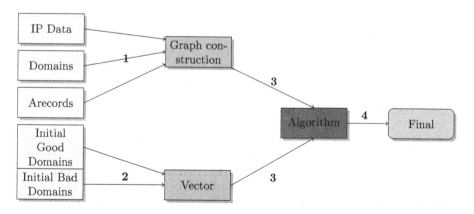

Fig. 1. The process for computing reputation scores: (1) Create the topology graph, assign weights and represent as a matrix; (2) Create the initial vector used for propagation; (3) Use the vector and the matrix as input to the flow algorithm; (4) output final reputation scores.

Figure 1 outlines the preparation steps prior to the execution of the basic algorithm. The **Basic Flow** algorithm starts with an initial set of domains which are labeled either bad or good. The parameters of the algorithm are:

1. A matrix M, where each entry represents a weighted edge between the vertices (domains or IPs); M^T denotes the transpose of the matrix M.
2. $V_{initial}$ - a vector representing the initial reputation value of each vertex, based on the initial set of labeled vertices.
3. $n \in \mathcal{N}$ - the number of iterations.
4. $atten \in [0,1]$ - the attenuation factor.
5. $\theta \in [0,1]$ - a reputation threshold above which a vertex is considered bad.

Algorithm 1 outlines the basic flow algorithm that propagates the reputation from a node to its neighbors and is carried out in three steps:

1. Calculate the matrix for the ith iteration: $M_i = (M^T \cdot atten)^i$
2. Calculate the final Matrix after n iterations as the sum of all the matrices with attenuation: $M_{final} = \sum_{i=0}^{n}(M^T \cdot atten)^i$
3. Calculate the final reputation vector: $V_{final} = M_n \cdot V_{initial}$, the reputation scores of all vertices after the propagation.

Applying the algorithm separately to propagate bad and good reputation may result in a node that is labeled both as good and bad. The final labeling of such node depends on the relative importance given to each label as done in the combined algorithm.

Algorithm 1. Basic

---

    procedure BASIC($M, n, atten, V_{initial}$)
        for $i = 0$ to n **do**
            $M_i \leftarrow (atten \cdot M^T)^i$
        $M_{final} \leftarrow \sum_{i=0}^{n} M_i$
        $V_{final} \leftarrow M_{final} \cdot V_{initial}$
        return V_{final}

The **combined algorithm** runs the basic flow algorithm twice with $V_{initial} = V_{good}$ and $V_{initial} = V_{bad}$. Each flow is configured independently with the following parameters: factor, threshold, and number of iterations. We denote $n_{good}, n_{bad} \in \mathcal{N}$ as the number of iterations for the good and bad flow respectively; $atten_{good}, atten_{bad} \in \mathcal{R}$, as the attenuation factor for the good and bad flow respectively; and $w \in \mathcal{R}$ the weight of the "good" reputation used when combining the results. Algorithm 2 uses of the basic flow algorithm to compute the good and bad reputation of each vertex and merge the results. Set_{Mal} is the result set of domains identified as bad.

The combined algorithms ignores the following observations which lead us to examine another approach:

Algorithm 2. Combined

1: $V_{good} \leftarrow basic(M, n_{good}, atten_{good}, V_{good})$
2: $V_{bad} \leftarrow basic(M, n_{bad}, atten_{bad}, V_{bad})$
3: $Set_{Mal} \leftarrow \emptyset$
4: **for** $d \in Domains$ **do**
5:     **if** $V_{bad}[d] + w \cdot V_{good}[d] > \theta$ **then** $Set_{Mal} \leftarrow Set_{Mal} \cup \{d\}$
6: return Set_{Mal}

- A reputation score is a value in the range of [0,1], therefore a vertex should not distribute a reputation score higher then 1 to it's neighbors.
- Initial labels are facts and therefore domains that were initially labeled as good or bad should maintain this label throughout the propagation process.
- A domain gaining a reputation value above a predefined threshold, bad or good, is labeled accordingly and maintain this label throughout the propagation process.

The extended algorithm shown as Algorithm 3 is proposed to address these observations. The main new procedure is the *Normalize* procedure which normalizes the scores after each iteration. The threshold used is the average of the scores so far (good or bad according to the actual procedure).

Algorithm 3. Extended

1: **for** $x \in Domains$ **do**
2:     $V_{bad}[x] \leftarrow 0; V_{good}[x] \leftarrow 0$
3:     **if** $x \in Set_{bad}$ **then** $V_{bad}[x] \leftarrow 1$
4:     **if** $x \in Set_{good}$ **then** $V_{good}[x] \leftarrow 1$
5: **for** $i = 1$ *to* n **do**
6:     $V_{good} \leftarrow V_{good} + (M^T) \cdot V_{good}$
7:     $V_{bad} \leftarrow V_{bad} + (M^T) \cdot V_{bad}$
8:     $Normalize(Set_{good}, V_{bad}, V_{good})$
9:     $Normalize(Set_{bad}, V_{good}, V_{bad})$
10: $Set_{Mal} \leftarrow \emptyset$
11: **for** $d \in Domains$ **do**
12:     **if** $V_{bad}[d] + w \cdot V_{good}[d] > \theta$ **then** $Set_{Mal} \leftarrow Set_{Mal} \cup \{d\}$
13: return Set_{Mal}
14: **procedure** $Normalize(Set_1, V_1, V_2)$
15:     $avg_2 \leftarrow 0$
16:     **if** $\sum_{d \in Set_1} V_{good}[d] > 0$ **then** $avg_2 \leftarrow \frac{\sum_{d \in Set_1} V_2[d]}{|\{d \in Set_1 : V_2[d] > 0\}|}$
17:     **for** $x \in Domains$ **do**
18:         **if** $V_1[x] > 1$ **then** $V_1[x] \leftarrow 1$
19:         **if** $x \in Set_1$ **then** $V_2[x] \leftarrow 0$
20:         **if** $V_1[x] > 1 - avg_2$ **then** $V_1[x] \leftarrow 1$

3.3 Optimization for Large Graphs

As we deal with millions of domains and IPs we have to calculate the scores in an efficient way. The most computationally intensive step is the matrix multiplication (see Fig. 1). To speed it up we use a special property of our graph which is the existence of *Cliques*. There are two kinds of cliques in the graph: cliques of IPs which share the same set of common attributes and cliques of domains which share the same parent or the same name server. Since a clique can contain thousands of nodes we calculate the flow within it separately and not as part of the matrix multiplication. A *clique* in a graph is a subset of its vertices such that every two vertices in the subset are connected by an edge.

We define a **Balanced Clique** as a clique such that all vertices have the same attribute values. This necessarily leads to a clique with a single weight value on all of its edges.

Theorem 1. *Let M be a matrix representing a weighted directed graph and V a vector representing vertices values, and let BC be the set of vertices that form a balanced clique, such that the weight on every edge in BC is $const_{BC} \in R$; For a vertex $v \in BC$, connected only to vertices in BC*

$$((M^T) * V)[v] = const_{BC} \cdot \sum_{v \neq i \in BC} V[i] \tag{1}$$

Due to space limitation, the proof of this theorem is omitted.

Using the property of a balanced clique we devised the following algorithm for computing the scores. The reputation of every clique vertex is the sum of reputation scores of all other vertices of the clique, multiplied by the constant edge weight of the clique. This is shown in Algorithm 4.

Algorithm 4. AssignBCScores

---

    procedure AssignBCScores($BC, const_{BC}, V$)
        $Sum \leftarrow \sum_{i \in BC} V[i]$
        for $i \in BC$ **do**
            $V_{result}[i] = (Sum - V[i]) \cdot const_{BC}$
        return $V_{result}[i]$

The complexity of this algorithm is $O(|BC|)$ which is a significant improvement to $O(|BC|^2)$, the complexity of the matrix multiplication approach. In our graph, all edges between the same type of vertices (IPs or domains) belong to balanced cliques and therefore this optimization plays a major factor.

4 Experiment Results

The evaluation of the algorithm uses real data collected from several sources. To understand the experiments and the results, we first describe the data obtained for constructing the graph, and the criteria used for evaluating the results.

4.1 Data Sources

We used five sources of data to construct the graph.

- A-records: a database of successful mappings between IPs and domains, collected by Cyren [7] from a large ISP over several months. This data consists of over one milion domains and IPs which are used to construct the nodes of the graph.
- Feed-framework: a list of malicious domains collected and analyzed by Cyren over the same period of time as the collected A-records. This list is intersected with the domains that appeared in the A-records and serves as the initial known "bad" domains vector.
- Whois [15]: a query and response protocol that is widely used for querying databases that store the registered users or assigners of an Internet resource, such as a domain name, an IP address block, or an autonomous system. We use WHOIS to get the IP data, which consists of the five characteristics of IP (ASN, BGP prefix, registrar, country, registration date).
- VirusTotal [14] - a website that provides scanning of domains for viruses and other malware. It uses information from 52 different antivirus products and provides the time a malware domain was detected by one of them.
- Alexa: Alexa database ranks websites based on a combined measure of page views and distinct site users. Alexa lists the "top websites" based on this data averaged over a three-months period. We use the set of top domains as our initial benign domains, intersecting it with the domains in the A-records. This set is filtered to remove domains which appeared as malicious in VirusTotal.

We conducted two sets of experiments *Tuning-test* and *Time-test*. In the *Tuning-test* experiment, the DNS graph is built from the entire set of A-records, but the domains obtained by the Feed-Framework are divided into two subsets: an *Initial set* and a *Test set*. The Initial set is used as the initial vector of "bad" domains for the flow algorithm. The test set is left out to be identified as bad by the algorithm. Obviously, not all bad domains of the test set can be identified, mainly because the division of domains was done randomly and some of the domains in the test set are not connected to the initial set. Yet, this experiment was very useful to determine the best parameters of the algorithm which were used later in the Time-Test experiment. The *time-test* experiment, is carried out in two steps corresponding to two consecutive time periods. In the first step, we construct the graph from the data sources described above. We use the feed-framework data to set the initial vector of bad domains in the first time period and the Alexa data to set the initial vector of good domains. We execute the flow algorithm (combined or extended) and assign the final score for each node of the graph.

To validate the results of the Time-test, we check the domains detected as malicious by the algorithm against data from VirusTotal for the period following the time period used in the first step. We sort the domains by descending bad reputation score and use the score of the domain on the k-th position as the threshold. As the evaluation criteria for this test, we define a *Prediction Factor*

(PF) which evaluate the ability of our algorithm to detect bad domains identified later by VirusTotal. We compute this factor as the ratio of domains labeled as bad that were tagged by VirusTotal and a random set of domains of the same size, that were tagged by VirusTotal.

A domain tested with VirusTotal, is considered as tagged only if it was tagged by at least one anti-virus program. A PF_i factor considers a domain as tagged by VirusTotal if at least i anti viruses tagged the domain.

To compute the prediction factor we extract the set of domains with the k-highest bad reputation scores $HSet_k$ found by the algorithm and select randomly a set of k domains $RSet_k$:

$$PF_i = \frac{|HSet_k \cap Set_{tagged}^i|}{|RSet_k \cap Set_{tagged}^i|} \qquad (2)$$

where set_{tagged}^i is the set of all domains tagged by at least i anti viruses.

A value of PF_i indicates the extent to which our algorithm identifies correctly bad domains, compared to the performance of randomly selected domains. A similar approach was used by Cohen et al. [5] that compared the precision of a list of suspicious accounts returned by a spam detector against a randomly generated list. Next we describe the results of the two experiments.

4.2   The Tuning Test

There are two main objectives to the Tuning test. The first is to verify that domains with higher bad reputation values are more likely to be detected as bad domains. The second objective is to understand the impact of the different parameters on the final results and configure the evaluation experiment accordingly. We tested the different weight functions discussed in Sect. 3.1. The following combination was found best and was selected to compute the weights on the graph edges:

- IP to domain - for $ip \in Set_{IP}$ and $d \in D_{ip}$, $w(ip, d) = \frac{1}{|D_{ip}|}$.
- Domain to IP - for $d \in Set_{domain}$ and $ip \in I_d$, $w(d, ip) = \frac{1}{|I_d|}$.
- IP to IP - for $ip_1, ip_2 \in Set_{commonAtt}$, s.t. $ip_2 \neq ip_1$, $w(ip_1, ip_2) = \frac{1}{|Set_{commonAtt}|}$.
- Domain to Domain - for $d_1, d_2 \in Set_{domain}$, parents $P_d \subset Set_{parent}$, and $d_1, d2 \in P_d$, s.t. $d_1 \neq d_2$, $w(d_1, d_2) = \frac{1}{|P_d|}$.

The most effective combination of features for IP data turned to be (none, ASN, BGP-Prefix, Registrar, none), which derives cliques of IPs with the same ASN, BGP-Prefix and Registrar.

The tuning test also examines the attenuation of the flow, the number of iterations, and the relative importance of the good domains used to calculate the final score. The tuning test repeats the following steps:

1. Construct the graph from the entire A-records database.
2. Divide the set of 2580 tagged malicious domains from the feed-framework into two sets: an initial set of 2080 domains and a test set consisting of 500 domains.
3. Apply the flow algorithm (combined or extended) using the Initial set to initiate the vector of bad domains and the data from Alexa to initiate the vector of good (as described above).

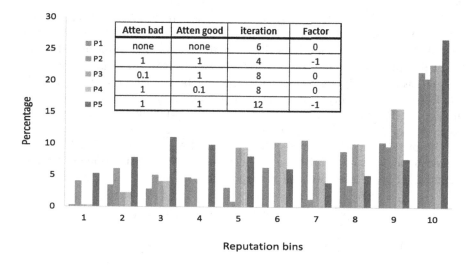

	Atten bad	Atten good	iteration	Factor
P1	none	none	6	0
P2	1	1	4	-1
P3	0.1	1	8	0
P4	1	0.1	8	0
P5	1	1	12	-1

Reputation bins

Fig. 2. The percentage of malicious domains by reputation score

We repeat these steps with different combinations of parameters (see Fig. 2). We then compute the reputation scores of all domains, sort the domains by these scores and divide them into 10 bins of equal size. For each bin S_i, $i = 1..10$ we measure the presence of domains that belong to the test set S_{test} (known malicious domains), as $\frac{|S_i \cap S_{test}|}{|S_{test}|}$.

In Fig. 2 we can see that the 10 % of domains with the highest 'bad' reputation score contain the highest amount of malicious domains. Moreover, in all five type of experiments, the bin of domains with the highest scores consists of 20–25 percents of all known malicious domains of S_{test}.

The tests we conducted demonstrate the following three claims:

1. Domains with high 'bad' scores have a higher probability to be malicious.
2. The combinations of the "good" and "bad" reputation scores improve the results.
3. After a relatively small number of iterations the results converge.

4.3   Time-Test

The time test experiment uses the best parameters as determined by the Tuning test. The first step of the experiment uses data collected during three months: September-November 2014 while the second step uses data collected during the following two months (i.e., December 2014- January 2015). After the first step in which we apply the flow algorithm (either the combined or the extended), and assign bad reputation scores to domains, we validate the domains with the highest 'bad' reputation scores that did not appear in the initial set of malicious domains against the information provided by VirusTotal.

The data we used for the time test consists of $2,385,432$ Domains and $933,001$ IPs constructing the nodes of the graph, from which 956 are tagged as maliciouse and $1,322$ are tagged as benign (Alexa). The resulting edges are $2,814,963$ Ip to Domain edges, $13,052,917,356$ Domain to Domain edges and $289,097,046$ IP to IP edges. The very large numbers of edges between IP to IP and Domain to Domain, emphasize the importance of the optimized Algorithm 4 in Sect. 3.3. For the validation test we selected the 1000-highest bad reputation domains and calculated the prediction factor PF_i for $i \in \{1, 2\}$ (see Eq. 2).

Out of 1000 random domains checked against VirusTotal, only 2.775% were tagged by at least one anti virus product and 0.875% of the random domains were tagged by at least two anti virus product.

Table 1. Results for time test experiment

	Atten bad	Atten good	Algorithm	Tagged by one	Tagged by two
1	0.8	1	combined	334	212
2	1	1	combined	323	203
3	none	none	extended	247	136

Table 1 presents the results of the experiment using the Combined and Extended algorithms. We used only 5 iterations since the Tuning test results indicates that this number is sufficient. For the combined algorithm the weight of good reputation score was set to $w = -1$ and the bad attenuation was set to 1 and 0.8 in tests 1 and 2 respectively.

We can see from the table that with the parameters of P2, that from the 1000 domains with the highest score, 323 were tagged by at least one of the anti viruses in VirusTotal (tagged by one), and 203 were tagged by at least two anti viruses (tagged by two) which derive the prediction factor of $PF_1 = 11.61$ and $PF_2 = 23.2$, respectively.

Due to space limitations we do not present all the results, however the best results were achieved in the second test. For example, out of 200 domains with the highest scores in test 2, 107 domains were tagged which reflect 53.5% of all known malicious domains.

Figure 3 demonstrates the ability of our algorithms to predict malicious domains, using the prediction factor (Eq. 2). The figure shows that if we consider

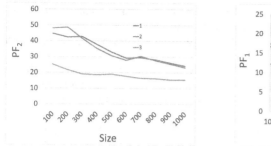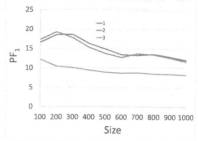

Fig. 3. Prediction factor with respect to the number of highest bad domains

smaller size of domains with the highest score the prediction rate is better but the overall predicted malicious domains are less. If we consider a larger size we end up with a larger number of domains that we suspect as malicious by mistake (i.e., false positives).

5   Conclusions

This paper discusses the problem of detecting unknown malicious domains by estimating their reputation score. It applies a classical flow algorithms for propagating trust, on a DNS topology graph database, for computing reputation of domains and thus discovering new suspicious domains. Our work faces two major challenges: the first is building a DNS graph to represent connections between IPs and domains based on the network topology only and not on the dynamic behavior. The second challenge was the design and implementation of a flow algorithm similar to those used for computing trust and distrust between people. We presented an algorithm that can be deployed easily by an ISP using non private DNS records. The algorithm was evaluated to demonstrate its effectiveness in real-life situations. The results presented in this paper are quite encouraging. In future work we intend to further improve the results by taking more data features into consideration and by conducting further tests with more parameters.

Acknowledgement. This research was supported by a grant from the Israeli Ministry of Economics, The Israeli Ministry of Science, Technology and Space and the Computer Science Frankel center.

References

1. Alexa: Websites Ranking (2014). https://www.alexa.com/
2. Antonakakis, M., Perdisc, R., Dagon, D., Lee, W., Feamster, N.: Building a dynamic reputation model for dns. In: USENIX Security Symposium, pp. 273–290 (2010)

3. Antonakakis, M., Perdisci, R., Le, W.: Detecting malware domains at the upper dns hierarchy. In: USENIX Security Symposium (2011)
4. Choi, H., Lee, H.: Identifying botnets by capturing group activities in dns traffic. Comput. Netw. **56**, 20–33 (2012)
5. Cohen, Y., Gordon, D., Hendler, D.: Early detection of outgoing spammers in large-scale service provider networks. In: Rieck, K., Stewin, P., Seifert, J.-P. (eds.) DIMVA 2013. LNCS, vol. 7967, pp. 83–101. Springer, Heidelberg (2013)
6. Coskun, B., Dietrich, S., Memon, N.D.: Friends of an enemy: identifying local members of peer-to-peer botnets using mutual contacts. In: ACSAC, pp. 131–140 (2010)
7. Cyren: A provider of cloud-based security solutions (2014). https://www.cyren.com/
8. Kamvar, S.D., Schlosser, M.T., Garcia-Molina, H.: The eigentrust algorithm for reputation management in p2p networks. In: WWW, pp. 640–651 (2003)
9. Guha, R., Kumar, R., Raghavan, P., Tomkins, A.: Propagation of trust and distrus. In: WWW, pp. 403–412 (2004)
10. Leyla, B., Engin, K., Christopher, K., Marco, B.: Exposure finding malicious domains using passive dns analysis. In: NDSS (2011)
11. Mui, L., Mohtashemi, M., Halberstadt, A.: A computational model of trust and reputation for e-businesses. In: Proceedings of the 35th Annual Hawaii International Conference on System Sciences HICSS02, Washington, DC, USA, vol. 7, p. 188 (2002)
12. Page, L., Brin, S., Motwani, R., Winograd, T.: Pagerank citation ranking: bringing order to the web. In: Technical report. Stanford Digital Library Technologies Projext (1998)
13. Villamarin-Salomon, R., Brustolon, J.C.: Bayesian bot detection based on dns traffic similarity. In: SAC, pp. 2035–2041 (2009)
14. VirusTotal: A free virus, malware and URL online scanning service (2014). https://www.virustotal.com/
15. Whois: IP data (2014). https://who.is
16. Witten, I., Frank, E.: Data Mining: Practical Machine Learning Tools and Techniquel. Morgan Kaufmann, San Francisco (2005)
17. Wu, B., Goel, V., Davison, B.D.: Propagating trust and distrust to demote web spam. In: WWW Workshop on Models of Trust for the Web and MTW (2006)
18. Yadav, S., Reddy, A.K.K., Reddy, A.L.N., Ranjan, S.: Detecting algorithmically generated malicious domain names. In: Internet Measurement Conference, pp. 48–61 (2010)

FPGuard: Detection and Prevention of Browser Fingerprinting

Amin FaizKhademi[1]([✉]), Mohammad Zulkernine[1],
and Komminist Weldemariam[1,2]

[1] School of Computing, Queen's University, Kingston, Canada
{khademi,mzulker,weldemar}@cs.queensu.ca
[2] IBM Research-Africa, Nairobi, Kenya
k.weldemariam@ke.ibm.com

Abstract. Fingerprinting is an identification method used by enterprises to personalize services for their end-users and detect online fraud or by adversaries to launch targeted attacks. Various tools have been proposed to protect online users from undesired identification probes to enhance the privacy and security of the users. However, we have observed that new fingerprinting methods can easily evade the existing protection mechanisms. This paper presents a runtime fingerprinting detection and prevention approach, called FPGuard. FPGuard relies on the analysis of predefined metrics to identify fingerprinting attempts. While FPGuard's detection capability is evaluated using the top 10,000 Alexa websites, its prevention mechanism is evaluated against four fingerprinting providers. Our evaluation results show that FPGuard can effectively recognize and mitigate fingerprinting-related activities and distinguish normal from abnormal webpages (or fingerprinters).

Keywords: Fingerprinting · User privacy · Detection · Prevention · FPGuard

1 Introduction

Web tracking involves monitoring and recording a user's browsing experience across different websites or multiple visits of the user to a website. Based on the recorded information, a user profile can be created for delivering personalized and targeted services (e.g., advertisements). In fact, many advertisers collect information about the users' interests, location, browsing habit, etc. without asking for their users' consent by employing either active or passive tracking methods [1]. An attentive user can prevent or permanently stop the active trackers —which store an identifier in a user's browser or computer so that they can identify the user in future visits— by just deleting the client-side identifiers or operating in the private mode of browsers. However, clearing client-side identifiers is no longer sufficient to prevent the user from being identified or tracked. The reason is that passive tracking methods such as browser fingerprinting [2] and history

© IFIP International Federation for Information Processing 2015
P. Samarati (Ed.): DBSec 2015, LNCS 9149, pp. 293–308, 2015.
DOI: 10.1007/978-3-319-20810-7_21

sniffing [3] do not rely on client-side identifiers and hence can easily evade the existing anti-tracking tools (e.g., [4,5]).

To identify a browser, fingerprinters systematically send multiple queries to the underlying environment (through the browser) to extract various system properties such as screen resolution, list of installed plugins, system fonts, timezone, etc. Then, they combine the collected properties to generate an identifier (or fingerprint) for the browser [2]. Fingerprinting process is invisible to users and thus they are unaware of the trackers' queries and underlying logics. In addition, unlike client-side identifiers, fingerprinting does not leave any footprint (on the browser). These features (i.e., invisibility and no footprint) make fingerprinting as a reliable source of user identification. While fingerprinting is becoming more prevalent than before [6,7], according to several studies (e.g., [8–11]), Web users prefer to have control over their privacy and thus prefer to stay anonymous to unknown or hidden tracking service providers.

To preserve user's privacy, a number of fingerprinting providers offer an opt-out solution (e.g., bluecava [12], AddThis [13]) [14]. They provide an opt-out page in which a user can choose to stay anonymous by not sharing her browser fingerprint. This solution mostly relies on server side (i.e., tracker) for collecting the browser's fingerprint, without sharing it with third-parties (e.g., advertising companies). However, the fingerprinting provider might still share the browser's fingerprint with clients who are exploiting fingerprinting for fraud detection purposes [12]. In addition, the existing anti-fingerprinting solutions [15–17] lack a detection mechanism (at runtime), therefore can disable browser functionalities for both normal and fingerprinting webpages.

In this paper, we present an approach for runtime detection and prevention of Web-based fingerprinting, named *FPGuard*. With respect to detection, FPGuard monitors running Web objects on the user's browser, collects fine-grained data related to fingerprinting activities and analyzes them to search for patterns of fingerprinting attempts. In case fingerprinting activities are detected, FPGuard notifies the user by raising an alert. It then labels the URL of the website as fingerprinter and adds it to a blacklist database as an evidence for future use. With respect to prevention, FPGuard combats fingerprinting attempts by combining randomization and filtering techniques. In particular, we employ four different randomization policies and two filtering techniques to protect users from being fingerprinted while keeping the browser's functionality for normal websites. FPGuard is implemented as a combination of a Chrome browser extension and an instrumented Chromium browser. We evaluate its detection capability using the top 10,000 Alexa websites. The prevention mechanism of FPGuard is also evaluated against four fingerprinting providers: two popular commercial fingerprinters and two proof-of-concept fingerprinters. As compared to existing approaches, our evaluation results show that FPGuard first detects and then prevents fingerprinting attempts, thereby it does not affect the user's browsing experience.

The next section discusses the related work on fingerprinting. While Sect. 3 introduces our proposed approach, Sect. 4 discusses its implementation details and our experimental analysis. In Sect. 5, we compare FPGuard with the existing work and Sect. 6 concludes the paper.

2   Related Work

There are several techniques employed for fingerprinting a browser instance with the purpose of identification. These methods mainly use especial JavaScript objects (i.e., `navigator` and `screen` objects (or *infromative* objects)) [2,14,18], Flash plugin [2], HTML5 canvas element [19], browsing history [20], performance and design difference of JavaScript engines of web browsers [19,21], IP address and HTTP accept headers [22] (accessible though network analysis) for identification. Not all of the mentioned methods exist in real-life fingerprinting products [14]. However, they can increase the identification accuracy.

With respect to detection, to the best of our knowledge, FPdetective [6] is the first large-scale study on detecting browser fingerprinting attempts by combining dynamic and manual analysis techniques. The approach focused on finding JavaScript-based font detection and Flash-based fingerprinting-related activities. The authors found that Flash-based fingerprinting (97 websites) is more prevalent than JavaScript-based font detection (51 websites) among the top 10 K websites of Alexa. They also embedded the discovered URLs of scripts and Flash objects in a browser extension, which can be used as a blacklist-based approach for finding previously recognized fingerprinting attempts. In addition to FPdetective, a large-scale study on the prevalence of canvas fingerprinting among the Alexa's top 100 K websites is presented in [7]. The authors modified the Chromium browser to log the accesses (writes and reads) to canvas elements. They combined manual and dynamic analysis to identify fingerprinting attempts and found that more than 5 % of the visited websites leveraged this type of fingerprinting.

For prevention, *Tor* [15], *Privaricator* [16], and *Firegloves* [17] are widely used anti-fingerprinting tools. Tor is a browser used to connect to the Tor network. The Tor network is an anonymous network for hiding the user's online activities and traffic by encrypting the data and passing it through a number of nodes (or relays). In addition to providing such an anonymous network, Tor is equipped with features for combating browser fingerprinting. The reason is that browser fingerprinting works well on the anonymous network and could effectively be used for identification. As explained by Perry et al. [23], Tor makes the browsers' fingerprints identical, meaning that the properties of the browser are fixed and identical for all users. In addition, it disables all browser plugins except the Flash plugin (due to high market penetration of Flash). For the Flash files, it offers a "click-to-play" option in which the user has to authorize a Flash file to be executed. Similarly, canvas elements in Tor should be authorized by users. Otherwise, the canvas elements are disabled and represent empty white images. Moreover, Tor limits the number of fonts that a website can load. In case a document exceeds the limit, Tor does not allow the website to load more fonts. This ultimately reduces the functionality of the browser.

Privaricator enhances the private-mode of browsers [16]. It implements randomization policies on two properties of the browser by randomly changing the browser's fingerprint upon each visit to a website. Thus, every visit of a user with the same browser is considered as a new user visiting the website. However, authors only focused on the plugin list of the browser and the offset properties of HTML elements to prevent *JavaScript Objects Fingerprinting* and the *JavaScript-based Font Detection* attempts, receptively. To do so, Privaricator randomly hides a number of plugins from the browser's plugin list. Moreover, it adds noises to the offset properties of HTML elements, when the properties are looked up more than 50 times.

Firegloves [17] is a proof-of-concept Mozilla Firefox extension. It returns random values for the browser properties (e.g., screen resolution). It also disables all plugins and MIME types on the browser. To prevent JavaScript-based font detection attempts, Firegloves limits the number of available fonts on each tab and also returns random values for the `offsetWidth` and `offsetHeight` properties of the HTML elements. However, it is also possible to get the width and height of the HTML elements using the `width` and `height` properties of the `getBoundingClientRect` method. Finally, *ExtensionCanvasFingerprintBlock* [24] is a recently developed browser extension for protecting users against canvas fingerprinting by returning an empty image for canvas elements that are accessed programmatically.

Finally, as noted, the above solutions reduce the fingerprinting surface by disabling browser functionalities (e.g., diabling Flash plugin). In fact, they block both normal and fingerprinting websites as they do not have detection capability to perform prior to blocking. This ultimately will create unpleasant experience (e.g., Facebook does not load Flash resources if the Flash plugin is hidden) to users due to functionality loss of the browser.

3   Detection and Prevention Approach

In this section, we present our approach named *FPGuard* for the detection and prevention of four major fingerprinting methods discussed in previous in studies [6,7,14,25]: *JavaScript Objects Fingerprinting*, *JavaScript-based Font Detection*, *Canvas Fingerprinting*, and *Flash-based Fingerprinting*. With respect to detection, FPGuard relies on recently discovered fingerprinting metrics [25] as listed in Table 1. These metrics are indicators for fingerprinting attempts and can be used for detection purposes.

Figure 1 shows an overview of FPGuard. Given a webpage running on the user's browser, FPGuard monitors and records its activities on the user's browser from the time the webpage has started loading. Then, it extracts the metrics relative to each fingerprinting method and builds a signature for the webpage. Next, it uses various algorithms to distinguish normal webpages from fingerprinters. In case, a webpage is flagged as fingerprinter, FPGuard notifies the user with an

Table 1. Metrics that are indicators for fingerprinting attempts.

Metric	Description
Metric 1	the number of accesses to the `navigator` and `screen` objects' properties
Metric 2	the number of accesses to the properties of the `Plugin` and `MimeType` objects
Metric 3	the number of fonts loaded using JavaScript
Metric 4	the number of accesses to the offset properties of HTML elements
Metric 5	a boolean specifying whether a canvas element is programmatically accessed (writes and reads)
Metric 6	a boolean specifying the visibility status (hidden or visible) of a canvas element that is programmatically accessed
Metric 7	a boolean specifying the existence of methods for enumerating system fonts and collecting system-related information in the source code of a Flash file
Metric 8	a boolean specifying the existence of methods for transferring the collected information
Metric 9	a boolean specifying the visibility status of a Flash file (hidden, visible, or small)

alert and stores the URL of the webpage in a blacklist. The user has the option to either trust the webpage and let it run as is or prevent it from fingerprinting the user's browser using one of the designed prevention techniques. FPGuard runs in two phases: *detection* and *prevention*. In what follows, we describe these two phases in detail.

3.1   Phase I: Detection

In this phase, FPGuard identifies the fingerprinting-related activities. The core components of this phase are (see Fig. 1): *Monitor*, *Logger*, and *Analyzer*. The Monitor component is responsible for collecting browser activities. First, it injects the Logger component to the DOM tree of the webpage before the loading of other resources. The Logger component runs at the background of the browser and records all the activities of the webpage. This component then parses the logs and extracts metrics (nine metrics in total, see Table 1) for each corresponding fingerprinting method. These metrics will be used by the Analyzer component to look for fingerprinting evidences. Once the Analyzer flags the webpage as a fingerprinter, FPGuard displays an alert to the user and stores the URL of the webpage with the observed metrics into the blacklist database. Using the collected nine metrics, the Analyzer assigns a score (Score in Fig. 1) depending on the level of suspicion. Thus, we define three levels of suspiciousness for performing fingerprinting using those metrics. For example, for the *JavaScript Objects Fingerprinting* method, the Analyzer assigns three levels of suspiciousness for accesses to the informative objects (i.e., `navigator` and `screen` objects)

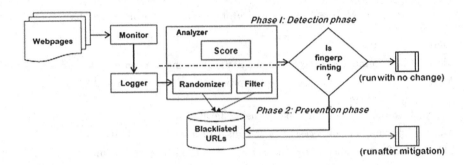

Fig. 1. An overview of FPGuard.

as well as `Plugin` and `MimeType` objects. A webpage has the first and second level suspicious access to the mentioned JavaScript objects if *Metric 1* and *Metric 2* surpass the corresponding predefined thresholds. A webpage has also third-level suspicious access when it has first-level and second-level suspicious accesses.

Similarly, for *JavaScript-based Font Detection*, using *Metrics 3 &4*, the Analyzer compares the obtained metrics against predefined thresholds and any attempt that surpasses to a given threshold value is flagged as fingerprinting. The Analyzer checks *Metrics 5 &6* and considers a canvas element as first-level suspicious, if they indicate writes and reads performed on the canvas element. The Analyzer considers a canvas element as second-level suspicious if the canvas element is first-level suspicious and is also hidden or dynamically created. Finally, the Analyzer labels each Flash file with a suspiciousness level from one to three where level three suspiciousness indicates a high probability of a fingerprinting attempt. In particular, it encodes as first-level suspicious when *Metric 7* is true. When *Metric 8* is true in the context of the first-level suspicious Flash file, then we consider it as a second-level suspicious Flash file. A second-level suspicious Flash file that is hidden or small (i.e., *Metric 9* is true) is considered as a third-level suspicious Flash file.

3.2   Phase II: Prevention

In this phase, the Analyzer module is responsible for preventing fingerprinting attempts by changing the browser's fingerprint every time the user visits a website. For this purpose, we combine randomization (*Randomizer* in Fig. 1) and filtering (*Filter* in Fig. 1) techniques. Note that many websites need information about the browser (e.g., userAgent string, screen resolution, etc.) to customize their service for different browser or operating system configurations to run properly. As a result, we need a robust randomization technique which is able to: (i) change the browser's fingerprint between multiple visits and (ii) return values that represent the properties of the browser almost correctly. For example, the contents of a canvas element are pixels while the content of a `userAgent` property is a string representing the browser's name, version, and the underlying platform. Therefore, a suitable randomization technique is needed for each property. Moreover, our filtering technique should be able to remove fingerprinting attempts (e.g., suspicious Flash files) for mitigation instead of disabling a plugin (e.g., the Flash plugin) for the whole webpage or the whole browser. In what follows, we describe the modules that we implemented in detail.

The Randomizer component implements four core engines: *objectRand*, *pluginRand*, *CanvasRand*, and *fontRand* to handle the respective fingerprinting attempts. The *objectRand* engine generates a random object at runtime to change the objects' properties between multiple visits. In this way, the objects' properties become an unreliable source of identity due to their randomized values. For this purpose, the Randomizer retrieves the `navigator` and `screen` objects of the browser, applies some changes on the properties shown to be important for fingerprinting (e.g., changing the subversion of the browser or adding noises to the current location of the user) [25], and replaces the generated objects with the native objects. However, for `plugins` and `mimeTypes` properties, this approach does not work, because changing the information of a browser's plugin might disable the plugin and cause loss of functionality. Therefore, the *pluginRand* engine adds a number of non-existing virtual `Plugin` and `MimeType` objects to the list of the current `plugins` and `mimeTypes` of the browser. It also changes the order of these lists upon every visit of the user to the URls in the blacklist.

Similarly, as canvas fingerprinting depends on the contents of canvas elements, the *CanvasRand* engine simply adds minor noises to the contents of a canvas element that is considered suspicious by the Analyzer component. Finally, the *fontRand* engine randomly reports the loaded available fonts as unavailable after the defined threshold has passed a limit. In this way, it changes the list of available fonts on the system and thus changes the fingerprint randomly. As a result, it assures that the webpage cannot employ JavaScript-based font detection for fingerprinting.

For combating Flash-based fingerprinting, instead of disabling the Flash plugin for the browser, we adopt two approaches (*flashFilter*): (i) filtering a Flash file that is identified as suspicious by the Analyzer component, and (ii) disabling the Flash plugin for each fingerprinter individually. In the former case, the Logger stores the URL of the suspicious Flash file in the blacklist. Then, the Analyzer watches for the URLs of the existing Flash files in the blacklist and prevents the browser from loading them. In the latter case, based on the Monitor (the component that flags the webpage as fingerprinter), the Logger stores the URL of the webpage in the blacklist. In subsequent visits, FPGuard disables the Flash plugin for the URL of the webpages that are present in the blacklist. For example, the Flash plugin can be disabled for a fingerprinter included as an `iframe` (which is considered as third-party) in another webpage. However, the Flash plugin can be enabled for the webpage that the user directly interacts with.

4   Implementation and Experimental Evaluation

In this section, we discuss the implementation of the FPGuard and its experimental evaluation in detail.

4.1 Implementation

FPGuard is developed as a combination of an instrumented version of the Chromium browser (version 38.0.2090.0) and a browser extension integrated with the Google Chrome browser. The FPGuard extension runs on the background of the browser and silently monitors and logs any activities related to fingerprinting on the browser. For example, to log the access to the `navigator`, `screen`, `Plugin`, and `MimeType` objects' properties, we override the getter method of these properties using the `Object.defineProperty` method. In order to record suspicious canvas elements, we override the methods of the `Object.prototype` of canvas elements that are used for writing (e.g., `fillText`) and retrieving the canvas contents (e.g., `getDataURL`). We add our implementation codes (in JavaScript) for recording the writes, reads, and the visibility status of the canvas elements (of the `Object.prototype` of canvas elements).

To record the suspicious Flash files that are loaded by the webpage, we first collect the URL of the Flash files that are loaded by the webpage. We use the *as3-commons* libraries [26] for parsing and decompiling Flash files. To do so, the FPGuard extension injects the decompiler's file (with the size of 132.4 KB) to the beginning of the webpage's DOM after the webpage is loaded. Next, the Logger sends the URL of Flash files to the decompiler. The decompiler decompiles the Flash files, traverses the obtained source codes for extracting the related metrics (see Sect. 3.1) and then sends back the obtained metrics for each URL to the Logger.

A fingerprinter might be able to check if FPGuard is installed or not by probing the getter method of the JavaScript objects' properties. However, the fingerprinter cannot invade FPGuard. Therefore, even if the fingerprinter finds out about the randomized attributes and skips them (because they are randomized and their actual value is not accessible), it generates a less unique fingerprint for the browser.

We should be clear that we were unable to find a way for having control on the browser fonts using JavaScript to prevent the JavaScript-based font detection method. The reason is that the style (i.e., font) is a property of each instance of JavaScript object not the prototype object. Thus it is not possible to filter a font on an HTML element before the loading of the font. Therefore, we modified the source code of a Chromium browser with the purpose of detecting and mitigating JavaScript-based font detection attempts. To this end, we identified the spots in the source code of the Chromium browser in which the browser loads the system fonts for HTML elements as well as the spots where the offset properties of HTML elements are returned upon being called through JavaScript. For this purpose, we modified the `CSSFontSelector.cpp` and `Element.cpp` classes. The `CSSFontSelector.cpp` class contains methods which are called upon the loading of the fonts for HTML elements (for prevention). The `Element.cpp` class contains methods for obtaining information about HTML elements such as offset properties (e.g.,width and height) using JavaScript (for detection).

Table 2. Presence of fingerprinting methods (i.e., JavaScript Objects (JSO), JavaScript-based Font Detection (JSFD), Canvas Fingerprinting (CF), and Flash-based Fingerprinting (FF)) in fingerprinters.

Fingerprinter	JSO	JSFD	CF	FF
bluecava	Yes	Yes	No	Yes
coinbase	Yes	Yes	No	No
browserleaks	No	No	Yes	No
fingerprintjs	Yes	No	Yes	No

4.2 Experimental Evaluation

Our evaluation of FPGuard is twofold: (i) measuring its effectiveness in correctly identifying fingerprinting-related activities at runtime, and (ii) measuring its effectiveness in protecting users from fingerprinters. With respect to the first part of our evaluation, similar to previous studies [6,7], we evaluate FPGuard using the top 10,000 websites from Alexa [27]. For the second part, whereas we use two types of fingerprinting providers in which the generated fingerprint is obtainable as an ID: a popular commercial fingerprinting provider named bluecava [12] and coinbase [28] and proof-of-concept fingerprinters named browserleaks [29] and fingerprintjs [30]. (see also Table 2)

Analysis of Detection. To automate the process of visiting the websites and data collection, we use the *iMacros* [31] extension for the Google Chrome browser. Using iMacros, we visit each website (of 10 K websites). Once the website is fully loaded, FPGuard records the metrics and identifies the activities of the website as either fingerprinting or normal. This way, we collected metrics for 9,264 websites (out of the 10 K websites). The remaining websites (736 websites) were not accessible at the time of our experiment. Next, we report the number of fingerprinting attempts that are discovered by FPGuard for each fingerprinting method.

JavaScript Objects fingerprinting. By using *Metric 1* and *Metric 2* (see Sect. 3.1), respectively, we enumerate the number of calls for the `navigator` and `screen` objects and the number of calls for the `Plugin` and `MimType` objects. The related thresholds for both metrics are defined accordingly. The maximum thresholds are when the websites look for all properties of the `navigator` and `screen` objects, and when they access a property for all plugins or MIME types, respectively. On average, the visited websites have looked up more than 5 properties of the `navigator` object and 3 properties of the `screen` object. In fact, more than 39 % of the visited websites have called the properties of the informative objects with more than the average (i.e., more than 5 properties of the `navigator` object and 3 properties of the `screen` object). As a result, returning invalid values for the properties of these objects might cause functionality loss of the browser as mentioned before. We also computed the suspiciousness level in performing fingerprinting based on the number of accesses to the properties of the informative

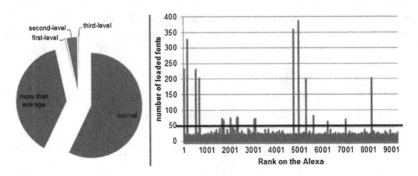

Fig. 2. Suspicious access level distribution for the Alexa's top 10 K websites (Left) and number of fonts that are loaded by the Alexa's top 10 K websites (Right).

objects for each individual website from our dataset. Figure 2 (left side) shows the result of measuring the suspiciousness level where most of the websites have normal (less than average) number of accesses to the properties of the informative objects (57.4 %). However, the number of websites that have suspicious access of first, second, and third level is considerably low in comparison to the number of websites that have the average number of accesses to the properties. Among the visited websites, only 101 of them requested for more than 80 % properties of the informative objects. That is to say, more than 17 properties of all 22 properties have been called. For example, Letitbit.net is one of the websites requested for most properties of the informative objects and the detailed information of all plugins and MIME types. This is due to, as we manually investigated, the fact that Letitbit contains a third-party script from MaxMind [32], which offers an online fraud prevention solution using fingerprinting. In addition, we visited bluecava and coinbase and for both, FPGuard reported second-level suspiciousness access to the informative objects' properties.

Finally, 15 websites from the dataset looked up for all the properties of the `navigator` and the `screen` objects plus the detailed information of all browser plugins and MIME types. Accessing all the information of `plugins` and `mimeTypes` is the characteristic of fingerprinting attempts. According to [25], using only these two properties, it is possible to identify a browser instance in a dataset of 1,523 browsers with almost 90 % accuracy.

JavaScript-based Font Detection. Based on our empirical studies, we revealed that most of the websites (92.76 % of 9,264 websites) request less than 50 fonts. Figure 2 (right side) shows the number of fonts that are loaded using JavaScript. Thus, we set 50 as the threshold for the number of fonts that a website can load. In addition, according to our analysis, the threshold for the average number of accesses to the offset properties of HTML elements is set to 65. Therefore, a given website that loads more than 50 fonts and the number of its accesses to the offset properties of HTML elements surpasses 65 is considered as a fingerprinting candidate. FPGuard identified 22 websites that were loading more than 50 fonts and accessed more than 69 times to the offset properties of HTML elements. Among the 22 websites that loaded more than 300 different fonts with more than 69 accesses to the offset properties of HTML elements are: www.yad2.co.il (388), www.junkmail. co.za (359), www.vube.com (327), and www.people.com.cn (325). These websites either employ fingerprinting themselves or contain a third-party script from a fingerprinting provider.

Canvas Fingerprinting. Figure 3 (left side) shows the distribution of suspicious (first and second-level) canvas elements among the visited websites. FPGuard found 191 websites from our dataset with first and second-level suspicious canvas elements. However, by analyzing their image data, only 85 out of 191 are second-level suspicious elements performing canvas fingerprinting. As shown in Fig. 3 (right side), in all cases, the fingerprinter inserts an arbitrary text, often a pangram with different colors to increase the uniqueness of the fingerprint.

However, a recent study identified canvas fingerprinting as the most prevalent type of fingerprinting among the top 10 K websites of Alexa (4.93 %) [7]. The study found that 95 % of the canvas fingerprinting attempts come from a third-party script which belongs to a single fingerprinting provider (i.e., AddThis [33]). In fact, after manual investigation, we found that AddThis disabled canvas fingerprinting as of mid July, 2014 [34]. Websites that use canvas fingerprinting belong to categories such as dating (e.g., www.pof.com), news (e.g., www.reuters.com), file sharing (e.g., www.letitbit.com), deal-of-the-day (e.g., www.groupon.com), etc. These websites either include a third-party script whose main job is fingerprinting (e.g., www.reuters.com and www.letitbit.com) or they actually perform fingerprinting (e.g., pof.com and groupon.com). For example, reuters.com includes a script from Audience Science [35] which is an advertising company (from revsci.net domain) that implements canvas fingerprinting. This company uses Fingerprintjs [30], which implements canvas fingerprinting.

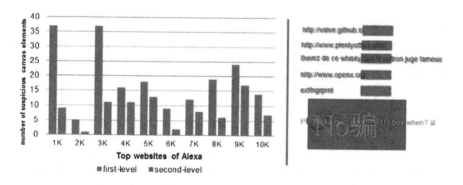

Fig. 3. Number of suspicious canvas elements that are found from our dataset (Left) and different canvas images used for fingerprinting browsers (Right).

Flash-based Fingerprinting. FPGuard found 124 websites which included Flash files in their homepage that contain methods for enumerating system fonts and considered them as first-level suspicious. We revealed that 120 out of the 124 websites loaded Flash files that include methods for storing information on the user's system, sending information to a remote server, or interacting with JavaScript programs. Hence, they are marked as second-level suspicious Flash files. From the 120 websites, only 59 of them contain third-level suspicious Flash files, meaning that the Flash files are hidden, small (less than 2×2 pixels), or added dynamically. We manually investigated the source code of the third-level suspicious Flash files and observed that they indeed perform fingerprinting. In addition, four second-level suspicious Flash files are observed to perform fingerprinting.

Discussion on FPGuard's Detection Accuracy. As for detection accuracy of FPGuard, we attempted to calculate its false-positive and false-negative rates. A false-negative error occurs when FPGuard improperly identifies a webpage as normal while the webpage is fingerprinter. On the other hand, a false-positive error occurs when FPGuard identifies a webpage as fingerprinter while the webpage is normal. Regarding the false-negative rate, FPGuard identified all fingerprinting websites (known as fingerprinter) as fingerprinters (false-negative rate is 0 %). However, for the false- positive rate, we find that it is challenging to define this value for fingerprinting-related topics. The reason is that fingerprinting is just collecting data from the users' browsers. That is to say, unless we know the name of the company (and identify it as tracker), we cannot say they are performing fingerprinting. However, we observed that many websites in our database are performing fingerprinting-related activities while they used their own scripts (mostly obfuscated), and they did not have a script from a known tracker. As a result, we cannot label them as fingerpriner; instead, we consider these websites as candidates for performing fingerprinting attempts. Accordingly, it is difficult if not impossible to evaluate the false-positive rate in our database.

Analysis of Prevention. To assess the accuracy of FPGuard's prevention technique, we repeatedly visited each fingerprinter for 100 consecutive times and collected the generated IDs. Then, we checked the uniqueness of the generated IDs with the goal of achieving the highest unique value from the list of IDs. In other words, a single browser can have 100 different IDs when one prevention technique is enabled; and, thus, the fingerprinter cannot uniquely identify the browser upon multiple visits. We define uniqueness as the fraction of the number of unique IDs and the total number of IDs. We found that the fingerprinters generate a unique ID for the browser upon each visit when FPGuard is enabled (i.e., 100 different fingerprints for a given browser upon each visit when visiting each fingerprinter for 100 times). This means that the fingerprinter is not able to uniquely identify the browser between multiple visits.

To evaluate the capability of the two popular commercial fingerprinters (i.e., bluecava and coinbase), we slightly modified some browser information (e.g., version of the browser) to change the browser's fingerprint in order to check whether the fingerprinter can detect the changes and thus generate an identical ID for the same browser. Surprisingly, none of the fingerprinting providers could detect slight changes made to the fingerprint. For example, bluecava generated different IDs for a browser instance upon every visit when the order of the elements in the browser's plugin list was changed randomly. Moreover, Bluecava could not detect the changes in the browser's version and generated different IDs when changes were performed on the browser's version. Similarly, we evaluated browserleaks and fingerprintjs by adding a single-pixel random noise to the content of canvas elements and checked whether they generate an identical ID for the browser or not. They both generated new IDs, demonstrating that they highly depend on the canvas contents and cannot detect minor changes. Our analysis of the four fingerprinters showed that the current fingerprinting algorithms are not capable of detecting slight changes of a fingerprint. In addition, gradual changes such as updating the browser version cannot be detected by even popular fingerprinters. The main point here is that our randomization and filtering engines are used to make the changes even undetectable to prevent fingerprinting.

5   Comparative Discussion

As mentioned earlier, FPdetective browser extension is a blacklist-based approach for detecting previously discovered fingerprinting objects. To compare FPGuard with FPdetective, we first included the blacklisted URLs that exist in the FPdetective extension in FPGuard. After visiting each website from our dataset, FPGuard identified 36 websites that contain URLs from the blacklist. This means that these 36 websites contain methods for fingerprinting (i.e., using *JavaScript-based Font Detection* and *Flash-based Fingerprinting* methods) and are detected by FPdetective. FPdetective identified 9 websites (out of 36 websites) as fingerprinter but we did not find any fingerprinting-related activities within these websites. We manually investigated the URLs that are identified by FPdetective as sources of fingerprinting and did not find any fingerprinting attempts which match with fingerprinting patterns of *JavaScript-based Font Detection* and *Flash-based Fingerprinting* methods. Furthermore, we observed that each of the identified websites (i.e., the 9 websites) include a Flash file[1,2] which is identified as suspicious by FPdetective. However, our analysis of these files showed that they contain methods for storing evercookies [36] or Flash cookies on the user's system (i.e., there are neither any attempts for collecting system-related information nor for enumerating system fonts). Finally, compared to FPGuard, the FPdetective extension cannot detect newly added fingerprinting scripts or Flash objects due to its blacklist-based nature.

From the prevention point of view, Tor and Firegloves block both normal and fingerprinting websites as they are not equipped with a detection mechanism. However, FPGuard first detects fingerprinting attempts and then applies a suitable prevention technique. Moreover, as mentioned earlier, FPGuard returns neither fixed nor empty values for the browser properties. Conversely, Tor and

---

[1] http://bbcdn-bbnaut.ibillboard.com/server-static-files/bbnaut.swf.
[2] https://aa.online-metrix.net/fpc.swf.

Firegloves return empty values for the plugin list. In our experiments, a property of the browser's plugin list is looked up by nearly 75.2 % of Alexa's top 10 K websites. Thus, returning an empty value for the plugins list can cause functionality loss. While Tor disables all plugins in the browser, PriVaricator employs a randomization-based solution by randomly hiding some plugins from the browser's plugin list upon every visit of a user to a webpage. Hiding a number of plugins still causes functionality loss of the browser. In contrast, FPGuard adds non-existing plugins with real names and properties to the browser's plugins list and permutes the order of the plugins upon every visit.

In addition, Tor, Firegloves and ExtensionCanvasFingerprintBlock return empty contents for all canvas elements. However, FPGuard keeps the browser's functionality by first identifying suspicious canvas elements and then adding minor noises to their contents. For preventing *JavaScript-based Font Detection* attempts, both Tor and Firegloves limit the number of system fonts for all websites. PriVaricator adds random noises to the offset properties of HTML elements after they are looked up more than 50 times. As mentioned earlier, this approach might interfere with the design of certain websites. FPGuard, on the other hand, first detects *JavaScript-based Font Detection* attempts and then after a predefined threshold (50 fonts), it randomly announces the available fonts as unavailable. In this way, it assures the randomness of browser's fingerprint on multiple visits. Moreover, it does not interfere with the webpage's design since it has no effect on the offset properties of the HTML elements and it only randomly changes the available fonts after a predefined threshold.

6 Conclusion

In this paper, we have presented the design and implementation of FPGuard — an approach to detect and combat fingerprinters at runtime. For detection of browser fingerprinting, we used a number of algorithms to analyze the metrics related to each fingerprinting method. In the detection phase, we set the threshold values based on our definition of abnormal behavior. For example, we selected 50 fonts as the threshold for JavaScript-based font detection, because we found that top websites (99.7 % of top 10 K websites) asked for less than 50 fonts. As for fingerprinting prevention, we combined randomization and filtering techniques to change the browser fingerprint in every visit the user makes to a webpage. In particular, we applied suitable randomization policies (4 policies) and filtering techniques to keep the browser functionality and combat fingerprinting attempts.

We evaluated FPGuard's detection approach on Alexa's top 10,000 websites and identified *Canvas Fingerprinting* as the most prevalent type of fingerprinting method on the Web (85 websites out of 10,000 websites). In addition, we evaluated FPGuard against a blacklist-based fingerprinting detector (i.e., FPdetective) and showed that FPGuard outperformed FPdetective's capability in correctly identifying the fingerprinters. More specifically, FPdetective identified 9 websites as fingerprinters exploiting the *Flash-based Fingerprinting* method, but we could not find any fingerprinting-related attempts in the source code of the Flash files that were identified as evidences of fingerprinting.

We also evaluated FPGuard's prevention approach against four fingerprinting providers. FPGuard successfully (with a negligible overhead) changed the browser's fingerprint upon each visit to the fingerprinters. This is to say, the fingerprinters were not able to uniquely identify the browser between multiple visits. We also compared FPGuard with the existing anti-fingerprinting tools and pointed out the strengths and weaknesses of each tool. We observed that the existing solutions cause functionality loss of the browser for both normal and fingerprinter webpages. However, FPGuard wins over fingerprinting attempts by keeping the browser functionality for the normal websites. It does by first detecting fingerprinting attempts and then preventing them using randomization policies and filtering techniques. Finally, we analyzed the existing fingerprinting algorithms used in popular fingerprinting providers.

References

1. Boda, K., Földes, Á.M., Gulyás, G.G., Imre, S.: User tracking on the web via cross-browser fingerprinting. In: Laud, P. (ed.) NordSec 2011. LNCS, vol. 7161, pp. 31–46. Springer, Heidelberg (2012)
2. Eckersley, P.: How unique is your web browser? In: Atallah, M.J., Hopper, N.J. (eds.) PETS 2010. LNCS, vol. 6205, pp. 1–18. Springer, Heidelberg (2010)
3. Wondracek, G., Holz, T., Kirda, E., Kruegel, C.: A practical attack to de-anonymize social network users. In: Proceedings of the 2010 IEEE Symposium on Security and Privacy, SP 2010, pp. 223–238. IEEE Computer Society, Washington, DC, USA (2010)
4. Ghostery. Ghostery — home (2014). https://www.ghostery.com/en/
5. AdblockPlus. Adblock plus — home (2014). https://adblockplus.org/
6. Acar, G., Juarez, M., Nikiforakis, N., Diaz, C., Gürses, S., Piessens, F., Preneel, B.: Fpdetective: dusting the web for fingerprinters. In: Proceedings of the 2013 ACM SIGSAC Conference on Computer & #38; Communications Security, CCS 2013, pp. 1129–1140. ACM, New York, NY, USA (2013)
7. Acar, G., Eubank, C., Englehardt, S., Juarez, M., Narayanan, A., Diaz, C.: The web never forgets: persistent tracking mechanisms in the wild. In: Proceedings of the 2014 ACM SIGSAC Conference on Computer and Communications Security, CCS 2014, pp. 674–689. ACM, New York, NY, USA (2014)
8. Hoofnagle, C.J., Urban, J.M., Li, S.: Privacy and modern advertising: most us internet users want'do not track'to stop collection of data about their online activities. In: Amsterdam Privacy Conference (2012)
9. McDonald, A.M., Cranor, L.F.: Beliefs and behaviors: internet users? understanding of behavioral advertising. In: Proceedings of the 2010 Research Conference on Communication, Information and Internet Policy. Carnegie Mellon University, Pittsburgh (2010)
10. Turow, J., King, J., Hoofnagle, C.J., Bleakley, A., Hennessy, M.: Americans reject tailored advertising and three activities that enable it (2009). (SSRN 1478214)
11. TRUSTe. 2009 study: Consumer attitudes about behavioral targeting (2009). http://goo.gl/LO2QEm
12. Bluecava. Bluecava — opt-out (2014). http://bluecava.com/opt-out
13. AddThis. Addthis - terms of service, July 2014. http://www.addthis.com/tos

14. Nikiforakis, N., Kapravelos, A., Joosen, W., Kruegel, C., Piessens, F., Vigna, G.: Cookieless monster: exploring the ecosystem of web-based device fingerprinting. In: Proceedings of the 2013 IEEE Symposium on Security and Privacy, SP 2013, pp. 541–555. IEEE Computer Society, Washington, DC, USA (2013)

15. Perry, M., Clark, E., Murdoch, S.: The design and implementation of the tor browser[draft], July 2014. https://www.torproject.org/projects/torbrowser/design/

16. Nikiforakis, N., Joosen, W., Livshits, B.: Privaricator: Deceiving Fingerprinters with Little White Lies (2014). http://research.microsoft.com/apps/pubs/default.aspx?id=209989

17. Boda, K.: Firegloves (2014). http://fingerprint.pet-portal.eu/?menu=6

18. Mayer, J.R.: Any person... a aamphleteer?: Internet anonymity in the age of web 2.0. Undergraduate Senior Thesis, Princeton University (2009)

19. Mowery, K., Bogenreif, D., Yilek, S., Shacham, H.: Fingerprinting information in javascript implementations. In: Proceedings of W2SP (2011)

20. Olejnik, L., Castelluccia, C., Janc, A., et al.: Why johnny can't browse in peace: on the uniqueness of web browsing history patterns. In: 5th Workshop on Hot Topics in Privacy Enhancing Technologies (HotPETs 2012) (2012)

21. Mulazzani, M., Reschl, P., Huber, M., Leithner, M., Schrittwieser, S., Weippl, E., Wien, F.H.C.: Fast and reliable browser identification with javascript engine fingerprinting. In: Web 2.0 Workshop on Security and Privacy (W2SP), vol. 5 (2013)

22. Yen, T.-F., Xie, Y., Fang, Y., Yu, R.P., Abadi, M.: Privacy and security implications. In: NDSS, Host fingerprinting and tracking on the web (2012)

23. Murdoch, S., Perry, M., Clark, E.: Tor: Cross-origin fingerprinting unlinkability (2014). https://www.torproject.org/projects/torbrowser/design/#fingerprinting-linkability

24. Appodrome. Canvasfingerprintblock (2014). http://goo.gl/1ltNs4

25. Khademi, A.F., Zulkernine, M., Weldemariam, K.: Empirical evaluation of web-based fingerprinting (to appear in ieee software, 2015). IEEE Software's SWSI: Security & Privacy on the Web (2015)

26. as3commons. As3 commons bytecode (2014). http://www.as3commons.org/as3-commons-bytecode/index.html

27. Alexa. Alexa - actionable analytics for the web (2014). http://www.alexa.com/

28. CoinBase. Coinbase - an international digital wallet (2014). https://coinbase.com/

29. BrowserLeaks.com. Browserleaks (2014). https://www.browserleaks.com/

30. Valve. Fingerprintjs (2014). https://github.com/Valve/fingerprintjs

31. imacros. imacros for chrome (2014). https://chrome.google.com/webstore/detail/imacros-for-chrome/cplklnmnlbnpmjogncfgfijoopmnlemp?hl=en

32. MaxMind. Maxmind - ip geolocation and online fraud prevention (2014). https://www.maxmind.com/en/home

33. AddThis. Addthis - get likes, get shares, get followers (2014). http://www.addthis.com/privacy/opt-out

34. AddThis. The facts about our use of a canvas element in our recent r&d test (2014). http://goo.gl/qa0x1y

35. AudienceScience. Audiencescience - enterprise advertising management system (2014). http://www.audiencescience.com/

36. Kamkar, S.: Evercookie-never forget. New York Times (2010)

Information Flow and Inference

Stream Processing with Secure Information Flow Constraints

Indrakshi Ray[1]([✉]), Raman Adaikkalavan[2], Xing Xie[1], and Rose Gamble[3]

[1] Computer Science, Colorado State University, Fort Collins, Colorado
{iray,xing}@cs.colostate.edu
[2] Computer and Information Sciences and Informatics,
Indiana University South Bend, South Bend, Indiana
raman@cs.iusb.edu
[3] Computer Science, University of Tulsa, Tulsa, Oklahoma
gamble@utulsa.edu

Abstract. In the near future, clouds will provide situational monitoring services such as health monitoring, stock market monitoring, shopping cart monitoring, and emergency control and threat management. Offering such services requires securely processing data streams generated by multiple, possibly competing and/or complementing, organizations, such that there is no overt or covert leakage of sensitive information. We demonstrate how an information flow control model adapted from the Chinese Wall policy can be used to protect against sensitive data disclosure in data stream management system. We also develop a language based on Continuous Query Language that can be used to express information flow constraints in stream processing and provide its formal semantics.

1 Introduction

Data Stream Management Systems (DSMSs) [1,5,6,8,9,14,15] are needed for situation monitoring applications that collect high-speed data, run continuous queries to process them, and compute results on-the-fly to detect events of interest. Consider one potential situation monitoring application – collecting real-time streaming audit data to thwart various types of attacks in a cloud environment. Detecting such precursors to attacks may involve analyzing streaming audit data belonging to various, possibly competing and/or complementing, organizations. Sensitive information, such as, company policies and intellectual property, may be obtained by mining audit data and hence it must be protected from unauthorized disclosure and modification. Most research on secure data stream processing focuses on providing access control to streaming data [2,3,12,13,18,19,21]. Controlling access is crucial, but it is also important to prevent illegal information flow through overt and covert channels. Towards this end, we emphasize how lattice-based information flow control models can be adapted and used for streaming data and provide a query language that supports this model.

The research was funded in part by NIST under award no. 70NANB14H059 and by NSF under award no. CCF-1018711.

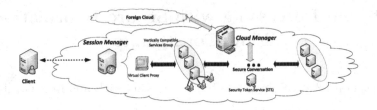

Fig. 1. Multi-Tier architecture of a cloud

In this work our main contribution is formalizing a new language based on CQL [6] for expressing continuous queries with information flow constraints. Query processing, in light of information flow constraints, differs from CQL as the security level of the user issuing the query impacts the responses returned. Our language allows for the specification of a set of partially ordered security levels that forms a lattice, where the ordering relation is referred to as the dominance relation, denoted by <. We provide the formal semantics of our language such that we can argue about query equivalences and optimization.

The rest of the paper is organized as follows. In Sect. 2, we present an architecture for processing continuous queries generated from the various tiers in the cloud. In Sect. 3, we present our information flow control model that formulates the rules for accessing data streams generated by various organizations in the cloud. In Sect. 4, we provide the formal semantics of our language. In Sect. 5, we discuss related work. In Sect. 6, we conclude the paper with pointers to future work.

2   Example Cloud Architecture

We have a service that aims to prevent and detect attacks in real-time in the cloud. Such a service provides warnings about various types of attacks, often involving multiple organizations. Figure 1 shows a multi-tier architecture of the cloud adopted from [29]. Various types of auditing may take place in the cloud. The first level is the *company auditing tier*, not explicitly shown in Fig. 1, that is represented by the users connected to some service. In this tier, the activities pertaining to an organization are analyzed in isolation. The next level is the *service auditing tier*, identified by shaded ellipses that contain sets of resources and services. Each shaded ellipse depicts vertically compatible services or resources; this implies the services or resources that can be functionally substituted for each other, possibly on demand. The *cloud auditing tier* is shown with connecting dark arrows, which depicts the internal communication within the cloud due to a service invocation chain.

Various types of audit streams must be captured to detect the different types of attacks that may take place in a cloud. The company auditing tier logs the activities of the various users in the organization. If the behavior of an authorized user does not follow his usual pattern, we can perform analysis to determine if the user's authentication information has been compromised. This tier is responsible for analyzing the audit streams of individual companies in isolation. Typically, at this layer, the audit streams generated by a single company are analyzed. The service auditing tier logs information pertaining to the various companies who provide similar services. Session Manager at this tier can detect whether there is a denial-of-service attack targeted at a specific type of service. Session Manager analyzes audit streams generated from multiple competing organizations, so we need to protect against information leakage and corruption. In short, the Session Manager needs to analyze data from one or more companies belonging to the same COI class. The cloud auditing tier collects audit information pertaining to a service invocation chain and is able to detect the presence of man-in-the-middle attack. Cloud Manager is responsible for analyzing audit streams from multiple organizations associated with service invocation chains, but the organizations may not have conflict of interest. Thus, at this tier, the audit streams from the companies belonging to one or more COI classes are analyzed.

In order to detect and warn against these attacks, continuous queries must be executed on the streaming data belonging to various organizations. Queries must be processed such that there are no overt or covert leakage of information across competing organizations. We assign security levels to categorize the various classes of data that are being generated and collected at the various tiers. The security level of the data determines who can access and modify it. In the next section, we discuss how security levels are assigned to various classes of data.

Audit data generated by the services are sent to the DSMS. For this paper, we consider a centralized DSMS architecture. Compatible services are grouped and they interact based on client needs. Servers contain event detectors that monitor and detect occurrence of interesting events. The detectors sanitize and propagate the events to the data stream management system, which arrive at the stream source operator. This operator checks for the level of the incoming audit events and propagates them to the appropriate query processor's input queue. The query processor architecture is based on the replicated model, where there is a one-to-one correspondence between query processors and security levels. A query specified by a user at a particular level is executed by the query processor running at that level. Also a query processor at some level can only process data that it is authorized to view. After processing, the query results are disseminated to authorized users via the output queues of queries. In addition to the query processors and stream source operator the data stream management system contains various other components (trusted and untrusted).

3   Continuous Queries with Information Flow Constraints

Secure Information Flow Model. We provide an information flow model that is adapted from the lattice structure for Chinese Wall proposed by Sandhu [23]. We have a set of companies that provide services in the clouds that are partitioned into conflict of interest classes based on the type of services they provide.

Companies providing the same type of service are in direct competition with each other. Consequently, it is important to protect against disclosure of sensitive information to competing organizations. We begin by defining how the conflict of interest classes are represented.

Definition 1 [Conflict of Interest Class Representation:]. *The set of companies providing service to the cloud are partitioned into a set of n conflict of interest classes, which we denote by COI_1, COI_2, ..., and COI_n. Each conflict of interest class is represented as COI_i, where $1 \leq i \leq n$. Conflict of interest class COI_i consists of a set of m_i companies, where $m_i \geq 1$, that is $COI_i = \{1, 2, 3, \ldots, m_i\}$.*

On the other hand, a set of companies, who are not in competition with each other, may provide complementing services in the cloud. A single company can provide some service, and sometimes multiple companies may together offer a set of services. In the following, we define the notion of complementing interest (CI) class and show how it is represented.

Definition 2 [Complementing Interest Class Representation:]. *The set of companies providing complementing services is represented as an n-element vector $[i_1, i_2, \ldots, i_n]$, where $i_k \in COI_k \cup \{\bot\}$ and $1 \leq k \leq n$. $i_k = \bot$ signifies that the CI class does not contain services from any company in the conflict of interest class COI_k. $i_k \in COI_k$ indicates that the CI class contains services from the corresponding company in conflict of interest class COI_k. Our representation forbids multiple companies that are part of the same COI class from being assigned to the same complementing interest class.*

We next define the security structure of our model. Each data stream, as well as the individual tuples constituting it, is associated with a security level that captures its sensitivity. Security level associated with a data stream dictates which entities can access or modify it. Input data stream generated by an individual organization offering some service has a security level that captures the organizational information. Input streams may be processed by the DSMS to generate *derived streams*. Derived data streams may contain information about multiple companies, some of which are in the same COI class and others may belong to different COI classes. Before describing how to assign security levels to derived data streams, we show how security levels are represented.

Definition 3 [Security Level Representation:]. *A security level is represented as an n-element vector $[i_1, i_2, \ldots, i_n]$, where $i_j \in COI_j \cup \{\bot\} \cup \{T\}$ and $1 \leq j \leq n$. $i_j = \bot$ signifies that the data stream does not contain information from any company in COI_j; $i_j = T$ signifies that the data stream contains information from two or more companies belonging to COI_j; $i_j \in COI_j$ denotes that the data stream contains information from the corresponding company in COI_j.*

Consider the case where we have 2 COI classes, namely, COI_1 and COI_2 as shown in Fig. 2. COI_1 has two companies denoted by 1 and 2 and COI_2 has

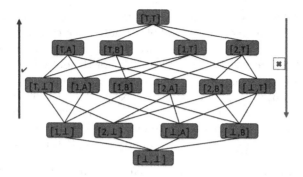

Fig. 2. Lattice-Based Information Flow for the Chinese Wall

two companies denoted by A and B. The audit stream generated by Company 2 in COI_1 has a security level of $[2, \bot]$. Similarly, the audit stream generated by Company B in COI_2 has a security level $[\bot, B]$. When audit streams generated from multiple companies are combined, the information contained in this derived stream has a higher security level. For example, audit stream having level $[1, B]$ contains information about Company 1 in COI_1 and Company B in COI_2. It is also possible for audit streams to have information from multiple companies belonging to the same COI class. For example, a security level of $[\bot, T]$ indicates that the data stream does not have information from any company in COI_1, but has information from both companies in COI_2. We also have a level $[\bot, \bot]$ which we call *public* and that has no company specific information. The level $[T, T]$ correspond to level *trusted* and it contains information pertaining to multiple companies in each COI class and can be only accessed by trusted entities. We next define dominance relation between security levels.

Definition 4 [Dominance Relation:]. *Let* **L** *be the set of security levels, L_1 and L_2 be two security levels, where $L_1, L_2 \in$ **L**. We say security level L_1 is dominated by L_2, denoted by $L_1 \preceq L_2$, when the following conditions hold: $(\forall i_k = 1, 2, \ldots, n)(L_1[i_k] = L_2[i_k] \vee L_1[i_k] =\bot \vee L_2[i_k] = T)$. For any two levels, $L_p, L_q \in$ **L**, if neither $L_p \preceq L_q$, nor $L_q \preceq L_p$, we say that L_p and L_q are incomparable.*

The dominance relation is reflexive, antisymmetric, and transitive. In Fig. 2 the level *public*, denoted by $[\bot, \bot]$, is dominated by all the other levels. Similarly, the level *trusted*, denoted by $[T, T]$, dominates all the other levels. Note that the dominance relation defines a lattice structure, where level *public* appears at the bottom and the level *trusted* appears at the top. Incomparable levels are not connected in this lattice structure. In our earlier example, level $[1, \bot]$ is dominated by $[1, B]$ and $[1, T]$. $[\bot, 2]$ is dominated by $[T, T]$. That is, $[1, \bot] \preceq [1, B]$ and $[1, \bot] \preceq [1, T]$. $[\bot, 2]$ and $[1, \bot]$ are incomparable.

Each data stream is associated with a security level. Each of the tuples constituting the data stream also has a security level assigned to it. Thus, the schema of the data stream has an attribute called level that captures the security level of tuples. The level attribute is generated automatically by the system and cannot be modified by the users. Note that, the security level of an individual tuple in a data stream is dominated by the level of the data stream. When a DSMS operation is executed on multiple input tuples, each having its own security level, an output tuple is produced. The security level of the output tuple is the least upper bound (LUB) of the security levels of the input tuples.

In our work, various types of queries are executed to detect security and performance problems. Each continuous query Q_i, submitted by a process, inherits the security level of the process. We require a query Q_i to obey the simple security property and the restricted $\star$-property of the Bell-Lapadula model [10].

1. Query Q_i with $L(Q_i) = C$ can read a data stream x only if $L(x) \preceq C$.
2. Query Q_i with $L(OP_i) = C$ can write a data stream x only if $L(x) = C$.

Note that, for our example, a process executing at level $[5, \perp, T]$ can read streams belonging to Company 5 in COI_1 and all companies in COI_3 and also streams derived from them. Thus, the process is trusted w.r.t. COI_3, but not w.r.t. the other COI classes. Our information flow model thus provides a finer granularity of trust than provided by the earlier models. Our goal is to allow information flow only from the dominated levels to the dominating ones. All other information flow, either overtly or covertly, should be disallowed by our architecture.

Continuous Queries for Motivating Example. Consider a simple application that tries to detect example denial-of-service attacks in the cloud. We have two conflict of interest classes denoted by COI_1 and COI_2. The constituent companies in each COI class is given by, $COI_1 = \{1, 2\}$ and $COI_2 = \{A, B, C\}$. Examples of security levels in our configuration are $[\perp, \perp]$ (public knowledge), $[T, T]$ (completely trusted), $[1, \perp]$ (data from 1), $[\perp, T]$ (trusted w.r.t. COI_2), $[1, B]$ (data from 1 and B), $[1, T]$ (data from 1 in COI_1 and trusted w.r.t. COI_2). Continuous queries are executed at various tiers to detect performance delays and possibly denial-of-service (DoS) attacks. In any given tier, different types of DoS attacks may occur – some involving the data belonging to single organizations, others involving data belonging to multiple organizations. Thus, a tier can have query processors at different levels, each of which executes queries on data that it is authorized to view and modify.

We consider a single data stream, called MessageLog, that contains the audit stream data associated with message events, such as send and receive. MessageLog is obtained from SystemLog by filtering the events related to sending and receiving the messages. Note that, MessageLog in reality may contain many other fields, but we only deal with those that are pertinent to this example. The various attributes in MessageLog are serviceId, msgType, sender, receiver, timestamp, outcome. serviceId is a unique identifier associated with each service; msgType gives the type of message which is either send or receive; sender (receiver) gives the id of the organization sending (receiving) the message; timestamp is the time when the event (send or receive) occurred; outcome denotes success or failure of the event. In addition to these attributes, we have an attribute referred to as level that represents the security level of the tuple. The level attribute is assigned by the system and it cannot be modified by the user.

```
MessageLog(serviceId, msgType, sender, receiver, timestamp, outcome)
```

The queries are expressed using the CQL language [6]. We describe the various types of queries that can be executed at the various tiers.

Company Auditing Tier. In the company auditing tier, companies have access only to their own audit records. We give some sample queries that are executed by *Company1* to detect performance delays and DoS attacks. All the queries are executed at level $[1, \bot]$.

Query 1 (Q1):

Company1 requests service from *CompanyB*. It is trying to check the times when such message could be successfully delivered.

```
SELECT timestamp FROM MessageLog WHERE msgType = "send" AND outcome = "success"
      AND receiver = "CompanyB"
```

Query 2 (Q2):

Company1 requests service from *CompanyB*. It is trying to check the times when such message could not be successfully delivered.

```
SELECT timestamp FROM MessageLog WHERE msgType = "send" AND outcome = "failure"
      AND receiver = "CompanyB"
```

Service Auditing Tier. Service auditing tier receives log records from all the companies making use of some service. However, as the queries below demonstrate, not all the queries need to access all the data from the same COI class.

Query 3 (Q3): Level $[\bot, B]$

Log records received at the service auditing tier can be analyzed by the Session Manager to find out whether *CompanyB* is not available for some service.

```
SELECT timestamp FROM MessageLog WHERE msgType = "send" AND outcome = "failure"
      AND receiver = "CompanyB"
```

Query 4 (Q4): Level $[\bot, T]$

Session Manager may wish to find out whether all companies in COI_2 are target of some DoS attacks.

```
SELECT timestamp FROM MessageLog WHERE msgType = "send" AND outcome = "failure"
      AND receiver = "CompanyB" OR receiver = "CompanyA" OR receiver = "CompanyC"
```

Cloud Auditing Tier. Cloud auditing tier gets log records pertaining to all the services. However, the various queries will have different types of security requirements.

Query 5 (Q5): Level $[1, B]$

Cloud Manager may want to look at all records pertaining to `serviceId` 5 and measure the delays in order to detect possible man-in-the-middle attack. `serviceId` 5 involves *Company1* from COI_1 and *CompanyB* from COI_2.

```
SELECT  MIN(timestamp), MAX(timestamp) FROM MessageLog [ROWS 100]
    WHERE outcome = "success" AND serviceId = "5"
```

Query 6 (Q6): Level $[1, B]$

Cloud Manager wants to find the delay encountered by *Company1* between sending the request and receiving the service from *CompanyB* for the last 100 tuples.

```
SELECT R.timestamp - S.timestamp AS  delay
    FROM MessageLog R[Rows 100], MessageLog S[Rows 100]
    WHERE S.msgType = "send" AND S.outcome = "success" AND R.msgType = "receive" AND
    R.outcome = "success" AND R.receiver = "Company1" AND R.sender = "CompanyB" AND
    S.receiver = "CompanyB" AND S.sender = "Company1" AND S.serviceId = R.serviceId
```

Query 7 (Q7): Level $[T, T]$

Cloud Manager may want to find out the delay incurred in the different service invocation chains.

```
SELECT MIN(timestamp), MAX(timestamp) FROM MessageLog[ROWS 100]
    WHERE outcome = "success" GROUP BY serviceId
```

Challenges of Continuous Queries with Information Flow Constraints. In this section, we describe why existing DSMS are unsuitable for handling continuous queries in the cloud. The audit queries may be handled by a DSMS that is processing streaming data generated by the various organizations. The DSMS receives data from various stream sources. The stream shepherd system operator [6] receives the incoming data, cleans them, and converts them into a stream with a well-defined schema that can be acted upon by the DSMS. For processing streaming data, CQL has three types of operators, in addition to the shepherd operator: (i) stream-to-relation (S2R), (ii) relation-to-relation (R2R), and (iii) relation-to-stream (R2S). The S2R operators (time, tuple, partitioned by sequential-window) convert input streams to relations. The R2R operators (select, project, join, aggregate) process tuples in the relations produced by the S2R operators and output relations. The R2S operators (istream, dstream, rstream) convert the relations produced by R2R operators back to streams.

In order to securely process queries, the basic requirement is to have an attribute that maintains the sensitivity level of a tuple and that cannot be tampered with by a user. We introduce an attribute termed *level* which is the security level of the tuple and is system generated. It can be queried or used as part of select condition, but *cannot* be modified by the user. Schemas of all relations and streams in our secure DSMS must have this attribute. The results returned depend on the query level. Thus, when the queries Q_i and Q_j, which look identical, but issued at levels $[1, \perp]$ and $[T, \perp]$ respectively are executed, different results are returned.

- $Q_i([1, \perp])$: SELECT COUNT FROM MessageLog [ROWS 100] WHERE msgType = "send" AND outcome = "success" AND receiver = "CompanyB"
- $Q_j([T, \perp])$: SELECT COUNT FROM MessageLog [ROWS 100] WHERE msgType = "send" AND outcome = "success" AND receiver = "CompanyB"

The response to Q_i only involve information sent by *Company1* whereas the response to Q_j involve information sent by all companies in COI_1. One may argue that rewriting Q_j by adding an additional clause involving the security level, shown below as query Q'_j, may produce the same result as Q_i.

- $Q'_j([T, \perp])$: SELECT COUNT FROM MessageLog [ROWS 100] WHERE msgType = "send" AND outcome = "success" AND receiver = "CompanyB" AND level = $[1, \perp]$"

In other words, rewriting Q_j as Q'_j, does not give the same result as Q_i. Thus, post-processing Q_j cannot give us Q_i. Moreover, the window operator in Q_i should not know about the existence of the other types of tuples as that may constitute leakage of sensitive information.

In order to handle the above and other cases, one or more of the operators of types S2R, R2R, or R2S must be modified. In order to process Q_i, the R2R operator (count) which is at the second stage should receive 100 tuples that only have level $[1, \perp]$ from the window operator at the first stage. This cannot be achieved by using another R2R operator such as select (via a filtering condition as shown in Q'_j) in the second stage as the window is created in the first stage. Thus, the S2R operator in the first stage should create time varying relations with 100 tuples that are at level $[1, \perp]$ from the input stream and propagate it to the R2R operator in the second stage. This cannot be done by existing S2R operators. Moreover, in existing systems, an S2R operator is shared by queries accessing the same input stream to reduce resource usage. The input streams may have tuples belonging to different sensitivity levels. Consequently, allowing queries at different levels to read from the same S2R operator violates the information flow policies.

The final issue is the processing of the specified queries. The query processor should be able to execute the queries with different sensitivity levels without leaking information. Leakage can occur through overt or covert channels. Overt channels occur when a process reads or writes data at a different sensitivity level. Covert channels occur when a process at some sensitivity level manipulates the use of shared resources (such as CPU and memory) to pass information on to a process at a different sensitivity level. Current DSMS query processors are not equipped to provide protection against such illegal channels. For example, the scheduler in a DSMS is responsible for executing all the queries – by manipulating the time taken to execute certain queries, information can be passed from one security level to another. We need to redesign query processors in light of information flow constraints.

4   Formal Semantics of the Language

We begin with discussing the formal semantics of the language used to express streaming queries with information flow constraints. We present our language and semantics in a manner similar to that proposed by Arasu and Widom [7]. We have adapted the approach for our language, which we call SIF-CQL (Secure Information Flow Continuous Query Language). To make the paper self contained, we have used some definitions from [7].

In our secure DSMS, we have two types of data: *streams* and *relations*. Each stream or relation is associated with a schema consisting of a set of attributes as in the traditional relational model together with a system defined security attribute which we refer to as a *level*. We also assume the existence of a discrete and totally ordered time domain $T = \{0, 1, \ldots\}$. An element in T is referred to as *time instant* or *instant*.

We can have two types of streams: *trusted* and *single level*. A trusted stream consists of inputs from various sources and is not associated with any specific security level, but consists of tuples each of which is associated with a security level. The assumption is that in a trusted stream the individual tuples are protected and information is not passed from one level to another. In contrast, we may have single level streams which are associated with a specific security level. A single level stream contains tuples, each of whose security level is dominated by the level of the stream. For example, a single level stream at $[1, \perp]$ level can contain tuples at $[\perp, \perp]$ or $[1, \perp]$ level. The formal definitions of these two types of streams appear below.

Definition 5 [Trusted Stream]. *A trusted stream SS is not associated with any security level and consists of a possibly infinite bag of elements $< s, l, \tau >$, where $< s, l >$ is a tuple belonging to the schema of S, $\tau \in T$ is a timestamp and $l \in \mathcal{L}$ is the security level of the tuple.*

Definition 6 [Single Level Stream]. *A single level stream S is associated with a single security level L_S and consists of a possibly infinite bag of elements $< s, l, \tau >$, where $< s, l >$ is a tuple belonging to the schema of S, $\tau \in T$ is a timestamp and l is the security level of the tuple such that $l \leq L_S$ and $L_S \in \mathcal{L}$.*

We have only single level relations (or just relations) that are associated with one security level.

Definition 7 [Single Level Relation]. *A single level relation or a relation R is a mapping from $T \times \mathcal{L}$ to a finite but unbounded bag of tuples belonging to the schema of R each of which is associated with a security level. A relation R is associated with a security level L_R which is the input to the mapping function. The security level of each tuple in R is dominated by $L_R \in \mathcal{L}$.*

A stream is a collection of timestamped tuples each of which is associated with a security level. The element $< s, l, \tau >$ signifies that tuple s arrives on S at time τ and is associated with the security level l. For a relation R, $R(\tau)$ denotes the bag of tuples, each associated with a security level, in the relation at time instant τ.

In secure DSMS, continuous queries submitted by users operate only on single level streams that have the same level as the query level. Continuous queries are composed from secure operators belonging to three classes: stream-to-relation (S2R), relation-to-relation (R2R), and relation-to-stream (R2S).

- A secure S2R operator takes an input stream, time instant τ, and security level l and produces a relation at level l. Each tuple of the relation is associated with a level that equals the level of the corresponding element in the stream as a stream can contain tuples at different levels. Note that, the level of each tuple of the relation is dominated by l. The bag of tuples in the output relation at time instant τ and security level l depends only on input stream elements with timestamps $\leq \tau$ and security level $\leq l$.
- A secure R2R operator takes one or more relations as input together with a security level l and produces another relation at level l as output. When the input has one relation, the level of each tuple in the output relation is same as the corresponding input tuples. When there is more than one input relation, the level of each output tuple is the least upper bound of the levels of the corresponding input tuples. Here again, the level of the output relation dominates the level of tuples in that relation. The bag of tuples in the output relation at time τ depends on the bag of tuples in the input relations at τ and their security levels.
- A secure R2S operator takes an input relation, timestamp τ, and a security level l, and produces a stream at level l. The security level of each element of the stream depends on the security level of the corresponding tuple in the relation. Note that, the security level of the elements of the stream is dominated by the level of the stream l. The elements of the stream with timestamp τ depend only on the relation tuples at time instants $\leq \tau$ and whose security level $\leq l$.

The trusted stream shepherd operator, a secure stream-to-stream operator (S2S-Op), takes as input a trusted stream and creates single level streams for each security level.

We define the following domains.

- *Time domain* $(\mathcal{T})$ is the domain of time instants. $\mathcal{T} = \{0, 1, \ldots\}$.
- *Security level domain* $(\mathcal{L})$ (defined in Sect. 3) is the domain of security levels. We use $l_i \leq l_j$ to denote that l_j dominates l_i where $l_i, l_j \in \mathcal{L}$.
- *Tuple domain* $(\mathcal{TP})$ is the domain of tuples consisting of all but the security attribute.
- *Tuple multiset domain* (Σ) is the domain of finite but unbounded bag of tuples.
- *Relation domain* $(\mathcal{R})$ is the domain of functions that map time instants and security levels to bags of tuples. The security levels of the bags equal the input security level. Each tuple in the bag is also associated with a security level that is dominated by the input security level. We denote this as $R = \mathcal{T} \times \mathcal{L} \rightarrow \Sigma \times \mathcal{L}$.
- *Trusted stream domain* $(\mathcal{SS})$ is the domain of possibly infinite multisets over $\mathcal{TP} \times \mathcal{L} \times \mathcal{T}$.

- *Single level stream domain* $(\mathcal{S})$ is the domain of functions that map security levels to possibly infinite multisets over $\mathcal{TP} \times \mathcal{L} \times \mathcal{T}$. We denote this as $\mathcal{S} = \mathcal{L} \to \mathcal{TP} \times \mathcal{L} \times \mathcal{T}$.
- *Relational operator domain* $(\mathcal{R}_{op})$ is the domain of functions that produce a bag of tuples from one or more bags of tuples and an input security level. Each input bag is associated with a security level which dominates the security level of tuples in the bag. The output bag is associated with a security level that is input to the operator. The security levels of the tuples in the output bag depend on the security levels of the corresponding input tuples. We formally denote this as: $\mathcal{R}_{op} = (\Sigma \times \mathcal{L})^n \times \mathcal{L} \to \Sigma \times \mathcal{L}$, where n represents the number of input bags.
- *Syntactic domains* are the domains associated with syntactic terms.
- *Relation lookup domain* $(RelLookUp)$ is the domain of functions that map an identifier to its corresponding relation. We denote it as: $RelLookUp = Identifier \to \mathcal{R}$
- *Stream lookup domain* $(StrLookUp)$ is the domain of functions that map an identifier to its corresponding stream. We denote it as: $StrLookUp = Identifier \to \mathcal{S}$

The abstract syntax for language is given below. Table 1 has the symbol descriptions and domains.

$$
\begin{aligned}
Q &::= Q_R \mid Q_S \\
Q_R &::= \text{RName} \mid \text{R2R-Op } (Q_R^1, \ldots, Q_R^n) \\
&\quad \mid \text{S2R-Op } (Q_S) \\
Q_S &::= \text{SName} \mid \text{R2S-Op } (Q_R) \\
\text{SName} &::= \text{S2S-Op } (\text{SSName}) \\
\text{SSName} &::= \text{Id} \\
\text{RName} &::= \text{Id}
\end{aligned}
$$

We are now ready to provide a denotational semantics [24], similar to the work in [7], for SIF Continuous Queries that are expressed using our language

Table 1. Symbol descriptions and domains

Symbol	Description	Domain
Q	Continuous Query (CQ) in $\mathcal{SIF} - \mathcal{CQL}$	*Query*
Q_R	CQ producing a relation	*RelQuery*
Q_S	CQ producing a stream	*StrQuery*
S2S-Op	Stream-to-Stream Operator	*S2SOp*
S2R-Op	Stream-to-Relation Operator	*S2ROp*
R2R-Op	Relation-to-Relation Operator	*R2ROp*
R2S-Op	Relation-to-Stream Operator	*R2SOp*
RName	Relation Name	*Identifier*
SSName	Stream Name	*Identifier*
Id	Identifier	*Identifier*

Table 2. Meaning Functions

Query Part	Meaning	Signature
Q	$\mathcal{M}$	$Query \rightarrow (RelLookUp \times StrLookUp \times \mathcal{L} \times \mathcal{T} \rightarrow$ $((\Sigma \cup \mathcal{S}) \times \mathcal{L}))$
Q_R	$\mathcal{M}_R$	$RelQuery \rightarrow (RelLookUp \times StrLookUp \times \mathcal{L} \times \mathcal{T} \rightarrow$ $\Sigma \times \mathcal{L})$
Q_S	$\mathcal{M}_S$	$StrQuery \rightarrow (RelLookUp \times StrLookUp \times \mathcal{L} \times \mathcal{T} \rightarrow$ $\mathcal{S} \times \mathcal{L})$
S2S-Op	$\mathcal{M}_{S2S}$	$S2SOP \rightarrow (\mathcal{SS} \times \mathcal{L} \rightarrow \mathcal{S} \times \mathcal{L})$
S2R-Op	$\mathcal{M}_{S2R}$	$S2ROp \rightarrow (\mathcal{S} \times \mathcal{L} \times \mathcal{T} \rightarrow \Sigma \times \mathcal{L})$
R2R-Op	$\mathcal{M}_{R2R}$	$R2ROp \rightarrow \mathcal{R}_{op}$
R2S-Op	$\mathcal{M}_{R2S}$	$R2SOp \rightarrow (\mathcal{R} \times \mathcal{L} \times \mathcal{T} \rightarrow \mathcal{S} \times \mathcal{L})$

which we denote as $\mathcal{S}$. A denotational semantics is specified by a meaning function that we denote as $\mathcal{M}$. Function $\mathcal{M}$ applied to a continuous query Q, which we represent as $\mathcal{M}[\![Q]\!]$, takes as input the streams and relations referred to in Q together with a time instant τ and security level l, and produces an output consisting of a new relation or stream corresponding to the time instant τ. The security level of this output relation or stream is l and it consists of tuples or elements each of whose security level is dominated by l. Table 2 describes the meaning functions that we use.

We use *lambda calculus* [22] notations for defining our functions. The expression $\lambda x_1, \ldots, \lambda x_n.E$ represents a function that takes arguments $v_1, \ldots v_n$, and returns the result of evaluating E by replacing all free occurrences of x_i in E by v_i where $1 \le i \le n$. We now present the details of the meaning functions.

– $\mathcal{M}$: The function $\mathcal{M}[\![Q]\!]$ produced by $\mathcal{M}$ for query Q takes four parameters. The first two parameters are functions that map the relation or stream names in the query to the appropriate relations or streams. The third and fourth parameters are security level and time instant respectively. $\mathcal{M}[\![Q]\!](r, s, l, \tau)$ specifies the output produced by Q at time instant τ and security level l. $\mathcal{M}[\![Q]\!](r, s, l, \tau)$ invokes $\mathcal{M}_R[\![Q_R]\!](r, s, l, \tau)$ if $Q = Q_R$ produces a relation as an output and calls $\mathcal{M}_S[\![Q_S]\!](r, s, l, \tau)$ if $Q = Q_S$ produces a stream as an output.
$$\mathcal{M}[\![Q_R]\!] = \lambda r.\lambda s.\lambda l.\lambda \tau.\mathcal{M}_R[\![Q_R]\!](r, s, l, \tau)$$

$$\mathcal{M}[\![Q_S]\!] = \lambda r.\lambda s.\lambda l.\lambda \tau.(\{\langle e, l', \tau \rangle : \langle e, l', \tau \rangle \in \mathcal{M}_S[\![Q_S]\!](r, s, l, \tau)\}, l)$$

– $\mathcal{M}_R$: If Q_R is a query producing a relation, $\mathcal{M}_R[\![Q_R]\!](r, s, l, \tau)$ specifies the bag of tuples in the output relation at time τ that are dominated by level l. Parameters r and s signify the stream and relation lookup functions. If $Q_R = $ RName, $\mathcal{M}_R[\![Q_R]\!](r, s, l, \tau)$ uses function r to look up the time-varying relation corresponding to RName and identifies the bag of tuples at time τ that are dominated by level l. The security level of the bag is l.
$$\mathcal{M}_R[\![\text{RName}]\!] = \lambda r.\lambda s.\lambda l.\lambda \tau.(\{\langle e, l' \rangle : \langle e, l' \rangle \in r(\text{RName})(\tau) \wedge l' \le l\}, l)$$

$$\mathcal{M}_R[\![\text{R2R-Op}(Q_R^1, \ldots, Q_R^n)]\!]$$
$$= \lambda r.\lambda s.\lambda l.\lambda \tau.\mathcal{M}_{R2R}[\![\text{R2R-Op}]\!](\mathcal{M}_R[\![Q_R^1]\!](r, s, l, \tau), \ldots, \mathcal{M}_R[\![Q_R^n]\!](r, s, l, \tau), l)$$

$$\mathcal{M}_R[\![\text{S2R-Op}(Q_S)]\!] = \lambda r.\lambda s.\lambda l.\lambda \tau.\mathcal{M}_{S2R}[\![\text{S2R-Op}]\!](\mathcal{M}_S[\![Q_S]\!](r, s, l, \tau), l, \tau)$$

- $\mathcal{M}_S$: If Q_S is a query producing a stream, $\mathcal{M}_S[\![Q_S]\!](r, s, \tau, l)$ specifies the bag of stream elements in the output stream with timestamp $\leq \tau$ and security level $\leq l$. The security level of the output stream is l.
  $$\mathcal{M}_S[\![\text{SName}]\!] = \lambda r.\lambda s.\lambda l.\lambda \tau.(\{\langle e, l', \tau' \rangle : \langle e, l', \tau' \rangle \in s(\text{SName}) \wedge \tau' \leq \tau \wedge l' \leq l\}, l)$$

$$\mathcal{M}_S[\![\text{R2S-Op}(Q_R)]\!] = \lambda r.\lambda s.\lambda l.\lambda \tau.\mathcal{M}_{R2S}[\![\text{R2S-Op}]\!]((\lambda \tau'.\mathcal{M}_R[\![Q_R]\!](r, s, l, \tau')), l, \tau)$$

4.1   Semantics for Example Operators

We present the abstract syntax for a few example operators. The abstract syntax for these operators presented in BNF like form appears below.

```
S2S-Op ::= StreamShepherd
R2S-Op ::= IStream | DStream | RStream
R2R-Op ::= SemiJoin(i, j) | Filter(i, v)
S2R-Op ::= Now Cond | Range(T) Cond
         | Row(N) Cond
Cond   ::= True | Filter(i, v)
```

- $\mathcal{M}_{S2S}$: We have only one stream-to-stream operator which is the `StreamShepherd`. The `StreamShepherd` operator takes a multilevel trusted stream and a security level as its input and creates a single level stream at the corresponding security level as the output.
  $$\mathcal{M}_{S2S}[\![StreamShepherd]\!] = \lambda SS.\lambda l.(\{\langle e, l' \rangle : \langle e, l' \rangle \in SS \wedge (l' \leq l)\}, l)$$
- $\mathcal{M}_{R2S}$: We have three relation-to-stream operators in SIF-CQL. The `IStream` operator takes a time-varying relation R, security level l, and a time instant τ and streams the new tuples inserted into R at time τ, that is, only those tuples that appear in $R(\tau)$ but not in $R(\tau - 1)$ whose security level is dominated by l. The `DStream` operator streams the tuples that were deleted from R at time τ, that is, tuples that appear in $R(\tau - 1)$ but not in $R(\tau)$. Here again only the tuples whose security level is dominated by l are reported. The `RStream` operator streams all tuples in $R(\tau)$ whose security levels are dominated by l. The security levels of the output streams in each case equals l.
  $$\mathcal{M}_{R2S}[\![\text{IStream}]\!] = \lambda R.\lambda \tau.\lambda l.(\{\langle e, l', \tau' \rangle : \tau' \leq \tau \wedge l' \leq l \wedge \langle e, l' \rangle \in R(\tau) \wedge \langle e, l' \rangle \notin R(\tau - 1)\}, l)$$

  $$\mathcal{M}_{R2S}[\![\text{DStream}]\!] = \lambda R.\lambda l.\lambda \tau.(\{\langle e, l', \tau' \rangle : \tau' \leq \tau \wedge l' \leq l \wedge \langle e, l' \rangle \notin R(\tau) \wedge \langle e, l' \rangle \in R(\tau - 1)\}, l)$$

  $$\mathcal{M}_{R2S}[\![\text{RStream}]\!] = \lambda R.\lambda l.\lambda \tau.(\{\langle e, l', \tau' \rangle : \tau' \leq \tau \wedge l' \leq l \wedge \langle e, l' \rangle \in R(\tau)\}, l)$$

- $\mathcal{M}_{R2R}$: We do not give the semantics of all relational operators, but just present only two as examples. $\texttt{SemiJoin}(i, j)$ performs a semijoin on the ith attribute of its first input with the jth attribute of the second input, where both inputs are bags of tuples together with the security levels of the tuples. $\texttt{Filter}(i, v)$ returns all tuples from its input bag having value v in the ith attribute. The notation $e.i$ denotes the value in the ith attribute of a tuple e.

$\mathcal{M}_{R2R}[\![\texttt{SemiJoin}(i, v)]\!] = \lambda E_1.\lambda E_2.\lambda l.(\{\langle e_1, l_3 \rangle :$
$\quad \langle e_1, l_1 \rangle \in E_1 \wedge (\exists \langle e_2, l_2 \rangle \in E_2 \wedge l_1 \leq l \wedge l_2 \leq l \wedge e_1.i = e_2.j \wedge l_3 = lub(l_1, l_2))\}, l)$

$\mathcal{M}_{R2R}[\![\texttt{Filter}(i, v)]\!] = \lambda E.\lambda l.(\{\langle e, l' \rangle : \langle e, l' \rangle \in E \wedge l' \leq l \wedge e.i = v\}, l)$

- $\mathcal{M}_{S2R}$: We first consider three basic sliding window operators. All three operators take a stream S, a timestamp τ, and security level l as input and return a bag of tuples together with their security levels as output. The $\texttt{Now}$ operator returns the tuples with timestamp τ and security level l' where $l' \leq l$. The $\texttt{Range}$ operator specified with parameter T returns the tuples of S with timestamps in the range $[\tau - T, \tau]$ with security level l' where $l' \leq l$. The $\texttt{Row}$ operator specified using an integer parameter N, returns the N most recent tuples of S with timestamps $\leq \tau$ and security level $\leq l$.

We then augment the basic operators with filtering conditions. The $\texttt{Now Filter}(i, v)$ operator returns the tuples with timestamp τ and security level l' where $l' \leq l$ such that the ith attribute of the tuple equals the value v. The other window operators are augmented with a condition in a similar manner.

$\mathcal{M}_{S2R}[\![\texttt{Now}]\!] = \lambda S.\lambda l.\lambda \tau.(\{\langle e, l' \rangle : \langle e, l', \tau \rangle \in S \wedge (l' \leq l)\}, l)$

$\mathcal{M}_{S2R}[\![\texttt{Now Filter}(i, v)]\!] = \lambda S.\lambda l.\lambda \tau.(\{\langle e, l' \rangle : \langle e, l', \tau, \rangle \in S \wedge (l' \leq l) \wedge (e.i = v)\}, l)$

$\mathcal{M}_{S2R}[\![\texttt{Range}(T)]\!] = \lambda S.\lambda \tau.\lambda l.(\{\langle e, l' \rangle : \langle e, l', \tau \rangle \in S \wedge (l' \leq l) \wedge (\texttt{max}(\tau - T, 0) \leq \tau' \leq \tau)\}, l)$

$\mathcal{M}_{S2R}[\![\texttt{Range}(T) \texttt{ Filter}(i, v)]\!] = \lambda S.\lambda \tau.\lambda l.(\{\langle e, l' \rangle : \langle e, l', \tau \rangle \in S \wedge (l' \leq l)$
$\quad \wedge (\texttt{max}(\tau - T, 0) \leq \tau' \leq \tau) \wedge (e.i = v)\}, l)$

$\mathcal{M}_{S2R}[\![\texttt{Row}(N)]\!] = \lambda S.\lambda \tau.\lambda l.(\{\langle e, l' \rangle : \langle e, l', \tau' \rangle \in S \wedge (l' \leq l) \wedge (\tau' \leq \tau) \wedge (N \geq | \{\langle e, l'', \tau'' \rangle \in S :$
$\quad (\tau' \leq \tau'' \leq \tau) \wedge (l' \leq l) \wedge (l'' \leq l)\} |)\}, l)$

$\mathcal{M}_{S2R}[\![\texttt{Row}(N) \texttt{ Filter}(u, v)]\!] = \lambda S.\lambda \tau.\lambda l.(\{\langle e, l' \rangle : \langle e, l', \tau' \rangle \in S \wedge (l' \leq l) \wedge (\tau' \leq \tau) \wedge$
$\quad (e.i = v) \wedge (N \geq \quad | \{\langle e, l'', \tau'' \rangle \in S : (e.i = v) \wedge (\tau' \leq \tau'' \leq \tau) \wedge (l' \leq l) \wedge (l'' \leq l)\} |)\}, l)$

5 Related Work

DSMS Security: Most works on securing DSMSs [2,12,13,18,19,21] focus on how role-based access control policies can be supported in stream processing. Punctuation-based enforcement of RBAC over data streams is proposed in [21]. Access control policies are transmitted every time using one or more security punctuations before the actual data tuple is transmitted. Query punctuations define the privileges for a CQ. Both punctuations are processed by a special filter operator (stream shield) that is part of the query plan. Punctuations have been used to enforce continuous access control for both data and queries [20,21] where security restrictions can change while the continuous queries are being executed. While security punctuations are used for enforcing dynamic access control, our work in this paper is focused on preventing unauthorized access and illegal information flow. Secure shared continuous query processing is proposed in [2]. The authors present a three-stage framework to enforce access control without introducing special operators, rewriting query plans, or affecting QoS delivery mechanisms. Supporting role-based access control via query rewriting techniques is proposed in [12,13]. To enforce access control policies, query plans are rewritten and policies are mapped to a set of map and filter operations. When a query is activated, the privileges of the query submitter are used to produce the resultant query plan. The architecture proposed in [18] uses a post-query filter to enforce stream level access control policies. The filter applies security policies after query processing but before a user receives the results from the DSMS. Designing DSMS taking into account multilevel security constraints has been addressed by researchers [3,4] and the impact of information flow constraints on the performance has also been presented [30,31].

Chinese Wall Policy and Cloud Computing: Wu et al. [28], show how the Chinese Wall policy, originally proposed by Brewer and Nash [11] and later refined by Sandhu [23] can be used for information flow control in cloud computing. The authors enforce the policies at the Infrastructure-as-a-Service layer and develop a prototype to demonstrate the feasibility of their approach. She et al. [25] provide a protocol for doing access validation during service compositions for ensuring information flow control. Each service is required to specify its information flow policy with respect to the other services in the service-chain. However, the authors shed little light on the structure of the policies themselves. Hung and Qui [17] also address COI issues using Chinese Wall policy. Each COI has a set of operations and each service does not perform more than one operation in the same COI class. However, history information is not maintained which makes COI possible due to interleaved operation invocation by multiple services. Hsiao and Hwang [16] demonstrate how the Chinese Wall can be used in the context of workflows. Shen et al. [26] address COI issues in storage clouds to ensure isolation of data belonging to several companies. If a violation occurs because of data collaboration, the individual tenants have the right to approve or disapprove the violations. Tsai et al. [27] discusses how the Chinese Wall policy can be used to prevent competing organizations virtual machines to be placed on the same physical machine. Graph coloring is used for allocating virtual machines to physical machines such that the Chinese Wall policies are satisfied and better utilization of cloud resources is achieved. In an earlier work [31] we proposed an information flow control model suitable for cloud environments that was adapted from the Chinese Wall policy [23]. Our current work extends this by providing a formal semantics of the language used to express continuous queries with information flow constraints.

6   Conclusions and Future Work

Data streams generated by various organizations in a cloud may need to be analyzed in real-time for detecting critical events of interest. Processing of such data streams should be done in a careful and controlled manner such that company sensitive information is not disclosed to competing organizations. We propose a secure information flow control model, adapted from the Chinese Wall policy, to be used for protecting sensitive company information. We formalized the language for expressing continuous queries using denotational semantics. Our future plans include doing secure processing over encrypted streams and investigating how information flow constraints can be maintained while processing such data.

Acknowledgement. This work was partially supported by the U.S. NSF under Grants No. 0905232, CCF-1018711, by the NIST under Grant No. 70NANB14H059 and by Colorado State University under an internal research grant.

References

1. Abadi, D.J., Ahmad, Y., Balazinska, M., Çetintemel, U., Cherniack, M., Hwang, J., Lindner, W., Maskey, A., Rasin, A., Ryvkina, E., Tatbul, N., Xing, Y., Zdonik, S.B.: The design of the borealis stream processing engine. In: Proceedings of the CIDR, pp. 277–289 (2005)
2. Adaikkalavan, R., Perez, T.: Secure shared continuous query processing. In: Proceedings of the ACM SAC (Data Streams Track), pp. 1005–1011, Taiwan, March 2011
3. Adaikkalavan, R., Ray, I., Xie, X.: Multilevel secure data stream processing. In: Li, Y. (ed.) DBSec. LNCS, vol. 6818, pp. 122–137. Springer, Heidelberg (2011)
4. Adaikkalavan, R., Xie, X., Ray, I.: Multilevel secure data stream processing: architecture and implementation. J. Comput. Secur. **20**(5), 547–581 (2012)
5. Arasu, A., Babcock, B., Babu, S., Cieslewicz, J., Datar, M., Ito, K., Motwani, R., Srivastava, U., Widom, J.: STREAM: The Stanford Data Stream Management System. Technical Report 2004–20, Stanford InfoLab (2004)
6. Arasu, A., Babu, S., Widom, J.: The CQL Continuous Query Language: semantic foundations and query execution. VLDB J. **15**(2), 121–142 (2006)
7. Arasu, A., Widom, J.: A denotational semantics for continuous queries over streams and relations. SIGMOD Rec. **33**, 6–11 (2004)
8. Babcock, B., Babu, S., Datar, M., Motwani, R., Widom, J.: Models and issues in data stream systems. In: Proceedings of the PODS, pp. 1–16, June 2002

328   I. Ray et al.

9. Balakrishnan, H., Balazinska, M., Carney, D., Çetintemel, U., Cherniack, M., Convey, C., Galvez, E., Salz, J., Stonebraker, M., Tatbul, N., Tibbetts, R., Zdonik, S.B.: Retrospective on aurora. VLDB J.: Spec. Issue Data Stream Process. **13**(4), 370–383 (2004)
10. Bell, D.E., LaPadula, L.J.: Secure Computer System: Unified Exposition and MULTICS Interpretation. Technical Report MTR-2997 Rev. 1 and ESD-TR-75-306, rev. 1, The MITRE Corporation, Bedford, MA 01730, March 1976
11. Brewer, D.F.C., Nash, M.J.: The chinese wall security policy. In: Proceedings of the IEEE S & P, pp. 206–214, May 1989
12. Cao, J., Carminati, B., Ferrari, E., Tan, K.: Acstream: enforcing access control over data streams. In: Proceedings of the ICDE, pp. 1495–1498 (2009)
13. Carminati, B., Ferrari, E., Tan, K.L.: Enforcing access control over data streams. In: Proceedings of the ACM SACMAT, pp. 21–30 (2007)
14. Carney, D., Çetintemel, U., Cherniack, M., Convey, C., Lee, S., Seidman, G., Stonebraker, M., Tatbul, N., Zdonik, S.B.: Monitoring streams - a new class of data management applications. In: Proceedings of the VLDB, pp. 215–226, August 2002
15. Chakravarthy, S., Jiang, Q.: Stream Data Processing: A Quality of Service Perspective: Modeling, Scheduling, Load Shedding, and Complex Event Processing. Advances in Database Systems. Springer, Heidelberg (2009)
16. Hsiao, Y.-C., Hwang, G.-H.: Implementing the chinese wall security model in workflow management systems. In: Proceedings of the ISPA, pp. 574–581 (2010)
17. Hung, P.C.K., Qiu, G.-S.: Specifying conflict of interest assertions in WS-policy with chinese wall security policy. SIGecom Exchanges **4**(1), 11–19 (2003)
18. Lindner, W., Meier, J.: Securing the borealis data stream engine. In: Proceedings of the IDEAS, pp. 137–147 (2006)
19. Nehme, R.V., Lim, H., Bertino, E., Rundensteiner, E.A.: StreamShield: a stream-centric approach towards security and privacy in data stream environments. In: Proceedings of the ACM SIGMOD, pp. 1027–1030 (2009)
20. Nehme, R.V., Lim, H.-S., Bertino, E.: Fence: Continuous access control enforcement in dynamic data stream environments. In: Proceedings of the ACM CODASPY 2013, pp. 243–254 (2013)
21. Nehme, R.V., Rundensteiner, E.A., Bertino, E.: A security punctuation framework for enforcing access control on streaming data. In: Proceedings of the ICDE, pp. 406–415 (2008)
22. Pierce, B.C.: The Computer Science and Engineering Handbook. In: Tucker, A.B. (ed.) chapter Foundational Calculi for Programming Languages, pp. 2190–2207. CRC Press, US (1997)
23. Sandhu, R.: Lattice-based enforcement of chinese walls. Comput. Secur. **11**(8), 753–763 (1992)
24. Schmidt, D.A.: Programming language semantics. In: Tucker, A.B. (ed.) The Computer Science and Engineering Handbook, pp. 2237–2254. CRC Press, US (1997)
25. She, W., Yen, I.-L., Thuraisingham, B.M., Bertino, E.: Security-aware service composition with fine-grained information flow control. IEEE TDSC **6**(3), 330–343 (2013)
26. Shen, Q., Yang, X., Sun, P., Yang, Y., Wu, Z.: Towards data isolation & collaboration in storage cloud. In: Proceedings of the APSCC, pp. 139–146 (2011)
27. Tsai, T., Chen, Y., Huang, H., Huang, P., Chou, K.: A practical chinese wall security model in cloud computing. In: Proceedings of the APNOMS, pp. 1–4 (2011)
28. Wu, R., Ahn, G., Hu, H., Singhal, M.: Information flow control in cloud computing. In: Proceedings of the CollaborateCom, pp. 1–7 (2010)

29. Xie, R., Gamble, R.: A tiered strategy for auditing in the cloud. In: IEEE International Conference on Cloud Computing, June 2012
30. Xie, X., Ray, I., Adaikkalavan, R.: On the efficient processing of multilevel secure continuous queries. In: Proceedings of Social Computing, pp. 417–422 (2013)
31. Xie, X., Ray, I., Adaikkalavan, R., Gamble, R.: Information flow control for stream processing in clouds. In: Proceedings of the ACM SACMAT, pp. 89–100 (2013)

Optimal Constructions for Chain-Based Cryptographic Enforcement of Information Flow Policies

Jason Crampton$^{(\boxtimes)}$, Naomi Farley, Gregory Gutin, and Mark Jones

Royal Holloway, University of London, London, UK
jason.crampton@rhul.ac.uk

Abstract. The simple security property in an information flow policy can be enforced by encrypting data objects and distributing an appropriate secret to each user. A user derives a suitable decryption key from the secret and publicly available information. A chain-based enforcement scheme provides an alternative method of cryptographic enforcement that does not require any public information, the trade-off being that a user may require more than one secret. For a given information flow policy, there will be many different possible chain-based enforcement schemes. In this paper, we provide a polynomial-time algorithm for selecting a chain-based scheme which uses the minimum possible number of secrets. We also compute the number of secrets that will be required and establish an upper bound on the number of secrets required by any user.

1 Introduction

Access control is a fundamental security service in modern computing systems and seeks to restrict the interactions between users of the system and the resources provided by the system. Generally speaking, access control is policy-based, in the sense that a policy is defined by the resource owner(s) specifying those interactions that are authorized. An attempt by a user to interact with a protected resource, typically called an *access request*, is evaluated by a trusted software component, the *policy decision point* (or *authorization decision function*), to determine whether the request should be permitted (if authorized) or denied (otherwise). The use of a policy decision point is entirely appropriate when we can assume the policy will be enforced by the same organization that defined it. However, use of third-party storage, privacy policies controlling access to personal data, and digital rights management all give rise to scenarios where this assumption does not hold.

An alternative approach to policy enforcement, and one that has attracted considerable interest in recent years, is to encrypt the protected object and enable authorized users to derive decryption keys. This approach is particularly suitable for data that changes infrequently, for read-only policies, and for policies that can be represented in terms of user attributes. Research into cryptographic access

© IFIP International Federation for Information Processing 2015
P. Samarati (Ed.): DBSec 2015, LNCS 9149, pp. 330–345, 2015.
DOI: 10.1007/978-3-319-20810-7_23

control began with the seminal work of Akl and Taylor [2] on the enforcement of information flow policies, and has seen a resurgence of interest in recent years.

Generally, it is undesirable to provide a user with all the keys she requires to decrypt protected objects. Instead, a user is given a small number of secrets from which she is able to derive all keys required. Thus a cryptographic enforcement scheme may be characterized by (i) the number of secrets each user has to store, (ii) the total number of secrets, (iii) the amount of auxiliary (public) information required for key derivation, and (iv) the amount of time required for key derivation.

Many schemes in the literature provide each user with a single secret [3,11], the trade-off being that the amount of public information and derivation time may be substantial. In contrast, chain-based schemes require no public information but each user may require more than one secret [9,14,15]. In addition, chain-based schemes can achieve very strong security properties [15]. There are many different ways to instantiate a chain-based scheme for a given policy, each instantiation being defined by a chain partition of the partially ordered set that defines the policy.

However, existing work on chain-based CESs assumes the existence of a chain partition and simply generates the required secrets and keys for this partition [9,14,15]. This approach ignores the fact that there will be (exponentially) many choices of chain partition. Thus, it is important, if we are to make best use of chain-based CESs, that we know which chain partition to use for a given information flow policy. It is this issue that we address in this paper.

Contributions. Our first contribution (Theorem 2) is to show how $\widehat{K}(\Pi)$, the (total) number of secrets for a chain partition Π, is related to the set of edges in the representation of Π as an acyclic directed graph. We then prove that $\widehat{K}(\Pi)$ is determined by the end-points of the chains in Π (Lemma 2). This, in turn, allows us to prove there exists a chain partition that simultaneously minimizes the number of secrets required and the number of chains in the partition (Theorem 3). The last result is somewhat unexpected, as it is not usually possible to simultaneously minimize two different parameters. The result is also of practical importance, since the number of chains in Π provides a tight upper bound on the number of secrets required by any one user. Our main contribution (Theorem 1 and Sect. 4) is to develop a polynomial-time algorithm that enables us to find a chain partition Π such that $\widehat{K}(\Pi)$ and the number of chains is minimized (with respect to all chain partitions). Our algorithm is based on finding an optimal feasible flow in a network and makes use of the characterization of the number of secrets in terms of the set of edges (established in Theorem 2) to define the capacities of the edges in the network. We thereby provide rigorous foundations for the development of efficient chain-based enforcement schemes.

Paper structure. In the next section, we provide the relevant background on cryptographic enforcement schemes, formally define the problem, and state Theorem 1. In Sect. 3, we state and prove Theorems 2 and 3 and Lemma 2. In Sect. 4, we develop an efficient algorithm to derive the best chain partition and prove

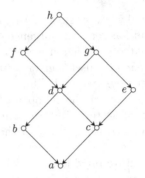

Fig. 1. The Hasse diagram of a simple poset

Theorem 1. We conclude the paper with a summary of our contributions and some ideas for future work.

2 Background and Problem Statement

A *partially ordered set* (or *poset*) is a pair $(X, \leqslant)$, where $\leqslant$ is a reflexive, antisymmetric, transitive binary relation on X. We may write $x \geqslant y$ whenever $y \leqslant x$, and $y < x$ whenever $y \leqslant x$ and $y \neq x$. Given a poset $(X, \leqslant)$, it is convenient to introduce the following notation.

$$\downarrow x \stackrel{\text{def}}{=} \{y \in X : y \leqslant x\} \qquad \text{and} \qquad \uparrow x \stackrel{\text{def}}{=} \{y \in X : y \geqslant x\}$$

We will also make use of the following terminology and notation.

- We say x *covers* y, denoted $y \lessdot x$, if $y < x$ and there does not exist $z \in X$ such that $y < z < x$. We say y is a *child* of x if $y \lessdot x$ (and x is a *parent* of y).
- The *Hasse diagram* of a poset is the directed acyclic graph $H = (X, E_0)$, where $xy \in E_0$ if and only if $y \lessdot x$.
- X is a *tree* if no element of X has more than one parent and X has a unique maximum element.
- $Y \subseteq X$ is a *chain* (or *total order*) if for $x, y \in Y$, $x < y$ or $x = y$ or $y < x$. $\{C_1, \ldots, C_\ell\}$ is a *chain partition* (of $(X, \leqslant)$) if $C_i \subseteq X$ is a chain, $C_i \cap C_j = \emptyset$ if $i \neq j$, and $C_1 \cup \cdots \cup C_\ell = X$.
- $Y \subseteq X$ is an *antichain* if for $x, y \in Y$, $x \leqslant y$ if and only if $x = y$. (In other words, for $x \neq y$ in an antichain, $x \not\leqslant y$ and $y \not\leqslant x$.) The *width* of a poset is the cardinality of an antichain of maximum size.

An illustrative Hasse diagram is shown in Fig. 1. In the poset depicted, $\{a, d, f\}$ is a chain, for example, and $\{d, e\}$ is an antichain of maximum size. Thus the width of this poset is 2 and one chain partition of cardinality 2 is $\{\{a, c, e, g, h\}, \{b, d, f\}\}$.

Definition 1. *An* information flow policy *is a tuple* $(X, \leqslant, U, O, \lambda)$, *where:*

- $(X, \leqslant)$ is a (finite) partially ordered set of *security labels*;
- U is a set of *users* and O is a set of *objects*;
- $\lambda : U \cup O \to X$ is a *security function* that associates users and objects with security labels.

The simple security property *requires that user* $u \in U$ can read an object $o \in O$ if and only if $\lambda(u) \geqslant \lambda(o)$.

We may define an equivalence relation $\sim$ on U, where $u \sim v$ if and only if $\lambda(u) = \lambda(v)$. We write U_x to denote $\{u \in U : \lambda(u) = x\}$; U is partitioned into the set of equivalence classes $\{U_x : x \in X\}$. Similarly, $O_x \subseteq O$ is the set of objects having security label $x \in X$. Thus, the simple security property guarantees that any $o \in O_x$ can be read by a user $u \in U_y$ for any $y \geqslant x$. Conversely, $u \in U_y$ can read $o \in O_x$ for any $x \leqslant y$. Henceforth, we will represent an information flow policy $(X, \leqslant, U, O, \lambda)$ as a pair $(X, \leqslant)$ with the tacit understanding that U, O and λ are given.

2.1   Cryptographic Enforcement of Information Flow Policies

One way of enforcing the simple security property (for policy $(X, \leqslant)$) is to encrypt $o \in O_y$ with a (symmetric) key $k(y)$ and provide all users in U_x, where $x \geqslant y$ with the key $k(y)$. An alternative is to provide a user u in U_x with a smaller number of keys (typically a single key for label x) and enable u to derive keys for all y such that $y < x$. However, this introduces the possibility that users may be able to collude and use their keys to derive a key that no single user could derive.

More formally, there exists the notion of a *cryptographic enforcement scheme* (CES), defined by the SetUp and Derive algorithms, SetUp being used to generate secrets and keys and the data used to derive secrets and keys, and Derive being used to compute secrets and keys. Let $\mathcal{K}$ denote an arbitrary key space (typically $\mathcal{K} = \{0, 1\}^l$ for some $l \in \mathbb{N}$). Then SetUp and Derive have the following characteristics.

- SetUp takes as input a security parameter ρ and information flow policy $(X, \leqslant)$. It outputs, for each element $x \in X$, a pair $(\sigma(x), \kappa(x))$: the *secret* $\sigma(x)$ is given to all users in U_x; $\sigma(x)$ is used to derive secrets and/or keys for labels $y \leqslant x$; and the *key* $\kappa(x) \in \mathcal{K}$ is used to encrypt data objects in O_x.
  The SetUp algorithm also outputs a set of public information Pub, which is used for the derivation of secrets and keys.
- Derive takes as input $(X, \leqslant)$, Pub, start and end points $x, y \in X$ and $\sigma(x)$. It outputs $\kappa(y) \in \mathcal{K}$ if and only if $y \leqslant x$. (In particular, $\kappa(x)$ can be derived from $\sigma(x)$.)

The requirement that Derive outputs $\kappa(y)$ (given $\sigma(x)$) if $y \leqslant x$ is a correctness criterion, which ensures an authorized user can derive the keys required to decrypt objects. We also require a security criterion. Informally, the *strong key-indistinguishability* criterion requires the following.

There is no polynomial time algorithm, given $z \in X$, a set of secrets $\sigma(Y) = \{\sigma(y) : y \in Y\}$ such that $z \not\leqslant y$ for any $y \in Y$, and $\kappa(x)$ for all $x \neq z$ (and the public information Pub), that can distinguish between $\kappa(z)$ and a random key in $\mathcal{K}$.

That is, an adversary cannot distinguish a key from random unless it may be computed from one of the secrets or keys known to the adversary (which implies, in particular, that the adversary can only compute such a key if it can be computed from one of those secrets); see Freire et al. [15] for further details.

2.2   Chain-Based Enforcement

For certain classes of cryptographic enforcement schemes, public information is not required. In particular, if X is a chain, then (by definition) there is a unique directed path from x to y (in the Hasse diagram of X) whenever $y < x$. Then for $y \lessdot x$, we may define the secret $\sigma(y)$ to be $F(\sigma(x))$, and $\kappa(y) = H(\sigma(y))$, where F and H are suitable one-way functions. Thus, if $y < x$, there exist $z_1, \ldots, z_\ell \in X$ with $y = z_1 \lessdot z_2 \lessdot \cdots \lessdot z_\ell = x$; $\kappa(y)$ may be derived from $\sigma(x)$ by iteratively deriving $\sigma(z_i) = F(\sigma(z_{i+1}))$, $i = \ell - 1, \ldots, 1$, and then deriving $\kappa(y) = H(\sigma(y)) = H(\sigma(z_1))$.

This observation has led to the development of chain-based CESs [9,14,15] for arbitrary information flow policies. The basic idea is to partition the information flow policy $(X, \leqslant)$ into chains and then construct multiple CESs, one for each chain.

More formally, let $(X, \leqslant)$ be a poset and $C = x_1 > x_2 > \cdots > x_m$ be a chain in X. Then we say any chain of the form $x_j > x_{j+1} > \cdots > x_m$, $1 \leqslant j \leqslant m$, is a *suffix* of C; the empty chain is (vacuously) also a suffix of C.

Proposition 1. *For all $x \in X$ and any chain $C \subseteq X$, $\downarrow x \cap C$ is a suffix of C.*

The above result (due to Crampton et al [9, Proposition 4]) enables us to define, for a given chain partition Π, the secrets that should be given to a user $u \in U_x$, since $\downarrow x$ defines the labels for which u is authorized. Given a chain partition $\Pi = \{C_1, \ldots, C_\ell\}$, $\{\downarrow x \cap C_1, \ldots, \downarrow x \cap C_\ell\}$ is a disjoint collection of chain suffixes. Hence, a user in U_x must be given the secrets for the maximal elements in the non-empty suffixes $\downarrow x \cap C_1, \ldots, \downarrow x \cap C_\ell$. Thus, any user requires at most ℓ secrets. Let $\phi(x, \Pi) \subseteq X$ denote this set of maximal elements. (Clearly, $x \in \phi(x, \Pi)$ for all chain partitions Π and all $x \in X$.)

Remark 1. Let w be the width of a poset $(X, \leqslant)$. Clearly, $(X, \leqslant)$ cannot have a chain partition with less than w chains. Dilworth's theorem asserts that there exists a chain partition of $(X, \leqslant)$ into w chains [13]. Thus, if we can find a chain partition of X into w chains, no user will require more than w secrets. (If u were to have more secrets than there are chains in the partition, then there must exist a chain containing y and z for which u has secrets and one of the secrets may be derived from the other.)

Freire *et al* [15] provide a formal description of the SetUp and Derive algorithms. Informally, the SetUp algorithm performs the following steps:

1. For each chain C_i in Π, select a secret for the top element in C_i and generate a secret for each element in the chain by applying the one-way function F to the secret of its parent in C_i;
2. For each element $x \in X$, generate $\kappa(x)$ by applying the one-way function H to $\sigma(x)$;
3. Assign the secrets $\sigma(\phi(x, \Pi)) \overset{\text{def}}{=} \{\sigma(z) : z \in \phi(x, \Pi)\}$ to each user in U_x.

The Derive algorithm performs the following steps, given $x, y \in X$ and $\sigma(\phi(x, \Pi))$:

1. if $x = y$, then output $H(\sigma(x))$;
2. if $y < x$, then find $z \in \phi(x, \Pi)$ such that $z \geqslant y$, so there exist $z = z_0 >_\Pi \cdots >_\Pi z_t = y$, and compute $F(\sigma(z_0)) = \sigma(z_1), \ldots, F(\sigma(z_{t-1})) = \sigma(y)$; output $H(\sigma(y))$.

This scheme has the strong key-indistinguishability property; see Freire *et al* [15] for further details.

A user in U_x will need to be given $|\phi(x, \Pi)|$ secrets, in contrast to most CESs in the literature in which each user receives a single secret [3, 11]. However, chain-based CESs have substantial benefits: (i) they require no public information [9]; (ii) they can use cryptographic primitives that are very easy to compute; and (iii) it is easy to construct schemes with the strong key-indistinguishability property [15].

2.3   Problem Statement

Certain aspects of chain-based CESs are not well understood. As we have already noted, some users will require multiple secrets, each of which corresponds to a unique label in X. In particular, a user u in U_x will require a secret for each chain that contains an element y such that $y < x$. Three chain partitions of the poset in Fig. 1 are shown in Fig. 2. We have, for example, $\phi(g, \Pi_1) = \{b, e, g\}$, $\phi(g, \Pi_2) = \{b, d, g\}$, and $\phi(g, \Pi_3) = \{d, g\}$. Hence, the number of secrets required, on a per-user basis and in total, will vary, depending on the chain partition chosen. Thus, considering various chain partitions of X, we may ask:

- How do we minimize $k_{\max}$, the maximum number of secrets a user may require?
- How do we minimize K, the total number of secrets required?
- How do we minimize $\widehat{K}$, the total number of secrets that need to be issued to users?

More formally, given a chain partition Π of $(X, \leqslant)$, we may regard ϕ as a function from X to 2^X that is completely determined by Π. Thus, given a chain partition Π, we can define the following values.

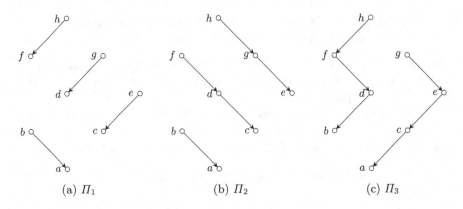

(a) Π_1 (b) Π_2 (c) Π_3

Fig. 2. Three chain partitions of the poset in Fig. 1

$$k_{\max}(\Pi) \overset{\text{def}}{=} \max\{|\phi(x,\Pi)| : x \in X\}$$

$$K(\Pi) \overset{\text{def}}{=} \sum_{x \in X} |\phi(x,\Pi)|$$

$$\widehat{K}(\Pi) \overset{\text{def}}{=} \sum_{x \in X} |U_x| \cdot |\phi(x,\Pi)|$$

Values of $k_{\max}$ and K for the chain partitions in Fig. 2 are shown in Table 1; node h is used for illustrative purposes.[1]

Table 1. $\phi(h)$, $k_{\max}$ and K for the chain partitions in Fig. 2

Partition	$\phi(h)$	$k_{\max}$	K
Π_1	$\{b,e,g,h\}$	4	20
Π_2	$\{b,f,h\}$	3	17
Π_3	$\{g,h\}$	2	13

The important question is: Can we minimize these parameters (over all choices of chain partition Π for X)? In short, given an information flow policy $(X, \leqslant)$, how do we determine Π for use in a chain-based CES?[2] It is this question we address in the remainder of the paper. In particular, at the end of Sect. 4, we prove the following result.

---

[1] Note that we can deduce K from $\widehat{K}$ by letting $|U_x| = 1$ for all $x \in X$.

[2] Crampton *et al* [9] observed that further research was needed to identify the best choice of chain partition for a given information flow policy. While subsequent research has formalized [14] and strengthened the security properties of chain-based CESs [15], we are not aware of any research that specifies how to select a chain partition.

Theorem 1. *Let* $(X, \leqslant)$ *be an information flow policy of width* w *and let* $\widehat{K}$ *denote the minimum number of secrets required by a chain-based enforcement scheme for* X. *Then in* $O(|X|^4 w)$ *time, we can find a chain partition* Π *for which the corresponding chain-based enforcement scheme only requires* $\widehat{K}$ *secrets and* $k_{\max} \leqslant w$.

Remark 2. We assume throughout that our information flow policy has a maximum element. We may assume this without loss of generality: given an information flow policy $(X, \leqslant)$ without a maximum element, we simply add a maximum element r and define $r > m$ for all maximal elements m in X; no users are assigned to r. Observe that such a transformation does not affect the values of $k_{\max}$ and $\widehat{K}$.

3   Computing $k_{\max}$ and $\widehat{K}$

Informally, we take a poset $(X, \leqslant)$ and construct a second poset $(X, \leqslant')$, where $x <' y$ implies $x < y$ (but $x < y$ does not necessarily imply $x <' y$). We will say $\leqslant'$ is *contained* in $\leqslant$. In particular, any chain partition Π of $(X, \leqslant)$ defines a second poset $(X, \leqslant_\Pi)$, where $x <_\Pi y$ if and only if x and y belong to the same chain and $x < y$; thus $\leqslant_\Pi$ is contained in $\leqslant$ for any Π. Note, however, that $x <_\Pi y$ does not necessarily imply $x \lessdot y$.[3]

Given a poset $(X, \leqslant)$ and $z < y$, we define

$$\gamma(yz) = \{x \in X : x \geqslant z, x \not\geqslant y\}.$$

Thus $z \in \gamma(yz)$ and $y \notin \gamma(yz)$. For the maximum element $r \in X$ and any $y, z \in X$ such that $z < y$, $r \notin \gamma(yz)$. Informally, the intuition behind γ is that its cardinality measures the "damage" that would be done by creating a chain partition Π such that $z <_\Pi y$, because having $z <_\Pi y$ means that $z \not\leqslant_\Pi x$ for any $x \in \gamma(yz)$. Thus, every user in U_x will require an extra secret in order to derive $\kappa(z)$. We will capture this intuition more precisely in Lemma 1.

Remark 3. For maximum element r and any chain partition $\Pi = \{C_1, \ldots, C_\ell\}$, $\phi(r, \Pi) = \{t_1, \ldots, t_\ell\}$, where t_i is the maximum element in chain C_i. Moreover, $r = t_i$ for some i. Hence, we can construct a tree $\widetilde{\Pi} = (X, \leqslant_{\widetilde{\Pi}})$, where $y <_{\widetilde{\Pi}} x$ if and only if one of the following conditions holds: (i) $y = t_j$, $j \neq i$, and $x = r$; (ii) $y <_\Pi x$.

Figure 3 illustrates the construction of two such trees, using chain partitions from Fig. 2; the arcs used to create the trees are shown as dashed lines.

Lemma 1. *Let* $(X, \leqslant)$ *be a poset and let* Π *be a chain partition of* X. *Then, for all* $x, y, z \in X$ *such that* $x \neq r$ *and* $z <_{\widetilde{\Pi}} y$,

$$z \in \phi(x, \Pi) \text{ if and only if } x \in \gamma(yz).$$

---

[3] To see this, consider the poset of four elements, in which $a \lessdot b \lessdot d$ and $a \lessdot c \lessdot d$ with $b \not\leqslant c, c \not\leqslant b$. Then $\{\{b\}, \{c\}, \{a, d\}\}$ is a chain partition and $a <_\Pi d$, but $a \not\lessdot d$.

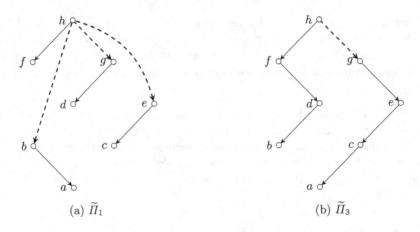

Fig. 3. Creating trees from partitions Π_1 and Π_3 in Fig. 2

Proof. Given $z \in \phi(x, \Pi)$ and chain partition $\Pi = \{C_1, \ldots, C_\ell\}$, $y_i \in \phi(x, \Pi) \cap C_i$ if and only if $C_i \cap \downarrow x$ is non-empty and y_i is the maximum element in $C_i \cap \downarrow x$ (Sect. 2.3). Thus, $z \leqslant x$. Moreover, $x \not\geqslant y$ (otherwise there would exist $t \in \phi(x)$ such that $y \leqslant_{\widetilde{\Pi}} t$ and hence $z <_{\widetilde{\Pi}} y \leqslant_{\widetilde{\Pi}} t$, violating the condition that z is the maximum element in the suffix $C_i \cap \downarrow x$). That is, $x \in \gamma(yz)$.

Now suppose $x \in \gamma(yz)$. Then $x \not\geqslant y$, by definition, and hence y does not belong to $\downarrow x \cap C_i$ for any i. However, $x \geqslant z$; hence, there exists $t \in \phi(x)$ such that $z \leqslant_{\widetilde{\Pi}} t$. Since Π is a chain partition, the only parent of z in $\widetilde{\Pi}$ is y. Hence it must be the case that $z = t$ (and thus $z \in \phi(x)$). $\qquad\square$

Let $(X, \leqslant)$ be an information flow policy and let $y, z \in X$ with $z < y$. Then, following Crampton *et al* [10], we define

$$\omega(yz) \stackrel{\text{def}}{=} \sum_{x \in \gamma(yz)} |U_x|.$$

We will be interested in minimizing the $\sum \omega(yz)$, where the sum is taken over all pairs (y, z) such that $z <_{\widetilde{\Pi}} y$. The intuition behind this definition is that it captures, in some appropriate sense, the connectivity that is lost from $(X, \leqslant)$ by using $(X, \leqslant_\Pi)$. Since every element in $(X, \leqslant_\Pi)$ has at most one parent, $\gamma(yz)$ represents those elements in X that become "disconnected" from z by defining $z <_\Pi y$. The next result establishes an exact correspondence between $\phi(x, \Pi)$ and $\gamma(yz)$, and enables us to use network flow techniques to compute a chain partition that minimizes $\widehat{K}$ (as we explain in Sect. 4).

Theorem 2. *Let $(X, \leqslant_\Pi)$ be a chain partition of $(X, \leqslant)$ with maximum element r. Then*

$$\widehat{K}(\Pi) = \ell \, |U_r| + \sum_{z <_{\widetilde{\Pi}} y} \omega(yz).$$

where ℓ is the number of chains in Π.

Proof. By definition,

$$\widehat{K}(\Pi) = \sum_{x \in X} |U_x| |\phi(x, \Pi)| = |U_r| |\phi(r, \Pi)| + \sum_{x \in X \setminus r} \sum_{z \in X} |U_x| \delta(x, z),$$

where $\delta(x, z)$ equals 1 if $z \in \phi(x, \Pi)$ and 0 otherwise. By Lemma 1, we have $\delta(x, z) = 1$ if and only if $x \in \gamma(yz)$ for $z \lessdot_{\widetilde{\Pi}} y$. Moreover, y is unique, since $\widetilde{\Pi}$ is a tree. Therefore,

$$\sum_{x \in X \setminus r} \sum_{z \in X} |U_x| \delta(x, z) = \sum_{z \lessdot_{\widetilde{\Pi}} y} \sum_{x \in \gamma(yz)} |U_x| = \sum_{z \lessdot_{\widetilde{\Pi}} y} \omega(yz)$$

As $r \geqslant x$ for all $x \in X$, $\phi(r, \Pi)$ must contain exactly one element from each chain in Π. Therefore $|U_r| |\phi(r, \Pi)| = \ell |U_r|$, as required. $\qquad\square$

The following result shows that the number of secrets required by a chain partition can be computed by considering only the minimum elements in the chain partition.

Lemma 2. *Let $\Pi = \{C_1, \ldots, C_\ell\}$ be a chain partition of $(X, \leqslant)$ and let chain C_i have bottom element b_i, $1 \leqslant i \leqslant \ell$. Then*

$$K(\Pi) = \sum_{i=1}^{\ell} |\uparrow b_i| \qquad and \qquad \widehat{K}(\Pi) = \sum_{i=1}^{\ell} \sum_{x \in \uparrow b_i} |U_x|.$$

Proof. We have, by definition,

$$\widehat{K}(\Pi) = \sum_{x \in X} |U_x| |\phi(x, \Pi)| = \sum_{x \in X} |U_x| |\{C_i : C_i \cap \downarrow x \neq \emptyset, 1 \leqslant i \leqslant \ell\}|$$

$$= \sum_{x \in X} |U_x| |\{b_i : x \geqslant b_i, 1 \leqslant i \leqslant \ell\}|$$

$$= \sum_{x \in X} \sum_{i=1}^{\ell} |U_x| \delta(x, b_i) \qquad \text{where } \delta(x, b_i) = 1 \text{ if } x \geqslant b_i \text{ and 0 otherwise}$$

$$= \sum_{i=1}^{\ell} \sum_{x \in X} |U_x| \delta(x, b_i) = \sum_{i=1}^{\ell} \sum_{x \in \uparrow b_i} |U_x|$$

Clearly, we may prove the result for K in an analogous fashion. $\qquad\square$

In Fig. 2a, for example, the bottom elements are a, c, d and f and $|\uparrow a| = 8$, $|\uparrow c| = 6$, $|\uparrow d| = 4$ and $|\uparrow f| = 2$. Thus, the number of secrets required in total is 20.

Theorem 3. *Let $(X, \leqslant)$ be an information flow policy of width w and let $\widehat{K}$ denote the minimum number of secrets required by a chain-based enforcement scheme for X. Then there exists a chain partition containing w chains such that $\widehat{K}(\Pi) = \widehat{K}$.*

Proof. Let Π be a chain partition of X into $t \geqslant w$ chains such that $\widehat{K}(\Pi) = \widehat{K}$ and let B be the set of bottom vertices in the chains of Π. A result of Gallai and Milgram asserts that if a chain partition Π of a poset $(X, \leqslant)$ contains t chains, where $t > w$, then there exists a chain partition Π' into $t - 1$ chains such that the set of bottom vertices in Π' is a subset of B [16].[4] Hence, by iterated applications of the Gallai-Milgram result, there exists a chain partition Π^* of width w such that the set of bottom vertices B^* in Π^* is a subset of B. Moreover, by Lemma 2,

$$\widehat{K}(\Pi^*) = \sum_{b \in B^*} \sum_{x \in \uparrow b} |U_x| \leqslant \sum_{b \in B} \sum_{x \in \uparrow b} |U_x|$$

By the minimality of $\widehat{K}$, we deduce that $\widehat{K}(\Pi^*) = \widehat{K}$.   □

Corollary 1. *Let $(X, \leqslant)$ be an information flow policy. There exists a chain partition such that the total number of secrets $\widehat{K}$ is minimized and $k_{\max} \leqslant w$.*

Proof. The result follows immediately from Theorem 3, the definition of $k_{\max} = \max \{|\phi(x, \Pi)| : x \in X\}$, and the fact that $|\phi(x, \Pi)|$ is bounded above by the number of chains in Π for all $x \in X$.   □

4   Finding a Chain Partition Requiring $\widehat{K}$ Keys

Suppose $(X, \leqslant)$ is a poset of width w. In general, a chain partition of X has $\ell \geqslant w$ chains. Theorem 3 asserts that there exists a partition of X into w chains such that the corresponding enforcement scheme requires the minimum number of secrets. We now show how such a chain partition may be constructed. In particular, we show how to transform the problem of finding a chain partition Π such that $\widehat{K}(\Pi)$ attains the minimum value into a problem of finding a minimum cost flow in a network.

Informally, a *network* is a directed graph in which each edge is associated with a *capacity*. A *network flow* associates each edge in a given network with a flow, which must not exceed the capacity of the edge. Networks are widely used to model systems in which some quantity passes through channels (edges in the network) that meet at junctions (vertices); examples include traffic in a road system, fluids in pipes, or electrical current in circuits. In our setting, we model an information flow policy as a network in which the capacities are determined by the weights ω. Our definitions for networks and network flows follow the presentation of Bang-Jensen and Gutin [5].

Definition 2. *A network is a tuple $\mathcal{N} = (D, l, u, c, b)$, where:*

- *$D = (V, A)$ is a directed graph with vertex set V and arc set A;*
- *$l : V \times V \to \mathbb{N}$ such that $l(vv') = 0$ if $vv' \notin A$ and $l(vv') \geqslant 0$ otherwise;*

---

[4] The result is phrased in the language of digraphs, but every poset may be represented by an equivalent transitive acyclic digraph.

- $u : V \times V \to \mathbb{N}$ such that $u(vv') = 0$ if $vv' \notin A$ and $u(vv') \geqslant l(vv') \geqslant 0$ otherwise;
- $c : V \times V \to \mathbb{R}$;
- $b : V \to \mathbb{R}$ such that $\sum_{v \in V} b(v) = 0$.

Intuitively, l and u represent lower and upper bounds, respectively, on how much flow can pass through each arc, and c represents the cost associated with each unit of flow in each arc. The function b represents how much flow should enter or leave the network at a given vertex. If $b(x) = 0$, then the flow going into x should be equal to the flow going out of x. If $b(x) > 0$, then there should be $b(x)$ more flow coming out of x than going into x. If $b(x) < 0$, there should be $|b(x)|$ more flow going into x than coming out of x.

Definition 3. Given a network $\mathcal{N} = (D, l, u, c, b)$, a function $f : V \to \mathbb{N}$ is a *feasible flow* for $\mathcal{N}$ if the following conditions are satisfied:

- $u(vv') \geqslant f(vv') \geqslant l(vv')$ for every $vv' \in V \times V$;
- $\sum_{v' \in V} (f(vv') - f(v'v)) = b(v)$ for every $v \in V$.

The *cost* of f is defined to be

$$\sum_{vv' \in A} c(vv') f(vv').$$

Our aim is to find a tree $\widetilde{\Pi}$ such that Π is a chain partition of X with w chains that minimizes $\widehat{K}$. To do this, we will construct a network $\mathcal{N}$ such that the minimum cost flow of $\mathcal{N}$ corresponds to the desired tree. We can then find the minimum cost flow of $\mathcal{N}$ in polynomial time.

In $\widetilde{\Pi}$, we want every vertex except r to have at most one parent and at most one child. We cannot represent this requirement directly in a network. However, we can use the *vertex splitting procedure* [5] to simulate it. Specifically, given poset $(X, \leqslant)$, define $X_{in} = \{x_{in} : x \in X \setminus \{r\}\}$ and $X_{out} = \{x_{out} : x \in X\}$; and define $v' \prec v$ if and only if either $v = x_{in}$ and $v' = x_{out}$ for some $x \in X \setminus r$, or $v = x_{out}$ and $v' = y_{in}$ for some $x, y \in X$ such that $y < x$. We now add a minimum element $\perp$, where $\perp \prec x_{out}$ for all $x \in X$.

Then define $D = (X_{in} \cup X_{out} \cup \{\perp\}, A)$, where $xy \in A$ if and only if $y \prec x$, and the network (D, l, u, c, b), where

$$l(vv') = \begin{cases} 1 & \text{if } v = x_{in}, v' = x_{out}, x \in X \setminus r \\ 0 & \text{otherwise;} \end{cases}$$

$$u(vv') = \begin{cases} 1 & \text{if } v' \prec v \\ 0 & \text{otherwise;} \end{cases}$$

$$c(vv') = \begin{cases} w(xy) & \text{if } v = x_{out}, v' = y_{in}, y \leqslant x \\ 0 & \text{otherwise;} \end{cases}$$

$$b(v) = \begin{cases} w & \text{if } v = r_{out} \\ -w & \text{if } v = \perp \\ 0 & \text{otherwise.} \end{cases}$$

We call this network the *network chain-representation of* $(X, \leqslant)$. Note that any feasible flow f for this network must have $0 \leqslant f(xy) \leqslant 1$ for all $xy \in A$.

Lemma 3. *Let* $\mathcal{N}$ *be the network chain-representation of poset* $(X, \leqslant)$*. Then the minimum number of secrets required by a chain-based enforcement scheme for* $(X, \leqslant)$ *with* w *chains is* $w\,|U_r| + \widehat{f}$*, where* $\widehat{f}$ *is the minimum cost of a feasible flow in* $\mathcal{N}$.

Proof. Suppose we are given a chain partition Π with w chains. Then we may construct the tree $\widetilde{\Pi}$. Consider the following flow:

$$
\begin{aligned}
f(x_{\mathrm{in}}x_{\mathrm{out}}) &= 1 && \text{for all } x \in X \setminus r; \\
f(x_{\mathrm{out}}y_{\mathrm{in}}) &= 1 && \text{if } y <_{\widetilde{\Pi}} x; \\
f(x_{\mathrm{out}}\bot) &= 1 && \text{if } x \text{ is a bottom element in a chain in } \Pi; \\
f &= 0 && \text{otherwise.}
\end{aligned}
$$

Then we can show that f is a feasible flow. Indeed, by construction all arcs xy satisfy $u(xy) \geqslant f(xy) \geqslant l(xy)$. In the graph formed by arcs xy with $f(xy) = 1$, it is clear that every vertex x has in-degree and out-degree 1, except for r_{out} and $\bot$. As there is one element y such that $y <_{\widetilde{\Pi}} r$ for each chain in Π, r_{out} has in-degree 0 and out-degree w in this graph, and similarly $\bot$ has in-degree w and out-degree 0. As all arcs xy have $f(xy) = 1$ or $f(xy) = 0$, we have that

$$
\sum_{v \in V(D)} (f(xv) - f(vx)) = b(x)
$$

for all x, as required. Moreover, the cost of f equals $\sum_{x <_{\widetilde{\Pi}} y} w(yx)$.

Conversely, suppose f is a feasible flow for $\mathcal{N}$. Then we define $y <_f x$ if and only if $f(x_{\mathrm{out}}, y_{\mathrm{in}}) = 1$. For each $x \in X \setminus r$, the arc $x_{\mathrm{in}}x_{\mathrm{out}}$ is the only in-coming arc for x_{out} and the only out-going arc for x_{in} in D, and by definition of $\mathcal{N}$, $f(x_{\mathrm{in}}x_{\mathrm{out}}) = 1$. As $b(x_{\mathrm{in}}) = b(x_{\mathrm{out}}) = 0$ and all in-coming arcs for x_{in} are of the form $y_{\mathrm{out}}x_{\mathrm{in}}$, it follows that there is exactly one element $y \in X$ such that $x <_f y$, and at most one element $z \in X$ such that $z <_f x$. As $b(r_{\mathrm{out}}) = w$ and r_{out} has no in-coming arcs in D, and all its out-going arcs are of the form $r_{\mathrm{out}}x_{\mathrm{in}}$, there are exactly w elements y such that $y <_f r$. Let these elements be labelled $t_1, \ldots, t_w$.

Now choose an arbitrary i, $1 \leqslant i \leqslant w$, and define $y <_\Pi x$ if and only if $x = r$ and $y = t_i$, or $x \neq r$ and $y <_f x$. Then for every element $x \in X$, there is at most one element $y \in X$ such that $x <_\Pi y$, and at most one element $z \in X$ such that $z <_\Pi x$.

It is easy to see that $\leqslant_\Pi$, the reflexive, transitive closure of $<_\Pi$, defines a chain partition of X. (Observe that as D is an acyclic digraph, the transitive reflexive closure of $<_\Pi$ is antisymmetric, and therefore a partial order. The fact that $(X, \leqslant_\Pi)$ is a chain partition can be shown by induction on $|X|$, considering X with a minimal element removed for the induction step.) By construction, the only maximal elements for $\leqslant_\Pi$ are r and the elements t_j for $j \neq i$. Thus, $(X, \leqslant_\Pi)$ has w chains.

Recall the definition of $<_{\widetilde{\Pi}}$, that $y <_{\widetilde{\Pi}} x$ if and only if either $y <_{\Pi} x$, or $y = t_j$, $j \neq i$, and $x = r$. Note that $<_{\widetilde{\Pi}}$ is exactly the relation $<_f$. By Theorem 2, the number of secrets required by $\widetilde{\Pi}$ is

$$w\,|U_r| + \sum_{z <_{\widetilde{\Pi}} y} \omega(yz).$$

As $z <_{\widetilde{\Pi}} y$ if and only if $f(y_{\text{out}} z_{\text{in}}) = 1$, $c(y_{\text{out}} z_{\text{in}}) = \omega(yz)$, and $c(uv) = 0$ for all other arcs with $f(uv) = 1$, we have that $\sum_{z <_{\widetilde{\Pi}} y} \omega(yz)$ is exactly the cost of f, as required. $\qquad\square$

Lemma 4. *We can find a minimum cost flow for $\mathcal{N}$ in $O(|X|^4 w)$ time.*

Proof. The Negative Cycle algorithm (see [1, Sect.5.3], for example) finds a minimum cost flow for a network with n vertices and m arcs in time $O(nm^2 CU)$, where C denotes the maximum cost on an arc, and U denotes the maximum of all upper bounds on arcs and the absolute values of all balance demands on vertices. By construction of $\mathcal{N}$, we have that $n = 2|X| = O(|X|)$, $m = O(n^2) = O(|X|^2)$, $C = \max\{\omega(xy) : xy \in E_0^*\} = O(|X|)$, $U = 1$ and $C = w$. Thus we get the desired running time. $\qquad\square$

Remark 4. Strictly speaking, the Negative Cycle algorithm assumes that all lower bounds on arcs are 0. However, we can satisfy this assumption, given $\mathcal{N} = (D, l, u, c, b)$, by defining the network $\mathcal{N}' = (D, l', u', c, b')$, where

$$l'(xy) = 0 \qquad\qquad b'(x) = b(x) - l(xy)$$
$$u'(xy) = u(xy) - l(xy) \qquad b'(y) = b(y) + l(xy)$$

Then the minimum cost flow f' for $\mathcal{N}'$ will have cost exactly $\sum_{xy} l(xy)c(xy)$ less than the minimum cost flow for $\mathcal{N}$, and f' can be transformed into a minimum cost feasible flow f for $\mathcal{N}$ by setting $f(xy) = f'(xy) + l(xy)$.

We are now able to prove our main result, which is, essentially, a corollary of Theorem 3 and Lemmas 3 and 4.

Proof (of Theorem 1). By Theorem 3, there exists a chain partition that has exactly w chains, for which the corresponding chain-based enforcement scheme only requires $\widehat{K}$ secrets. Then by Lemma 3, $\widehat{K}$ is equal to the minimum cost of a feasible flow in $\mathcal{N}$, the network chain-representation of $(X, \leqslant)$. By Lemma 4, such a flow can be found in $O(|X|^4 w)$ time, and this flow can be easily transformed into the corresponding chain partition Π. Finally, by definition of $\phi(x, \Pi)$, $|\phi(x, \Pi)| \leq w$ for each $x \in X$ and therefore $k_{\max} \leqslant w$. $\qquad\square$

5 Concluding Remarks

Cryptographic enforcement schemes (CESs) fall into two broad categories: those that use symmetric cryptographic primitives and those that use asymmetric ones (notably attribute-based encryption [6,17]). The focus of this paper is on symmetric schemes, which may be characterized by (i) the total number of secrets required, (ii) the number of secrets required per user, (iii) the total amount of public information required for the derivation of secrets, and (iv) the number of derivation steps required.

Until recently, symmetric CESs for information flow policies have assumed each user would be given a single secret, from which other secrets and decryption keys would be derived using public information generated by the scheme administrator (see, for example, [3,11]). In this setting, there is a considerable literature on the trade-offs that are possible by reducing the number of steps required for the derivation of secrets, at the cost of increasing the amount of public information (see, for example, [4,8,12]).

One drawback of these types of CESs is that the administrator must generate and publish information to facilitate the derivation of secrets (and decryption keys). Moreover, the amount of public information required may be substantial, particularly when security labels are defined in terms of (subsets of) attributes. Chain-based CESs obviate the requirement for public information, the trade-off being that each user may require several secrets. The chain-based approach may well be much more practical, particularly if the poset is large and its Hasse diagram contains many edges (as in a powerset, for example). Moreover, chain-based CESs may be implemented using one-way functions, typically the fastest of cryptographic primitives in practice.

However, it was not known which choice of chain partition was most appropriate for a given information flow policy. Our work provides formal and practical methods for constructing a chain partition with the smallest number of keys in total, with the additional property that no user is required to have more than w keys, where w is the width of the information flow policy.

One question remains: If there exist multiple chain partitions that minimize the number of keys in total and per-user, which of these should we choose and can we compute it efficiently? The one parameter that our work does not address is the number of derivation steps d required by a user in the worst case. Our future work, then, will attempt to find a polynomial-time or fixed-parameter algorithm that takes a poset as input and outputs a chain partition into w chains that minimizes d. We also hope to investigate whether the insight provided by Lemma 2—that $\widehat{K}(\Pi)$ is completely determined by the bottom elements in Π—can be exploited to design an algorithm whose performance improves on that of the algorithm described in Sect. 4.

Acknowledgements. The authors would like to thank Betram Poettering for his valuable feedback and the reviewers for their comments.

References

1. Ahuja, R.K., Magnanti, T.L., Orlin, J.B.: Network Flows: Theory, Algorithms, and Applications. Prentice Hall, Englewood Cliffs (1993)

2. Akl, S., Taylor, P.: Cryptographic solution to a problem of access control in a hierarchy. ACM Trans. Comput. Syst. **1**(3), 239–248 (1983)
3. Atallah, M.J., Blanton, M., Fazio, N., Frikken, K.B.: Dynamic and efficient key management for access hierarchies. ACM Trans. Inf. Syst. Secur. **12**(3), 1–43 (2009)
4. Atallah, M.J., Blanton, M., Frikken, K.B.: Incorporating temporal capabilities in existing key management schemes. In: Biskup, J., López, J. (eds.) ESORICS 2007. LNCS, vol. 4734, pp. 515–530. Springer, Heidelberg (2007)
5. Bang-Jensen, J., Gutin, G.: Digraphs: Theory, Algorithms and Applications, 2nd edn. Springer, London (2009)
6. Bethencourt, J., Sahai, A., Waters, B.: Ciphertext-policy attribute-based encryption. In: 2007 IEEE Symposium on Security and Privacy (S&P 2007), 20–23 May 2007, Oakland, California, USA, pp. 321–334. IEEE Computer Society (2007)
7. Ciriani, V., De Capitani di Vimercati, S., Foresti, S., Jajodia, S., Paraboschi, S., Samarati, P.: Combining fragmentation and encryption to protect privacy in data storage. ACM Trans. Inf. Syst. Secur. **13**(3), 22:1–22:33 (2010)
8. Crampton, J.: Practical and efficient cryptographic enforcement of interval-based access control policies. ACM Trans. Inf. Syst. Secur. **14**(1), 14:1–14:30 (2011)
9. Crampton, J., Daud, R., Martin, K.M.: Constructing key assignment schemes from chain partitions. In: Foresti, S., Jajodia, S. (eds.) Data and Applications Security and Privacy XXIV. LNCS, vol. 6166, pp. 130–145. Springer, Heidelberg (2010)
10. Crampton, J., Farley, N., Gutin, G., Jones, M., Poettering, B.: Cryptographic enforcement of information flow policies without public information. CoRR abs/1410.5567 (2014). http://arxiv.org/abs/1410.5567. To appear in Proceedings of ACNS 2015
11. Crampton, J., Martin, K.M., Wild, P.R.: On key assignment for hierarchical access control. In: 19th IEEE Computer Security Foundations Workshop, (CSFW-19 2006), 5–7 July 2006, Venice, Italy, pp. 98–111. IEEE Computer Society (2006)
12. D'Arco, P., De Santis, A., Ferrara, A.L., Masucci, B.: Security and tradeoffs of the Akl-Taylor scheme and its variants. In: Královič, R., Niwiński, D. (eds.) MFCS 2009. LNCS, vol. 5734, pp. 247–257. Springer, Heidelberg (2009)
13. Dilworth, R.: A decomposition theorem for partially ordered sets. Ann. Math. **51**, 161–166 (1950)
14. Freire, E.S.V., Paterson, K.G.: Provably secure key assignment schemes from factoring. In: Parampalli, U., Hawkes, P. (eds.) ACISP 2011. LNCS, vol. 6812, pp. 292–309. Springer, Heidelberg (2011)
15. Freire, E.S.V., Paterson, K.G., Poettering, B.: Simple, efficient and strongly KI-secure hierarchical key assignment schemes. In: Dawson, E. (ed.) CT-RSA 2013. LNCS, vol. 7779, pp. 101–114. Springer, Heidelberg (2013)
16. Gallai, T., Milgram, A.N.: Verallgemeinerung eines Graphentheoretischen Satzes von Rédei. Acta Sci. Math. **21**, 181–186 (1960)
17. Ostrovsky, R., Sahai, A., Waters, B.: Attribute-based encryption with non-monotonic access structures. In: Ning, P., di Vimercati, S.D.C., Syverson, P.F. (eds.) Proceedings of the 2007 ACM Conference on Computer and Communications Security, CCS 2007, 28–31 October 2007, Alexandria, Virginia, USA, pp. 195–203. ACM (2007)

Inference Leakage Detection for Authorization Policies over RDF Data

Tarek Sayah[✉], Emmanuel Coquery, Romuald Thion,
and Mohand-Saïd Hacid

Université de Lyon, CNRS, Université Lyon 1, LIRIS, UMR5205,
69622 Lyon, France
{tarek.sayah,emmanuel.coquery,romuald.thion,
mohand-said.hacid}@liris.cnrs.fr

Abstract. The Semantic Web technologies include entailment regimes that produce new RDF data from existing ones. In the presence of access control, once a user has legitimately received the answer of a query, she/he can derive new data entailed from the answer that should have been forbidden if carried out inside of the RDF store. In this paper, we define a fine-grained authorization model for which it is possible to check in advance whether such a problem will arise. To this end, we provide a static analysis algorithm which can be used at the time of writing the authorization policy and does not require access to the data. We illustrate the expressiveness of the access control model with several conflict resolution strategies including *most specific takes precedence* as well as the applicability of the algorithm for diagnosis purposes.

Keywords: Authorization · Semantic reasoning · Inference leakage

1 Introduction

According to World Wide Web Consortium (W3C), inference on the Semantic Web using the Resource Description Framework (RDF) *"improve the quality of data integration on the Web, by discovering new relationships, automatically analyzing the content of the data"*. Inference rules are used to derive new triples from those explicitly asserted in a RDF store. In particular, a set of inference rules known as RDF *Schema* (RDFS) is standardized [6]. Authorization models for RDF data have been proposed to control accesses to RDF data, both in the presence of inference rules [7,8,10,15] or not [1,5,13]. However, the issue is that inference capabilities can be used by a malicious user to infer sensitive information from public ones. We call this problem the *inference leakage* problem.

To illustrate the so-called inference leakage problem, suppose that RDF triples stating that someone has a cancer are labeled as confidential (*e.g.*, triples similar to (?p ; rdf :type ; :cancerous) with ?p denoting a person), while the ones stating that a person has a tumor are public (*e.g.*, triples of the form (?p; :hasTumor; ?t)). If there exists a public triple stating that the domain of the

© IFIP International Federation for Information Processing 2015
P. Samarati (Ed.): DBSec 2015, LNCS 9149, pp. 346–361, 2015.
DOI: 10.1007/978-3-319-20810-7_24

:hasTumor predicate is :cancerous (*e.g.*, (:hasTumor ; rdfs :dom ; :cancerous))
then, using the RDFS rule that relates the domain of a predicate to the type
of its subjects, sensitive information can be inferred from the authorized triples.
The situation is even worse when RDFS is enriched with user-defined rules.

The issue is that such inferences can be performed outside the RDF store,
using only authorized data. One way of preventing inference leakages could be to
dynamically deny queries that may provide too much information, at the price
of a (possibly) quite high runtime overhead. In this paper, we propose an alternative approach based on a static analysis. The idea is to detect, at the time of
specifying the confidentiality policy, whether authorizations and inference rules
interact in such a way they can lead to disclose sensitive information. Several
authorization models for RDF which consider inference use annotations to determine whether the inferred triples are accessible or not [8,10,15]. The problem
is that these approaches do not guarantee that forbidden information cannot be
inferred again, once the data have been disclosed. The inference leakage problem
in the case of RDFS has been investigated by Jain and Farkas [7], but the base
RDF graph kept in the RDF store is needed and conflict resolution strategies
are hard-coded in their algorithm. Related works are discussed in Sect. 6.

We highlight the main contributions of this paper and detail its organization. First of all, by using standard machinery for RDF query and entailment
defined in Sect. 2, we propose a flexible access control framework for RDF data
in Sect. 3. The access control semantics is defined by computing the *authorized
subgraph* G^+ of a base RDF graph G, and hence it is independent of the query
language used by the RDF store. In Sect. 3.2, we identify and formalize a *consistency property* that captures the information leakage arising when inference
rules and authorizations interact, as exemplified informally in this introduction.
Intuitively, a policy is consistent w.r.t. a set of inference rules **R** if the authorized
subgraph G^+ of a closed graph G is itself *closed*, that is, no new facts can be
produced using **R** another time. In Sect. 4, we illustrate the applicability of the
authorization model by showing that usual conflict resolution strategies can be
expressed in our framework. In particular, we show that the *most specific takes
precedence* strategy can be modeled, this strategy being particularly useful to
capture exceptions in authorizations. In Sect. 5, we propose an algorithm that,
given a policy P and a set of inference rules **R**, but without any prior knowledge
of G, checks if the consistency property holds. The algorithm is proved correct[1]
and it is constructive: whenever the answer is positive, a counterexample graph
is computed. This answer can be used by the administrator to analyze and then
solve the issue, as illustrated in Sect. 5.2. We conclude and discuss ongoing and
future work in Sect. 7.

2   Data Model

2.1   RDF and SPARQL

RDF is a generic, graph-oriented data model that represents information based
on triples of the form "(subject ; predicate ; object)" built from pairwise

---

[1] Proofs are provided at http://liris.cnrs.fr/~tsayah/DBSEC2015/.

disjoint countably infinite sets I , V , and L for IRIs, variables, and literals respectively. A set of RDF triples is called an RDF graph. RDF graphs are stored into repositories usually called RDF stores. In this paper, we reuse the formal definitions and notation used by Pérez and Gutierrez [11]. Throughout the paper, $\mathcal{P}(\mathsf{E})$ denotes the *finite powerset* of a set E and $\mathsf{F} \subseteq \mathsf{E}$ denotes a *finite subset* F.

We do not explicitly use blank nodes which are replaced by *variables*. Blank nodes of RDF are semantically equivalent to existentially quantified variables [12]. Not to distinguish between blank nodes and variables significantly reduces the overhead of formal definitions but it does not change the expressiveness of the framework.

RDF graphs are queried using SPARQL which is the RDF counterpart of the SQL query language used in relational databases. We focus on a subset of SPARQL called *basic graph patterns* used in Sect. 3 to define authorizations and policies.

Definition 1 (Triple Pattern, Graph Pattern). *A term* t *is either an IRI, a variable or a literal. Formally* $\mathsf{t} \in \mathsf{T} = \mathsf{I} \cup \mathsf{V} \cup \mathsf{L}$ *. A tuple* $t \in \mathsf{TP} = \mathsf{T} \times \mathsf{T} \times \mathsf{T}$ *is called a* Triple Pattern (TP). *A Basic Graph Pattern (BGP), or simply a graph, is a finite set of triple patterns. Formally, the set of all BGPs is* $\mathsf{BGP} = \mathcal{P}(\mathsf{TP})$.

Given a triple pattern $tp \in \mathsf{TP}$, var(tp) *is the set of variables occurring in tp. Similarly, given a basic graph pattern* $B \in \mathsf{BGP}$, var(B) *is the set of variables occurring in the BGP defined by* var$(B) = \{v \mid \exists tp \in B \wedge v \in \mathsf{var}(tp)\}$.

When graph patterns are considered as instances stored in an RDF store, we simply call them *graphs*. In this paper, we do not make any formal difference between a basic graph pattern and a graph. Also, note that Definition 1 is slightly more liberal than usual because variables are allowed in property positions.

Example 1. Figure 1 depicts a graph G_0 constituted by triples et_1 to et_5, both pictorially and textually. We explicitly write rdf and rdfs when the term is from the RDF or the RDFS standard vocabulary. However, we do not prefix the other terms for the sake of simplicity. Triples it_1 an it_2 are depicted by dashed arrow in Fig. 1. They are part of the closure $\mathsf{Cl}(G_0)$ of G_0 that we will introduce in Sect. 2.2.

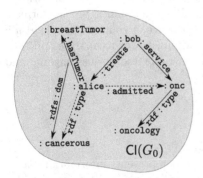

	Subject	Predicate	Object
et_1	:hasTumor	rdfs :dom	:cancerous
et_2	:onc	rdf :type	:oncology
et_3	:alice	:hasTumor	:breastTumor
et_4	:bob	:service	:onc
et_5	:bob	:treats	:alice
it_1	:alice	rdf :type	:cancerous
it_2	:alice	:admitted	:onc

Fig. 1. An example of an RDF graph G_0 and its closure $\mathsf{Cl}(G_0)$

The evaluation of a graph pattern B on another graph pattern G is given by mapping the variables of B to the terms of G such that the structure of B is preserved. First, we define the substitution mappings as usual. Then, we define the evaluation of B on G as the set of substitutions that embed B into G.

Definition 2 (Substitution Mappings). *A* substitution (mapping) η *is a partial function* $\eta : V \rightarrow T$. *The domain of* η, $\mathsf{dom}(\eta)$, *is the subset of* V *where* η *is defined. We overload notation and also write* η *for the partial function* $\eta^* : T \rightarrow T$ *that extends* η *with the identity on terms. Given two substitutions* η_1 *and* η_2, *we write* $\eta = \eta_1 \eta_2$ *for the substitution* $\eta : ?v \mapsto \eta_2(\eta_1(?v))$.

Given a triple pattern $tp = (\mathsf{s};\mathsf{p};\mathsf{o}) \in TP$ *and a substitution* η *such that* $\mathsf{var}(tp) \subseteq \mathsf{dom}(\eta)$, $(tp)\eta$ *is defined as* $(\eta(\mathsf{s});\eta(\mathsf{p});\eta(\mathsf{o}))$. *Similarly, given a graph pattern* $B \in BGP$ *and a substitution* η *such that* $\mathsf{var}(B) \subseteq \mathsf{dom}(\eta)$, *we extend* η *to graph pattern by defining* $(B)\eta = \{(tp)\eta \mid tp \in B\}$.

Definition 3 (BGP Evaluation). *Let* $G \in BGP$ *be a graph, and* $B \in BGP$ *a graph pattern. The evaluation of* B *over* G *denoted by* $[\![B]\!]_G$ *is defined as the following set of substitution mappings:*

$$[\![B]\!]_G = \{\eta : V \rightarrow T \mid \mathsf{dom}(\eta) = \mathsf{var}(B) \wedge (B)\eta \subseteq G\}$$

Example 2. Let B be defined as $B = \{(?\mathsf{d};:\mathtt{service};?\mathsf{s}),(?\mathsf{d};:\mathtt{treats};?\mathsf{p})\}$. The evaluation of B on the example graph G_0 of Fig. 1 is $[\![B]\!]_{G_0} = \{\eta\}$, where η is defined as $\eta : ?\mathsf{d} \mapsto :\mathtt{bob}$, $?\mathsf{s} \mapsto :\mathtt{onc}$ and $?\mathsf{p} \mapsto :\mathtt{alice}$.

Formally, the definition of BGP evaluation captures the semantics of SPARQL restricted to the conjunctive fragment of SELECT queries that do not use FILTER, OPT and UNION operators (see [11] for further details). Please note that this fragment is basically used to define the access control model itself, and it is not meant to replace the generic SPARQL query language on RDF stores.

2.2 Inference Rules and RDFS

Inference rules are used to add triples to a graph when it contains triples conforming to a graph pattern. Thus, inference rules turn an RDF store into a *deductive database* similar to positive Datalog that extends traditional (non-deductive) relational databases.

Definition 4 (Inference Rule). *An* inference rule $\mathbf{r}$ *is a formal expression of the form* $(tp \leftarrow tp_1, \ldots, tp_k)$ *where* $tp, tp_0, \ldots, tp_k \in TP$ *that is subjected to the condition* $\mathsf{var}(tp) \subseteq \mathsf{var}(\{tp_0, \ldots, tp_k\})$. *The sets of inference rules are denoted by* $\mathbf{R}$.

For a rule $(tp \leftarrow tp_1, \ldots, tp_k)$, the condition $\mathsf{var}(tp) \subseteq \mathsf{var}(\{tp_0, \ldots, tp_k\})$ ensures that it does not introduce fresh uninstantiated variables when applied to a graph. When useful, we also use the notation $\frac{tp_1, \ldots, tp_k}{tp}$ for inference rules. We define an operational semantics for the rules, inspired by the *fixpoint semantics* of Datalog. It is known that the closure of a finite graph is finite and the operator is increasing, monotonic and idempotent [2, Chap. 12].

Definition 5 (Rule Semantics, Closure). *Given a graph pattern* $G \in$ BGP *and an inference rule* $\mathbf{r} = (tp \leftarrow tp_1, \ldots, tp_k)$, *the set of triples (immediately) deduced from* G *by* $\mathbf{r}$ *is* $\phi_{\mathbf{r}}(G) = \{(tp)\sigma \mid \sigma \in [\![\{tp_1, \ldots, tp_k\}]\!]_G\}$. *We extend the operator* $\phi(G)$ *to sets of inference rules* $\mathbf{R}$, $\phi_{\mathbf{R}}(G) = \bigcup_{\mathbf{r} \in \mathbf{R}} \phi_{\mathbf{r}}(G)$.

Given a set of inference rules $\mathbf{R}$, *let* $(G_i)_{i \in \mathbb{N}}$ *be the infinite sequence of basic graph patterns defined by* $G_0 = G$ *and for any* $i \in \mathbb{N}$, $G_{i+1} = G_i \cup \phi_{\mathbf{R}}(G_i)$. *The closure of* G *w.r.t.* $\mathbf{R}$ *is* $\mathsf{Cl}_{\mathbf{R}}(G) = \bigcup_{i \in \mathbb{N}} G_i$. *We write* $\mathsf{Cl}(G)$ *when* $\mathbf{R}$ *is clear from the context. We say that a graph is* closed *when* $\mathsf{Cl}_{\mathbf{R}}(G) = G$

Example 3. The following RDFS rule named **RDom** states that the type of a triple's subject is the class defined by its predicate's domain. Let us consider the graph G_0 of Fig. 1. If we apply the inference rule **RDom** using triples et_1 and et_3 then we infer it_1. Thus, $\mathsf{Cl}_{\{\mathbf{RDom}\}}(G_0) = G_0 \cup \{it_1\}$.

$$\frac{(?\mathsf{p}\,;\mathtt{rdfs:dom}\,;?\mathsf{d})(?\mathsf{x}\,;?\mathsf{p}\,;?\mathsf{y})}{(?\mathsf{x}\,;\mathtt{rdfs:type}\,;?\mathsf{d})} = \mathbf{RDom}$$

Assume that we add an extra rule name **RAdm** which states that if a doctor is assigned to a service and treats a patient, then this patient is admitted to the doctor's service. Referring to the graph G_0 of Fig. 1, its closure now contains a new inferred triple $\mathsf{Cl}_{\{\mathbf{RDom},\mathbf{RAdm}\}}(G_0) = G_0 \cup \{it_1, it_2\}$.

$$\frac{(?\mathsf{d}\,;:\mathtt{service}\,;?\mathsf{s})(?\mathsf{d}\,;:\mathtt{treats}\,;?\mathsf{p})}{(?\mathsf{p}\,;:\mathtt{admitted}\,;?\mathsf{s})} = \mathbf{RAdm}$$

3   Access Control

In this section, we define an access control model for RDF that uses the ingredients from Sect. 2 and we formalize a consistency property between authorizations and inference rules that captures the absence of information leakage.

We assume that the Policy Decision Point (PDP) knows what are the authorizations applicable to a given authenticated requester. The entity to which authorizations are granted or denied is left implicit in this paper. The upstream mapping from requesters to authorizations may use any model from the literature, for instance using users' identifiers, groups, roles or set of attributes. In other words, we assume that the PDP is able to produce a set of authorizations in our formalism for each requester. Moreover, we restrict ourselves to the read action on RDF graphs, because the information leakage issue in the presence of RDF inference already exists in this minimal setting. The investigations on upstream policy definitions, their administration as well as update, delete and insert actions are left for future work.

3.1   Authorization Policy

We define authorizations using basic SPARQL constructions, namely basic graph patterns, in order to facilitate the administration of access control and to include homogeneously authorizations into concrete RDF stores with minimal effort.

Definition 6 (Authorization). *Let* Eff $= \{+,-\}$ *be the set of applicable effects. Formally, an* authorization $\mathfrak{a} = (e, h, b)$ *is a element of* Auth $=$ Eff $\times$ TP $\times$ BGP. *The component* e *is called* the effect *of the authorization* $\mathfrak{a}$, h *and* b *are called its* head *and* body *respectively. We use the function* effect $:$ Auth $\rightarrow$ Eff *(resp.,* head $:$ Auth $\rightarrow$ TP, body $:$ Auth $\rightarrow$ BGP*) to denote the first (resp., second, third) projection function. We call* hb$(\mathfrak{a}) = \{\text{head}(\mathfrak{a})\} \cup$ body$(\mathfrak{a})$ *the underlying graph pattern of the authorization* $\mathfrak{a}$. *Given a finite set of authorizations* $\mathfrak{A}$, *we introduce* $\mathfrak{A}^{+} = \{\mathfrak{a} \in \mathfrak{A} \mid \text{effect}(\mathfrak{a}) = +\}$ *and* $\mathfrak{A}^{-} = \{\mathfrak{a} \in \mathfrak{A} \mid \text{effect}(\mathfrak{a}) = -\}$ *for the positive and negative subsets of* $\mathfrak{A}$.

We use the concrete syntax "GRANT/DENY h WHERE b" to represent an authorization $\mathfrak{a} = (e, h, b)$. We use the GRANT keyword when $e = +$ and the DENY keyword when $e = -$. Condition WHERE $\emptyset$ is elided when b is empty.

Example 4. Consider the set of authorizations shown in Table. 1. Authorization $\mathfrak{a}_1$ grants access to triples with predicate :hasTumor. Authorization $\mathfrak{a}_5$ states that triples about admission to the oncology service are specifically denied, whereas the authorization $\mathfrak{a}_6$ states that such information are allowed in the general case. Finally, authorization $\mathfrak{a}_9$ denies access to any triple, it is meant to be a default authorization.

Given an authorization $\mathfrak{a} \in$ Auth and a graph G, we say that $\mathfrak{a}$ is *applicable on* a triple $t \in G$ if there exists a substitution θ such that the head of $\mathfrak{a}$ is mapped to t and all the conditions expressed in the body of $\mathfrak{a}$ are satisfied as well. In other words, we evaluate the underlying graph pattern hb$(\mathfrak{a}) = \{\text{head}(\mathfrak{a})\} \cup$ body$(\mathfrak{a})$ against G and we apply all the answers of $[\![hb(\mathfrak{a})]\!]_G$ to head$(\mathfrak{a})$. In a concrete system, this evaluation step would be computed using the mechanisms used to evaluate SPARQL queries.

Definition 7 (Applicable Authorizations). *Given a finite set of authorization* $\mathfrak{A} \in \mathcal{P}(\text{Auth})$ *and a graph* $G \in$ BGP, *the function* ar *assigns to each triple* $t \in G$, *the subset of* applicable authorizations *from* $\mathfrak{A}$:

$$\text{ar}(G, \mathfrak{A})(t) = \{\mathfrak{a} \in \mathfrak{A} \mid \exists \theta \in [\![hb(\mathfrak{a})]\!]_G . t = (\text{head}(\mathfrak{a}))\theta\}$$

Example 5. Consider the graph $\text{Cl}(G_0)$ shown in Fig. 1 and the set of authorizations $\mathfrak{A}$ shown in Table 1. The applicable authorizations on triple it_2 are computed as follows : $\text{ar}(G, \mathfrak{A})(it_2) = \{\mathfrak{a}_5, \mathfrak{a}_6, \mathfrak{a}_9\}$. The mappings from hb$(\mathfrak{a}_5)$, hb$(\mathfrak{a}_6)$ and hb$(\mathfrak{a}_9)$ to $\text{Cl}(G_0)$ are illustrated by Fig. 2.

As exemplified above, there may exist some t such that the set $\text{ar}(G, \mathfrak{A})(t)$ is not a singleton authorization. If the set of applicable authorizations is empty, then a solution to ensure that the decision function is total is to specify a *default decision*. When several authorizations with different effects are applicable, one has to specify a *conflict resolution strategy* that defines which of the effects has to be selected.

To prevent us from defining many extra parameters, arbitrarily fixing some conflict resolution strategies or running into considerations on conflict resolution

Table 1. Example of authorizations

a_1 = GRANT(?p ; :hasTumor ; ?t)
a_2 = DENY (?p ; rdf :type ; :cancerous)
a_3 = GRANT(?d ; :service ; ?s)
a_4 = GRANT(?d ; :treats ; ?p)
a_5 = DENY (?p ; :admitted ; ?s)
    WHERE {(?s ; rdf :type ; :oncology)}
a_6 = GRANT(?p ; :admitted ; ?s)
a_7 = GRANT(?p ; rdfs :dom ; ?s)
a_8 = DENY (?s ; ?p ; :cancerous)
a_9 = DENY (?s ; ?p ; ?o)

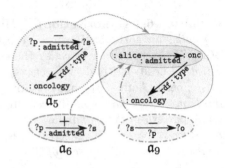

Fig. 2. Authorizations applicable to it_2

that are out of the scope of this paper, we abstract from the details of the concrete
resolution strategies by assuming that there exists a choice function that, given
a finite set of possibly conflicting authorizations, picks a unique one out. This
design choice as well as the issues related to the modeling of classical conflict
resolution strategies are discussed in Sect. 4.

Definition 8 (Conflict Resolution Function, Policy). *A conflict resolution
function* ch *for authorizations is a function* ch $\in \mathcal{P}(\mathsf{Auth}) \to \mathsf{Auth}$. *An (authorization) policy* P *is a pair* $P = (\mathfrak{A}, \mathsf{ch})$, *where* $\mathfrak{A}$ *is a finite set of authorizations
and* ch *is a conflict resolution function, which satisfies the following coherence
conditions:*

- *Closedness:* $\forall \mathfrak{A}' \subseteq \mathfrak{A}.\mathfrak{A}' \neq \emptyset \Rightarrow \mathsf{ch}(\mathfrak{A}') \in \mathfrak{A}'$
- *Totality:* $\forall G \in \mathsf{BGP}.\forall t \in G.\,\mathsf{ar}(G, \mathfrak{A})(t) \neq \emptyset$
- *Monotony:* $\forall \mathfrak{A} \subseteq \mathsf{Auth}.\,\mathsf{ch}(\mathfrak{A}) = a \Rightarrow (\forall \mathfrak{A}' \subseteq \mathfrak{A}.a \in \mathfrak{A}' \Rightarrow \mathsf{ch}(\mathfrak{A}') = a)$

The subset of $\mathcal{P}(\mathsf{Auth}) \times (\mathcal{P}(\mathsf{Auth}) \to \mathsf{Auth})$ *that satisfies the above coherence
conditions is denoted by* Pol.

The coherence conditions are properties which ensure that the conflict resolution functions behave well when applied to set of authorizations. The *Closedness*
property guarantees that the selected rule is taken from the input. The *Totality*
property avoids a corner case. We explain in Sect. 4 how to enforce *default decisions* that ensure this property. The *Monotony* property is more technical but it
captures an intuitive requirement that is: *the conflict resolution function makes
consistent choices*, which means its answer is kept the same when lesser choices
are available.

Example 6. An example policy is $P = (\mathfrak{A}, \mathsf{ch})$ where $\mathfrak{A}$ is the set authorizations
in Table 1 and ch is defined as follows. For all non-empty subset $\mathfrak{B}$ of $\mathfrak{A}$, $\mathsf{ch}(\mathfrak{B})$
is the first authorization (using syntactical order of Table 1) of $\mathfrak{A}$ that appears
in $\mathfrak{B}$. For $\mathfrak{B} = \emptyset$, $\mathsf{ch}(\emptyset) = a_9$. *Closedness* and *Monotony* directly stem from the
definition of ch. *Totality* stems from a_9, as it is applicable to any triple.

We are ready to give semantics to policies by composing the functions ar, ch and
then effect in order to compute the authorized subgraph of a given graph.

Definition 9 (Policy Evaluation, Positive Subgraph). *Given a policy* $P = (\mathfrak{A}, \text{ch}) \in \text{Pol}$ *and a graph* $G \in \text{BGP}$, *the set of authorized triples that constitutes the positive subgraph of* G *according to* P *is defined as follows, writing* G^+ *when* P *is clear from the context:*

$$G_P^+ = \{t \in G \mid (\text{effect} \circ \text{ch})(\text{ar}(G, \mathfrak{A})(t)) = +\}$$

Example 7. Let us consider the policy $P = (\mathfrak{A}, \text{ch})$ defined in Example 6, the graph G_0 of Fig. 1, and the triple $it_2 = (\text{:alice};\text{::admitted};\text{::onc})$. As we can see in Fig. 2, $\text{ar}(\text{Cl}(G_0), \mathfrak{A})(it_2) = \{\mathfrak{a}_5, \mathfrak{a}_6, \mathfrak{a}_9\}$. Since $\mathfrak{a}_5$ is the first among authorization in Table 1 and its effect is -, we deduce that $it_2 \notin \text{Cl}(G_0)_P^+$. By applying a similar reasoning on all triples in $\text{Cl}(G)$, we obtain $\text{Cl}(G_0)_P^+ = \{et_1, et_3, et_4, et_5\}$. Note that et_2 is not authorized.

3.2 Consistency Property

The inference rules which are applied to a graph reflect the particular knowledge conveyed by the graph. Hence, the real semantics of a graph are represented by its closure, regardless it is materialized or not. Thus, information leakage has to be considered in the closure of a graph, rather than considering only the base graph which is under control of a trusted RDF store. A malicious user who knows the inference rules could use a local reasoner and apply the inference rules over his accessible triples to infer triples she/he is not supposed to access. To illustrate this issue, consider the following example.

Example 8. Assume a of inference rules $\mathbf{R} = \{\mathbf{RDom}, \mathbf{RAdm}\}$, as shown in Example 3. We want to apply the policy defined in Example 7 on the graph $\text{Cl}_{\mathbf{R}}(G_0)$ of Fig. 1. According to Example 7, the authorized subgraph is $(\text{Cl}_{\mathbf{R}}(G_0))_P^+ = \{et_1, et_3, et_4, et_5\}$. If one computes the closure of $(\text{Cl}_{\mathbf{R}}(G_0))_P^+$, she/he obtains $(\text{Cl}_{\mathbf{R}}(G_0))_P^+ \cup \{it_1, it_2\}$. Whereas the policy states that triples it_1 and it_2 must be denied, they are deduced from the authorized subgraph, hence the information leakage.

We formally characterize the issue that arises when inference rules produce facts that would have been forbidden otherwise. This issue occurs when the positive subset of a closed graph is not, itself, closed.

Definition 10 (Consistency between Rules and Policies). *An authorization policy* $P = (\mathfrak{A}, \text{ch})$ *is consistent w.r.t. a set of inference rules* $\mathbf{R}$ *if, for any graph* $G \in \text{BGP}$, *the following holds:*

$$\text{Cl}_{\mathbf{R}}((\text{Cl}_{\mathbf{R}}(G))_P^+) = (\text{Cl}_{\mathbf{R}}(G))_P^+$$

The consistency property has to hold for all graphs. Therefore, it does not have to be checked when stored graphs are updated, but solely at the policy design-time or when the inference rules change. Given that the stored graphs are updated on a regular basis, we consider that policies and inference rules are more stable over time.

4   Building Policies

First, we illustrate the applicability of policies as defined in Definition 8 by showing how to construct motivating conflict resolution functions. Then, we show that the default decisions and common conflict resolution strategies can be modeled in our framework. In particular, we illustrate how the *Most Specific Takes Precedence* (MSTP) principle can be defined.

First of all, we notice that if there exists a *total order* denoted by $\preccurlyeq$ between authorizations of a set $\mathfrak{A}$, we can construct its associated conflict resolution function $\min_{\preccurlyeq}$ that selects the smallest element from a subset $\mathfrak{B} \subseteq \mathfrak{A}$. The *Closedness* and the *Monotony* conditions of Definition 8 are satisfied by construction. There are several ways to equip $\mathfrak{A}$ with a total order. For instance, the administrator can explicitly assign a unique prevalence level to each authorization or she/he can rely on the *syntactical order*. When one writes a set of authorizations such as the one shown in Table 1, there is a total order given by the order of the statements. The syntactical order is always available and it is used, for example, in firewalls, so that no ambiguity arises.

4.1   Default Policy

A default policy is a decision that is selected when no other authorization is applicable that is $\mathsf{ar}(G, \mathfrak{A})(t) = \emptyset$. Such a default policy can either be *deny by default* or *permit by default*. In order to respect the *Totality* coherence condition of Definition 8, we cannot simply apply a default *decision*. However, we have to identify a default *authorization*. The following lemma shows that the *Totality* condition can be ensured by adding a *universal authorization* which is applicable to any triple.

Lemma 1. *Let $\mathfrak{A}$ be a set of authorizations, the condition $\forall G.\forall t \in G.\, \mathsf{ar}(G, \mathfrak{A})(t) \neq \emptyset$ is equivalent to $\exists \mathfrak{a}_u \in \mathfrak{A}.\forall G.\forall t \in G.\mathfrak{a}_u \in \mathsf{ar}(G, \mathfrak{A})(t).$*

We enforce the default policy by adding a universal authorization such as authorization $\mathfrak{a}_9$ as shown in Table 1. There may be several different universal authorizations in the set $\mathfrak{A}$. Therefore, conflicts will be systematically triggered. Even though it is formally possible to have several universal authorizations, we can assume that such a rule is *unique*. Note that the addition of a default rule at the end of a rule set is standard practice in firewall policies.

4.2   Precedence Strategies

The *Denials Take Precedence* (DTP) principle resolves conflicts by stating that the negative authorizations prevail over the positive ones; the *Permissions Take Precedence* (PTP) principle being its dual. The idea to capture the DTP (resp. PTP) strategy is to transform a policy $P = (\mathfrak{A}, \mathsf{ch})$ into a policy $P^- = (\mathfrak{A}, \mathsf{ch}^-)$ where ch^- privileges negative (resp. positive) effects. Considering the previous discussion on default policies, we assume that there is a unique universal authorization $\mathfrak{a}_u \in \mathfrak{A}$. As $\mathfrak{a}_u$ is assumed to be a default authorization, we require that

$\mathfrak{B} \setminus \{a_u\} = \emptyset$ if and only if $ch(\mathfrak{B}) = a_u$. Remind that $\mathfrak{B}^-$ (resp. $\mathfrak{B}^+$) is the subset of $\mathfrak{B}$ with a negative (resp. positive) effect. With $\mathfrak{B} \subseteq \mathfrak{A}$, the ch^- function is formally defined as follows:

$$ch^-(\mathfrak{B}) = \begin{cases} ch(\mathfrak{B}^- \setminus \{a_u\}) & \text{if } \mathfrak{B}^- \setminus \{a_u\} \neq \emptyset & (1) \\ ch(\mathfrak{B}^+ \setminus \{a_u\}) & \text{if } \mathfrak{B}^- \setminus \{a_u\} = \emptyset \wedge \mathfrak{B}^+ \setminus \{a_u\} \neq \emptyset & (2) \\ a_u & \text{if } \mathfrak{B} \setminus \{a_u\} = \emptyset & (3) \end{cases}$$

Similarly, the dual function ch^+ is defined by flipping $+$ and $-$ in the definition of P^-. The next lemma ensures that the construction is correct.

Lemma 2 (Correctness of P^-). *Given $P = (\mathfrak{A}, ch)$ a policy according to Definition 8 with a unique universal authorization $a_u \in \mathfrak{A}$ such that $\forall \mathfrak{B} \subseteq \mathfrak{A}. ch(\mathfrak{B}) = a_u \Rightarrow \mathfrak{B} \setminus \{a_u\} = \emptyset$, the structure $P^- = (\mathfrak{A}, ch^-)$ is a policy as well.*

Example 9. Consider the graph $Cl(G_0)$ shown in Fig. 1 and the set of authorizations $\mathfrak{A}$ shown in Table 1. Let us consider the authorizations applicable to triple et_1, that is $ar(Cl(G_0), \mathfrak{A})(et_1) = \{a_7, a_8, a_9\}$. If we consider the ch given in Example 6, that is, the syntactical order, authorization a_7, a positive one, is selected. However, with the DTP construction, we have that $ch^-(\{a_7, a_8, a_9\}) = ch(\{a_8\}) = a_8$.

4.3   Most Specific Takes Precedence (MSTP)

The MSTP strategy *partially* solves conflicts by choosing most specific authorizations first, then remaining conflicts are solved afterwards. This strategy is particularly adequate to capture exceptions in policies in a natural way. For instance, in Table 1, the authorization a_5 that denies admissions to oncology service is an exception to the authorization a_6 which allows admissions in general. According to the MSTP strategy, a_5 should prevail over a_6.

We say that an authorization a_1 *is more specific* than authorization a_2 denoted by $a_1 \sqsubseteq a_2$ when the underlying graph pattern of a_2 can be matched to the one of a_1 with the restriction that the head of a_2 is mapped to the head of a_1. More formally, $a_1 \sqsubseteq a_2 \equiv \exists \theta. hb(a_2)\theta \subseteq hb(a_1) \wedge head(a_2)\theta = head(a_1)$.

Clearly, the identity substitution makes the $\sqsubseteq$ relation reflexive and composition of substitution makes it transitive. Therefore, it is a preorder. We can define a function $mins_\sqsubseteq$, from sets of authorizations to sets of authorizations, which keeps the most specific ones: $mins_\sqsubseteq(\mathfrak{A}) = \{a \in \mathfrak{A} \mid \forall a' \in \mathfrak{A}. a' \sqsubseteq a \Rightarrow a' \sqsupseteq a\}$.

At this stage, the pair $(\mathfrak{A}, mins_\sqsubseteq)$ is not a policy yet: $mins_\sqsubseteq$ is ambiguous. Therefore, it does not comply with coherence conditions of Definition 8. However, we can rely on the previous constructions for the DTP precedence strategy to define a more precise policy, by composing $mins_\sqsubseteq$ with $min^-_{\preccurlyeq_{lex}}$ (resp. $min^+_{\preccurlyeq_{lex}}$ for PTP), where $min_{\preccurlyeq_{lex}}$ is the conflict resolution function using the syntactical order. Finally, we obtain the structure $P = (\mathfrak{A}, min^-_{\preccurlyeq_{lex}} \circ mins_\sqsubseteq)$ which is a fully-fledged policy.

Algorithm 1. Algorithm for enumerating inconsistency patterns

Input: a set of inference rules $\mathbf{R}$, an authorization policy $P = (\mathfrak{A}, \mathrm{ch})$
Output: a collection $BGPs$ of counterexample basic graph patterns
1: **function** RDFLEAKS($\mathbf{R}$, P)
2: $\quad$ $BGPs \leftarrow \emptyset$
3: $\quad$ **for all** $\mathbf{r} = (tp \leftarrow tp_1, \ldots, tp_k) \in \mathbf{R}$ **do**
4: $\quad\quad$ **for all** $(\mathfrak{a}_1, \ldots, \mathfrak{a}_k, \mathfrak{a}) \in \mathfrak{A}^{+^k} \times \mathfrak{A}^-$ **do**
5: $\quad\quad\quad$ let $\rho_1, \ldots, \rho_k, \rho$ be renaming substitutions for $\mathfrak{a}_1, \ldots, \mathfrak{a}_k, \mathfrak{a}$
6: $\quad\quad\quad$ let $(ha_1, \ldots, ha_k, ha) = (\mathrm{head}(\mathfrak{a}_1)\rho_1, \ldots, \mathrm{head}(\mathfrak{a}_k)\rho_k, \mathrm{head}(\mathfrak{a})\rho)$
7: $\quad\quad\quad$ **if** $\exists \mu = \mathrm{mgu}((ha_1, \ldots, ha_k, ha), (tp_1, \ldots, tp_k, tp))$ **then**
8: $\quad\quad\quad\quad$ let $B = \bigcup_{i=1}^{k} \mathrm{hb}(\mathfrak{a}_i)\rho_i\mu \cup \mathrm{hb}(\mathfrak{a})\rho\mu$
9: $\quad\quad\quad\quad$ **if** $\{(tp_1)\mu, \ldots, (tp_k)\mu\} \subseteq (\mathrm{Cl}_{\mathbf{R}}(B))^+_P$ and $(tp)\mu \notin (\mathrm{Cl}_{\mathbf{R}}(B))^+_P$ **then**
10: $\quad\quad\quad\quad\quad$ $BGPs \leftarrow BGPs \cup \{B\}$
11: $\quad\quad\quad\quad$ **end if**
12: $\quad\quad\quad$ **end if**
13: $\quad\quad$ **end for**
14: $\quad$ **end for**
15: $\quad$ **return** $BGPs$
16: **end function**

Example 10. Given a policy $P = (\mathfrak{A}, \min^-_{\preccurlyeq_{lex}} \circ \min s_{\sqsubseteq})$, the selected authorization for the triple it_2 is computed as follows : $(\min^-_{\preccurlyeq_{lex}} \circ \min s_{\sqsubseteq})(\mathrm{ar}(G, \mathfrak{A})(it_2)) = (\min^-_{\preccurlyeq_{lex}} \circ \min s_{\sqsubseteq})(\{\mathfrak{a}_5, \mathfrak{a}_6, \mathfrak{a}_9\}) = \min^-_{\preccurlyeq_{lex}}(\{\mathfrak{a}_5\}) = \mathfrak{a}_5$. If we consider et_1, we have $\mathrm{ar}(G, \mathfrak{A})(et_1) = \{\mathfrak{a}_7, \mathfrak{a}_8, \mathfrak{a}_9\}$ and $\min s_{\sqsubseteq}(\{\mathfrak{a}_7, \mathfrak{a}_8, \mathfrak{a}_9\}) = \{\mathfrak{a}_7, \mathfrak{a}_8\}$: the most specific authorization is not unique. Therefore, we rely on $\min^-_{\preccurlyeq_{lex}}$ to finally select $\mathfrak{a}_8$.

5 Static Verification

In this section, we show a key property of the framework introduced so far: it is possible to check, without any knowledge of a base graph, if a policy is consistent w.r.t. a set of inference rules. In other words, we define Algorithm 1 that, given an authorization policy $P = (\mathfrak{A}, \mathrm{ch})$ and a set of inference rules $\mathbf{R}$, checks whether Definition 10 holds. In fact, Algorithm 1 is an enumeration algorithm and not a mere decision algorithm: it is constructive and finds all possible counterexamples to the consistency property.

The principle of Algorithm 1 is to find an inference rule $(tp \leftarrow tp_1, \ldots, tp_k) \in \mathbf{R}$ and related sets of authorizations $(\mathfrak{a}_1, \ldots, \mathfrak{a}_k, \mathfrak{a})$ such that $\mathfrak{a}$ is negative and its head is unifiable with tp and all authorizations $\mathfrak{a}_i$ for $i \in \{1, \ldots, k\}$ are positive and their heads are unifiable with $\{tp_1, \ldots, tp_k\}$. Pictorially:

$$\mathbf{r} = \frac{\overbrace{\mathrm{hb}(\mathfrak{a}_1)}^{tp_1} \ldots \overbrace{\mathrm{hb}(\mathfrak{a}_k)}^{tp_k}}{\underbrace{\frac{tp}{\mathrm{hb}(\mathfrak{a})}}} \text{ with } \mathfrak{a}_i \in \mathfrak{A}^+ \text{ and } \mathfrak{a} \in \mathfrak{A}^-$$

Let us consider the graph B built by considering the union of the underlying graphs $hb(\mathfrak{a}_1) \dots hb(\mathfrak{a}_k)$ and $hb(\mathfrak{a})$, properly renamed and unified. By construction, the inference rule $\mathbf{r}$ is applicable, thus $B \subsetneq Cl_{\mathbf{R}}(B)$. Moreover, all authorizations are applicable as well. On the one hand, triples tp_1 to tp_k are authorized by some positive authorizations. On the other hand, tp is inferred using rule $\mathbf{r}$ but is forbidden by authorization $\mathfrak{a}$: an inconsistency.

The key idea that ensures the completeness of Algorithm 1 is that all counterexamples of the consistency property have to arise this way. Theorems 1 and 2 formally state the correctness of the algorithm: P is not consistent w.r.t. $\mathbf{R}$ *if and only if* Algorithm 1 returns a non empty collection. We rely on the usual definitions of unifiers and most general unifiers (mgu) as stated by Martelli and Montanari for instance, [9].

Theorem 1 (Soundness of Algorithm 1). *If Algorithm 1 returns a non empty collection then P is not consistent w.r.t. $\mathbf{R}$.*

Theorem 2 (Completeness of Algorithm 1). *Given a basic graph pattern G, if $Cl_{\mathbf{R}}((Cl_{\mathbf{R}}(G))_P^+) \neq (Cl_{\mathbf{R}}(G))_P^+$, then there exists a basic graph pattern $B \in$ RDFLEAKS$(\mathbf{R}, P)$ such that $[\![B]\!]_{Cl_{\mathbf{R}}(G)} \neq \emptyset$.*

Theorem 1 holds by construction: Line 9 of Algorithm 1 ensures that B is a counterexample. Next, we prove Theorem 2 and discuss counterexample usage.

5.1 Main Theorem

To show that Theorem 2 holds, we first introduce two lemmas. Intuitively, Lemma 3 ensures that the Definition 7 of applicable authorization behaves well according to instantiation of graphs. Lemma 4 is its counterpart for the closure of a graph according to a set of inference rules.

Lemma 3. *Let $P = (\mathfrak{A}, ch)$ be an authorization policy, $B, G \in$ BGP are basic graph patterns, and η is a substitution such that $B\eta \subseteq G$. For any $t \in B$, $ar(B, \mathfrak{A})(t) \subseteq ar(G, \mathfrak{A})((t)\eta)$.*

Lemma 4. *Let $P = (\mathfrak{A}, ch)$ be an authorization policy, $\mathbf{R}$ is a set of inference rules, $B, G \in$ BGP are basic graph patterns, and η is a substitution such that $B\eta \subseteq G$. For any $t \in Cl_{\mathbf{R}}(B)$, $(t)\eta \in Cl_{\mathbf{R}}(G)$.*

Proof (Sketch of Proof of Theorem 2). Let G^{ex} be a counterexample graph as in the hypothesis of Theorem 2. First, we note that if a graph is not closed $Cl_{\mathbf{R}}(G) \neq G$ then there are some triples not in G that are produced at the first step of the closure algorithm. By applying it to $(Cl_{\mathbf{R}}(G^{ex}))_P^+$, we know that there exists a triple $t^{ex} = (tp)\sigma$ produced by some rule $\mathbf{r} = (tp \leftarrow tp_1, \dots, tp_k) \in \mathbf{R}$ with $(tp_i)\sigma \in (Cl_{\mathbf{R}}(G^{ex}))_P^+$. By making hypothesis on $(Cl_{\mathbf{R}}(G^{ex}))_P^+$ and t^{ex}, we build the tuple $(\mathfrak{a}_1, \dots, \mathfrak{a}_k, \mathfrak{a})$ of authorizations that were selected by ch for tp_1, $\dots$, tp_k and tp. Then, by considering the heads of these authorizations, we can construct a unifier μ' between $\mathbf{r}$ and the authorizations once the authorizations

Table 2. Corrected authorization policy

a_1 = GRANT(?p ; :hasTumor ; ?t) a_5 = DENY (?p ; :admitted ; ?s)
a_2 = DENY (?p ; rdf :type ; ::cancerous)   WHERE {(?s ; rdf :type ; ::oncology)}
a_3 = GRANT(?d ; :service ; ?s) a_6 = GRANT(?p ; :admitted ; ?s)
a_3' = DENY (?d ; :treats ; ?p) a_8 = DENY (?s ; ?p ; ::cancerous)
   WHERE {(?d ; ::service ; ?s), a_7 = GRANT(?p ; rdfs :dom ; ?s)
          (?s ; rdf :type ; ::oncology)} a_8' = GRANT (?x0 ; rdf :type ; ?x1)
a_4 = GRANT(?d ; ::treats ; ?p) a_9 = DENY (?s ; ?p ; ?o)

are renamed. If there exists a unifier, so does the most general one, say μ, thus the condition at Line 7 is satisfied.

We construct B at Line 8 and consider its evaluation on $\mathsf{Cl_R}(G^{ex})$. We know that $\mathsf{Cl_R}(G^{ex})$ contains an instance of B because of μ and μ'. Using Lemmas 3 and 4 and the *Monotony* condition of Definition 8, we conclude that authorizations $(a_1, \ldots, a_k, a)$ are also the ones selected by ch for the triples $(tp_1)\mu, \ldots (tp_k)\mu$, and $(tp)\mu$ in $\mathsf{Cl}_R(B)$. This means that the condition in Line 9 evaluates to true and B is in the result.

5.2   Understanding the Counterexamples

As Algorithm 1 enumerates inconsistency patterns, its output can be used to correct access control policy. A proof of concept of the algorithm has been implemented in Prolog[2]. The methodology to correct an inconsistent policy is to iteratively apply the following two steps: (1) use Algorithm 1 to obtain counterexample graph patterns; (2) change the authorization policy to correct inconsistencies illustrated by these graph patterns. The iteration stops when the authorization policy is consistent w.r.t. the set of inference rules. We illustrate this methodology on the inference rules of Example 3 and the policy defined in Table 1 with syntactical order. After three iterations, no inconsistency subsists anymore. The complete policy once corrected is given in Table 2.

The first two runs point out interactions between rule **RDom** and predicate rdf :type. The policy can be corrected by adding authorization a_8' and switching authorizations a_7 and a_8. We give more details about the third run that produces a single counterexample graph $B = \{(?d ; :service ; ?s), (?d ; :treats ; ?p),$ $(?p; :admitted; ?s), (?s; rdf :type; ::oncology)\}$ which involves the rule **RAdm** together with authorizations a_3, a_4 and a_5. A first and simple solution would be to change the effect of authorization a_4 to deny access to triples matching $(?d ; :treats ; ?p)$. However, such an authorization would be extreme while the counterexample suggests to add a finer authorization a_3' just before a_4. Note that we can alternatively switch $(?d ; :treats ; ?p)$ and $(?d ; :service ; ?s)$ in a_3', but such a choice should be discussed with the experts first. After adding a_3', a final execution of the algorithm confirms that the new policy is consistent w.r.t $\{\mathbf{RDom}, \mathbf{RAdm}\}$ as it returns no counterexample.

---

[2] http://liris.cnrs.fr/~tsayah/DBSEC2015/.

Another way of using the counterexamples is to keep the policy unchanged, but to check if they occur in the actual closed graph managed by the RDF store. By Theorem 2, if there is no such instance, no information leakage will occur. Thus, one could use each B produced by Algorithm 1 as an integrity constraint in the RDF store, thereby reject updates that may lead to information leakage.

6 Related Work

The importance of confidentiality problems have been recognized for long. As such, access control models for different data models data have been proposed. RDF graphs can be written in a standard XML format, but there can be many different syntactical expressions that denote the same graph. Thus access control models for XML are quite difficult to transpose, if feasible, when applied to RDF graphs [7]. The Datalog model extends the relational one with deductive rules, thus one may devise a transformation that encodes graphs and rules into a Datalog program that uses a unique 3-ary relation symbol for triples [12], and then rely on access control mechanisms for deductive databases, such as the one by Barker [3]. Unfortunately, it seems that problems that arise when dealing with RDF data, the information leakage in particular, has not received much attention from the database community. We argue this because RDF is thought to be openly used between independent web sources, with shared or even standardized inference rules. In contrast, the Datalog model is more centralized, with rules and data under the control of a single authority.

Several access control models related to RDF data *without* inference rules have been proposed [1,5,13]. Abel et al. [1] propose a query rewriting mechanism to enforce authorizations. The authors do not present the formal semantics of the authorization language and their conflict resolution strategies are hard-coded. Flouris et al. [5] propose an annotation based access control language with its formal semantics for fine-grained authorizations on RDF data. The definition of authorizations in this paper is clearly inspired by Flouris et al. However, they used a fixed set of conflict resolution strategies (deny/permit by default and deny/permit takes precedence) without *most specific takes precedence*. In contrast, we advocate a more liberal approach. These models are sources of inspiration, but the problems related to inference rules are not addressed.

Other approaches consider inference rules and use propagation techniques to compute authorizations that are applicable to inferred triples [8,10,15]. Reddivari et al. [15] propose an access control language for RDF stores that considers update operations. They use meta-rules to define conflict resolution strategies and default policies but they do not provide formal semantics of their language. A similar approach inspired from provenance which has been proposed by Lopes et al. [8], where each triple is annotated with a label and labels are propagated through inference rule with a fixed conflict resolution strategy. Papakonstantinou et al. [10] propose a flexible model that defines the access label of a triple as an algebraic expression. They considered a fixed subset of RDFS rules only, but not user-defined rules. To sum up, the label-based techniques may use more expressive authorization languages or may consider updates, however they need some base graphs and they do not consider the information leakage.

Jain et al. [7] propose a label-based propagation technique for RDF data. They propose an algorithm that detects unauthorized inferences where higher security triples may be inferred from lower security triples. Nevertheless, a graph is needed to detect such violation, and their conflict resolution strategies and the default strategy are hard-coded. In contrast, we favor static analysis without knowledge of the graph and allow more flexible conflict resolution strategies. It would be interesting to check if their technique could be used to parallelize the computation of applicable authorizations with closure.

As a concluding remark, the inference problem we consider in this paper is a particular case of a more general one that is instantiated to the RDF data model [4]. Other orthogonal methods developed to deal with the general case, e.g., statistical ones or dynamic monitoring, may complement our statical verification technique.

7   Conclusion

In this paper, we introduced a fine-grained access control model for RDF stores with inference capabilities. We showed how concrete resolution strategies, notably *most specific takes precedence*, can be instances of our abstract framework. Whereas some models allow or deny *queries*, we gave semantics to authorizations by means of the *authorized subgraph* of a base graph, doing so we are independent of a given query language. We formalized an information leakage problem that arises when inferred triples are computed out of the RDF store by a (potentially) malicious user. We showed that, whenever the inference system can be expressed in a set of Datalog-like rules without negation, this property can be statically verified at the time of writing the authorization policy without the need of a base graph. Dealing with other inference systems such as OWL reasoning has to be further investigated.

The main issue related to the performance about our enforcement model stems from the definition of the applicable authorizations function (Definition 7). We propose the following technique using quad store technology, which adds a fourth attribute to triples. Given a policy $P = (\mathfrak{A}, \mathsf{ch})$, for each $\mathfrak{a} \in \mathfrak{A}$, compute $[\![\mathsf{hb}(\mathfrak{a})]\!]_G$. Then, we add authorization $\mathfrak{a}$ to the fourth attribute of each triple $(\mathsf{head}(\mathfrak{a}))\theta$ produced by some θ in $[\![\mathsf{hb}(\mathfrak{a})]\!]_G$. This technique assumes that the fourth attribute can be used to store the sets of identifiers, by means of the named graphs. This implementation is an ongoing work.

As for future work, we will study alternatives to the existence of a total order between authorizations to build the ch function. We plan to relax this condition with a user-defined partial order on authorizations. In order to build the ch function, an interesting perspective is to define it using the meet operator of a lower semilattice that extends the given partial order.

Additionally, we will compare our policy model against the existing ones. We envision to translate some well-known policy languages, e.g., XACML, into our formalism. As other models' semantics are usually expressed in terms of allowed or denied *queries* and not in terms of authorized *subgraphs*, verifying the correctness of such a translation would lead us to relate these different semantics.

As an example, for a query Q and an XACML policy X, the condition may be that $Q(G^+_{\alpha(X)}) = Q(G)$ if and only if $[\![X]\!]_X(Q) = \top$ where α is the translation function and $[\![\_]\!]_X$ is the interpretation function of XACML [14].

Finally, we plan to study the impact of RDF data updates, indeed, new issues arise from updates. For instance, a user may be allowed to insert a triple, but she/he may not be allowed to insert some of its consequences that can be inferred. We would like to characterize this problem with a new consistency property for updates, inspired by the one given in Sect. 3.2.

Acknowledgements. This work is supported by Thomson Reuters in the framework of the Partner University Fund project : *"Cybersecurity Collaboratory: Cyberspace Threat Identification, Analysis and Proactive Response"*. The Partner University Fund is a program of the French Embassy in the United States and the FACE Foundation and is supported by American donors and the French government.

References

1. Abel, F., De Coi, J.L., Henze, N., Koesling, A.W., Krause, D., Olmedilla, D.: Enabling advanced and context-dependent access control in RDF stores. In: Aberer, K., et al. (eds.) ASWC 2007 and ISWC 2007. LNCS, vol. 4825, pp. 1–14. Springer, Heidelberg (2007)
2. Abiteboul, S., Hull, R., Vianu, V.: Foundations of Databases. Addison-Wesley, Boston (1995). http://webdam.inria.fr/Alice/
3. Barker, S.: Protecting deductive databases from unauthorized retrieval and update requests. Data Knowl. Eng. **43**(3), 293–315 (2002)
4. Farkas, C., Jajodia, S.: The inference problem: a survey. SIGKDD Explor. Newsl. **4**(2), 6–11 (2002)
5. Flouris, G., Fundulaki, I., Michou, M., Antoniou, G.: Controlling access to RDF graphs. In: Berre, A.J., Gómez-Pérez, A., Tutschku, K., Fensel, D. (eds.) FIS 2010. LNCS, vol. 6369, pp. 107–117. Springer, Heidelberg (2010)
6. Hayes, P., McBride, B.: RDF semantics. Technical report, W3C (2004)
7. Jain, A., Farkas, C.: Secure resource description framework: an access control model. In: SACMAT, pp. 121–129. ACM (2006)
8. Lopes, N., Kirrane, S., Zimmermann, A., Polleres, A., Mileo, A.: A logic programming approach for access control over RDF. In: ICLP, pp. 381–392 (2012)
9. Martelli, A., Montanari, U.: An efficient unification algorithm. ACM Trans. Program. Lang. Syst. **4**, 258–282 (1982)
10. Papakonstantinou, V., Michou, M., Fundulaki, I., Flouris, G., Antoniou, G.: Access control for RDF graphs using abstract models. In: SACMAT, pp. 103–112 (2012)
11. Pérez, J., Arenas, M., Gutierrez, C.: Semantics and complexity of SPARQL. ACM Trans. Database Syst. **34**(3), 16:1–16:45 (2009)
12. Polleres, A.: From SPARQL to rules (and back). In: WWW, pp. 787–796 (2007)
13. Rachapalli, J., Khadilkar, V., Kantarcioglu, M., Thuraisingham, B.: Towards fine grained RDF access control. In: SACMAT, pp. 165–176. ACM (2014)
14. Kencana Ramli, C.D.P., Nielson, H.R., Nielson, F.: The logic of XACML. In: Arbab, F., Ölveczky, P.C. (eds.) FACS 2011. LNCS, vol. 7253, pp. 205–222. Springer, Heidelberg (2012)
15. Reddivari, P., Finin, T., Joshi, A.: Policy-based access control for an RDF store. In: Policy Management for the Web workshop, WWW. pp. 78–81 (2005)

Author Index

Printed in the United States
By Bookmasters